SEX IN LITERATURE

The Erotic Impulse in Literature

by

JOHN ATKINS

GROVE PRESS, INC.
NEW YORK

First published in Great Britain 1970
by Calder and Boyars Ltd.
18 Brewer Street, London W1

Library of Congress Catalog Card Number: 73-187580

ISBN: 0-394-17769-x

Manufactured in the United States of America

First Evergreen Black Cat Edition, 1972

Distributed by Random House, Inc., New York

First Printing

CONTENTS

Glory be to him who joins the hearts of men and women, and brings young lovers together in the night!

> (*Arabian Nights*, trs. Mathers)

Let the chaste be driven forth from Islam, for they corrupt the people. Let there be no abstention from women among the priests of Islam.

> (Attributed to the Prophet, on whom be prayer and peace)

But mercy, lady bright, that knowest weel
My thought, and seest what harmes that I feel,
Considere al this, and rewe up-on my sore,
As wisely as I shal for evermore,
Emforth my might, thy trewe servant be,
And holden werre alwey with chastitee.

> (Palamon's prayer to Venus, 'The Knightes Tale', Chaucer)

Save wyn and wommen, no-thing mighte aswage
His hye entente in armes and labour.

> (De Alexandro, 'The Monkes Tale')

Who beauty loveth and created hath
With the same breath which bade us fear Thy wrath,
*   Lover and Lord, we pray thee to remove*
Either restraint or beauty from our path.

> ('Tale of Kamar and the Expert Halimah', *Arabian Nights*)

Madame, shall we undress you for the fight?
The wars are naked that we make tonight.

> (Quoted by George Moore in *Memoirs of My Dead Life*: from 'the old poet')

Horsus:
　　'Tis her cunning,
　　The love of her own lust, which makes a woman
　　Gallop down hill as fearless as a drunkard.
　　There's no true loadstone in the world but that;
　　It draws them through all storms by sea or shame:
　　Life's loss is thought too small to pay that game.

(Thomas Middleton, *Mayor of Queenborough*)

1: *Introduction*

Definitions

It is usual to state, when dealing with this subject, that *erotic* does not mean either *obscene* or *pornographic*. Turning to the *Shorter Oxford English Dictionary* we find that *erotic* is an adjective, of or pertaining to the sexual passion; treating of love, *amatory*. As a matter of interest *amatory*, according to the same authority, is an adjective, of or pertaining to a lover, love-making, or sexual love. We may presume that *sexual* implies physical, with as little intrusion of the spiritual as man's complicated nature will allow. *Amatory* is a polite word, used in genteel sonnets, and it is quite probable that I will not use it again. Coming to *obscene*, this is a horror word: it is always offensive (i) to modesty or decency, expressing or suggesting lewd thoughts, and (ii) to the senses or the mind; disgusting, filthy (but this latter use is 'arch'). Finally, *pornographic*: of, pertaining to, or of the nature of *pornography*—which, upon seeing, turns out to be the expression or suggestion of obscene or unchaste subjects in literature or art.

Various writers have wrestled with definitions of these words, with results almost as various. Alec Craig quotes Havelock Ellis on *obscene*, which is that which is 'off the scene' in life and normally hidden. 'If we apply this idea to literature we may say that an "obscene book" is one that at any given time is not permitted to circulate openly by reason of erotic subject matter or manner of treatment of erotic subject matter. The time factor is important because what is obscene to one generation may not be so to another.' In addition to being a splendid example of the empiric spirit at its peak, this is not very helpful to reader, critic or censor: it does not tell us in advance whether a book is likely to be considered obscene.

There is no more agreement about the term *pornography*. Literally it means a 'description of harlotry'. It is frequently equated with sexual stimulation. But, as writers never tire of pointing out, what stimulates one person will not stimulate another. If I hear that Mr X is stimulated by *Cranford* I learn quite a lot about Mr X and next to nothing about *Cranford*. It also implies that sexual stimulation is always and every-where undesirable. Craig suggests that pornography is 'writing or drawing executed with the *intention* of exciting sexuality and without a sense of moral responsibility.' But intention? Who is to look into the mind of the author? Everyone sees what his prejudices dictate. Even then we cannot be sure that a prejudice is for or against.

Personally, I think it's a hopeless business and also pointless. It holds up the real business in hand, which is coming to a closer knowledge and understanding of what everyone, by and large, agrees is erotic literature. But some more than others. Just as not every man is equally equipped in a sexual sense, so is he not in an imaginative, censorial or self-hating sense. (Self-hatred is probably a most important factor in the appreci-ation or otherwise of sexual matters.) I also suspect that the urge to define, to refine, and to re-define is allied to the narrow-ness of temper that heaps obloquy on sexual pleasure. I will keep away from it henceforth. I will note, however, before going on that the Greek Muse of Love Poetry was named Erato, which may invite a pun from word-lovers, Brownists and Partridgeites.

Just a word about Dr C. S. Lewis, author of *The Four Loves*. One of the loves is Eros, of which Lewis has a highly personal interpretation. He doubts if Eros usually grows out of Venus (sex). It is more likely that a delightful preoccupation with the Beloved in her totality comes first. 'A man in this state really hasn't leisure to think of sex. He is too busy thinking of a person.' Eros enters the lover and reorganises him, including his sex. Lewis illustrates his point from Orwell's *1984* where the 'dreadful hero' insists on hearing from the girl whether she likes sex. He is not satisfied till he gets the answer, 'I adore it'. He concludes that sexual desire, without Eros, wants *it*, the *thing in itself*; Eros wants the Beloved. I have great sympathy with this point of view. In fact, I agree entirely with the attitude towards woman and sex expressed, but it is not a true definition of Eros. The original Greek word meant sexual love. Lewis suggests that sex is an afterthought. There is some intellectual dishonesty here, though venial.

My subtitle is the Erotic Impulse in Literature. This element at first comprises awe and wonder at man's procreative powers. This is naïvely expressed in primitive folklore, boastfully in the general run of nineteenth century literature, where sexual exhaustion is practically unknown. After wonder come the refinements: delight, disgust and amusement. Of course, I am not sure of the priorities. I simply know that some writing about sex is very merry and that some is very horrid.

A decision I had to make was what *qualifies* as erotic literature. This word allows a certain amount of sidestepping. Dr E. J. Dingwall, in his essay on Erotic Literature in Cassell's *Encyclopaedia of Literature*, cites *The Golden Lotus* as Chinese erotica. In fact, it is a fairly orthodox novel (though very long) with some highly erotic passages. I employ the term 'erotic literature' in this fashion in this study. It is not necessarily a *genre* of its own but a part of the total literary pattern. Sometimes the part becomes the whole, as in the nineteenth century *Tableaux Vivants*, but more often it remains merely a part, as in *Lady Chatterley's Lover*. The latter type has a better literary balance. The former is for the specialist, and naturally tends to obsession.

I intend to treat the idea of eroticism in the very broadest fashion. The limits of 'love' are uncertain. There is considerably more agreement about what is sexual, or has a sexual affiliation. For example, Swift's disgust is frequently sexual. Whether it was a by-product of his erotic impulse is a question we must leave to the psychologist. But it is an illustration of the kind of thing I have chosen to include rather than exclude. To confine my study to the positive and the harmonious would be to ignore a large portion of a very complex field of behaviour. No one denies that Sade's fantasies are erotic, and I think we must therefore give the benefit of the doubt to all writings where the centre of interest appears to be the generative and pleasure-giving organs (even if sometimes the object is pain-giving). I have decided not to be too much concerned with erotic purpose, erotic effect or erotic stimulation. Having made a general statement about these things, it is best to forget them. I wish to think of erotic literature as writing about sexual activity and the erogenous zones, otherwise we will be halting constantly to ask whether the Zambe Creation Stories, let us say, when written down, constitute erotic literature, or whether they are merely quasi-scientific statements or mythological explanations. I take my stand on the bald statement that whatever bears a relation to sex, in any form, is erotic in essence. A whirling spray is not a sexual symbol but its existence derives absolutely from sexual activity. There is one other thing: it must be read by non-specialists. For this reason the greater part of scientific literature about sex is omitted. (If it weren't I would be in danger of suffocation.) Some scientific works, however, have attracted the non-scientist: certain seventeenth century productions have always been regarded as 'curious', the Kinsey Report was a best-seller, marriage manuals are often read by people who have no intention of marriage. So my rough definition is that erotic literature is writing about sexual activity and sexual organs that is read by many or few non-specialist members of the general public. But this is little more than a bow to convention. A child can pick holes in it, and it doesn't matter. I note a growing tendency these days, even among philosophers, to exclaim with irritation: 'Finally, we all know what is meant by *x*.' I should say we do.

The dean of English Erotic Studies, H. S. Ashbee, who wrote under the pseudonym of Pisanus Fraxi, excused his interest in the subject (in his *Index*, 1877) on the grounds that historians and psychologists could not ignore the evidence afforded by such writing. It is comforting to think that no product of the human brain should be afforded—after all, psychoanalysis itself rests on the singular interest Freud took in exceptional phenomena. All writing has some value for the student but blasphemous or indecent books should not be put in the hands of young people. In his *Catena*, 1885, Ashbee concludes his Preliminary Remarks thus:

> The view that I take of Erotic Literature has already been expressed. Better were it that such literature did not exist. I consider it pernicious and hurtful to the immature, but at the same time I hold that, in certain circumstances, its study is necessary, if not beneficial.

In a footnote he says: 'The multitude and divergence of opinion on the subject may be urged as a *raison d'être* for the present study.'

There is more than a change of emphasis here; there is actually a change of attitude and one wonders if this really was Ashbee's opinion. Perhaps pressures had been put on him from influential quarters but it is more likely that, in preparing the *Catena*, he had had to wade through such a morass of sordid popular English erotica he was feeling sickened. It seems hardly likely that some of the more graceful erotic writings in other literatures would have come under his denunciation. And the greater part of erotic writing in the eighteenth century, even in England, could not justly be called pernicious and hurtful. In fact, if challenged to produce the right adjectives I would suggest merry and uncomplicated. The end was pleasure and the pleasure was regarded simply as man's right. Poor Ashbee lived in an age that had bowed to shame. Sex had been pronounced dirty, hence it took place under cover, hence it often became nasty. The pleasure was often unpleasant. Ashbee was spared our own century. We are still trying to throw off the slime of Victorian respectability and it is no easy matter. We want to feel free but too many voices tell us freedom is only fit for animals. Men and women regret that they need each other, and seek to inflict pain. The exceptions are all the more interesting: the loathsome William King in the time of Swift and the cavalier Henry Miller in our own.

Treatment
We have to be rather careful about how we treat this subject,

though there have been improvements lately. The rules have changed even while I have been reading for and planning this study. At one time you could use Latin where English was forbidden. Sexual intercourse was high and dry and perfectly safe but—was utterly reprehensible. Now I may write, quite simply, fuck—and society still stands! But there are still limits, as Fanny Hill's experience in the courts showed. You can probably get away with any foreign language, just as you can price your information out of the ordinary man's reach, the rich being incorruptible. Indian terms such as *lingam* and *yoni* are thoroughly respectable. No one minds *phallus*. Elsewhere in this work I will make use of certain African words and they will be all right too. But when it comes to English you have to be more careful, though it is no longer necessary to use asterisks—although I note, delightedly I admit, that some writers (or perhaps it is their publishers) still choose to put obfuscation before clarity. The odd thing about this practice is that everyone knows what is meant but the manner of calling it appears to be regarded as more important than the thing itself. Scientists are allowed ♂ and ♀, although they are much more direct and to the point than anything on my typewriter. I intend to use the words themselves but you don't have to be heroic these days. The battles have been won.

As for situations, etc., one can usually get away with anything if one is careful, and yet—there were no bad words in *Fanny Hill*. What is allowed? And, even more interesting, why? Here is one of my favourite jokes. A clergyman went to a South Coast resort on his honeymoon. Next morning he went down to breakfast alone and there met another clergyman who was on the same business. They discreetly exchanged notes, then decided to have a walk together on the cliff. The scene before them was beautiful—green grass, blue sea and sky. Ah, sighed one clergyman, what a beautiful spot! Yes, said the other eagerly, and how cunningly concealed!

Now is this filthy? Certainly not. On the contrary, it is charming. Is it erotic? Mildly, because it hinges on the female sexual organ. Could it be told in polite society? I tried it once and was rewarded by a freeze. But they were U.N. experts, feeling their way through higher salaries, unaccustomed cheese and wine. In general I think my little story would pass today. But for long periods in our history, no. Who is right? If this joke is permissible, much in this volume is also permissible. Where objection can be raised it will be on the grounds of deliberate coarseness.

Here is a message for puritans. This is not for you, so do not disturb yourselves by reading it. What is more, do not attempt to disturb others who may enjoy it by making a great fuss about obscenity. There is nothing here to corrupt, unless you are anxious to be corrupted, and nothing that can disturb a normally healthy person. Weak people are advised against over-strenuous activity; the physically sick must be careful of what they eat; the spiritually sick must be careful of what they read.

Materials

It would be absolutely unreasonable to expect a single author to make a balanced and comprehensive study of erotic literature. Even if he were the kind of linguist one hears about but never meets (knows a dozen languages, fluent in six) he would still be under-equipped. He would still have to depend on translations in many cases, and the bare fact remains that many sublime works (we are told) remain untranslated. Unless he were a millionaire or a Ford Foundation scholar he could not expect to consult the many libraries scattered over the globe, where the world's erotica are confined. Millionaires are rarely scholars. Big Foundation grants never go to mavericks. Only a committee could encompass the work and although this would be better than nothing, committees usually produce work that is either deadly dull or jerkily variable. And so, although I can do no more than offer a few bites at the erotic apple, I hope I will not be thought presumptuous in trying to describe the taste.

This is largely a book about erotic literature that is available in English. This is not a bad foundation for there is probably as much work of this type available in English as in

any other language, despite the fact that very little of the best
quality originated in English. Also, because of the liberalisa-
tion in publishing that has taken place since the last war, far
more work is generally available than ever before. You can
now buy the *Kama Sutra* and the *Perfumed Garden* quite
openly. There are still one or two works which, so far as I
know, have not appeared in English and yet have an intrinsic
value and, in some cases, have been influential beyond the
country of origin. In these cases I have tried to correct the
balance by making some translations of my own (from French
and Latin) and using those of friends (Arabic). An excellent
example of this type of work is afforded by the elegant novels
of Nerciat who, to the best of my knowledge, has only been
partially (and poorly) translated into English—and then in a
periodical. This still leaves many languages untapped, however, and I don't see how this can be overcome, except by
committees, organisation and finance. This book has to pay
its way. Circumstances compel me to base my study on availa-
bility in English. The reader may find an unexpected amount
of Arabic writing referred to. It happens that I have spent the
greater part of the last fifteen years in an Arabic-speaking
country and it seemed foolish to reject the opportunity.

I don't wish to compartmentalise literature more than the
situation requires. I have tried to avoid making a rigid distinction between erotic literature and the Rest. Some has been
written entirely for its erotic effect, but much highly erotic
writing can be found embedded in non-erotic material. If I
wanted to write a study of travel literature I wouldn't confine
myself to those books listed under Travel in the Public Library.
How does Johnson's *Tour of the Hebrides* qualify? It is the
puritan who tries to seal off *Lady Chatterley's Lover* as Erotic
Literature, instead of allowing it to stay where it belongs: an
interesting and valuable station on the general line. In fiction
I find love and sex, food and drink, ships and railways, frogs
and cows, courage and cowardice, cheese and bacon, tables and
chairs, trust and treachery—the good novel is the one that is
concerned with life, not a totem. Sex interests me, but how
could it not? Sometimes I gaze at my foot (or her foot) with

wonder. Any person of normal instincts must feel the same reactions. One person I mentioned this book to told me loftily that he preferred to act sex than read about it. This is the arrogance that comes of false values. Act sex! I'd rather walk to Rome than read about it but I'm not going to prudishly forego the latter because of it. But there it is, poor Western man. Look at sex and shudder with guilt.

So much of what can be considered important to this study was a by-product of observation, reportage or even scientific interest. I would never deny the existence of the specifically erotic purpose on occasion, resulting in titillation, provocation, stimulation, *épatisme*. But what are we to say about the diaries and the letters? None of these (the best ones) were written for the general view. Today they are literature and are studied alongside the more selfconscious product of the novelist and critic. Yet one is Pepys (who belongs to us here) and another is Evelyn, whom we can't squeeze in; one is Boswell and another is Creevey (ditto). Also I haven't hesitated to forget literature on occasion and take a look at the society that produced it. I feel sympathy here for Malinowski who was disappointed that sex should be abstracted and isolated by the critics from the social whole in his study of savages. True, he called it *The Sexual Life of Savages* but he was trying to show that the sexual organ was the stone and the sexual life the ripples on the pond. Similarly, a study of the erotic element in literature can only be made fully meaningful in its actual context: the erotic element in society.

I have paid very little attention to the publishing history of the books mentioned: how many editions, dates of various editions, in some cases the author's name. These are matters which often require considerable research; they are the stuff of another book—a book, in fact, which I know one expert has for some time been trying to persuade another expert to write. I imagine the general public has little idea of how deeply shrouded in mystery these matters are in the field of erotic writing. I remember how sternly one weekly reviewer chided Ginzburg for not always putting the author or the date in the bibliography to his *Unhurried View of Erotica*. I am putting

a bibliography to this book but it won't be terribly expert. It
is largely for the curious amateur.

Erotic Types

Dr Dingwall suggests there are three kinds:

  (i) Intimate relations merely suggested or mentioned in
      passing.
 (ii) Sexual details are filled in, but still subsidiary.
(iii) Purely pornographic (the writing of harlots), where
      sex details are the main theme and the intention is
      to arouse lust.

In this classification intention seems to be one of the major
factors, as in the English law of obscene libel. But our first
concern should be aesthetic satisfaction. The perfect work of
art demands physical, intellectual, spiritual and emotional
reaction. Where the interest is sensual only, the work is of
medical, psychological or anthropological value only. The
erotic element can only play a subordinate part in fully realised
literature. For this reason *The Golden Lotus* (type ii) is artisti-
cally superior to *Fanny Hill* (type iii), both being excellent of
their kind. (For an inferior type ii is certainly not automati-
cally superior to a first-rate type iii.)

This classification is perfectly sound but a more analytical
one could be made, based less on intention than on treatment.
I would suggest the following:

  (i) Accounts of genuine sensual pleasure: joy, exuber-
      ance, and essentially healthy (Henry Miller).
 (ii) Stimulating, pornographic (Cleland).
(iii) Philosophic, with an axe to grind (Sade).
(iv) Dramatic, emphasis on situation (Boccaccio).
  (v) Bawdy and rumbustious (Rabelais).
 (vi) Surrealist (Piombo).
(vii) Instructional manual (Kama Sutra).
(viii) Scientific enquiry (Kinsey).

Not all writers or works fall neatly into any one classification.

Tennessee Williams, for instance, is a serious writer yet there are times when I feel he enters type ii. Type viii was never intended to be listed in a book of this character but such books are in fact read by some people for what stimulation they can get out of them.

Existing Bibliography

Anyone working in this field must acknowledge his debt to Pisanus Fraxi (Henry Spencer Ashbee), whose *Index Librorum Prohibitorum*, followed by the *Catena* and the *Register*, is absolutely indispensable. In his introduction he stated that the only bibliography of erotic literature that existed at the time (1877) was the *Bibliographie des Ouvrages relatifs a l'Amour, aux Femmes, au Mariage et des Livres Facétieux, Pantagruéliques, Scatologiques, Satyriques, etc., par M. Le C. D'I. . . .* His purpose had been to embrace the erotic books of all European languages, ancient and modern. It was useful for French and Italian but worthless for English. It is redundant, padded with irrelevant material and omits much that should be included. (In an appendix Fraxi also noted the *Bibliotheka Germanorum Erotica*, published at Leipzig two years before his own volume.)

> The English nation (writes Fraxi) possesses an ultra-squeamishness and hyper-prudery peculiar to itself, sufficient alone to deter any author of position and talent from taking in hand so tabooed a subject.

He turns, in a footnote, to the authors of *The Index Expurgatorius of Martial* for support:

> But there is a superficial morality among the English of the present day which unhappily bears all before it, and those who dare to write in the teeth of this bring upon themselves most unmerited obloquy; the consequence of this is shown in all our translations of the classics. Mr Bohn's classical series might have been a most splendid

introduction to the pursuit of Latin and Greek Literature, but unfortunately when an obscene passage occurs, it is either omitted *without asterisks* or simply and purposely mistranslated.

In the name of virtue, of course. Fraxi notes that the most eminent authors in England rarely attempted licentious work, unlike their French, Italian and German counterparts. Consequently our greatest name in this field is Cleland. It is possible that Fraxi had some idea of how Swinburne wrote to his friends but it is practically certain that he did not know that Thackeray, even prudent clean-minded Thackeray, was unable to resist the temptation on at least one occasion.

A rather maligned publication called the *Bibliotheca Arcana seu Catalogus Librorum Penetralium* appeared in 1885. It contained 'brief notices of books that have been secretly printed, prohibited by law, seized, anathematised, burnt or Bowdlerised', and was by Speculator Morum. From one source I learn that it was anonymously edited by Sir William Laird Clowes and that S.M. was the Rev. John B. McClellan. From another source I learn that S.M. was Ashbee. I say it is usually maligned because it is held to be an abridgment of Ashbee, with some additions, but the additions are often of considerable interest.

Speculator Morum stated that the arts were beginning to concern themselves, not with picturesqueness or conventional piety, but with truth. (*Germinal* appeared at about the time these words were written.) He pointed out that Buckle believed that for an understanding of history the lives of debauchees and harlots were as valuable as the writings of divines and statesmen, and went straight to the proscribed documents which were afterwards secretly printed and published as The Library of Social Progress. *Bibliotheca Arcana*, he claimed, bore much the same relation to literature as the *Newgate Calendar* did to the record of London life. A Buckle of the future might well be grateful to it. Some statistics follow. At least 2,000 erotic works were published in France between 1750 and 1825. In America, a single Irish bookseller issued 320 between 1846 and 1871. According to Pisanus Fraxi,

100,000 volumes were sold annually in New York alone. In Europe the major producer was Belgium. In France the law permitted more freedom than in England, and the national humour of the French (*gauloiserie*) helped the process. None of these books were as cynically objectionable as W. H. Mallock's *Romance of the Nineteenth Century*, which was accepted in the most genteel English drawing room. Germany once produced a great deal, until the authorities intervened. A good deal was produced in Portugal and Italy. The English production was smaller and largely secret.

Two more bibliographies are worth a brief mention. Louis Perceau's *Bibliographie du Roman Erotique* (Paris, 1930) claims to give a complete description of every prose work published *sous le manteau* in French since 1800. The *Registrum Librorum Eroticorum* (1936) combines titles taken from Ashbee, Clowes, the Private Case of the British Museum and the Enfer of the Bibliothèque Nationale. It was compiled by Alfred Rose under the anagrammatic pseudonym Rolf S. Reade but was messed up by W. J. Stanislaus after Rose's death on the eve of publication. There is also an imitation of Ashbee, not really worth separate mention, by the Paris publisher, Charles Carrington, entitled *Forbidden Books*, by an Old Bibliophile (Paris 1902, New York 1929). Short bibliographies are to be found in *Sexual Life in England*, by Dr Ivan Bloch, and *An Unhurried View of Erotica*, by Ralph Ginzburg.

Acknowledgments

Obviously I owe acknowledgments to many people, known and unknown, living and dead. I prefer not to single out any particular individuals—it would be invidious and well nigh impossible to do fairly, and I am certain many of them would not thank me. Therefore a list, in alphabetical order, of those who have given me assistance, ranging from the slightest encouragement at the right moment to the loan of books and the offering of much needed advice.

Ahmed Abdalla Sami; Mrs Hortense Sonia Bardwell; Antony

Borrow; A. F. J. Brown; Professor J. L. Cloudsley-Thompson;
Alec Craig; Margaret Crosland; Dr E. J. Dingwall; Leon
Drucker; El Nur Ibrahim; Comte d'Estegnes; Albert Gailani;
Geoffrey Gorer; V. Slingsby Gort; Bernard Hanison; Michael
Jolliffe and his assistants at the Newbould Library, Khartoum
University; K. J. Lace; G. Legman; Jack Lindsay; Harry
Loshak; Mahgoub Omer Beshery; Mahomed Abdel Gadir
Karaf; Alfred Perlès; Dr Richard Pankhurst; P'ing Lin Hao;
Raymond Postgate; Bernard Raymund; Rashid Ibn Mansour;
Professor W. Simon; Dr Edvard Skok; Roger Staples; Lady
Hermione Stott; G. J. Yorke.

2: *Primitives*

The Discovery of Sex

Margaret Mead, in a book written primarily for children, wrote: 'Wherever we find human beings, we find that they wonder about other people.' We can, with perfect justice, paraphrase this: 'Wherever we find human beings, we find that they wonder about the making of other people.' Every people has its creation mythology.

It is difficult to imagine primitive people expressing an interest in sex for itself. Apart from a few groups who had not developed sufficiently to link copulation with procreation, they looked upon sex as an instrument of racial survival, and hence ringed it round with ceremonies and tabus. They were not amused by it—they were probably amused by very few things in their nasty, brutish circumstances. The capacity to be amused premisses a high degree of civilisation. Amusement at sex is still rare and demands considerable mental sophistication. Yet sex as an element in literature is closely related with the expression of pleasure, and along with it the sensation of amusement. We laugh at two classes of phenomena: those which strike us as funny and those that give pleasure. Realism, that is, the impulse to describe things as they are, is a late literary development. The earliest writings (in fact, folk sayings, which are later written down—but there is no essential distinction) on sex come mostly out of wonder. Unless there has been a fantastic physiological change in man during historic times, sex experiences gave pleasure, but the pleasure is rarely referred to. The surrender to pleasure, felt as a sense of fun, developed later; in fact, I have a suspicion that man willed it. If I suggested that the sexual experience is what you make it, pain, pleasure or nothing, I would be anticipating the Marquis de Sade. After fun came the disgusting seriousness of the professional puritan and life-hater, for these also are sophisticated attitudes, deriving from a philosophy of existence. It seems likely that life-hatred has intensified in modern times as life (that is, the way we choose to live it) becomes more complicated and difficult. On the other hand, life-hatred is not entirely modern, as can be seen from a study of some African and South American masks, but primitive life-hatred rarely (perhaps never) centred on sex.

Wonder caused primitive people to theorise about the separation of the sexes—for the idea that originally there was no distinction was widespread. Some of the North American tribes believed that men were separated from women in the underworld before they came to earth. One of the Apache tribes tried to establish why the separation took place: it was caused by female infidelity—a charming instance of primitive illogicality, since the woman would have to exist before she could do the act which brought her into existence. Or she might scold a chief, who could call all the men to him, even the baby boys, male dogs and horses, and take them to the other side of a river. (Women couldn't cross rivers.) They remained separated in this way for four years, by which time the women were starving, as they didn't plant crops in the final year. (Women need supervision.) Finally that admirable creature of North American folklore, Coyote, brought the two sexes together again.

So far, no mention of what we think of as sex. A Kabyl (Berber) legend of creation provides a representative account. Their Adam and Eve lived under the earth and did not know that they were different. They came to a well together to drink and quarrelled about who should have first go. They quarrelled and fought, the woman fell and her clothing fell apart. The man saw that she had a *taschunt* and felt that he had a *thabuscht*—our first erection, gentle reader. It was the woman who told him what to do. They did it for eight days.

Later we hear of fifty youths bathing in a stream, watched

from afar by fifty maidens. Three crept close to watch and one, a prototype of the bold hussy, went right up to them without being seen.

> The maiden returned to the other maidens, who gathered around her and asked: 'What have you seen?' The bold maiden replied: 'Come, we'll bathe too, and then I can tell you and show you.' The fifty maidens undressed and stepped down into their spring. The bold maiden told them: 'The people over there are not as we are. Where our breasts are, they have nothing. Where our *taschunt* is they have something else. The hair on their heads is not long like ours, but short. And when one sees them naked one's heart pounds and one wishes to embrace them. When one has seen them naked one can never forget it.' The other maidens replied: 'You lie.' But the bold maiden said: 'Go and see for yourselves and you'll come back feeling as I do.'
>
> *African Genesis*, LEO FROBENIUS and DOUGLAS C. FOX

The bold maiden is finally discovered snooping, there is a chase, she screams and the other maidens run to her. The fifty maidens meet the fifty youths in the bush. It was dark and they fought in pairs. The maidens were strong and threw the youths down. Feeling between their thighs, they found the *thabuscht*, which began to swell. The youths lay still. The fifty maidens inserted the fifty *thabuschts* and began to ravish the fifty youths. But slowly the youths became more active than the maidens. Each youth took a maiden to his house. Then he said: 'It is not right that the woman lies on the man. In the future we shall see to it that the man lies on the woman. In this way we will become your masters.' Since then the Kabyl men have always been on top.

This legend has many of the ingredients of the familiar erotic story. In addition to the more obvious aspects there is the scream, the chase—and the conviction of so many later writers, that woman's lust is the true lodestone.

The Centre of Life

Sex is at the centre of the body and at the centre of life. All
man's activities must be related to it: not to money or ideals
or a thousand substitutes. For a quick survey of modern man's
approach to his own nature, we cannot do better than turn to
Havelock Ellis's preface to Bronislaw Malinowski's *The
Sexual Life of Savages*. This book opened the eyes of honest
men and women to the reality of their own sexual being.

Ellis drew attention to the spurt of interest experienced in
the eighteenth century, particularly in France, in the customs
of 'Primitive Man'. French voyagers and missionaries were
intoxicated by the strange manners and customs which they
encountered and could not understand. Yet they came as a
revelation to the Parisian world, for intelligent Frenchmen
were beginning to realise that their own manners and customs
were extraordinarily artificial. The conception of the 'noble
savage' whom Tacitus had glimpsed in the primeval German
forests gathered force. Rousseau studied the narratives of the
explorers carefully even if his conclusions were superficial. But
Diderot went a step further. In his *Supplément au Voyage de
Bougainville* he declared the superior reasonableness of the
Tahitians in sexual ethics.

In the nineteenth century it was English explorers and
missionaries who took the lead, with a consequent change in
outlook. Unfamiliar sexual customs were branded without
question as shocking or obscene. A urethral subincision
practised by Australian tribes was named 'the terrible rite'.
Similar incisions of nose and ear in other tribes were not
terrible. The twentieth century has managed to discover a
calmer and more rational approach. Our own sex tabus are
breaking down. Ellis pointed out that cultural development
is often unequal. Absorption in other fields of culture, such
as the mechanical arts or intellectual matters, can be detri-
mental to sexual development. It is possible that the
Trobriand Islander has in some respects reached a finer
degree of civilisation than 'civilised' man.

But Rome wasn't built in a day and it took seven marches

to bring down the walls of Jericho. In a special foreword to the
third edition Malinowski expressed his disappointment with
the reception of his book. The reviewers had been invariably
kind and pleasant but usually missed the point. Malinowski
wanted his book to be regarded as an achievement in field-
work, to show that only a synthesis of facts concerning sex can
give an idea of what sexual life means to a people. 'The effect
of the book, on the other hand, was that merely sensational
details were picked out, and wondered or laughed at, while the
synthesis, the integration of details, the correlation of aspects,
the whole functional mechanism in short was missed.' Two
sorts of people, making up the great majority, could not grasp
that they were being shown the centre. The peripheral people
are the sniggerers and the life-haters. The first creep round the
edges via the smutty joke, the second run for their lives (or
anti-lives).

When a people see sex in its true perspective they put it in
the centre of their folklore. The Legend of Inuvayla'u, told
by Malinowski, is typical. It is an interpretation of a human
mystery; it is humourless; and it is related to the contemporary
story-teller and his audience by material evidence. Inuvayla'u
was the head of his clan. He had an abnormally long penis
with which he used to assail the wives of his younger brothers
and maternal nephews. When the men went fishing he would
stand outside their houses, make a hole in the thatch and push
his penis through. It was like a long snake. When the women
were cleaning the ground or weeding he would go into the
garden and stand behind a fence in the uncut bush while his
penis wriggled like a snake, creeping all the way. It would
approach a woman from behind as she bent over—and surprise
her. When they went bathing it would go under the water like
an eel. The women complained until at last the men hid and
watched him, and then ducked him in the head pool of the
tidal creek. After this he decided to leave, but first he cut pieces
off his penis, and then his testicles, and when they fell they
turned into stone. They can still be seen. After long voyages
through the islands with his mother he returned to his native
village and taught the tribesmen a song and dance which has

remained the song and dance of the people of Kwabulo. The stones are still to be seen—the testicles in the creek, large round boulders, just awash at low tide, and the glans penis, a pointed helmet-shaped piece of white coral, in the centre of the village. Inuvayla'u means 'the thief of women'.

The story supports the idea of an old-time gerontocracy, where the old patriarch trespasses on the rights of the younger men, maintaining his power symbolically with an enormous organ. While the women are engaged in privileged occupations, such as communal weeding and fetching water, they are tabu. No man may even approach them, let alone make love. It was felt natural to relate the landmarks of the village to the sexual apparatus of one of the great men of the tribe.

Our ancestors always asserted the centrality of sex, and symbolised the relationship. Whenever they were compelled to think of the major realities of life, whether power, tribal cohesion, food supply, crops, health and long life, they turned instinctively and unerringly to the sexual basis, their sexual nature. They weren't yet clever or cynical enough to feel shame. Primitive men still behave in this way. Sex is so integral to them that it informs every vital process; cruelty will be riddled with it as much as joy. This is evident from the Mau Mau oaths. Here is part of a statement made by a Mau Mau detainee:

I found a circle of banana leaves, potatoes and sugar cane leaves and sorghim leaves. There was a girl there and Karanja. The ram which was used had been killed yesterday at General Charles's camp, and had been used for the fourth oath there.

I was put into the circle and made to take off all my clothes. The whole breast of the ram had been cut off including the penis. I was made to squat down on the ground within the circle. The meat was placed on my penis and chest. I held it in place and ate one end of the meat. The ndito stood on one side and the meat and penis of the ram was then placed in the vagina of the ndito, who was having her monthlies. It was given back to me and I was made to eat parts of it including parts of the penis and the testicle.[1]

Most Europeans will consider this disgusting. We have in fact been trained too consider it disgusting. It is doubtful whether disgust is a primitive emotion or whether it is one man has evolved. Anyway, the fact that sex as a fundamental factor in man's make-up relates equally to the light and the dark in his nature precipitates us into the extremely complex field of sexual psychology, expressed in literature in writings as diverse as the joyful Miller, the sinister Sade and the business-like *Kama Sutra*.

Growth of Sophistication

What we call licentiousness was rare among many but not all primitive people. The cultural history school claims that totemism was not a universal phase affecting all races. It was originally unknown to the Indo-Germans, Hamo-Semites and Ural-Altaic peoples, until they came into contact with it in their wanderings. Sexual matters did not appear to dominate their mores. The investigators have not always been as scientific in their approach as might be wished, however. One, for example, lived for fourteen years among the Malayan pygmies and claims he never saw a single 'indecent scene'.[2] Indecency is a relative quantity, and it is possible that the investigator himself often committed 'indecencies', though unwittingly, by eating a banana in public. Another investigator asserted that sexual passion did not play a decisive role among the Andaman tribes. Such statements tell us next to nothing about the significance of the sex act among these people, except that it occurred in private. Very few apostles of sexual freedom advocate public love. Public love in fact has one of two origins: it is either part of a fertility rite or it is the consequence of intoxication.

What we today think of as licentiousness was extremely rare among primitives. Sex was regarded as a normal activity to be naturally indulged in, by some; by others it was regarded as the fount of life, at times a sacred symbol, even to the point of being rigorously limited and circumscribed according to the demands of a semi-mystical ritual. Generalisation is impossible, except for this: it was never fudged aside into a corner.

For one class sex was never a joking matter. It was they who gave the subject the taint of humourlessness that characterises so much primitive ritual. But the others, the 'naturalists', were free of such a burden. They could, and did, tell each other funny sex stories to pass the time just as chaps do in bars and offices today. I think the distribution of such folklore was very uneven, judging by the literature I have managed to read, but where it does occur it strikes a familiar note. Malinowski gives examples from Melanesia. There is the story of the giant stingaree which used to terrify a mother of five boys who rejoiced in five clitorises. The stingaree used to copulate with her and then cut off a clitoris. She complained to each of her sons in turn but it was only the fifth and youngest, when she had one remaining clitoris only, who faced the creature and killed it. That must have been worth a lot of laughs.

Digawina had such a capacious vagina (her name means Store-cunt) that when she went to the food distribution after a man's death she used to pack it to bursting with coconuts, yams, taro, areca nuts, betel pods, large chunks of sugar cane and whole bunches of bananas. She met her match, however, when the master of the next distribution concealed a large black mangrove crab among the food. This lady is the first of a long line, renowned in sexual lore; she is even a character in Voltaire.

Then there is the story of Monovala who sends his daughter up a tree, sees her genitals spread out before him and screams lustfully. When she asks why he says he saw a green lorry bird. It happens again and again and each time he claims he sees a different bird. When she comes down he has an erection and has her. The girl is so ashamed she tells her mother, then goes to the shore and asks a shark to eat her up, which it does. Monovala's reaction to the news is to set about fucking the mother, but he does it so vigorously she complains. He takes

no notice and she dies. Next day he cuts off his penis and
also dies.

By the time this stage is reached sex has become a subject.
It is something to talk about, something to raise a laugh—and
the link with death and brutality, two other commonplaces of
existence, is stressed. (The extremely odd thing about Western
society in recent times is that whereas it is perfectly respectable to talk about and write about killing and murder, it is not
done to talk and write frankly about sex and loving. But this
may be changing.) Once sex had become a subject for discussion
and verbal appreciation (on the whole unlike eating and
excreting) the familiar treatments of civilised literature follow,
long before pen has been put to paper.

For example, the Mande used to tell this tale. A maiden
refused to marry. A man who wanted her changed into a flute
and lay by her door. On her mother's advice she took it and
leaned it against the wall. When she bathed the flute said, 'I
want to bathe too.' The maiden said it must surely be a man
but her mother told her not to worry as it was the prettiest
flute in the village. The same thing happened when the maiden
lay on her bed; first the flute wanted to lie with her, then it
wanted to lie between her breasts. On each occasion the
maiden's doubts were stilled by her mother's reflection that it
was the best flute in the village. The maiden lay down and
put the flute between her breasts, whereupon it turned into a
strong man with a mighty *fosso* which it put into the maiden's
bie. Next morning the maiden went to her mother and said:
'Now I'm married after all, for the flute was naturally a man.
But I'm glad.' Rather enigmatically the mother replied:
'Didn't I tell you?'

If Boccaccio had been an animist he might have told that
story. It is noticeable that all these stories have an element that
today we might call surrealist. The subject calls out, perhaps
more than any other, the human love of hyperbole and exaggeration, sometimes verbal, sometimes fantastic. Even the
Eskimos have their version of the woman with the enormous
cunt—and a particularly charming one. Miller, Perlès and
Durrell printed it in their magazine *Booster*. Durrell discovered

it in an anthology collected in Greenland by Holm in 1884, and the very notion of such a magnificently soft and warm resting place must have delighted Miller. Nukarpiartekak visits a girl in an igloo. She is so beautiful he keeps fainting. He starts getting into her and can't stop. First his legs, then his arms, then his body and finally all of him disappeared completely. In the morning there was no Nukarpiartekak, only his kayak lying on the river. The story ends on a refinement. The girl went out of the igloo to make water and out came N's skeleton.

A Soninke legend gives us a darker story of a lover's revenge. Mamadi Sefe Dekote loved Sia Jatta Bari to distraction (as they say) until he had lavished all his wealth on her, with nothing in return. Then she got a headache. She announced that it could only be cured if he cut off one of his little toes and washed her forehead with the blood. This failed and he was required to offer a finger. She then wrote a letter saying she could not possibly love anyone with only nine fingers and nine toes. Mamadi now managed to get a love potion which made Sia mad for him, but he refused her because of his regrettable deficiencies. Apparently relenting, he now agreed that she should visit him in the night, but put his young slave Blali in his bed. In the morning he entered the bedroom, saying: 'Why haven't you groomed my horse this morning instead of sleeping with this disreputable Sia?' Sia stayed inside all that day, then crept out through the shadows to her own house, but she died on the way of shame.

All the same, there is in general a difference of tone between the primitive sex story and the sophisticated one. The latter has a wider range, is more suggestive, more cunning, more naughty, more evocative. And one often reads a primitive tale and says to oneself: 'Imagine this if told by Boccaccio or Chaucer or La Fontaine!' An Ibo story tells of a wealthy man who set before his guests a mound of foo-foo so high that those who sat on one side could not see what was happening on the other. It was not until late in the evening that one of them saw for the first time an in-law who had arrived during the course of the meal and fallen to on the other side. It was only then that they exchanged greetings and shook hands over what was left of the food. Now imagine the *dénouement* if this story had been told in Europe. The guest would have discovered, late in the day, another man seducing his wife. Even then the possibilities of the situation would not have been exhausted, for he would have been persuaded that what he saw was in fact an illusion caused by magical properties in the foo-foo.

FOOTNOTES

1. From information supplied by R. W. Forrest.
2. Reported in *Woman's Experience of the Male*, by Dr Sofie Lazarsfeld.

3: *Stimulation by Word*

What causes erotic arousal in literature? What is it that causes no doubt well-meaning, if warped, people to believe fervently that written descriptions or suggestions can rouse people to greater sexual activity than would otherwise occur? (Whether increased sexual activity is evil is another question and beyond the scope of my enquiry.) Another question that always arises: supposing the written word can be proved to rouse desire, will its withdrawal cause the desire to lie dormant, or will another type of stimulus be found?

It is pointless to state, bluntly and uncritically, what rouses desire. Quite simply, one man's meat is another man's poison. Naylor, in Cyril Connolly's *The Rock Pool*, remembers how he used to hold hands with an old school friend and experience a sentimental erotic thrill as they read together this translation of some Latin verses:

> *Little brown brother, little brown brother,*
> *Are you awake in the dark?*
> *Here we lie cosily close to each other,*
> *Hark to the song of the lark!*

It turns out to be a potato talking. Sir Walter Scott warned a female relation off reading Aphra Behn. Dr Johnson said of Matthew Prior: 'There is nothing in Prior that will excite to lewdness. If Lord Hailes thinks there is, he is more combustible than other people.' I know a young man who confessed to me that he had an erection while reading *Bonjour Tristesse*, by Françoise Sagan. Yet it is not an erotic book. People make love but the love-making is not described. There is an atmosphere of sexual frankness but it is cheapened by frivolity. In fact, the main theme of the book is conspiracy. Eroticism seems to be ninety per cent in the observer, depending on his age, circumstances, maturity and state of health.

Two more examples. Lord Brougham, attacking Lord Campbell's Obscenity Bill in 1857, said that in Pope's *Eloisa to Abelard* there were lines that 'I would be ashamed to read aloud.' Read the poem and one is baffled—the only possible candidate for censorship appears to be these lines:

> *Then my conscience sleeps, and leaving Nature free*
> *All my loose soul unbounded springs to thee.*
> *O cursed, dear horrors of all-conscious night!*
> *How glowing guilt exalts the keen delight!*
> *Provoking demons all restraint remove,*
> *And stir within me ev'ry source of love,*
> *I hear thee, view thee, gaze o'er all thy charms,*
> *And round thy phantom glue my clasping arms.*

The reader in those days supplied more imaginative effort than we do, with the result that this might well have been thought too fleshly, even if he was cuddling a ghost. And yet Brougham might equally well have quailed before the blasphemy of the following couplet rather than any expression of erotic passion:

> *Snatch me, just mounting, from the bless'd abode;*
> *Assist the fiends and tear me from my God!*

Certainly the reader in Pope's day, and much later, would have considered this the more terrible of the two. As I remarked in the previous chapter, most people today appear to think fornication more terrible than murder—judging by our popular literature, anyway.

The truth is, that old ogre, Point of View, is at work. Sir Walter Scott, and his aunt who appears to have put him up to it, were typical victims. I was once lambasted by a weekly reviewer for not worshipping at this shrine, and I trust these examples will deter my readers from such saurian attitudes.

For nine times out of ten Point of View is a comforting rampart behind which the mind can hide. It provides an automatic response to any situation that arises.

When Charles Bradlaugh and Annie Besant were prosecuted for the publication of their pamphlet, *The Fruits of Philosophy*, a typical confusion between heterodoxy and lubricity were in action. This was a serious work but the fact that a prosecution was laid indicates that many people could not recognise the seriousness of the motive or, worse, refused to believe that it was possible. Such people usually announce their own purity and put themselves forward as guardians of yours and mine. In fact, the only thing that can be asserted without doubt is that the prosecutors must have felt some kind of erotic arousal in themselves. Combustible, as Johnson would have said. The English record in these matters is a sorry one, though no sorrier than elsewhere, but in this case sanity triumphed. The jury exonerated the authors from any imputation of corrupt motive.

On the other hand there is a class of reader who searches literature eagerly for erotic symbols and allusions. The morality of such action is not in question here. It is, however, a practice that we must take cognisance of, for such a reader will ultimately get more satisfaction from a child's book about ponies than from the *Decameron*. After a while, Sade, Nerciat, *Fanny Hill*, Henry Miller and the *Kama Sutra* begin to pall. The reader wants something more subtle—and naturally finds it. He especially delights in uncovering erotic interests in popular authors such as Gilbert Frankau and Ethel M. Dell. Innocent-seeming novels of the past, juvenilia such as *Eric, or Little by Little* and *Tom Brown's Schooldays*, or romantic epics, such as *The Count of Monte Cristo*, yield up unexpected treasures. Or the amatory passages of a respectable writer such as Angus Wilson are closely investigated, to get the thrill of powdered and flaking corpses jangling in febrile copulation, trying to beat the years.

According to Kinsey, men respond far more freely to stimulation by erotic stories than women—but then, they appear to respond more freely to most things compared with women. But women do respond more freely to literary material than to pictures of erotic action or photographs of nude figures. It is also rare for women actually to write pornography. Among 'the hundreds and probably thousands' (there is a strain of vagueness running all through the Kinsey Reports, despite the statistics) of unpublished, amateur documents examined over fifteen years, only three written by females contained erotic elements of the sort normally found in male documents. The same can be said about drawings. Females in fact produce another type of erotic literature, dealing with more general emotional situations, affectional relationships and love. It is akin to Shelleyan eroticism. It does not bring specifically erotic responses from males and only minimal responses from females. The unwary may sometimes be misled by the pseudonyms of authors, particularly in the field of flagellation literature, where it is common for male authors to adopt female names—a kind of psychological transvestism which in many cases appears to aid the thrill. Women on the whole are not interested in detailed descriptions of genital organs and activity, so that much scientific and physiological literature becomes pornographic (i.e., is used pornographically) for men but not for women. The women in pornographic literature extol the males's sexual capacity, and the female's insatiability is always stressed. There is no reality in such works, only a phantasy of the kind of female men would like a living woman to be— or think they would. Men in general woefully misinterpret the woman's approach to sex; it is not true, for instance, that a woman will swoon at the mere thought or sight of a phallus. Erotic literary folklore will have it so, however. It is important to remember that pornography is written by males for a male public.

There is a class difference among men, according to Kinsey. The upper level male (we are speaking economically) is roused erotically by a much greater number of stimuli than his lower level counterpart. There may be some connection with the fact that lower level males have more pre-marital intercourse and more extra-marital intercourse during the early years of marriage—in America, anyway. It may be the comparative in-

hibition of the better-off American that causes him to react to
a greater variety of stimuli. It is also likely that the more highly
educated male has a greater capacity for visualising situations
from hints and suggestions. It is the upper level male who is
the chief reader of erotic literature, who is more affected by
thinking about females, by burlesque shows, obscene stories,
love stories in good literature, love stories in moving pictures,
animals in coitus and sadomasochistic literature. Another factor is that erotic literature in the past has usually been highly
priced.

The American Sex Obsession

American literature has had a particularly powerful effect on
contemporary British literature for the obvious reason that
anyone can read it. It is a direct rival to the home product. If
the British author does not give his reader what he wants, or
what publicity and advertising have decided he shall want, the
reader can turn elsewhere. Therefore the following statement
by the literary adviser to an American publishing company is
significant:

> Some years ago . . . I asked an American novelist, in
> many ways a good one and deservedly successful, why he
> found it necessary three or four times in every novel he
> wrote to bring in, often gratuitously, and describe a sexual
> encounter with a crudity and vulgarity that was plainly
> below his normal level of sensitivity. He replied that that
> was the way his American publishers, who knew what sold
> fiction, had taught him to write novels.

One might guess this, of course. It is always doubtful to
what extent novelists can be trusted in their descriptions of
manners and customs. (Is the picture of Restoration society
given by the playwrights accurate? Almost certainly not for the
greater part even of fashionable society.) It is noticeable, for
instance, that Henry Miller never concerns himself with courting. He makes the direct sexual assault. But on the other hand,
it is unwise to assume that fictional pictures are necessarily
false. According to an English lady of my acquaintance, who

has spent several years in America, Miller's sexual technique
is standard American practice. From the European point of
view their approach is blatant and crude. It is interesting to
find the same criticisms made of Russian males. The anonymous author of *A Woman in Berlin* noticed how a Russian
soldier appeared to pay no attention whatever to the appearance of the woman he took. He just took the first. Americans
are certainly much more selective, but having made the choice
they have little time for finesse. These are obviously generalisa-
tions and are not to be taken too seriously, but there is a likeli-
hood that both races find in sex an aspect of power. This is one
side of the erotic impulse, but only one. It is particularly noticeable in modern American fiction, and in fiction that has been
influenced by the Americans. It is not yet found in the typical
Russian novel. There is nothing surprising in this. The Russians are still treading a cultural path some way in the wake
of the Americans. There are already signs that the social and
economic situation that is slowly providing the Russians with
more refrigerators and more attractive dwellings is also leading
to a demand for pop music and abstract art. It is likely that
their literature will become not only freer in expression but
also more violent in its approach to sex. The insistence on sex,
beneath which often lies a bewildered hatred of sex, is a station
in our civilisational development.

The modern writer in America and England feels compelled
to describe the physical sensation of sex. He describes people
eating, sweating, even relieving themselves and he tries to
present the feelings. Modern literature is full of burps and
belches. Why not sex? Of course, the law is still watching,
though it watches much less carefully than of old. Nowadays
not even the law causes much inhibition. What there is comes
from personal taste and, increasingly, boredom. And a skilled
novelist can do so much. In Faulkner's *Soldier's Pay* Emmy
tells Mrs Powers how Donald seduced her. They had been bathing and suddenly she saw him looming over her—he was
panting from running 'and I could feel something inside me
panting, too'. Now it's no good your running round to the
police station with this little piece of lubricity. You can be

sure that, if trouble threatens, that 'something inside me'
wasn't necessarily Donald but the rhythm of her desire. Of
course, we know Donald did put it in but no one can say
Faulkner was crude enough to describe it.

Geoffrey Gorer has noted how enormously popular erotic
books are in America ('The Erotic Myth of America', *Partisan
Review*, July-August 1950). They must represent fulfilments
of deeply felt but furtive wishes. The thought of gratifying
such reprehensible wishes must also arouse a great deal of
guilt. He makes a comparison with the prostitutes who, in the
heyday of Victorian morality, gratified in a more concrete way
the wishes of respectable gentlemen and were then accused by
the same gentlemen of being the sources of their sin. This is
what is happening today with thousands of lonely readers. If
and when they commit sins while reading these books, then the
books and ultimately the culture are responsible. The fantastic
orgies described by American novelists are readily believed—
there are no facts to set against them.

Some American authorities profess themselves worried. The
F.B.I. Director, J. Edgar Hoover, said that the trade in pornography had a turnover of $500 million a year, but in fact cost
the nation much more than money. 'It is robbing our country
and particularly our younger generation of decency—it is a
seedbed for delinquency among juveniles and depravity among
all ages.' *Contact*, the organ of the General Board of Temper-
ance of the Methodist Church, claimed that sex had become a
selling tool for papers such as *Coronet*, which featured in its
advertising these headlines: 'Diet and Fertility', 'Marriage
Failures', 'How Women Hurt Men Most', 'The Woman Behind
Castro', 'What are the Real Differences Between Men and
Women?' In fact, most reputable magazines today candidly
discuss contraception, homosexuality, incompatibility, impotence and abortion. According to *Newsweek*, Margaret Mead
blames the Kinsey Report, and adds bluntly that the trend will
increase because it sells magazines.

The chief characteristic of such allegations is wildness of
assumption. No one stops to explain why it is a bad thing to
discuss homosexuality and incompatibility openly. No one

stops to consider whether the moral corruption, if it exists, is really caused by the publications or whether the publications, if they are corrupt, may not be part of a wider complex. And very often the critics appear to miss the point badly. Crane Brinton refers in one of his books to 'the latest American novelist attempting to be a clinician'. It is this kind of dishonesty that is the real, tangible vice. Writing about sex is bad when it is false. As I said earlier, the facts about private lives are hard to come by but a critic can develop an extra sense from his reading. Brinton names no names but I'll name one: Grace Metalious. Let's look at *The Tight White Collar* in some detail. Reviewing this book in the *Spectator*, Geoffrey Grigson wrote (6 June 1961):

> It is one of those novels which show how detestable people are in the tight white collar of respectability. But show this for no good reason, or only for titillating reasons, and lace with decidedly sexual connection and with little bits and spurts and gobbets of sadomasochism, adding a Mongolian offspring just to teach two of the pleasanter characters that life is life.

Most of it is regulation work—for instance, the young man who has been dominated by his mother, grew up wondering what was wrong with him, was disgusted and committed suicide. The impulse to commit suicide is something we are never made to feel. Miss M. likes to say that certain things are but she has not the skill to explain why they are, except in textbook fashion. There is routine sex and routine writing to go with it. First, the sexual act has to be done as frankly as possible.

> She felt the grind of his teeth against her left nipple so she gasped and moaned loudly enough to please him but not loudly enough to wake the children who slept in the next room. . . . He put his hands under her hips and pressed himself inside her . . . . in the next few seconds she felt his wet stickiness and then he went limp and heavy on top of her.

Don't imagine for one moment that Lisa was enjoying this.
She was busy hoping her husband wouldn't louse up his new
job. But long before this happened, before they were married,
Chris used to lie on his bed 'with a thumping heart and an
ache in his groin. Lover's nuts, he told himself as he rubbed his
sore parts gently. But every time he rubbed he had an erection
and had to run quickly to the bathroom and finish behind the
locked door.' You see, his mum used to examine the sheets.

Miss M. loves copulation—at least, she loves describing it
and the arts that lead to it. But the orgasm is her chief joy,
and contact is not necessary. Mr Justine used to tell Doris,
his Irish maid, to lie naked on the bed so that he could gloat
at her. 'She made her body curve, so that one hip was thrust
up higher than the other and when she looked at Theo, he had
moved his hands from the door panels and was holding his
groin. Doris sighed deeply and moved a little on the bed and
with one gigantic breath that was almost a sob, Theo Justine
reached his climax and it was over.'

Anthony Cooper didn't like slop in his love, either. Business-
like and matter-of-fact he was. He liked going to penthouses
and air-conditioned rooms and meeting sleek girls who didn't
fall in love with you. When you got tired of them 'you could
always go to a whorehouse or get a fancy call girl who knew
all the perversions and loved the extra money that practising
brought them in. Those girls didn't scream and pant and
moan and faint. They practised their art coolly, with precision,
while you watched and reluctantly admired them for the master
craftsmen they were. Even if they didn't excite you particularly
you still had to admire them. After all, what was sex anyway
but just another appetite to be appeased, like hunger. So you
might as well be a gourmet about it and get the best money
could buy.' Another thing: when the sleek girls wanted it
they wanted it coldly and neatly with a good strong condom
between you and them.

What all writers like Miss M. are dying to do is describe
copulation with all the stops out. When this is eventually
done (i.e., in public, for it has often been done for private
sale) it will show no merit in the author but just a shift in

social morality. Towards the end of this novel Chris and Lisa make it up and her heart begins to pound when he says he loves her. 'His fingers rubbed gently until her nipples hardened and stood up under the thin material of her nightgown. "You've got the most exciting pair of tits in the whole world," said Chris.' Now in the meantime Lisa has been having an affair with Anthony Cooper (whose desire for cool, sleek girls was largely a reaction from Lisa) and she has learnt a lot of new tricks which excite Chris immensely. (Which just shows what we chaps can do for one another.) But she puts off his curiosity by telling him that he was the one who brought home the Kinsey Report . . . so Margaret Mead may be right after all. And then 'the tip of him was touching the maddeningly elusive, excitingly secret place deep inside her and she could feel it starting.'

What is wrong with all this? We have demanded greater frankness for writers for years and now we've got it. Well, to begin with, the whole thing is so joyless. Then writers like Miss M. do not really know the facts of life, as another American writer once said. They have the feeling that they must make up for all the lost opportunities of generations of writers who preceded them. On the other hand, American society may be like this, weighted like this, in which case Miss M. becomes a good documentary writer—but she tells us more about society than about the individual. Compare this with Pierre Louÿs's *Aphrodite*. In ancient Alexandria (or Louÿs's Alexandria) sex gave people joy, release from their worries, a tremendous psychological lift. In Miss M.'s America sex is a rather unpleasant weapon for the furtherance of shady aims. And here is the real immorality. *Lady Chatterley* was prosecuted—and a thousand, thousand slimy things (like this) were not.

A Few Definitions

The word pornography is of Greek origin, meaning literally 'the writing of harlots'. The Greeks used it in a different way from us. Athenaeos quotes Cynulcus saying to a sophist: 'You lounge in low-class dives, not in the company of friends but

of harlots, you are surrounded by numerous pimps and carry
writings of Aristophanes, Apollodorus, Ammonius, Antiphanes
and the Athenian Gorgias around, all dealing with the harlots
of Athens. You really deserve to be called a pornographer like
the painters Aristides, Pausanias and Nicophanes.' That seems
to be the guest list of a wild party, classical style.

Switch to modern times. Zola comes to London and wants to
know why *La Terre* is regarded as pornographic. He was
incensed. 'If they knew how much worse life is,' he cried, 'they
would stop talking such nonsense.' And Hardy said that his
account of village life was mild compared with reality.

These references point to three important facts about sex:
some are roused by the mere existence of it, some wish to
examine it, others just accept it. Set against all three of these
a fourth type who disapproves of each: the excitement, the
investigation, the indifference. This type wishes to establish
the obscenity of any attitude but a careful abiding by the
rules of an established morality.

> If anyone was so great a lover of purity as to wish not only
> that no immodest desire should arise in his mind, but also
> that his imagination should be constantly free from every
> obscene idea, he could not attain his end without closing
> his eyes and ears, and the remembrance of many things
> which he could not choose but see and hear. Such perfec-
> tion could not be hoped for whilst we see men and beasts
> and know the signification of certain words that make a
> necessary part of our language. It is not in our power either
> to have, or not to have, certain ideas when certain objects
> strike our senses; they are imprinted in our imagination
> whether we will or not. Chastity is not endangered by
> them, providing we don't grow fond of them and approve
> of them.

These words are from the English translation (1738) of Pierre
Bayle's *Dictionnaire Historique et Critique*. Bayle, who came
in for a lot of criticism on account of his freedom of expression,
stops well this side of obsession. He might have added that

chastity is equally not endangered provided we don't grow over
fond of *dis*approving, for this is the condition of the extreme
sort of puritan, and it is a moot point whether a man is
maddened more by sex or by its denial.

Nobody discussed sex in terms of obscenity or pornography
(in the modern sense) until the nineteenth century. Although
the eighteenth century has a reputation for lustiness and bawdiness writers were nevertheless on their guard. La Fontaine,
for instance, was at pains to refute in advance accusations that
might be levelled against his work's air of levity and licentiousness, and its lack of respect for the fair sex. In the preface to
an English edition of his *Tales and Novels in Verse,* edited
by Samuel Humphreys, 1762, he claims that you can't write
a tale that isn't light-hearted and licentious, and as for the
ladies, he was never serious. He was only indulging a 'few
sportive sallies of fancy. . . . There is no reason to be appre-
hensive that they will cause marriages to be less frequent in the
future, and make husbands more circumspect and suspicious
than they were before.'

Moral conservatives such as Burke held that human beings
needed restraining rather than stimulating. He believed that
if they were left to themselves their natural desires would drive
them to all sorts of irresponsible excesses. Crane Brinton, the
historian of Western morals, believes that the *agon,* or com-
petitive struggle for a prize, sexual as well as economic, has
been fairly constant in our civilisation. It was softened in
some respects by Christianity but the Enlightenment released
it. At certain times in history there is more pornography in
print and in illustration than at others, but this is only because
the puritan ban has been stronger or weaker at different times.
When Brinton was writing (the late nineteen-fifties) he said
this material had been driven further underground than at
many times in the past, but so rapidly is the situation changing
that now, less than ten years later, it is doubtful if this is still
true.

The legal story has been told and retold so many times there
is no need to recount it here. I am more concerned with the
ideas of obscenity and pornography. It required the analytical

temper of the nineteenth century to enquire into their nature,
and not only for legislative purposes. Such enquiry is partly
the natural consequence of self-knowledge and it is only in
modern times that psychology has been pursued scientifically.
Hence I will end this section with a few random comments on
these two ideas, culminating in a fairly detailed analysis of
their ingredients.

D. H. Lawrence. The element of pornography enters when
there is sex excitement with a desire to spite, humiliate and
degrade the sexual feeling. 'For this reason there is an element
of pornography in nearly all nineteenth-century literature and
very many so-called pure people have a nasty pornographical
side to them, and never was the pornographical appetite
stronger than it is today. It is a sign of a diseased condition of
the body politic. But the way to treat the disease is to come
out into the open with sex and sex stimulus. The real pornographer truly dislikes Boccaccio, because the fresh healthy
naturalness of the Italian story-teller makes the modern pornographical shrimp feel the dirty worm he is. Today Boccaccio
should be given to everyone young or old, to read if they like.
Only a natural fresh openness about sex will do any good, now
we are being swamped by secret or semi-secret pornography.
And perhaps the Renaissance story-tellers, Boccaccio, Lasca
and the rest, are the best antidote we can find now, just as
more plasters of Puritanism are the most harmful remedy we
can resort to.' (*Pornography and Obscenity*, 1929).

This is a very personal point of view. If taken seriously it
would follow that sex should be a joy and writing and reading
about sex should also be joys—as they often have been. It does
not appear in Lawrence's own writings. Secret pornography
turns to the Ophelia Press, semi-secret to Kinsey.

Ronald Duncan. 'Pornography is the art which attracts you
towards sex; obscenity the nauseous substitute for sex which
repels you from the actual experience. The former moves you
towards sex, the latter from it.' (Introduction to *Selected Lyrics
and Satires of John, second Earl of Rochester*, 1948).

Again, a very personal view. Some writers would reverse these values, say that pornography disgusts and obscenity is, by definition, merely the other side of the picture.

Geoffrey Gorer. 'Pornography is, no doubt, the opposite face, the shadow, of prudery, whereas obscenity is an aspect of seemliness.' The rules of seemliness vary from society to society, from age to age. In one place I may not watch you eat; in another I may not address my paternal grandfather. 'Everywhere and at all times there are words and actions which, when misplaced, can produce shock, social embarrassment and laughter. Pornography, on the other hand, the description of tabooed activities to produce hallucination or delusion, seems to be a very much rarer phenomenon. It probably can only arise in literate societies, and we certainly have no records of it for non-literate ones; for whereas the enjoyment of obscenity is predominantly social, the enjoyment of pornography is predominantly private.' ('The Pornography of Death', *Encounter*, October 1955).

Lionel Trilling. A definition of pornography. 'I take it to mean the explicit representation in literature (or the graphic arts—or music, for that matter) of the actual sexual conduct of human beings. (I suppose I should include anthropomorphic gods, demons, etc.) It seems to me that this representation is a perfectly acceptable artistic enterprise. I expect that, if it is carried out with some skill, it will raise lustful thoughts in the reader, and I believe that this in itself provides no ground for objection.' ('The Last Lover', *Encounter*, October 1958).

He continues that it is one of the effects, perhaps functions, of literature, to arouse desire, 'and I can discover no ground for saying that sexual pleasure should not be among the objects of desire which literature presents to us, along with heroism, virtue, peace, death, food, wisdom, God, etc.'

An interesting thought: supposing the puritans had directed their venom against heroism instead of sex? Might not most of us be rather happier than we are, released of the necessity of trying desperately to live up to impossible standards?

Norman Mailer. This *enfant terrible* thinks that pornography may be less crippling to the mind than the respectable products of a respectable community. 'A sixteen-year-old boy closeted in the bathroom with the photo of a prostitute is laying the physical ground of his neurosis—he will pay later in bad reflex, pinched orgasm and nervous guilt, but at least he is not looking for a fetish—on the contrary, he is beginning his search for a mate. If he paralyses most of his chances by looking for satisfaction to come out of himself, he is at least still staring out—his dream is how climactic it would be to find such a woman in the real.

'That much deserved to be said for pornography. It must also be said that pornography gives no preparation for sex. In the pornographic dream, all comings come together, the torso is lithe, the smell is clean, pleasure arrives like manna. What a shock for the sensitive adolescent when he finds the courage to capture his first sex. For good, by times, as it may be, there are dead small corners for which he is not prepared, and responsibility he never knew. Nothing in the life of his fantasy prepared him for tenderness, for war, for the tragic need of sex to move into love or be chilled to something less.' ('A Note on Comparative Pornography', from *Advertisements for Myself*, 1958-9).

If this is the state of the pornographer, how much more alarming is that of the puritanical sex-hater (who naturally masquerades as a love-lover)?

Walter Allen. One man's obscenity is another man's pornography. Obscenity once meant that which could not be represented on the stage, e.g., the plucking out of Gloucester's eyes in *King Lear*. In origin pornography is a concept in morals, obscenity in aesthetics. 'Observation seems to show that in literature the obscene almost invariably cancels out the pornographic. Swift is often undeniably obscene but when he is, the effect is the reverse of pornographic: it inhibits rather than inflames lust. To take a more recent instance, I assume that if James Joyce had stood trial at the Old Bailey the Gerty MacDowell episode in *Ulysses* is one of the passages he would

have had to justify. It is a description of female exhibitionism
and Bloom's masturbation in consequence. It could have been
pornographic. It is anything but that, for the scene is rendered
throughout in terms of irony, is disinfected, as it were, by
comedy. It is satire on pornography.' (From his essay in *To
Deprave and Corrupt*).

A good general statement but it allows a lot of little fish to
escape. We know from the confessions of prostitutes that some
men can only be roused by what Allen would call the obscene:
the woman must be eight months pregnant, or have halitosis,
or five breasts.

No one to my knowledge has come closer to a satisfactory definition of these terms than Drs Eberhard and Phyllis Kronhausen.
In their book, *Pornography and the Law*, they attempt to distinguish between erotic realism and what they call 'hardcore
pornography'—as an illustration of the difficulties inherent in
this field, they frequently refer to this latter category as
'obscenity'. They make a plea for unrestricted access to erotic
realism, i.e., writing which deals with sexual matters with a
serious purpose (which can include humour) as distinct from
writing whose sole aim is the stimulation of the sex impulse.
It will be seen that in this respect they are in disagreement
with Trilling.

This book suffers from the usual American weaknesses in
this type of study—it is inclined to be portentous, at times
owlish. It is somehow symptomatic that, instead of being content with one piece of prefatory writing, it should have a
Foreword, an Introduction and a Preface. Maybe this is symbolic of the love play before the act. As for the act, this is
what the authors have to say:

> In pornography (hardcore obscenity) the main purpose is
> to stimulate erotic response in the reader. And that is all.
> In erotic realism, truthful description of the basic realities
> of life, as the individual experiences it, is of the essence
> . . . it is axiomatic that the reader should respond erotic-
> ally to such writing.

The authors have an odd habit of being unable to use the
word 'pornography' without immediately throwing in the
bonus 'hardcore obscenity' or, conversely using the word
'obscenity' without throwing in 'hardcore pornography',
which leads to confusion. The obscene (hardcore pornographic)
book must not have any superfluous non-erotic descriptions of
scenery, character portrayals, etc. The sole purpose of the
pornographic (hardcore obscene) book is the build-up of
erotic excitement. Erotic realism represents an expression of
the acceptance of life in its totality, of which the sexual drive
is an important part, rather than the retort of the repressed,
resulting in over-emphasis on the sexual. It is seen in the
difference between *The Golden Lotus* and *Gynecocracy*. *Fanny
Hill* stands left of centre.

The Kronhausens' most valuable contribution is their list
of the characteristics of obscene literature:

(a) Seduction. The 'Victim' is a willing collaborator. As a
    result seduction scenes are extremely brief. Foreplay
    starts immediately.

(b) Defloration. Usually with a strong sadistic element.
    The girl rarely admits to pain. It is often accom-
    plished with the help of others.

(c) Incest. Rare in open literature, frequent in porno-
    graphy. Rarely any qualms of guilt or emotional con-
    flict.

(d) Permissive-seductive parent figure. Not only condones
    but often participates—in some cases actually seduces
    or initiates the child.

(e) Profaning the sacred. Intermingling of the sacred and
    profane is commonplace. An intuitive grasp of psycho-
    logical ground here (as in *c* and *d*). Heightens erotic
    tension.

(f) 'Dirty' words. Use of taboo words serves same purpose
    as in *e*. Open defiance of superego.

(g) Supersexed males. Emphasis on exaggerated size of
    male organ and copiousness of semen ejaculated.
    Almost limitless potency. (In *The Strange Cult* a man

exhibits his huge penis, masturbates in front of a
girl, and drenches her nude body. In *Lustful Stories*
the hero causes his darling Norah to writhe in holy
joy no less than eleven times in one night. This
approaches sex worship—in another story in the
same book the woman has a household god, 'an exact
replica of my penis, gold mounted on a velvet stand
of convenient height.' Convenient enough for the
girls to immolate themselves.)

(h) Nymphomaniac females. Just as the men want them to
be: highly passionate, sensual and sexually insatiable,
who enjoy uninterrupted coitus.

(i) Negroes and Asiatics as sex symbols. In keeping with
popular prejudice that they are extraordinarily virile
and given to perversion.

(j) Homosexuality. Strong element, if not direct references. (In this case I think the authors are mistaken—
in the majority of 'hardcore pornography' of the kind
they are describing, there is little differentiation between homosexual and heterosexual.)

(k) Flagellation. Authors refer to long history of sado-
masochism in Western sex practice and literature, but
do not mention the extreme brutality of much literary
flagellation, and the heroic fortitude displayed by the
victims.

I would add one further characteristic to this list:

(l) Sexual aberration. This is nearly always present. There
is little agreement on what is aberrant, but it can be
agreed that certain practices are not orthodox. Chief
among these are sodomy, pederasty and irrumation.

In conclusion, my own definitions are as follows: *Erotic
literature*, a description of sexual activity. Motives may be
various but they include normal literary intention of reducing
the outer world to words; a description of sex is of the same
quality as the description of the harvest, a funeral or a cricket
match. *Pornography* is part of erotic literature but is written
with the express purpose of stimulating sexually. Later, after

the rise of opposition, the desire to shock appears. Erotic literature is co-eternal with all other forms. Pornography was partly
produced by the puritan repression of pleasure, sport and
'pastimes'. Rochester's *Sodom* was the first truly pornographic
work in English, with the possible exception of Nashe's dildo
poem.[1]

The Development of Pornography

But the Romans had their pornographic authors, although
few of them have survived. Elephantis, Musaeus and Labellus
were often praised—yes, praised—for works which served as
stimulants to excite the passions. Ovid alludes to a work
entitled *Opus Sybaritis* which must have been sheer pornography. Information is scanty, however. The *Priapeia* were less
pornography than witty occasional verses. Again, we know
very little of the Greek 'harlots' writings'. Orthodox Greek
literature has a high degree of salaciousness and gives the impression of frequently being intended to titillate. The endless
series of divine fornications and adulteries are never detailed,
never shocking in the modern manner, but certainly give the
impression that such activities were to be condoned. Lucian
recounts a dialogue between Mercury and Helios, in which
Mercury instructs the other not to go out for three days because Jupiter is visiting Amphitryon and wishes to produce
a hero—it cannot be done in one night. Helios is annoyed but
largely because his routine has been disturbed. 'For the sake
of one graceless woman, all nature must be turned upside
down . . . poor mankind must live miserably in darkness all
the while and, thanks to the amorous temperament of the king
of the gods, there must they sit waiting in that long obscurity,
till this great athlete you speak of is finished.' Jupiter must be
regarded as the patron of all sexual athletes, but we are not
given his dimensions.

There was no overt pornography in the Middle Ages. It
requires a circle of readers with the necessary literary interests.
The educated of the Middle Ages, mainly clerical, probably
managed to satisfy their sexual needs by natural means, or
rejected the subject entirely, that is to say, sublimated their

energies into non-sexual channels. Certainly the official puritanism of the medieval Church was by no means as thoroughgoing as its modern descendants. People in general were neither complicated nor refined enough (pornography exists at many cultural levels) to appreciate it. The type of literature that did draw on the sexual for its effect was largely crude and ribald, without any deliberate pandering to sexuality. It was intended to make people laugh, not fornicate. Chaucer is an admirable English example.

Perhaps the first writer in English to be consciously erotic was Spenser. The *Faerie Queene* is a mine of sensuality. Scholars have missed this quality for the very good reason that they have not wished to see it. There are still large areas of our literature that need rescuing from the dead hand of Victorian criticism. It is difficult to see how anyone could read Stanza 73 in Canto XII of Book II without being impressed by its carnality. Spenser has the approach of the *voyeur*—he positively drools over a description of his mistress as an ivory table 'all spred with juncats', the centre piece of which is a silver dish containing two golden apples. Alan Brien, who calls himself 'a constant reader of Spenser', directs our attention (in an article in *Spectator*, 15 Nov. 1963) to this description of the lustful monster in Book IV, Canto VII:

> *His neather lip was not like man nor beast,*
> *But like a wide deepe poke, downe hanging low,*
> *In which he won the relics of his feast,*
> *And cruel spoyle, which he had spard, to stow:*
> *And over it his huge great nose did grow,*
> *Full dreadfully empurpled all with bloud;*
> *And down both sides two wide long ears did grow,*
> *And raught downe to his waste, when up he stood,*
> *More great than th'eares of Elephants by Indus flood.*

'You do not need any psychoanalytical training to see here a rather grisly amalgam of the male and female sexual organs', writes Brien.

There are many other examples: the twins who commit incest in the womb of a giantess; the undressing of Serena (in

five stanzas) by the 'salvage nation'—a slow, conducted tour
of the naked heroine; and Dame Hellenore, whose husband
creeps up to see how she enjoys a mass rape by Satyres:

> At night, when all they wente to sleepe, he vewd,
> Whereas his lovely wife amongst them lay,
> Embraced of a Satyre rough and rude,
> Who all night did minde his joyous play;
> Nine times he heard him come aloft ere day,
> That all his hart with jealousie did swell;
> But yet that night's ensample did bewray,
> That not for nought his wife them loved so well,
> When one so oft a night did ring his matins bell.

Spenser professed to be preaching chastity and religion, and
allowed his imagination to luxuriate in obscenities which
would have impressed both Shakespeare and Donne. And here
we are on the edge of something new, something trembling to
be born. Spenser licks his lips over those milk-white bodies.

It was in the following century, when puritanism had become a powerful force in Europe, that the literary sexual situation became dramatic. A powerful body of opinion forbids
the old lusty attitude towards the subject, especially forbids
laughter. Sex, unlike health and eating, has become sacred.
Naturally writers feel a new compulsion to write about these
carnal activities, and at the same time have a sense of wickedness. *The Historical and Critical Dictionary* of Peter Bayle
was a landmark. Bayle was a Fleming who lived from 1647-1706
and who published his great work in Rotterdam in 1697. The
best French editions were those in 1720 and 1746 in four
volumes folio and a later one in sixteen volumes octavo. The
best English translation is that of Des Maizeaux in five volumes
folio. Significantly, a selected and abridged English edition
was published in 1826.

Bayle realised that a book 'stuffed with Greek and Latin
quotations' would not sell unless it were leavened with 'actions
and reflections' which were 'free and gallant'. As a result he
was charged with obscenity by the consistory of Rotterdam. In

the second edition he defended himself, as thousands have defended themselves since, by maintaining that in a historical work the truth must be told. Also, if an action is represented in all its depravity the reader may be shocked into good resolutions. There is no doubt, however, that Bayle enjoyed telling a risqué story. He was quite unregenerate about his activities, and it is fair to regard his defence, even if true, as an early example of the rationalising process in this field, where it has flourished ever since. The pastors objected particularly to his articles on the Manichaean heresy, Pyrrho and David, and his comments on atheists and Epicureans. Bayle promised to make changes but in fact only rewrote the article on David—and then included both versions in the second edition!

David's sexuality was emphasised and his polygamy criticised. The argument was that God excused it in those early days but it cannot be stretched far without indulging in sensuality. Because David chose the most handsome girls he could find Bayle says, rather quaintly, that 'we cannot say, with regard to the Pleasures of Love, that he took much pains to mortify Nature.' He was troubled by David's lying with a girl to keep warm. This was scarcely the action of a chaste man, and there is considerable doubt whether the natural instincts can be repressed in such circumstances. Later, after the publication of a new *Dictionary of the Bible*, Bayle added a note that even if David's sole purpose was to warm his hands and feet he would still be guilty of a sin.

There is nothing here to send young men to the brothels. The complaint was rather that Bayle discussed the actions of the great David in a manner altogether too free and easy. He saw through the moral twistings and turnings of the official apologists and showed them for what they were. The rock on which all sects, that tried to distinguish themselves by moral paradoxes, failed, was that of venereal pleasure; 'it is a worm which never dies, and a fire which never goes out', he says of the Adamists. He infuriated the casuists because he acknowledged the powerful allure of sexual pleasure. He is at his most delightful and roguish when discussing kissing, which he does in an article on Puteanus. Puteanus, he said, educated young

Italian gentlewomen and would not allow them to be kissed.
'That is dangerous for Italian girls. Our Flemish ones may do
it without any hazard or detriment; they do not understand
that there are any love-lessons in ogling and kisses; but those
of your country know very well the consequences of it, and
for this reason I have taught her our language, and all our
customs, except that of kissing.' One must not confuse cere-
monial with love kisses, however. 'Those familiarities which are
dangerous in Italy are very little, or not at all so, in the northern countries.' Socrates criticised Critobulus for kissing a
woman. After kissing you lose your liberty and engage in
excessive expenses to obtain a destructive pleasure. He compared a kiss with the poisonous bite of a spider. 'Do you think
that love-kisses are not venomous because you do not see the
poison? Know that a fair woman is an animal more dangerous
than scorpions, because they cannot hurt unless they touch us;
but beauty wounds us without coming near us.' A kiss which in
Turkey, Italy and Spain is the beginning of adultery is in
Paris a mere civility. He concludes by quoting Erasmus's enthusiastic report on the widespread habit of kissing in England.
'Wherever you meet them you feast on their rosy lips. In a
word, all places you enter are full of kisses which, my friend,
had you once but tasted, how soft, how fragrant they are, you
would not, I am positive, like Solon desire to live ten years,
but till death, in England.' Bayle's dry comment is: 'You see
that Erasmus did not like English women less than English-
men.'

Bayle applied his common sense about sex to the subject of
clerical celibacy, and its practical consequences (article on
Launoi):

> Either clergymen should be permitted to marry, or for-
> bidden to keep young servant maids; for the prodigious
> concubinage of priests, which has scandalised the public
> for so many ages, owes its origin to the permission of
> having women about them, to manage their houses. The
> intention of the superiors was that they should confine
> themselves to the business of servant maids; but they

easily suffered themselves to be persuaded to serve some other purpose. . . .

And in the article on Telemenus he gives us his view of love. It will be seen that he is not a libertine but his discussions of the subject are tinged throughout with tolerance and a sense of humour. These are the new notes.

We must not believe all that the poets and writers of romances make amorous people say; the descriptions of their sufferings are hyperbolical; however, it must be granted that love is an inexhaustible source of miseries and disorders. It is a very necessary passion upon earth for the preservation of animals; it is the soul of the world with respect to them; nay, it is certain that the Divine Providence has annexed a thousand charms and pleasures to so necessary a passion; but, on the other hand, it is attended with a thousand troubles.

Those whose love is not answered lose appetite, sleep, health and wits, even life. Those who are successful lose their reason, suffer agonies from jealousy. 'If there were a river in the world which could cure lovers, it would be more valuable than gold.' And this is like a voice from the classical past.

While readers in England were sniggering at Bayle's insinuations or feeling uncomfortable at his realistic approach, the first prosecutions for obscene libel were taking place. In 1708 a printer named Reid was indicted for publishing *Fifteen Plagues of a Maidenhead*, a dull, repetitious book. Sir John Holt, Lord Chief Justice, said he disliked the book but it was not illegal. The first conviction was of Edmund Curll, who was generally believed to have had his ears cut off for publishing *Venus in the Cloister, or the Nun in her Smock*. It appeared on 15 October 1724 as a translation from the French 'at the request of the Duchess of ——'. The respectable Samuel Garth's couplet prefaced it:

Vows of virginity should well be weigh'd;
Too oft they're cancelled, tho' in Convent made.

The Advertisement stated that 'the Amours herein display'd' were 'not to be parallel'd for their agreeable Entertainment in any Romance or Novel hitherto extant.' A second edition appeared in January. This was war. Sex was being used as a subject providing literary pleasure. It was the natural consequence of the Bayle approach. Curll always maintained he was not the author.

Someone made an official complaint. While the situation was being considered (no one knew exactly how to proceed, for this was totally new ground) Curll hastily printed *The Humble Representation of Edmund Curll, Bookseller and Stationer of London, concerning Five Books, complained of to the Secretary of State*. These five books were a *Treatise of Flogging*, which he claimed was a medical work translated from the Latin and which was far less lewd than another publication that was being sold without any action being taken; the Nun in question, the moral of whose story was 'inimitably instructive'; *The Praise of Drunkenness* (obviously satire); a manual for married ladies, translated from Albertus Magnus; and two modern renderings of Chaucer. Early in March several printers and publishers of obscene books were taken into custody. Curll was one of these, on account of *Flogging* and the *Nun*, but was released on bail in July. In the middle of November he was told to prepare for trial at the King's Bench Bar at Westminster. In his statement of defence Curll declared the prosecution was malicious, in that it was brought seven years after the first publication of a serious translation by a physician.

The question at issue was whether a book could be termed a 'libel'. Curll was found guilty but Strange, his counsel, moved an arrest of judgment on the ground that the offence was not a libel but *contra bonos mores* and therefore punishable only in the spiritual courts. The Attorney-General argued that it was an offence at Common Law as it tended to corrupt the morals of the King's subjects. If you destroyed morality you destroyed the peace of the Government. Mr Justice Fortesque stated that drunkenness, cursing and swearing were not punishable at Common Law but on the other hand the Spiritual Court ignored them. As a result of this discussion sentence was postponed and Curll was released on bail again.

On 3 December he announced his retirement, accompanied by an advertisement of the two books in question and two others. He sturdily maintained that he had not published the *Nun* but had merely sold a copy. The additional books were the *Works* of Andrew Marvell and *The Case of Seduction,* being the late proceedings in Paris against the Rev. Abbé des Rues, for committing rapes upon 133 virgins, written by himself. Less than a fortnight after the trial His Majesty's Messengers raided the shop and seized nine books and pamphlets. Curll was taken into custody again for six weeks, then transferred to the King's Bench Prison. There followed a further period on bail, then another in the custody of the King's Messengers, and again more bail. His enemies were closing in.

At this time many people guilty of 'unnatural lewdness' were being put in the Wooden Ruff (the pillory). Curll had now drawn more venom by publishing John Ker's 'scandalous and seditious' memoirs. On 27 November 1727 the judges of the King's Bench decided he must be committed to the King's Bench Prison in Southwark, without bail or mainprize, until next term when he would receive judgment. On 12 February 1728 Curll received sentence for 'his Amorous and Political Offences'. For the two amorous offences he was fined twenty-five marks each, and had to enter into a Recognizance of £100 for good behaviour for one year; for the political offence (Ker's *Memoirs*) he was fined twenty marks and sentenced to stand in the pillory for one hour, plus another Recognizance for good behaviour for another year. Eleven days later he was placed in the pillory at King's Cross. A broadside was handed to spectators in which he claimed he had had the Royal Warrant to publish Ker's *Memoirs*. Only one man threw an egg, and he was nearly lynched. When he was released Curll was taken on the shoulders of an admiring crowd to a tavern. He did not lose his ears. He was not stood in the pillory for obscene libel. Folklore always improves a story.

Curll's shop was in Holywell Street, which later became the centre of English pornography. While Bowdler was purifying Shakespeare and Plumptre was making English drama suitable for clergymen's daughters, Holywell Street boomed. The Society for the Suppression of Vice said there were 57 shops selling this type of literature in 1834. The first English magazines devoted entirely to obscenity were sold here. They differed from their eighteenth-century predecessors which had always concentrated on the joy of sex. A special literature concentrating on flagellation, fellatio and male homosexuality came into existence. By a series of prosecutions, nearly always successful, the Society claimed to reduce the number of shops to twenty, but it is doubtful if the total volume of business was reduced. Societies such as that for the Suppression of Vice bear a heavy responsibility for the unpleasant change of tone that is to be found in the modern approach to sex in some quarters, and, by giving it a scarcity value, for the persistence of pornography as opposed to erotic realism, which humanity needs and will have.

The Modern Eros

Guy de Maupassant, a master of the short story, whose work frequently resorts to sexual titillation but never becomes frankly pornographic, might well have been the hero of a Holywell Street novel. He suffered from satyriasis, or chronic hyperexcitability of the penis. He told Frank Harris he could make love six times in an hour. He made the same boast to Flaubert and, to prove his point, went to a brothel with a witness and did the trick. But Harris would not believe him and said he must be speaking metaphorically because such a power would be dangerous, leading to exhaustion and nervous breakdown. Maupassant retorted that he was no more tired after twenty times than after two. This claim seemed even more outrageous to Harris but Maupassant insisted he had done it twenty times and more without stopping. 'Surely you know,' he said, 'that in two or three times you exhaust your stock of semen, so that you can go on afterwards without further loss.'

I refer to this little achievement by one of the masters because it underlines one of the major characteristics of the

modern sex story. The man is inexhaustible. This is not
realistic for, despite Maupassant's argument, most men cannot
or do not wish to continue once they have run dry. But in the
cheaper type of novel they do not run dry. In serious works
they do, as in life. There is also another type of novel, the
humorous one, where copulation may be endless, but here the
effect is one of hyperbole. It is the equivalent of the Baron
Munchausen or Rabelais and the reader is required to accept
this approach if he is to get any benefit from his reading—the
benefit being a lightening of the spirit. But much pornography
is horribly grim and we feel that the hero is constantly proving
something as he ejaculates again and again. He is proving his
virility, just as he does when he beats the girl up.

The most famous modern dynasty in erotic publishing is
centred in Paris. Before the last war an Anglo-Irishman named
Jack Kahane founded the Obelisk Press and published Joyce's
Haveth Childers Everywhere (a foretaste of *Finnegan's Wake*),
Durrell's *The Black Book,* Connolly's *The Rock Pool* and
Harris's *My Life and Loves,* while he himself wrote under the
names of Cecil Barr and Basil Carr. It is obvious from these
titles that Kahane must not be dismissed as a pornographer.
His son, Maurice Girodias, has continued the family business
with the Olympia Press, and has equivalent publishing
triumphs on record: Nabokov's *Lolita,* Donleavy's *The Ginger
Man* and Burroughs's *The Naked Lunch* included. Here is a
statement made by Girodias to Kenneth Allsop and published
in the *Spectator* for 21 October 1960:

'The dirty books are not always bad, although I must
admit that some are awful. But I accept the title of pornographer with joy and pride. I enjoy annoying people,
people I dislike deeply—the bourgeois class which is
in power everywhere, in France, Britain and America. I
think it is very healthy to shock them. I don't believe that
dirty books corrupt young people. I don't think children
are interested in or can understand pornography. It is a
thing for adults. If my dirty books were sold freely in
Britain the word pornography would cease to exist. I am

quite aware of the poor quality of some of my dirty books —which is the only justification of the fight against pornography—but I think that some of them are well written. Frankly, I publish the worst kind just to annoy people who expect it of me. But I think, in general, our policy has been importantly helpful in the fight against censorship.'

He has reiterated this viewpoint on several occasions since.

A new element has been introduced since Curll's time: the desire to shock. I feel certain that Curll had no desire to shock —it was far too dangerous, anyway. There were two motives in his day: increased sales by providing material that you were told you mustn't read, and a genuine belief that the truth should be told about everything. Today the realist battle has been fought and, except for mopping-up operations, won. The desire to shock remains and is largely responsible for erotic hyperbole, which is often quite as amusing as Charlie Chaplin and James Thurber.

Incidentally, it is a common illusion that pornography can be published quite freely in France. It depends on the language. The French government has been just as busy in prosecuting pornography as the British and American governments, providing the offending article is in the French language. At the time Girodias made the above statement he had had forty-one books banned and had been indicted twenty-five times in thirteen years.

I now give a few examples of the better type of erotic publication during modern times. The first, *Fay and her Boy Friend* (no date), is completely unpretentious but is a cut above the average publication of this kind. It is pornographic (that is, not erotic realism in the Kronhausen acceptance of the phrase) but it has a pleasant lightness of touch: Bank Holiday reading. It is short, probably British, and tends to decline into 'hardcore obscenity' in its later chapters.

A gentleman seduces a virgin in a railway compartment— one of the old type without corridors which used to frighten our grandmothers so much, and with reason judging by this story. (Incidentally, this is the chief clue to the story's period.) Between stations the girl masturbates the man, is masturbated by him, allows him to perform cunnilingus, and herself performs fellatio (for five pounds). It starts thus:

'But there's a good deal of harm in your putting your hand up my clothes,' I said.

'Well, give us one kiss and I'll be good,' he retorted.

I let him have a kiss; he was a nice looking old man— and I always liked being kissed. As I expected, he put his tongue in my mouth, and I—well, I didn't jump away as I should have done; I gave the tongue just one little lick with mine.

It maddened him, as I expected it might.

'As you jolly knew it would,' puts in the typewriter.

'Nothing of the sort, you nasty-minded girl'; mind you, I was still a virgin at the time.

How long, o Lord, how long?

Well, he began putting his hand up my clothes again, so I jumped away and ran to the other end of the compartment.

He came after me, and pushed me down on the cushions of the carriage seat, standing over me and trying to force his legs between mine, but I escaped him again, and I think he saw then that it was no use trying to get me by force.

Now let's turn to something of an entirely different type, written by a young man who is today a revered novelist and is well stocked in the Public Library. *The Black Book*, by Lawrence Durrell, was first published by Kahane in 1937. In a preface to the American edition of 1960 Durrell says he sent it to Henry Miller who was instrumental in having it published. In a private letter Durrell told me that he now regards it as little more than a schoolboy excitement with naughty words and ideas.

There is a story though it has little dramatic value. It is periodically submerged beneath shoals of imagery, often sexual.

SEX IN LITERATURE

As uninhibited poetry it is often remarkable but it lacks the discipline that Durrell brings to his later novels. The subject is corruption, now and again referred to as the 'English death'. All the characters are corrupt and the corruption is that of idealism. The author (who writes in the first person) admits that he is part of the corruption. The sexual imagery runs riot: Durrell says he was born with an erection and will die with one. But despite its wildness the book is more subtle than many of its genre. None of the characters has faith in contemporary society or culture and they all attack it unceasingly —but, says Durrell (or Lawrence Lucifer), their criticisms are irrelevant. 'Let us stop all these corpses drinking their own pus like this.' The critics are part of the death they decry. To use the kind of imagery that fills *The Black Book*, it depicts exotic fungi growing in a rat-filled cellar.

This is certainly a more ambitious work than *Fay and her Boy Friend*. So far as literary values are concerned, they are just as likely to be found, good as well as bad, in erotic writing as in any other category. The number of respectable and honoured writers who have, at some time or other, added a personal portion to the stock of erotic literature, is imposing. It is also significant that some writers who have never knowingly written a dirty word have written many passages which are in fact thinly-disguised subconscious pornography. (Christina Rossetti is an example, and there will be others to come.) Sometimes a respectable writer feels the compulsion to write such a book but dare not admit authorship. The result is naturally a pseudonym. This may also be thinly disguised: could Peter Lewis be Pierre Louÿs? There are also occasions when the author is lost in admiration of his own work and compromises with an introduction under his own name. It is permissible to appreciate in others what one could not (publicly) admit to in oneself. Jean Paulhan is widely suspected of having written *L'Histoire d'O*, for which he wrote an introduction. Of this work Paul Claudel wrote: 'All priests should read it so they may have an exact sense of sin', and François Mauriac: 'Even to set the covers of *The Story of O* ajar is to open the gates of hell.' When Paulhan was being considered

for membership of the *Académie Française* members received
copies of the novel through the post. He was elected.

I will conclude this section with descriptions of two other
novels which may be regarded as typical of their time. The
first, *Mayfair with the Lid Off*, by Claude Swaine Kastinole,
was banned in 1938. Mr K. had an interesting problem before
him. He wanted to get away with as much as he could, in
public. This requires great qualities of judgment. To begin
with, certain words must not be used. Secondly, descriptions
must not be too factual; much of the effect must be gained
by suggestion and a skilful use of metaphor. Mr K. misjudged
and his book was banned in 1938. (It would pass today but is
not worth reviving.)

In a Foreword (spelt *Forward* in the Table of Contents—
this type of book is often characterised by illiteracy) the author
refers to the morals of the Mayfair Smart Set as being as
vicious as those of the decadent Roman Empire. The object of
the book is to let light in on the private lives, manners and
morals of the 'denizens of Mayfair'. This is an attempt to beat
the censor, used long ago by Peter Bayle. In his performance
of a public duty the author proposes a few random glances at
some of the most prominent personalities in the Society of his
day. They include:

> A Duke, whose chief hobby in life is collecting the filthiest
> pornographic films which can be bought for money.
> A brace of Earls who, burnt out with excesses, keep young
> women to perform vices too nauseating to be spoken,
> much less committed to print. (As if he could!)
> A Privy Counsellor, a Right Honourable gentleman, who
> revels in the same form of bestiality practised by the later
> Roman Emperors.
> A Baroness, who keeps half a dozen procuresses working
> overtime, to obtain young girls under ten years of age to
> give shameful exhibitions with her son, a mentally de-
> ficient degenerate boy of fifteen, for the amusement of
> the guests at her notorious cocktail parties.
> A prominent politician, whose chief delight is to give a

bachelor dinner party with a young girl placed under the
table for purposes which must be left to the imagination
of the reader.

Chapters are entitled The Negro, The Obscene Film, Lesbian-
ism, Flagellation and the Glamour Girl Racket.

My last novel is an Olympia Press publication, *Stradella*, by
James Sherwood, 1962, now available in Great Britain, in a
slightly edited version. Here the problem is quite different.
There is nothing that cannot be said, as the book is not intended for public sale, therefore literary values are important.
It is true many writers of pornography never consider literary
values, but that is partly because repression has created a
demand for anything obscene. But if he wishes to excel in the
genre the author must pay attention to the traditional considerations of theme, plot construction and characterisation.
One gets the impression that Sherwood was trying to give an
honest picture of a jazzily sordid Hollywood circle, but allows
the picture to get out of true and thus invites the charge of
mere salaciousness. There is great pathos in the story, some
good observation, but the patina is a trifle too glossy.

Stradella, the TV Amourella, takes up Archie Flum like a
pet. He is useful fixing her house. He can be played with and
insulted and he can give her sex when she wants, though there's
never any lack of what she calls studs. (She has been married
three times, never for long, and is maddeningly undependable
in her desires.) She can be very sentimental, like most people
who pit themselves flintily against the world, and she is occasionally capable of a deep perception. But by and large she is
an organism with strong reflex actions, and Archie discovers
that she is simply his own wayward mother all over again. His
mother is almost a whore but convinces herself she is not
common. This book is awkward and sincere. The author exudes
hopelessness (his Archie is a penniless poet). If Stradella believes in anything it is personal security; Archie believes in
love and fidelity and is terribly vulnerable because he can be
so easily hurt. The story jumps and pops along from one significant incident to the next. There is no attempt to show

the passage of time or the drag of humdrum action. The author's literary impatience rejects the realism of Forster, Greene, Faulkner and other mirrors of existence—for even Greene is slow by these standards, and Forster runs smoothly in comparison. Sherwood has a dry humour at times. 'Each room,' he writes of his two-roomed home, 'was half the size of the other.'

Stradella eventually reveals the dread secret that has deadened her to the normal joys of living. She was a Lolita Overplus who at the age of nine used to irrumate with dad. When she was seventeen a fellow fucked her on the radio-phonograph console while holding up her brother and parents with a gun. When he came he dropped the gun. Stradella now finds sex a bore. What excitement it brings (apart from occasional orgasmic spasms) comes from avoiding her brother, who thinks she is fair game. Like dad. She becomes a whore. It seems silly not to make money out of it if you get nothing else from it. The money will bring security for when the body gives out. 'No retreads yet, just a few blow-outs.' It sounds far-fetched in summary yet it does not go far beyond *Time Magazine's* crime section, William Faulkner and Tennessee Williams.

Stradella is a type we never meet in the literature of the past. For her sex is completely emptied of either pleasure or emotional fulfilment. She is possibly the end-product of two hundred years of pornography in which the aim has been not to depict the joys of sex (as other writers depict the joys of eating, travel, sport, meditation) but to present sex as something sensational and beyond the bounds of decent behaviour. The responsibility for this rests fairly and squarely on the shoulders of those who drove sex underground in the name of morality. What we have left is expressed thus by Roger Nimier, a young French novelist, speaking on the B.B.C.:

> We are reproached with eroticism—but already how can one pronounce that word without laughing? All our novels begin in such a scandalous fashion that it smacks of rosewater. Modern eroticism fancies itself serious and honest. It is indulged in with studied deliberation. Desper-

ately ñature is pursued, only to find it flee as fast as it is
approached. Oh, nature is capricious! But if it concerns
bodies alone, one might as well return to Rabelais.

Mr Nimier is as vague in his pronouncement as French writers
so often are but he does appear to be saying that what, say, the
eighteenth century considered erotic our own time will find
merely titillating. There has certainly been a change in the
level of acceptance, or seems to have been—and then the *Fanny
Hill* trial comes along to disprove it.

Oddities of Stimulation

An eroteur is a connoisseur of erotic art and literature. Full-
blown eroticism does not satisfy him for long. After the
straightforward account of orthodox sex he looks for aberration. But there is a limit to this, and in the end he is reduced
to something much more subtle—and to him, much more
satisfying. He develops a nose for the erotic, particularly when
it is unintended; he discovers a Lesbian relationship in a
respected Victorian masterpiece and searches out a 'tendency'
in some apparently innocent best-seller.[2]

The less sophisticated has in the past turned to the manual
of sexual instruction and psychology. Here he is allowed to
read (privately to wallow in) fairly frank accounts of sexual
activity and the difficulties encountered by others. Perhaps they
are his own also. There has always been a large section of our
population whose ignorance of sex is almost complete. John
O'Hara writes of one in his *Appointment in Samarra*. She is
assaulted by a little boy and completely mystified as to why he
had done it. It is something that everyone should know and
understand, why men and even little boys are sometimes driven
to such behaviour. She comes to the conclusion that 'that was
what you could expect of men'. But this explains nothing. She
had read case histories in Kraft-Ebing and Havelock Ellis but
had learned nothing. Now she knew that she had read them
as pornography.

This is the Lawrentian view of pornography. One hasn't

the courage to look upon sex as an integral part of one's nature and tries to put it behind with Satan, yet at the same time dabbles with it in dreary volumes which make of it something repulsive. Lawrence calls Trollope pornographic because his treatment of sex is one big blush. Others think the Dark Gods and a restoration of Phallic religion are pornographic, because they have none of the old pagan joy in them, but instead a gloomy worship. So there are at least three false ways of approaching sex: to ignore it, to treat it too seriously, and to make it rapt, intense and swoony, like the advertisements. There is a fourth way, too, which comes out of disgust and hatred. Only the emancipated few insist on the gaiety. The psychologists in particular have made a satisfactory sex life appear almost impossible. Instead of having cheery old Ovid on the parlour window seat, many modern couples seem to have Freud and Stopes on the bedside table. C. S. Lewis has this to say about over-solemnity in sex in his *The Four Loves*, 1960:

> I believe we are all being encouraged to take Venus too seriously; at any rate, with a wrong kind of seriousness. All my life a ludicrous and portentous solemnisation of sex has been going on.
>
> One author tells us that Venus should recur through the married life in a 'solemn, sacramental rhythm'. A young man to whom I had described as 'pornographic' a novel that he much admired, replied with genuine bewilderment, 'Pornographic? But how can it be? It treats the whole thing so seriously'—as if a long face were a sort of moral disinfectant.

The book of sex instruction, particularly that designed for the young and immature reader, often does exactly what the pornographic novel sets out to do: sets examples before the reader for emulation. The author who claims to have saved the health of a young lad by putting an end to his sexual excesses draws attention to the excesses, and puts them in the heroic light of martyrdom. Admittedly, this type of book is rare these days but the case-history of psychological vagrancy has taken its place. The pornographic novel owes its appeal partly to its dealing in forbidden goods. The sex manual can do exactly the same: it gives us facts and figures about the underworld of sex.

Dr Eustace Chesser outlines a typical modern sex affair in his *How to Make a Success of Your Marriage*. Two young people, who have discussed sex and read books about it and have slept together, decide to marry. They feel they have had the best advisers, they are mutually attracted, and they are absolutely determined to get the best out of it. Their lovemaking is very efficient, they do less of it every year, and finally only embrace when under the stimulus of alcohol. After four years they cannot bear the sight of each other and go their separate ways. This story represents the failure of eroticism pure and simple. It is never referred to in pornography because the basis of the pornographic attitude is that lovers never tire and that psychology does not exist. These two will probably become grim readers of hardcore pornography because it reflects their disillusion. The couples go on coupling but they do it out of boredom or habit. They persuade themselves that somebody else will be different—so he will be for a few nights. These lives and that literature are all of a piece. One of the books read by these two well-informed innocents was certainly Van de Velde's *Ideal Marriage: its Physiology and Technique*, probably the most famous of all such books. Its text comes from Balzac: 'Marriage is a science'—Balzac is, in fact, quoted fairly liberally throughout. There is a thorough account of the physical and physiological processes, with coloured plates, and due weight is given to the psychic aspect. It is hard to imagine anyone finding much erotic stimulation in these pages, but the seekers are an ingenious and persistent race. Representation and description is what they are after, and they naturally find it here.

Jeremy Taylor knew the type well and referred to it in *The Rule and Exercises of Holy Living* (1650). His fifth Rule for our Intentions warns the preacher not to be too ardent in his description of unchastity; his female auditor may be pleased with his language in a way he didn't bargain for. At the beginning of the chapter, 'Of Chastity', comes a warning to the lubricious:

> Reader, stay, and read not the advices of the following section, unless thou hast a chaste spirit, or desirest to be chaste, or at least art apt to consider whether you ought or no. For there are some spirits so atheistical, and some so wholly possessed with a spirit of uncleanness, that they turn the most prudent and chaste discourses into dirt and filthy apprehensions; like choleric stomachs, changing their very cordials and medicines into bitterness; and in a literal sense *turning the Grace of God into wantonness*. They study cases of conscience in the matter of carnal sins, not to avoid, but to learn ways how to offend God and pollute their own spirits; and search their houses with a sun-beam, that they may be instructed in all the corners of nastiness.

No modern reader who searched Taylor's work with a sunbeam would get much satisfaction, but there are rich rewards in, say, Van de Velde. For it is not tales of conscience that are searched now but psychological case-histories, and it is done in the name of science and knowledge. Books are written from the same motives, with a keen concern for the knowledge of mass-readership. The Comstocks and self-appointed censors even set up associations so that they will miss nothing juicy. How else would they know of the Attitude of Flexion and Vaginal Whistling (dubbed 'repulsive' by Van de Velde)?

To conclude, here is a passage from *Ideal Marriage* which is no doubt scientific in intent but becomes pornographic when the prude sets eyes on it:

> In coitus, the rush of air into the vagina has an unfortunate effect, for the distension of the walls and obliteration of folds much diminish the chance of stimulation by mutual friction for both partners. And the piston-like backwards and forwards motion of the phallos may occa-

sionally force some of the air out of the vaginal cavity
again, to the accompaniment of unpleasantly suggestive
and quite audible whistling sounds. Even when the air
leaves the vagina again on the resumption of a more
normal position after intercourse—or as much as some
hours later—the process is only too audible and extraordinarily repulsive in its effect.

In the case of a comparatively small and tight *introitus*,
the danger of this unpleasant phenomenon is much less,
as the phallos is at once enclosed and clasped by the
woman's organ. But in the case of a dilated orifice with
lax rim, an *audible* result is practically certain after knee-
elbow coitus, and so this attitude is best avoided under
such conditions.

Vagaries of Feeling

Writing about sex is confused these days. To begin with, no
one knows where it may not be lurking. This is due to a
vulgarisation of Freudian psychology. Anyone can now bandy
words such as *sublimation* and *inhibition* and have only the
flimsiest idea of how these processes operate. I think it was
Marghanita Laski who traced the obsession with the horse or
pony in much writing for children to unsatisfied sexuality. No
reasons were given. Anything you dislike in others can be
attributed to sexual insufficiency. There is a literary game
one can play which goes something like this: 'Will she, won't
she, will she, won't she, yes by God, she's actually gone and
done it!'—'Done what?'—'Attributed books about horses (or
sewing machines, or flint arrow heads, or dominant fifths) to
unsatisfied sexuality.'

Or the current nervousness about sexual expression and
reaction may lead to extraordinary statements such as the
following: 'Our desire was to show what part sexuality played
in the life of sects and *we hope that the results have probably
surpassed the expectations* of most of our readers.' The italics
are mine. These words come from a section on Secret Sects, by
Edward Bradley, in *The Five Books of Sex* (published about

1940). On the whole it is a serious book and does not masquerade prurience under a show of scientific intention. But how uncomfortable the author feels when he is required to adopt an attitude towards his work. The sentence quoted could be a prudish expression of faith in the reader's innocence, but it could equally be a shy expression of desire that the reader shall have his money's worth. Who knows what the author wished to do: publish information, pay homage to a noble human function, or shock?

When James Branch Cabell's Jurgen visited Anaitis's realm of Cocaigne he discovered that happiness was sought through curious pleasures. In the library he found *The System of Worshipping a Girl*, the unique manuscripts of Astyanassa and Elephantis and Sotades, the Dionysiac Formulae, the Chart of Postures, the *Litany of the Centre of Delight*, the Spintrian Treatises and the *Thirty-Two Gratifications*. 'Yet the deeper Jurgen investigated, and the longer he meditated, the more certain it seemed to him that all such employment was a peculiarly unimaginative pursuit of happiness.' He decided that they were the games of mental childhood.

Here, then, are three approaches to sex in life and literature, for one shadows the other. The first is so undefined it leaves an impression of nullity; the second is frankly bewildered; the third is whole hog, snatches at everything and catches nothing. No wonder then that some writers get impatient and persuade themselves that a world (and a literature) of concealed sex may be better after all. 'Sex is only interesting when it is not mentioned,' writes John Bayley in the *Spectator*, 27 July 1962. This is the direct antithesis of the eroteur's creed yet it has been followed by most writers of recent times. A Stendhal or a Turgeniev probably has gained more by restraint than a pornographer, even of the highest class, has gained by frankness. Yet nothing is proved. Certainly nothing is gained by a tacit acceptance of a situation in which one subject, and one only, out of the whole range of life is not to be mentioned. At least we need good reasons for such prohibitions.

The same author tries to justify the anomaly in his *The*

Characters of Love (1960). 'The muse of pornography is
blindfolded and cannot tell beforehand what will excite
desire.' He states that *The Faerie Queene* is more effectively
pornographic than Marlowe's *Ovid* or *Venus and Adonis*,
though both Marlowe and Shakespeare are doing their best
to be 'curious and wanton'. Spenser does not appear to
distinguish in his imagination between what appeals to his
sense of beauty and what appeals to his desire. It is at this
point that Bayley, it seems to me, draws the wrong conclusions. No one knows what will stimulate desire, hence it
is useless to attempt to do so by writing. But it is equally
true that no one knows what will be considered beautiful.
Would we therefore be justified in prohibiting the description of the beautiful? The truth is, even the subtlest prohibitions in literature are unwise.

There is no doubt that a rip-roaring pornographic account
gives as false a report of a sexual encounter as Rabelais, say,
gives of a banquet or Sterne of a lying-in. The best account
of a sexual encounter will give full weight to every nuance;
the body will be servant to the feelings instead of being the
tyrant. (There are, of course, occasions when it is the tyrant
and honesty must recognise them.) As an illustration of the
kind of relationship that can exist and must be faced without flinching, let us turn to Huysmans' *Là Bas*. Hyacinthe
agrees to 'give herself' to Durtal. He clutches her but it was
like embracing a dead woman. Yet she presses to him, clings
tightly and kisses fiercely. Then she says: 'Oh how I hate
you!' He notices how untidy his bedclothes are and feels
aggrieved as he foresees a cold night. He knows he is incapable of remaking the bed. Then she attacks him again, he
retaliates, and masters her. 'In a changed voice, deeper and
more guttural, she broke into a clamour of stupid venal cries
that almost shocked him, frantic exclamations of 'my darling',
'my soul'. When it is over he feels frightened, the ecstasies are
too wearing and terrible. He gets up to attend to the fire,
goes back to her; she kisses him passionately and asks if he
loves her better than he did. But he cannot reply. He is too
disillusioned. 'The satiety that came after well justified the

lack of appetite that went before. She now revolted him, and he was horrified at his own feelings.' He had idealised her and now knows that he cannot escape himself, that, despite his intentions, he is and always will be at the mercy of his sensuality.

This is not pornographic. It does not give a detailed description of the sexual act. Perhaps it does not suffer from the lack of it. It is certainly true—but it is only one truth out of a million possibilities. The world of love and sex is so vast and so intricate there must be freedom to map it. We are deceiving ourselves if we maintain that this is the only field in which concealment actually assists enlightenment. True erotic literature is a literature of the sensual pleasures. In general literature, as in the passage referred to above, we are given more: love as well as sex, 'attitudes of ravishment' as well as deep probings. Erotic literature naturally cloys, as does all unmitigated pleasure. The more comprehensive approach is more painful (the Huysmans passage contains a vast field of experience in a short space) and at the same time more satisfying. The combination of pleasure with satisfaction is best attained through some such work as *The Arabian Nights*, where bouts of sexual intercourse, frankly described, alternate with a hundred and one other human activities. But there is very little pain in the sex. The Huysmans illustrates complexity. It is not a model.

The Cult of Sterility

Sex produces two things: joy and babies, in that order. There are by-products, of course, such as pain and abortions, but they are secondary. An impressive aspect of sex literature is the high degree of sterility it celebrates. There is little joy, neither is there offspring. Why?

I have already referred to the change of tone that occurred in writing about sex during the seventeenth century. David Loth, in *The Erotic in Literature*, points out that shame first became noticeable in the literature of sex some time after the reign of Elizabeth. Previously writing about sex had been

mainly concerned with its beauty or joy. Now the object
seemed to be the sexual stimulation of the reader. Ever since,
society has been trying to repress it by censorship, motivated
by religious or moral principles, or by principles of taste. An
important result has been a shift in attitude towards sexual
perversion. Loth makes a valuable generalisation:

> Far more strictly than the law or the police, the moral
> taste and prejudices of the community govern erotic
> writings in these fields. Before there were any attempts
> to suppress such books officially, the perversions which
> society condemned were written about only in invectives
> against enemies. The most gifted artists indulged in no
> ribaldries on this score, but confined themselves to
> dignified treatment of problems and tragedies. Only
> when the law stepped in to condemn obscenity were
> perversions introduced into books as a routine bit of
> business aimed at erotic arousal.

Today pornography is more often about perversion than
about orthodox sex. The border-lines are vague and, to many
people, non-existent. But it would probably be agreed by
all but the hopelessly straitlaced that Henry Miller's attitude
to sex is a healthy one. When two Oslo booksellers were
proceeded against for selling his *Sexus*, the defence counsel
asked Miller for comment which might be passed on to the
court. In his reply (dated 27 February 1959) he said he did
not offer anything evil or poisonous but a dose of life which
he had administered first to himself. 'I can say one thing for
it unblushingly—compared to the atom bomb it is full of
lifegiving qualities.' In a world which accepts the atom bomb
(is not C.N.D. ridiculed by the majority?), literary sex is
aberrant when *sub rosa* and sadistic when offered for open
sale. Miller is a magnificent exception.

The approach to sex has become twisted in many minds
not because modern men and women are vicious but because
their natural instincts have been thwarted. Hence the cult of
sterility. So often one feels that sex activity and sex literature

is merely vengeful or the celebration of vengeance. Take the
apparent increase in prostitution and the use of prostitution
as a subject for discussion and enquiry. It seems likely that
many people today find erotic stimuli through reports such
as the Kinsey. Nothing else could explain the huge sales
among people who are not normally interested in sociology
or even the social aspects of sex. When magazines carry frank
sex stories, or reports on sexual behaviour carrying vivid
reportage, sales again rise. A report by Wayland Young in
Encounter (May 1959) entitled 'Sitting on a Fortune' was
serious and competent. It was carried out just before the
London prostitutes were driven from the streets, but it contained actual quotations from whores which were far more
likely to titillate the sex-starved or obsessed than many of
the sensational-looking paperbacks on the bookstalls. The
fact that it comes from the reader's own world, the world
that extends all around him, gives it an extra dimension. He
feels he has only to put out his hand and he will touch—
well, this:

> There's some of them (the whores) lies still as stones,
> they think it's more ladylike or something; but I say
> they don't know which side their bread's buttered.
> Listen: if you lie still the bloke may spend half the
> night sweating away. But if you bash it about a bit he'll
> come all the quicker and get out and away and leave
> you in peace. Stupid to spin it out longer than you need,
> isn't it. . . .

> And then, you know, there are all sorts of little gentle
> things you can do to a client so that with a bit of luck
> they come before they even get in to me. When they do
> I look ever so loving and gentle and say: 'Traitor.' Well,
> I'm not paid just to be a bag, am I? I'm paid to make
> them feel good. It's easy for me, so why not? That's how
> I see it.

Young asked one if she had ever come herself:

> Yes, I think so: twice. Twice in my life I've thought

to myself—now maybe this is what they talk about. That
was before I was on the game.

Young asked if she didn't want to keep him.

Keep him? No! I couldn't bear the sight of him afterwards. He couldn't get out quick enough for me.

And one girl had what seems to be a justifiable complaint:

You know, the young men seem to be getting bigger
and bigger. It must be the Welfare State. I hate it though;
it splits me.

Kinsey found that men in particular liked to read about
sexual aberration. There is far more discussion and a more
extensive literature about such things as incest, sado-
masochism and animal contacts than the actual occurrence of
these phenomena would justify. Another strongly marked
feature of erotic literature is the general absence of pregnancy.
It is a convention that it doesn't happen. It spoils the fun.
Women are 'objects' and when pregnant they cease to exist.
There are two exceptions to this rule. One type of pervert
insists on having a pregnant woman. You find this in Sade
and, according to the prostitutes, in life. The other occurrence of pregnancy is significant. In the monastery where Sade's
Justine is kept a prisoner, along with several other girls, it is
a serious crime to become pregnant. Such girls are punished
with a hundred strokes. Menstruation is also rarely mentioned,
although Miller has an account of copulation during menstruation. In the afore-mentioned monastery it is not regarded
as a crime, but failure to give warning is punished by sixty
strokes. In *The Golden Lotus* it is stated that bad luck will
attend the man who touches a woman 'in her blood'.

The interest in prostitution, the unreal emphasis on aberration and the rejection of pregnancy and menstruation are all
parts of the cult of sterility. The mere mention of the female
procreative functions enrages Sade. The Count de Gernande

explains to Justine why he abuses his wife so violently. Women are inferior, fit only to be slaves and to minister to the pleasures of the stronger male. Examples are cited from many countries of Nature's way of dealing with women. The Koreh of Arabia buried alive all girls at the age of seven, only keeping those needed for reproduction. Wives were immolated on their husband's funeral pyres in India, as they had lost their value. In Egypt they were sacrificed to the gods. In Formosa they were trampled to death when they became pregnant. A Greek playwright asked Zeus why he did not create a better means of reproducing the race without the agency of females. A Roman once said men could find true happiness if they could love without women.

Yet despite the examples from ancient civilisations there is a peculiarly modern tone to the sex hatred endemic in these attitudes. Sex is objectified, taken away from the woman, pursued for its own sake; the woman is spurned either because she possesses the sex or because she is not, after all, necessary. The gentleness and tenderness which we are taught to associate with loving and which we are capable of feeling evaporates. Elizabethan literature is full of hauntingly beautiful passages between man and woman; Fanny Hill feels; but already in the nineteenth century the gnashing of teeth can be heard. There are odd and unexpected exceptions, even in our own time. (I am at no time referring to romantic fiction, of course, which is concerned with dream sex—no part of an eroteur's business.) A clumsy and ill-written anonymous novel called *Three Mistresses*[3] is in these matters, as in some others, exceptional. Charles, the hero, shows tenderness. Occasionally his women have their periods. Aline even becomes pregnant and he is delighted. 'Thinking of my parenthood, I walked as proudly as a peacock, saying to myself that I was no more a baby.' He was fifteen.

Geoffrey Gorer writes of two pornographies, those of sex and death. Little of either class is aesthetically acceptable; he cites Andrea de Nerciat and Edgar Allan Poe. There can be no real development in pornography. It consists of the same thing happening again and again. The repetition may

be more refined or complicated or sensational but intrinsically
it is still the same act. A person is replaced by a set of genitals,
or perhaps a body capable of suffering pain. Most languages
are relatively poor in words or constructions expressing intense pleasure or pain, so that these pornographies abound
in onomatopaeic representations of sighs, gasps, groans and
screams. They rely heavily on adjective and simile. 'Both
types of fantasy are completely unrealistic since they ignore
all physical, social or legal limitations, and both types have
complete hallucination of the reader or viewer as their
object.' ('The Pornography of Death', *Encounter*, October
1955.)

Gorer says that the heyday of the pornography of death
was the nineteenth century. Children were encouraged to
think about death, their own deaths and the edifying or
cautionary death-beds of others. People paid their respects
to 'beautiful corpses'; funerals were the occasion of the greatest
display, irrespective of class; a death-bed scene was an essential
set-piece of any ambitious play or novel; and Thomas Hardy,
the complete representative of the ancient rural culture, used
solemnly to take his guests for a walk in the local graveyard.
Meanwhile copulation and birth went underground. Today
there has been a shift. Copulation is described and no novelist
considers it his duty to describe deaths in detail. Death there
is in plenty but it is the violence preceding death that exerts
the fascination. And the violence is often laced with sexual
assault or is sadistic in basis. The public gets its sex, but it
gets it in alienation. And that is exactly how it wants it.

FOOTNOTES

1. See page 394.
2. I see that Dr Alex Comfort finds 'the *motif* of shared bondage and
death as a decent and most ecstatic form of coition . . . in a muffled form'
in *The Last of the Mohicans* (*Anarchy*, March 1961).
3. An abbreviated version of the better known *Romance of Lust*.

4: *The Prevalence of Sex*

The simple fact stares you in the face, yet there are many who would willingly suffer any mutilation rather than admit it. Everyone does it, or nearly everyone.

Everyone wants to do it, including those who think they don't. It's a safe bet that everyone, unless he be maimed, has an urgent need to do it.

Those who persuade themselves that they don't want to do it come out in spots or are beastly to their colleagues or have hysterical fits. In extremis they kill rather than fuck.

This, then, is the justification (and a very powerful one) for the literature on the subject.

Marriage has been instituted partly to contain it, but it never has completely and never can. Two things war in a man and a woman: the continuing need and the slow rejection of monotony.

Man cannot escape his nature and there seems no good reason why he should. All other blueprints for mankind seem so unattractive. Axel Heyst, in his delicate *Words and Darkness*, recognised the call in the voices of the stags. 'These long cries of passion, sad and tragic, told me more about passion than thousands of impotent human words.' But men have to celebrate their passion just as once they had celebrated their victims on the cave-walls.

Rural culture acknowledges the need and the activity with a directness and a frankness that can only be called unhealthy by the sick. One of the last of the randy folk-singers in these islands was Jonathan Denwood, whose *Twinter's Wedding*, published in 1950, continues a tradition that must be as old as man. 'T' Ragman's Kiss', sung by Sunty Curry, starts with the blunt statement that something has gone wrong when a woman of thirty-five hasn't been bedded:

> *Quoth frisky Mag, Ah's thurty-five*
> *An hevn't hed a man;*
> *Yit Ah's as fit as owt alive*
> *An kittle reet ta t' bean;*
> *Ah's full o' luive fra top ta toe,*
> *Wid me theer nowt amiss.*
> *Ne doot o' that, said ragman Joe,*
> *An gev her gob a kiss.*

Exactly the same tone is to be found in the much older 'The Merry Hay-Makers, or Pleasant Pastime between the Youngmen and Maids in the Pleasant Meadows', which is to be found in the Douce Collection of Original Broadsides and was reprinted by De Sola Pinto and Rodway in *The Common Muse*:

> *There's Timmy and Tommy with bottle and bag,*
>   *as soon as the Lasses beheld them,*
> *Because they did not give them what they did lack,*
>   *adzuggers they swore they would geld 'em.*

In other words, a girl has her rights. How naturally did the husband of Juliet's nurse say to the little girl, 'Thou wilt fall backward when thou hast more wit'!

Women, of course, like to keep up a pretence that they are not really interested in this sort of thing. Whether this is natural cunning, intended to keep the man on his toes, or whether it actually represents a partial victory for the priest, prude and life-hater, is doubtful. But it serves literature well. Without complication literature would be in a poor way. Chevallier makes good use of this human perversity in his famous *Clochemerle*. When ex-Minister Bourdillat went into the new urinal to perform a personal initiation ceremony, 'the women broke into bursts of shrill laughter, as though they had been tickled; and this, likely enough, was at the thought of what Bourdillat, by way of symbol, held in his hand, which was in the minds of these buxom charmers more often than it would be seemly to admit.'

The degree of courting is one of the major differences in literature of this type. Where the need is frankly admitted, there is no courting. This is Zola's world. Mouquette (*Germinal*) has had every man in Montsou and is determined to have Etienne. She does. He tries to remain aloof but has no reply to her tremendous sexual gusto. She says: 'You know I'm dying for it. What about it? I should simply love it.' And when it was over she was the one overflowing with gratitude, not he. In *Germinal* the animal persistence in the face of every obstacle is perhaps the major theme. The novel ends with Etienne and Catherine clinging to each other in the complete darkness of the collapsed mine, with the water lapping round their knees and the dead body of Chaval floating up against them. This was how they had their wedding night. 'They loved each other in despair, in death itself'— for soon after consummation Etienne discovers that she is dead.

In Chaucer's *Knight's Tale* we are told that no law can constrain love. 'Whoever bound a lover by a law?' Arcita asks Palamon. 'Love is a law unto itself.' Cupid brooks no fellow-king. The mood shows itself again and again through our literature: in Chaucer and in Shakespeare, as we have seen, in Fielding and in Smollett, in Swinburne and in Lawrence. In a writer like Ronald Firbank, who was incapable of bad taste, yet who exudes a heavy air of exhausted lust. Everyone is after everybody else, especially negresses and holders of ancient titles. Sex or age do not matter. The very young are most appreciated. Pirelli dies naked in the cathedral, but for his mitre, having failed to catch a choir-boy. In his later years the poet Yeats betrays a peevishness at what he feels he has missed in his youth. The lech of desire crawls through his aging limbs, and he sighs for his youth. Could this have been the true self-abuse? Magic and spiritual power dominated his youth and when they faded he saw physical love as the ever-present basis of human experience.

In 1921 he made this statement in *Michael Robartes and the Dancer*:

> *Paul Veronese*
> *And all his sacred company*
> *Imagined bodies all their days*
> *By the lagoon you love so much,*
> *For proud, soft, ceremonious proof*
> *That all must come to sight and touch;*
> *While Michael Angelo's Sistine roof,*
> *His 'Morning' and his 'Night' disclose*
> *How sinew that has been pulled tight,*
> *Or it may be loosened in repose,*
> *Can rule by supernatural right*
> *Yet be but sinew.*

And let no one forget that ultimately desire builds up and pulls down empires.

> *A shudder in the loins engenders there*
> *The broken wall, the burning roof and tower*
> *And Agamemnon dead.*

For the loins belonged to a befeathered Zeus, trampling Leda.

Infidelity

No law constrains, marriage is helpless against the tide, fidelity is seen to be a miasma. For the breaking of one loyalty is the consequence of the creation of a second.

The Law Book of our culture, with its frightening authority, says 'Thou shalt not commit adultery' and 'Thou shalt not covet thy neighbour's wife'. And an ancient English nursery rhyme says:

> *Little Tommy Tittlemouse*
> *Lived in a little house;*
> *He caught fishes*
> *In other men's ditches.*

The first systematic collection of English nursery rhymes was made by Halliwell in 1844. Many of the examples that appeared to be pieces of inoffensive nonsense were recognised to be *double entendres* of this type.

The verdict of literature appears to be that adultery and infidelity are well-nigh universal. Iago tries to persuade Othello that Cassio has slept with Desdemona, but what of it?

> . . . *there's millions now alive*
> *That nightly lie in those unproper beds*
> *Which they dare swear peculiar: your case is better.*
> *O, 'tis the spite of hell, the fiend's arch-mock,*
> *To lip a wanton in a secure couch*
> *And to suppose her chaste!*

'Every man who believes that his honour depends upon that of his wife is a fool who torments himself, and drives her to despair', wrote Anthony Hamilton, author of *The Memoirs of the Count de Grammont*. It is true, he adds, that the Spaniards and even more so the Italians go to great lengths to keep their wives *incommunicado* but there is in fact only one sure method: assassination. 'Precaution is vain and useless before the evil (wedlock), and revenge odious afterwards.'

Chaucer refers to the nympholeptic passion which drives men on remorselessly. As soon as Arcite had gained the love of Anelida he was after someone else. Women are advised not to bestow too much affection if they want to keep their men:

> *The kinde of mannes herte is to delyte*
> *In thing that straunge is, also god me save!*
> *For what he may not gete, that wolde he have.*

Kinsey believed that curiosity is always a powerful stimulus, and not necessarily curiosity about another woman; how many men actually are unfaithful, are there many others like me, how do they manage it without legal difficulties or public scandal?

The *raison d'être* of one of the most interesting sources of
erotic literature, namely *The Arabian Nights*, is female
infidelity—which men consider a far more serious problem
than male infidelity. Two kings discovered that their wives
were unfaithful as soon as their backs were turned, and set
out to seek their destinies. They climb into a tree to escape
an Ifrit, who carries a box from which he takes a girl. He
lies down to sleep and the girl tells the kings to come down
from the tree. At first they are frightened but she insists, and
threatens to betray them. She requires them to pierce her
violently with their lances, which they do to her entire satisfaction. ('You are indeed experienced riders!') She then takes
from her pocket a necklace with 570 seal rings and explains
that each represents an infidelity to the Ifrit. They hand over
their own rings. King Shahryar was so horrified by her action
that he started his custom of beheading a wife every night.
Assassination, as Hamilton said, was the only remedy.

Women are the villains of the piece, of a hundred thousand
erotic pieces. They have a way of combining apparent virtue
with promiscuity. Their replies are equivocal, as in an English
traditional song, 'The Thankful Country Lass, or the Jolly
Batchelor Kindly Entertained' (*The Amanda Group of Bagford Poems*, ed. J. W. Ebsworth, 1880), where a lass from
Lynn meets a man and to every suggestion he makes she
replies, 'I, marry, and thank you too!'—which can mean
whatever she pleases. It also meant what the man pleased
because in a sequel ('The Lass of Lynn's New Joy, for Finding
a Father for her Child', *The Bagford Ballads*, c. 1600-1715,
B.M.) we find the girl pregnant and without a husband, but
she manages to get one and even persuade him by a trick that
the child is his.

The promiscuity of women is asserted by Villon, who
advises his audience to stick to one woman, a good woman,
if he can find her. But he adds with unexpected sympathy
that even the prostitutes were once good girls. Each woman
takes a husband and then finds consolation elsewhere. He
writes in his *Testament*, about 1460, in the McCaskie translation:

> *For their lovers followed the Decree,*
>   *That is quite clear: they found a hide*
> *Where they could take their love, and she*
>   *Wanted no other man beside;*
>   *But first love is not made to bide,*
> *And she, who loved one man, you find*
>   *Will part from him and wander wide,*
> *Preferring to love all mankind.*

> *What makes them do it? I should say,*
>   *Not meaning their good name to steal,*
> *That it's a woman's natural way*
>   *Warm love for every man to feel.*
>   *No other reason seems quite real,*
> *Though there's a saying, certainly,*
>   *In Rheims, Troyes, St Omer and Lille,*
> *'Six workmen do more work than three.'*

And, returning to Iago, it is not only in the French provinces that the women run wild.

> *I know our country disposition well;*
> *In Venice they do let heaven see the pranks*
> *They dare not show their husbands; their best*
>   *conscience*
> *Is not to leave't undone, but keep't unknown.*

Which is what Villon meant by the Decree: not the law of love but the Decree of Gratien which proclaimed that 'the fault is more pardonable if it be kept secret'.

Rank, of course, has nothing to do with it. Aubrey tells us of John Overall (1560-1618), a divine, who was famous because of his wife, who had 'the loveliest Eies that were ever seen', but was 'wondrous wanton'. Sir John Selby was charmed by her and one song ran:

> *The Deane of Paule's did search for his wife,*
>   *and where d'ee thinke ee found her?*

> *Even upon Sir John Selbye's bed,*
> *as flatte as any Flounder.*

Aubrey also quotes 'Pastorall verses' on this lady, all ending
with the 'hye nonny nonny noe' refrain, and with no doubt
as to its meaning. The last stanza runs:

> *But gonne she is the prettiest Lasse*
> *that ever trodde on plaine.*
> *What ever hath betide of her*
> *blame not the Shepherd Swayne*
> *For why? she was her own Foe,*
> *and gave herself the overthrowe*
> *By being so franke of her*
> *hye nonny nonny noe.*

Right up to our own times. The point I wish to make here
is not that women are unfaithful but that they are expected
to be. The men cannot hide their chagrin but they are
scarcely taken by surprise. Sergeant Brown, for instance, in
Mailer's *The Naked and the Dead*, is convinced that his wife
is being unfaithful. 'There isn't a woman you can trust', he
tells Stanley. Some of the other men demur but Brown supports his opinion with a certain degree of realism. 'Listen,
they're no different from you and me, especially the ones
that've had their screwing. They like it just as much as men
do, and it's a helluva sight easier for them to get it. . . .' He
asks Polack what he thinks his wife is doing at that moment.
'I'll tell you what. It's just about six a.m. now in America.
She's wakin' up in bed with a guy who can give her just as
much as you can and she's giving him the same goddam line
she handed you.' Polack agrees. This view is exactly the
same as the one expressed by the merchant in *The Decameron*.
It is also expressed by General Cummings in the same novel.
He tells Lieutenant Hearn that it is in woman's nature to
cheat.

Moralists and purists have loathed this particular divine
dispensation, and have tried to contain it by preaching

purdah, specially designed girdles and assassination. A different note is struck in the forester's song in *As You Like It*, the note of acceptance:

> *Take thou no scorn to wear the horn;*
> *It was a crest ere thou wast born. . . .*

The more tortured moderns seek desperately for an apology that will justify. Now if there is one thing more evident than female promiscuity it must be male promiscuity, yet there is strong resistance among men to allowing the sins of the male to justify those of the female. That is why Sergeant Brown's streak of honesty is so remarkable. Sergeant Croft takes his women where he can find them, but they waste a lot of good time excusing themselves. 'Everybody likes to have a good time. . . . That's it. That's my philosophy. You don't think a bit cheap of me, do you, soldier? . . . That's right, honey, I understand you. . . .' And all the time, as they drink, as they roll, Croft is smouldering with hatred (his wife did the same thing) and thinks: You're all fuggin whores. The sex guilt is induced, it is a load laid on by society, and in some cases it is a fearful task to remove. In Samuel Selvon's *Turn Again Tiger* (a West Indian novel) Tiger is worried because he has seduced Doreen. His friend Joe cannot understand his scruples. If there were any fear of punishment, then it would be natural, but Tiger is not concerned with legal or physical matters. His situation is complicated by the fact that Doreen is a white woman; he feels he should have more self-respect than to give way to the universal desire of a coloured man to have a woman of the ruling race. Joe finds no difficulty. 'Well you think you is the onliest man who unfaithful to his wife? Man, it aint have a married man I know who don't cut a stroke on the side. You know how much girls I have in town? You know how much nights I come in late after big bacchanal in town? . . . What you think you is? You just a drop of water in a river, boy, where the river go you have to go.'

To sum up this section, it is the conviction of most male

writers that there is a flaw in the female character which
causes them to be constantly unfaithful. The obvious fact
that men are as or even more frequently unfaithful is usually
glossed over. When men are aware of their own shortcomings
in this respect (or what they consider their shortcomings, for
it may be only a quirk of our particular society to regard
sexual freedom as wrong), they look for justification. This is
all the more remarkable when you consider that vast corpus
of male material which accepts male promiscuity as natural
and forgivable and even enviable: the 'smutty' story. (It's
smutty because we want to experience the joy of mildly
sinning.) Strictly speaking, such stories are (or were) not part
of literature, as they are not written down. It is truer to
regard them, however, in the same light as we regarded the
folk stories of Melanesia. These are eventually written down,
anyway, and so are the stories. With the recent increased
tolerance of the censorship books of bar-room stories have
begun to appear. Here is one, from an American collection
called *Over Sixteen*, edited by J. M. Elgart, which actually
focusses on male infidelity, and gets a laugh out of it.

> *Good Query, Dearie*: A group of men were in the club
> before dinner. The talk for no good reason turned to
> married life.
>
> 'Well,' said one fellow, 'the real comfort in life comes
> when you are settled down with one woman you love.
> You can argue all you want but it's my opinion that
> once they've settled down most men remain faithful.'
>
> Most of the men agreed with him but an older man
> in the group shook his head. 'I don't agree at all,' he
> asserted. 'And if you fellows are honest you'll know I
> am right. I'll bet any and all of you men a new hat there
> isn't one of you who hasn't strayed from the straight
> and narrow since he's married.'
>
> 'I'll take that bet,' cried one swiftly.
>
> 'How long have you been married?' asked the cynic.
>
> 'Since last Saturday,' was the reply.
>
> The crowd roared, of course—and one of the listeners

was so amused that he could hardly wait to get home
and tell his wife about it. At the end of the story he
laughed and laughed. But his laughter died as he noticed
a strange expression on his wife's face. 'Don't you think
the story very funny?'

'Very funny,' she replied quietly. 'But where is your
new hat?'

There used to be a curious belief that infidelity was
infectious. Aubrey quoted William Harvey, the great
physician: 'He that makes a widdowe makes himself Cuckold. *Exempli gratia*, if a good Bitch is first warded with a
Curre, let her ever be warded with a dog of a good straine
and yet she will bring curres as at first, her wombe being
first infected with a Curre. So, the children will be like the
first Husband (like raysing up children to your brother). So,
the Adulterer, though a crime in Law, the children are like
the husband.' This belief seems to have persisted, even in
reverse. My father had two red-headed boys by a woman who
was not red, although his wife was, and he once mentioned
this same theory to me to account for it.

Finally, a puzzle. This also comes out of Aubrey. Writing
of Beaumont and Fletcher, he said: 'They lived together on
the Banke side, not far from the Play-house, both batchelors;
lay together; had one Wench in the house between them,
which they did so admire. . . .' What could be more fitting
for such an intimate partnership? But there is a moral
problem: to whom was the Wench unfaithful?

Samuel Pepys, Average Man

'It is with us as with wives,' said Goethe to Eckermann:
'when they are brought to bed they for ever renounce sleeping
with men; and then, before you know where you are, they
are in the family way again.' (*Goethe's Conversations with
Eckermann*, trs J. Oxenford, 20 February 1829.)

Van de Velde urges the need for regular exercise of the
sex organs—on medical grounds, naturally. 'In our present

state of uncertainty, it seems advisable for a healthy man in
the fifties and sixties to prevent, so far as possible, the atrophy
of his organs, by exercising them *regularly and appropriately*,
i.e., not with excessive frequency, but also not too seldom.
*I assume, of course, that he will have always preserved them
from morbid infections!*'

The franker Greeks made no bones about it. The motive
is joy, and there is no need to refer to any 'state of uncertainty'. 'Thou grudgest thy maidenhead?' exclaims
Asclepiades in the *Greek Anthology*. 'What avails it? When
thou goest to Hades thou shalt find none to love thee there.
The joys of Love are in the land of the living, but in Acheron,
dear virgin, we shall lie dust and ashes.' The *Arabian Nights*
give the same advice. On the twenty-ninth night the barber
tries to persuade the young man to go to a feast, but the
young man is reluctant. The barber quotes a poet:

> *When pleasure offers, dear my friends,*
> *   Catch hands or feet or breasts of her,*
> *She is a woman and up-ends*
> *   The tantalising bests of her*
> *Perhaps three times a week. The other days*
> *'How gross a thing is man!' she says.*
>
>   'Tale of the Lame Young Man', MATHERS

That one girl is as good as another was certainly Pandarus's
opinion and he was baffled by Troilus's grief when Criseyde
leaves him. Not being in love himself, he failed to see that
Criseyde could satisfy a single desire that a dozen other ladies
of the town could not do as well.

> *What, god for-bede alwey that ech pleasaunce*
> *In o thing were, and in non other wight!*
> *If oon can singe, another can wel daunce;*
> *If this be goodly, she is glad and light;*
> *And this is fayr, and that can good a-right.*
> *Ech for his vertu holden is for dere,*
> *Both heroner and faucon for rivere.*

Troilus replies stiffly that he is not playing tennis. But he is outside our present terms of reference. His affections are involved.

The foregoing do suggest why the prevalence of sexual desire and sexual activity should in fact be masked. There is a tendency, especially among the moderns, to mistrust sexual joy. There is also a powerful urge, more often feminine than masculine, to disguise the instinct. Both Goethe and the Arabian poet refer to it. We do not know why Asclepiades's virgin resisted his advances, for the reasons can be many and complex, but both he and Pandarus were impatient with such scruples. This attitude is probably the characteristic one of most men, at all times, although we might read conventional literature in vain to find the evidence. There is probably no better example in literature of the ordinary man caught unawares, we might say with his trousers down, than Samuel Pepys.

Pepys, like most men in civilised society, was full of inhibitions. Most of his sexual adventures were strictly limited. Despite his untiring lusts, he was usually pulled up short by a sense of shame or a suspicion of danger. Despite his urge to keep a record of his adventures, there was little element of exhibitionism. He invented a peculiar language in which to recount his experiences—a strange jargon of tongues, French, Spanish, Greek, Italian, Latin, with little 'toy words' (as Arthur Bryant called them) scattered throughout. It is an inefficient device for no one who got hold of the diary could be in doubt of the meaning, but for Pepys it was better than stating boldly what he had been up to. Hence we read that 'she would not suffer that je should poner my mano above ses jupes which je endeavoured.' But here we see Pepys for what he was: a man whose social behaviour was as normal as can be imagined but who had been brought up to believe, first, that it was wicked, and second, that it was abnormal. And it is this fact that accounts for the failure of society to recognise the prevalence of sex activity. Wishing to keep it between the limits of the Ten Commandments, orthodoxy prefers to believe that nature actually is constrained.

Although Pepys wrote his sexual adventures down they were not for public consumption. He was as much a hypocrite in these matters as anyone else. This is illustrated by his reference to a book called *L'escholle des Filles*. He thought of getting it for his wife to translate but it was so lewd he felt ashamed, comparing it adversely with *Putana Errante*. 'We sat until almost night,' he wrote, 'and drank mighty good store of wine, and then they parted, and I to my chamber, where I did read through *L'escholle des Filles*, a lewd book but what do no wrong once to read it for information sake. . . . And after I had done it, I burned it, that it might not be among my books to my shame. . . .'

When Pepys devoted a large amount of energy to seducing maidservants, actresses and neighbours' wives, he was behaving as a very large number of men of all times have behaved. This is what Henry Miller says of himself, and it is corroborated by George Orwell's view of him: this is how I lived but so did nearly everyone else around me. One knows from one's own experience (and what one hears, from both male and female friends) that this is true, yet there is still a conspiracy of silence, a determination to maintain the fiction that sex is for special moments. How many millions of times has this happened since the world began:

> From thence walked towards Westminster, and being in an idle wanton humour, walked through Fleet Alley, and there stood a most pretty wench at one of the doors, so I took a turn or two, but what by sense of honour and conscience I would not go in, but much against my will took coach and got away, and away to Westminster Hall, and there 'light of Mrs Lane, and plotted with her to go over the water. So met at White's stairs in Chanel Row, and over to the old house at Lambeth Marsh, and there eat and drank, and had my pleasure of her twice, she being the strangest woman in talk of love of her husband sometimes, and sometimes again she do not care for him, and yet willing enough to allow me a liberty of doing what I would with her.

So spending 5s or 6s upon her, I could do .what I would. . . .

When he gets home his wife says she thinks she's pregnant and he is displeased—and anyway, doesn't believe her. He constantly affects to be amazed by the perfidy of woman (like all such double-livers, he cannot see his own), and recounts 'the best instance of a woman's falseness in the world'. This is Doll, who is furious with a Dutchman who 'pulled her into a stable by the Dog tavern, and there did tumble her and toss her, calling him all the rogues and toads in the world, when she knows that ell hath suffered me to do any thing with her a hundred times.'

No one would read the diary for an erotic thrill—he would have to have immense patience if he was to get it. As it is there are still portions which, according to Pepys's editor, Henry B. Wheatley, 'cannot possibly be printed'. (It is doubtful if this is still true.) Here is a selection of entries between August and November 1661, which give us the average man without the veils behind which he usually conceals his actions.

> *6 Aug.* Returning to London, the road was bad. He stopped at Baldwick (Baldock). 'The landlady being a pretty woman, but I durst take not notice of her, her husband being there.' Being a man of parts, he admired the church instead.
>
> *9 Sep.* '. . . and thence to Salisbury Court play house, where was acted the first time *'Tis Pity She's a Whore*, a simple play and ill acted, only it was my fortune to sit by a most pretty and most ingenious lady, which pleased me much.' He went to the play because he was too drunk to work, yet about this time he began to feel worried by the theatre's fascination for him.
>
> *10 Oct.* 'So home, and intended to be merry, it being my sixth wedding night; but by a late bruise . . . I am in so much pain that I eat my supper and in pain to bed, yet my wife and I pretty merry.' About this time there are many references to his disability, but all are omitted in the printed version.

11 Oct. 'All day in bed with a cataplasm . . . and at night rose a little, and to bed again in more ease than last night.'

17 Oct. Talking with Captain Lambert, just returned from Portugal. The King was a rude and simple fellow 'and, for reviling of somebody a little while ago, and calling of him cuckold, was run into . . . with a sword and had been killed, had he not told them that he was their king.'

25 Oct. 'Coming out of the house we met Mrs Pierce and her comrade Mrs Clifford, and I seeming willing to stay with them to talk my wife grew angry, and whether she be jealous or no I know not, but she loves not that I should speak of Mrs Pierce.'

13 Nov. 'To bed, and this night began to lie in the little green chamber, where the maids lie, but we could not a great while get Nell to lie there, because I lie there and my wife, but at last, when she saw she must lie there or sit up, she, with much ado, came to bed.' (Nell was new. It was not unusual for hosts, guests, servants, of both sexes, to share rooms in small houses—even beds. *Vide* 'Hob in the Well', *The Festival of Love*.)

18 Nov. Goes home with Moore. 'Here I dined and had a good dinner, and his wife a good pretty woman.'

19 Nov. 'At the office all the morning, and coming home found Mr Hunt with my wife in the chamber alone, which God forgive me did trouble my head, but remembering that it was washing and that there was no place else with a fire for him to be in, it being also cold weather, I was at ease again.'

(So they were both suspicious, but Mr Pepys with more reason, as he knew his own shortcomings. He had already seen Mr Lucy behaving very freely with Mrs Pierce as she lay in bed, and later Sir Charles Berkeley offered her £300 to be his mistress. The Pepyses had already had arguments about whether she was a beauty or not. A year later, however, Samuel changed his opinion on seeing her naked neck.)

22 *Nov.* Two new enthusiasms: Mrs Cocke ('a German lady, but a very great beauty') and a new maid.

This is the background: a continuing twitter of sexual excitement. The majority of cases lead to nothing, of course. In some cases there are doubts. In others, none at all. Here is Pepys with two of his girl friends. First, Mrs Knipp:

2 *Jan.* 1666: He longed for Knipp's company; after leaving a party he returned 'and met them coming home in coaches, so I got into the coach where Mrs Knipp was and got her upon my knee (the coach being full) and played with her breasts and sung. . . .'

24 *Jan.* 1667: 'The company being all gone to their houses, I up with Mrs Pierce to Knipp, who was in bed; and we waked her, and then I handled her breasts and did baiser la, and sing a song, lying by her on the bed. . . .' On the previous day he had felt mighty pleased with himself, having kissed Nell Gwyn at the King's theatre after the show ('a most pretty woman').

And here is Deb, one of a long line of maidservants whom Pepys lusted after.

30 *Sept.* 1667: The new maid, Willett, arrives. 'She is very pretty. . . . I wish my wife may use her well.'

15 *Oct.* At the play. 'Before the play begun, my wife began to complain to me of Willett's confidence in sitting cheek by jowl with us, which was a poor thing; but I perceive she is already jealous of my kindness to her, so that I begin to fear this girle is not likely to stay long with us.'

22 *Dec.* Goes down in morning, leaving wife in bed,' and thither come to me Willett with an errand from her mistress, and this time I first did give her a little kiss, she being a very pretty humoured girle, and so one that I do love mightily.'

11 Jan 1668: '. . . and so by the fireside to have my head
combed, as I do now often do, by Deb, whom I love
should be fiddling about me . . .'

On 25 October Mrs Pepys found him embracing the girl. On
12 November she was dismissed. She lasted longer than might
have been expected.

Pepys's medical condition did not help. He had a large
stone removed from his bladder (the size of a tennis ball,
according to Evelyn) in 1658, but he continued to suffer
pains from renal colic. This operation probably caused his
sterility, for the methods used in those days frequently caused
injury to the seminal ducts. He complained constantly of
pain and swelling in his testes, which remained functional
for many years, and his prostatic secretion was always
sufficiently abundant to prevent him suffering from any lack
of emission. The pain was caused by the blocked condition
of the *vasa deferentia*, which would not allow him to give
vent to his semen. These facts I take from a paper on *The
Medical History of Mr and Mrs Samuel Pepys*, read before
the Abernethian Society on 6 March 1895, by D'Arcy Power.
The author's conclusion was that 'his long spells of sedentary
office work and his rather gross habits of life tended to foster
his sexual feelings'. And if they fostered Pepys's it seems
likely that the same causes have fostered those of millions
of other men. I understand that country walks and tree fell-
ing are among the many activities that stimulate the sexual
impulse; long spells of reading and filling in ledgers do the
same. Perhaps it would be easier to compile a list of activities
that do not.

Statistics

No modern writer can ignore statistics. Here are a few to
illustrate the prevalence of sexual activity. Others will be
quoted in other parts of this book.

From the quantitative point of view none is more illustrious
than Madame de Saint-Ange. Her argument was that a woman
is ruined by lovers but that mere acts of libertinism are

quickly forgotten. 'That is the conduct I would always pre-
scribe to all women who would follow in my steps. In the
twelve years I have been married I have been had by perhaps
ten or twelve thousand individuals. . . .'

The Aphrodites were an eighteenth century Love Club,
very exclusive. Membership was £10,000 for a gentleman and
£5,000 for a lady, plus a gift compatible with economic status.
The Journal of a female member has been preserved. She gave
a list of 4,959 amorous rendezvous for a period of twenty
years—not excessive, according to Nina Epton, when one
considers the club's reputation. Among her lovers were:

>   272 princes and prelates
>   929 officers
>   93 rabbis
>   342 financiers
>   439 monks
>   420 society men
>   288 commoners
>   117 valets
>   2 uncles
>   12 cousins
>   119 musicians
>   47 negroes
>   1,614 foreigners

Pierre Louÿs, author of *Aphrodite*, 1896, realised that the
basic distinction between marital fidelity and sexual freedom
is numerical. Although this book is a novel it is written with
immense authority. It must come closer to the spirit of sexual
relations in the classical world than most histories. Chrysis,
the courtesan, taunts Demetrios with the number of men who
have had her. 'In seven years, Demetrios, I have slept alone
only three nights. Count how many lovers that makes:
around two thousand five hundred, and even more; for I
didn't include those I see by day.' At Bacchis's party Timon
speaks against marriage and says that when he dies three
thousand women will not have been enough for him. Chrysis,

however, thinks this ambitious.

One last example, taken at random. At the beginning of
the present century it is estimated that there were about
sixty thousand *insoumises* in Paris. These are the raw material
of the erotic life. They were free-lances who were not registered
with the police and had no card. They accepted a meal or a
gift, or they insisted on money, or they did it for fun. There
is always a large population of these in any big city. It may
be said that I have been quoting special cases. But when does
a case become special? How does an *insoumise* or a tart shade
off into a courtesan or a prostitute? And to what extent should
we retain a special category for the married women who
accept any lover who happens to come to the accommodation
address: the parachute women, as they are wittily called in
Omdurman?

It's All Nature

Mr Etaoin, the proof-reader (and corrector of errors) looks
at a sea serpent (in Charles Finney's *The Circus of Dr Lao*)
and they converse. The snake recalls its first affair. 'I slithered
after her; my passion warmed her; my ardour allayed her
coyness. Tell me, do men bite women on the neck when they
woo them?' 'Sometimes,' replies Etaoin. 'So do we,' says the
snake—and so the conversation proceeds, question, answer,
comment.

'Do men tire of women after they have lain with them?'

'After the period of surfeit wears off, do men again lust
after women?'

'Do men in cages . . .?'

It is the law of nature and the wise man accepts. Rosebud,
the American Negro hero in the story of that name (*Horizon*,
July 1949) died of pneumonia caught from making love to
a girl in the rain. He felt he was dying of love, and could
not complain. Better than being run over by an automobile
driven by a stranger. 'He had gotten only love out of life—
perhaps he had gotten life out of only love. . . .'

Much of man's social development and the literature that

mirrors it has been a resistance to this force. Men, with their
ache for morality, have often been at their wits' ends to
know how to categorise this force which they receive from
Nature—and Nature is a synonym for God. One easy way
out, perhaps the most familiar, has been to apportion the
blame. Man has not the power to resist; woman has. It is not
surprising that the most vigorous expression of this view
comes from Arab society, one of the most male-dominated of
all. *The Arabian Nights* are full of it. Halimah, for instance,
persuades Kamar to run away with her, although she is
married. Kamar's father is furious and shuts her up, then
says to his son: 'A man has nothing with which to reproach
himself when he is seduced by a woman, because Allah has
planted in him an instinct to yield; but when a woman is
tempted and does not repulse a man, she is most reprehensible.' ('Tale of Kamar and the Expert Halimah', trs. Mathers.)
Although these tales are supposedly told by a woman they
represent the male point of view. For the most part the
women are magnificent animals, openly bought and sold and
appraised like animals. Occasionally a freak is exhibited, a
paragon of learning such as the slave Sympathy. The *Nights*
have it both ways; male pleasure is the dominant principle
and the women carry the burden of immorality.

A word on climate. Much of the most salacious literature
of the world comes from the tropical or semi-tropical belt.
Europeans in Africa tend to be in a state of permanent sexual
excitement. Dr Julius Rosenbaum made a thesis out of this
and called it *Plague of Lust in Antiquity*—the point being
that known antiquity was almost entirely hot.

As a matter of fact we observe at the present day how
in hot climates, where the whole vegetative life presents
a luxuriant character, and all Nature appears to feel the
procreative impulse unceasingly, man too falls in with
the universal stress and strain of each species to maintain
its foothold. Yet as this must inevitably be done at the
expense of the individual life, we see the effort very
frequently resulting in the production of barren or sex-

less blossoms, and not fruit at all. The son of the South is like a tree growing in rich, rank soil; he ripens betimes to the sexual life, but equally early is constrained to abandon it again. . . .

We saw how in Asia lust and its abominable brood arose and extended thence over neighbouring lands, and how the rhythmic rites of the *Venus ebria* (drunken Venus) could indeed refine, but hardly increase their excesses. Babylon, Syria and Egypt were the nurseries of licentiousness, finding only at Rome a really self-taught and competent rival. The clear sky of Greece could cover only inhabitants of corresponding character in body and mind, and none but a Greek was capable of setting up the ideal, and verifying it in practice, of a fair soul in a fair body.

The heat of the sun, asserts the doctor, causes the mucous secretions to be lessened in quantity but more highly charged in quality. The genital secretions acquire an acid quality and exert a corrosive effect on things they come in contact with. Frequent working of the genital parts is essential for health in hot countries.

Being one of Nature's compulsions, we should not be surprised if it manifests itself early in life. Since Freud we have learned to accept infantile sexuality but actual memories are not so frequently published. Gide gives us one in *If It Die.* . . . On the first page he tells us how he used to crawl under a big table and play with the *concierge's* little boy. The nurse used to ask what they were up to and they would reply that they were playing—which indeed they were, but not in her understanding of the term. They used to take their playthings and make a great noise with them to allay her suspicions. Later he learnt that they were playing 'bad habits'. In fiction we get a glimpse of this underworld of precocious sexuality in John O'Hara's *Appointment in Samarra*. Caroline Walker, a rich man's daughter, taught poor Italians and Negroes for a while at the Gibbsville Mission. One red-headed little Irish boy used to fascinate her. One day, when she was

preparing to go home, the little fellow went for her: 'two
arms went around her legs and two hands slid up under her
skirt, and a red little head was burrowing into her stomach.'
She knocked him away but not before 'he had touched her
where he had wanted to with his vile little fingers'. This went
beyond 'bad habits', it was depravity. But he was a juvenile
and not responsible. It is doubtful if he understood that what
he did was wrong. And O'Hara uses the scene as an awakening for Caroline to the power of this force that is normally
held on a leash.

Zola was thoroughly aware of the precocity of sex. As soon
as it was dark the boys and girls of the village got up to their
tricks (Germinal). Their word for it (in L. W. Tancock's
translation) was 'up-ending', and they did it on the low,
sloping roofs of the sheds. That was where all the haulage
girls picked up their first babies. No one really minded,
except for the mothers of the boys, who would have to marry
and then bring in no more wages. This was real promiscuity
because it was done with anyone who happened along and
it was done in public. (But Hyde Park is no different.) 'It
was as though,' writes Zola, 'round this dead machine, by this
pit worn out with bringing forth coal, the life-force was taking
its revenge in the untrammelled love which used the lash of
instinct, and planted children in the wombs of those who
were scarcely more than children themselves.' Daddy Mouque
used to move among them tolerantly and they were not concerned with him. There was only one thing that used to
annoy him: one couple had got into the habit of doing it
against the wall of his shack and they pushed so hard they
were damaging the wall. As Mouque picks his way among
the sprawling limbs we recognise the plight of A. J. Leibling,
an American journalist, describing Green Park on a Bank
Holiday in the Observer (11 August 1957):

> The young, who fear neither aches nor grass stains, lie
> upon the turf heterosexually entangled in those bow-
> knots of limbs, flexing and tensing, that always amaze
> first visitors who have heard the English are a staid lot.

The dogs run among the lovers, only occasionally licking
an upturned palm, their owners, usually ladies old
enough to stay vertical, follow them, only occasionally
falling over an outflung amoring limb. . . .

No, it can't be stopped. Prohibitions are always broken.
Some societies have tried to make some accommodation.
Engagement is often regarded as a sanction. Wild young men
are married off quickly. The curious custom of bundling has
been resorted to in certain areas. Grose, in his *Dictionary of
the Vulgar Tongue*, defines it thus: 'A man and a woman
lying on the same bed with their clothes on; an expedient
practised in America on a scarcity of beds where, on such
occasions, husbands and parents frequently permitted
travellers to *bundle* with their wives and daughters'. The
couples were supposedly on their honour, but honour is a
weak prophylactic, and the custom was probably the equivalent of consent without responsibility.

This custom is described in an American publication
entitled *Bundling: its Origin, Progress and Decline in
America*, by Henry Reed Stiles (1871). It originated in the
British Isles, though whether this implies there has always
been a shortage of beds in that area I am uncertain. Undoubtedly comfortable sleeping places are fewer there than
in, say, the Middle East. There was also an ancient custom
called *handfasting*, according to which the heir of one chief
lived with the daughter of another for a year and a day. Sir
Walter Scott attributed it to a shortage, not of beds but of
priests. Monks used to be despatched on circuit to marry
such couples. The custom was common on the Isle of Portland and even more in Wales. This comes from *The Stranger
in Ireland* by John Carr, but he is writing of the Welsh:

The lower order of people do actually carry on their
love affairs in bed, and what would extremely astonish
more polished lovers, they are carried on honourably, it
being, at least, as usual for the Pastors of the mountains
to go from the bed of courtship to the bed of marriage

as unpolluted and maidenly as the Chloes of fashion;
and yet you are not to conclude that this proceeds from
their being less susceptible of the *belle passion* than their
betters; or that the cold air that they breathe has frozen
'the genial current of their souls'.

He describes a personal experience:

One evening, at an inn where we halted, we heard a
considerable bustle in the kitchen and, upon enquiring,
I was let into a secret worth knowing. The landlord had
been scolding one of his maids, a very pretty plump little
girl, for not having done her work; and the reason which
she alleged for her idleness was, that her master having
locked the street door at night, had prevented her lover
enjoying the rights and delights of *bundling*, an amatory
indulgence which, considering that it is sanctioned by
custom, may be regarded as somewhat singular, although
it is not exclusively of Welsh growth. . . . Habit has so
reconciled the mind to the comforts of *bundling*, that a
young lady who entered the coach soon after we left
Shrewsbury, about eighteen years of age, with a serene
and modest countenance, displayed considerable historical knowledge of the custom without one touch of bash-
fulness.

In Holland the custom was called *queesting*. Afghan tribes
(another place where comfortable sleeping places are not too
easy to find) had a similar practice called *namzat bezé*. Only
innocent endearments were allowed. There was also a variant
called *tarrying*, according to which a young man who wished
to marry might spend one night with the girl, fully clothed
and with the parents' consent.

The British were very critical of this custom in America,
overlooking it in their own country. The criticism was deeply
resented. It used to be customary at Westminster School to
perform a play of Terence annually. There was usually a
Latin prologue, especially composed for the occasion. In 1815,

when Anglo-American relations were hardly at their most cordial, the prologue was concerned with the American way of life, and contained this passage (in translation):

> Nor is it easy to say whether the tenor of their manners is more to be admired for simplicity or elegance; a negro wench, as we are told, will wait on her master at table in native nudity[1]; and a beau will strip himself to the waist, that he may dance unencumbered, and with more agility. There, too, we hear of the practice of *bundling* without any infraction of female modesty; and the chaste maiden, without any deception, but with right good will, ventures to share the bed with her chaste swain! Oh, what nights and banquets, worthy of the gods! What delightful customs among these pious people!

Bundling, as a literary subject, scarcely exists but for the reaction against it. The pious, the moralistic and the more sophisticated elements among the population united in their efforts to abolish the custom. For a long time tradition was too strong—and after all, no one undressed. Or did they? 'A New Bundling Song' which appeared in an almanack in 1785 suggests that the practice was not always as innocent as some hoped and believed.

> *Some really do, as I suppose,*
> *Upon design keep on some clothes,*
> *And yet in truth I'm not afraid*
> *For to describe a bundling maid;*
> *She'll sometimes say when she lies down,*
> *She can't be cumbered with a gown,*
> *And that the weather is so warm,*
> *To take it off can be no harm;*
> *The girl it seems had been at strift;*
> *For widest bosom to her shift,*
> *She gownless, when the bed they're in,*
> *The spark, nought feels but naked skin.*
> *But she is modest, also chaste,*
> *While only bare from neck to waist,*

And he of boasted freedom sings,
Of all above her apron strings.
And when such freedoms great are shared
And further freedoms feebly bared,
I leave for others to relate,
How long she'll keep her virgin state.

'A New Song in Favour of Courting' is equally ironical and worldly wise.

Nature's request is, grant me rest,
   Our bodies seek repose;
Night is the time, and 'tis no crime
   To bundle in your clothes.

Since in a bed a man and maid
   May bundle and be chaste,
It does no good to burn out wood,
   It is a needless waste.

Let coats and gowns be laid aside,
   And breeches take their flight
An honest man and woman can
   Lay quiet all the night.

'A Poem Against Bundling' by a clergyman of Massachusetts belongs to roughly the same period. Here are three (not consecutive) verses:

Let boars and swine lie down and twine,
And grunt, and sleep, and snore,
But modest girls should not wear tails
Nor bristles any more.

Dogs and bitches wear no breeches,
   Clothing for man was made,
Yet men and women strip to their linen,
   And tumble into bed.

A female meek, with blushing cheek,
  Seized in some lover's arms,
Has oft grown weak with Cupid's heat,
  And lost her virgin charms.

The power and prevalence of the sexual impulse has only
been fully recognised during this century. This has added a
new dimension to criticism, for it has allowed the critic to
turn more freely to the sexual impulse when he is baffled—
and often to be right. It has also allowed men to admit
personal fantasies which had previously remained hidden
behind the mask of social decency. In a discussion held at the
English P.E.N. Centre on 16 June 1959, for instance, Robert
Melville, the art critic, confessed that he frequently made
sweeping statements such as, 'If a picture looks meaningless
its meaning is almost bound to be erotic. . . .' It may well be
so. The mind tends to make this true, anyway. When faced
by obscurity, in literature as in art, the most likely channels
are explored first. Before the rational faculties can get to
work the intuitional apparatus is already relating the work
by which it is confronted with the basic drives of existence.
Like it or not, sex is one of these and is probably the most
powerful. And again, why does the mind resort to obscurity?
May it not be that it is trying to beat the censor which experience tells it is always lying in wait?

Male society is sex-orientated. Jokes and allusions are
almost invariably sexual in tone when men are together in
unbuttoned mood. Here is a perfectly innocent entry in a
book of Technical English (*Preparatory Technical English*,
by G. A. Pittman) describing a 'Situation': 'It needs ——ing.
It could do with a clean.' Show this to any man (except a
prude or a complete stranger) and he will laugh; you will
know why. The same relentless urge causes idle doodling to
cause later embarrassment to the doodler. Not everyone
doodles with a pencil. Many do it with the imagination. In
a mixed committee the male member (I mean of the committee) often imagines during the lulls and boring stretches
that everyone is stripped and, at the blow of the chairman's

gavel, rises and dances orgiastically round the table.

The Bye-Products of Promiscuity

The sexual impulse is promiscuous in most men and in some women. Society has tried to check the impulse. According to Remy de Gourmont this has been a powerful factor in causing the moral aberration that society wishes to avoid.

> There would be extremely few aberrant men and women if moral customs permitted a quite simple satisfaction of sexual needs, if it were possible for the two sexes to meet always at the opportune moment. There would remain aberration of anatomical order; they would be less frequent and less tyrannic if our customs, instead of contriving ways to make sexual relations very difficult, should favour them. But this easiness is only possible in promiscuity, which is possibly a worse ill than aberration.
> *The Natural Philosophy of Love.*

Various evils are attributed to promiscuity but it might be truer to attribute them to Checked, or Hindered, or Incomplete Promiscuity—I mean that just as the institution of marriage is a powerful progenitor of that unlovely human passion, jealousy,[2] so a promiscuity that has to hide its face and act in holes and corners gives rise to evils that a little frankness and common sense would soon eradicate—but the enemy don't want such evils eradicated except on their own terms. Here is a horrifying account of what promiscuity may lead to. It is taken from *Post-Office Intelligence*, or Universal Gallantry, being a Collection of Love-Letters (printed for the notorious Curll in 1736). It is on the model of *The Pacquet Broke Open*, a favourite eighteenth century literary ruse. Letter XXVI is addressed to Mr William Bastick, a gunsmith of Hereford, from his sincere well-wisher, James Wyborne:

> I expected a letter from you soon after you got to town, but I fear you follow so much the Pocky Comforts of

universal Copulation, that it has consumed your
Memory, and certainly will your Strength, if you go on
at the old rate; for there are many such true-bred Stallions
in this our Age, whose various inclinations give every
new Force a power of Temptation, and who are so
enamoured with every Female, that each fine petticoat,
or Turriferous Topknot kindles a new Fire to their
Leachery, which is no ways to be quenched or qualified
till his mercenary Bolt be shot in Nature's warm Staple;
till at last by a frequent Repetition of his beloved
Exercise, he thrusts his rustling Pole into an over-heated
Oven, where it takes such Fire, that half a year's Penance
with Ten pounds worth of the Doctor's assistance will
scarce quench, without having some remaining sparks,
which at Spring and Fall will still be blazing.

Then Aqua-Tetrachimagogon, Turpentine Potions,
Mercurial Pills, Sal Prunella, gentle Salivations, and
downright Fluxes, Diet-Drinks, Injections with all the
Engines of Chirurgery are set on Work to abate the
intolerable Symptoms, which afflict the repenting Sinner.
Now an aching Head, a gleeting *Penis*, with as many
Holes as the Bottom of a Cullender, and covered with
as many black patches as a Cheapside Crack; meagre
Faced, yellow Eyed, tottering Nose, and Jaws as thin
as a Spanish three-pence.

Then like a Woman in Labour, to hear his honest
Protestations, shewing all the Signs of Regeneration,
promising that if the Lord in his Mercy will be pleased
to bring him safe out of the Powdering Tub of Repent-
ance, he would never more be pickled in such a Salt
Bitche's Commodity. Thus he Raves and Frets, Prays
and Promises, till he has swallowed as many Pills as
there are Sheep-turds in a Common, and drank as much
Diet-Drink as will swim a Cock-Boat, by which means
Pego has shook off the Bridle, and begins to be finely
recovered; but our new Saint still finds an itching of the
old Devil about him, and begins to cast an Hawk's eye
at every handsome Woman, soon forgetting his poor

Miseries and pious Protestations; she ventures abroad in the Sunshine, drawing his Rowling-Pin-Legs after him, as if they were tied on with Whipcord; thus he walks like an Anatomy, moved by Clockwork, with a Complexion like a Christmas-Candle, that everyone may read his Distemper in his Looks, without the Skill of Physiognomy; then he re-assumes his old Course of Life (for what is bred in the Bone will never get out of the Flesh) till he gets Clap upon Clap, and Pox upon Pox; when after three or four gentle Salivations and downright Fluxes his radical moisture is so exhausted, that Nature can subsist no longer. Thus the poor Mortal pikes off with a Carcass as dry and hollow as an Old New River Pipe, with scarce Flesh enough on his Bones to give the Worms a Picking, leaving this character among his Neighbours Wives behind him, that he was as good a Woman's Man as ever handled a Merkin.

If this won't keep you off it, what will? Ah, but it won't! It may cause you to start agitation for better medical services.

The great danger to peace of mind is not promiscuity but promiscuity hounded by censors. If there were no check on promiscuity it is conceivable that some of the evils threatened by the moralists would assail us. On the other hand, many evils that are already with us would be successfully coped with—the Pox Problem, already alluded to, is one of them. Modern technology, in conjunction with modern promiscuity, has created another, which we can call the Pessary Problem. I can illustrate it from two modern novels. The first in time is Sherwood's *Stradella*, which I quoted earlier. Here we have the dilemma of the married woman—not that Stradella was either married or in a dilemma: she just didn't care. But Archie did. When Stradella tells him she is going away with a girl-friend for the weekend he has that sinking feeling. There is only one thing to do: look in the bathroom cupboard. He fumbled among the Kleenex and Kotex and the hot water bottle and the enema injector, but it was no use. It had gone —'the little pink plastic travel kit with the rubber bag and hose and nozzle and the jelly and the parachute.'

The problem is not insoluble. Moreover, the single girl has a similar problem but in reverse, so to speak. She must not let it be known (by mother, for example) that she *has* an outfit. Her best way out is to let the lover keep it. But the girl who doesn't have a regular lover may be in a more difficult position. She may even have to buy a fresh outfit for each performance—a costly business, though a self-respecting lover would at least help. When the performance is over the outfit has to be dumped somewhere—also on those sad occasions, so well described by Mary McCarthy in *The Group* when there is no performance and the little packet has to be left in the subway or on a park bench. The other novel I referred to is, in fact, *The Group*. Here we are told what the married woman does. She does what the single girl does, gets an extra outfit which is kept in the lover's apartment. Its very presence acts as a restraint if he is feeling disloyal. A man entrusted with such equipment was bonded like a bank clerk. If he did betray his trust he would be more likely to do it in the other woman's place or a hotel room or a taxi. A man of feeling would not be very comfortable in a seduction when the little bag was only a few feet away. The woman made a similar pledge, for 'only a married woman of very coarse fibre would use the same pessary for both husband and lover'. (Stradella was certainly of coarse fibre.) But you could never be sure. 'One adventurous wife . . . was said to have pessaries all over town, like a sailor with a wife in every port, while her husband, a busy stage director, assured himself of her good behaviour by a daily inspection of the little box in her medicine cabinet, where the conjugal pessary lay in its dusting of talcum powder.' For those who are more concerned with happiness than with ethics, this is an attractive story. How that husband was to be envied!

FOOTNOTES

1. See the anonymous *Memoirs of Dolly Morton*.
2. Last night a young lady informed me that gorillas exhibit sexual jealousy, and therefore I can hardly blame the institution of marriage, but I suspect they were Christian gorillas.

5: *Views of Love (Sex?)*

It is fashionable to speak and write of 'periods' in the sex relationship: the pagan, the classical, the romantic, the modern, and so on. One can scarcely avoid it. If one is to judge by literature one is driven to it, even though one may nurse a suspicion that the writers tended to be extremists (they do, and the critics urge them on relentlessly). There is a possibility that the attitude to love (or sex—this is *not* the place to go into that old debate) has not really varied during historic time. This is certainly the opinion of Crane Brinton who thinks that the behaviour of the Western male has varied much less since 600 B.C. than literary sources would have us believe and that there has been a rough constant. But our concern is erotic literature.

Writers have agreed that the attitude to physical love is not the same in both sexes. In No. 141 of his Miscellaneous Fragments (*Love*), Stendhal says that all women are susceptible to some kind of love. All men are not. From the age of fifteen a girl is secretly awaiting the onset of passion. A great passion will prove her importance. 'This expectation is twice as strong at about twenty, when she is past the earlier follies of life, whereas men have scarcely turned thirty before they're thinking love's impossible, or absurd.' At this age men tend to adopt a cynical attitude towards women, best expressed by the folklore of Sergeant William Brown in Mailer's *The Naked and the Dead*: 'If she won't lay she's frigid; if she does she's a whore.' Women can't win according to this philosophy, but there is nothing new in that. No woman, unless completely denatured, was ever able to win according to Christian philosophy. Such statements and attitudes are evidence of the defeatist immaturity of those who pronounce them; they are unfortunately extremely common.

Shakespeare's cynicism is far more realistic. It doesn't favour one sex against the other. None of us has much to boast about, he says, and by leaving out the rivalry and resultant hatred the temperature drops too. In *As You Like It* Orlando tells Rosalind that he intends to be faithful 'for ever and a day'. Rosalind replies:

> Say 'a day' without the 'ever'. No, no, Orlando; men are April when they woo, December when they wed: maids are May when they are maids, but the sky changes when they are wives. I will be more jealous of thee than a Barbary cock-pigeon over his hen, more clamorous than a parrot against rain, more new-fangled than an ape, more giddy in my desires than a monkey: I will weep for nothing, like Diana in the fountain, and I will do that when you are disposed to be merry; I will laugh like a hyena, and that when thou art inclined to sleep.

Beatrice in *Much Ado* had the same seasonal view of love. This is a solid basis for discussion.

The Spirit and the Body

The misery of so much Christian marriage has been caused by the Church's determination to regard the individual as a spirit to which a body is temporarily appended. It is extraordinary to what extent even anti-Christian writers have been influenced by this view. They have managed to detach from the theology a philosophy of love which could only be justified by esoteric argument, and they have done it without any sense of impropriety. It comes as something of a shock to find Huysmans, in his demonic *Là Bas*, claiming that hopeless love is the best love. But the satanists have always felt the attraction of the spiritual, and today it is doubtful if there is any force that works more strongly than Christianity for the maintenance of superstitious belief, including that of the devil-worshippers. Here is Huysmans:

> To love afar off and without hope, never to be one another's, to dream chastely of colourless allurements and impossible embraces, abortive caresses on forgotten brows of dead loves, ah! that is something akin to a delicious and incurable insanity! All else is ignoble or inane!

This is an attitude, I need hardly say, we are not likely to encounter very often in erotic literature. It is as absurd and as damnable as Sade's worst excesses, without his magnificent logic. James Branch Cabell seemed to believe that spiritual love was the invention of a woman, and although there are historical grounds for rejecting this view I must admit that there is a type of woman who rejoices in it more than any man. When Jurgen goes to heaven he finds it was invented by his grandmother—heaven, that is, and this is a theory that many will accept. God tells him that Koshchei, who made things as they are, talked to her and devised her illusions. He wanted to know what it was that came into her eyes when she spoke of her children. They told him it was love. Koshchei looked puzzled and asked if he had also created this love, for he made things as they are. They told him no, there were many sorts of love, but this especial sort was an illusion which women had invented for themselves, and which they exhibited in all dealings with their children. Also, we may add, with absent lovers.

Now that there is a sensation called love which is not the same as sex but which may contain it (must, in my view—which means we need another word for children and others with whom we don't or can't have physical connection, and there are such words), I do not deny. But the sensation has been expressed in language which does no justice to its reality, which stresses entirely the spiritual side, which may be the weakest, and at best is only a part. This has become such a powerful tradition few of our writers have been able to escape it, although it is becoming more common today. In

his *Physiologie du Mariage* Balzac compiled ninety-four
axioms, one section of which was called 'Matrimonial Catechism'. In the introduction he called love 'the poetry of the
senses'. He compared the reproductive need with hunger and
thirst (this was rapidly becoming the fashion), and lovers
with epicures. All are not called, he said. Our civilisation has
proved that taste is a science and only the privileged know
how to eat and drink properly. 'Pleasure, considered as an
art, awaits its physiologist.' This is not the spiritual aspect
of love, which is scarcely my province, but its reflection in the
mind of the ordinary, non-spiritual man. It is the heightening
of love, finally expressed in gallantry (a way of love which
deserves, and will get, separate consideration). Gallantry sees
love as technique, can be justified by the joy which skilful
techniques always bring, but has a flip side which is best
expressed (after Jurgen) as Venus Mechanitis. Spiritual love
can lead to the grossest cruelty, gallantry to the deepest
despair.

In this book I will refer frequently to gallant literature
but in essence it is not truly erotic. In the last resort gallantry
focusses on the emotion rather than the sensation, and often
on the most delicate emotion rather than those that exalt
or crush the soul. Modern man, particularly modern nineteenth century man, who laid the foundation for thought
and behaviour in this field, constantly showed himself to be
a hybrid. George Moore, who called himself a realist and
wrote that real love is physical love, nevertheless succumbed
to the delight of what he might have been expected to think
of as inessentials.[1] 'It is when lovers tell their illusions and
lonelinesses that they know each other', he wrote in *Memoirs
of My Dead Life*; 'the fiercest spasm tells us little, and it is
forgotten, whereas a simple confidence is remembered years
afterwards, and brings a lost love before us though she be
underground, or a thousand miles away.' Only a simpleton
could deny the truth of this. At the same time, it is equally
true that the confidence gains not only its force but even its
very existence from the previous intimacy.

One of the first to expound the notion that the basis of

love is physiological was the younger Crébillon (1707-1777). The intense and beautiful emotions which sex arouses cannot be philosophically justified or explained; they must simply be accepted for themselves, as feelings which are of the highest importance for those who experience them. *'Les plaisirs gagnent toujours à être ennoblis,'* says the Duke in *Le Hasard au Coin de Fer.* This is the man of science, the unprejudiced observer, who accepts facts and is too proud to explain them away. Pleasure gains by being ennobled, and that is the practical justification of all the seemingly infinite emotions evoked by sex. It has been argued against Crébillon that his view lacks balance, that he pays less attention to what ennobles than to pleasure pure and simple. It would have been difficult for him to have done otherwise, considering the times in which he lived. The Pompadour was his patroness.

But it was a hundred years later when the demands of the flesh were faced squarely by intelligent men. None did more to combat the false claims of the spirit than Remy de Gourmont, particularly in his *Physique de l'Amour: Essai sur l'Instinct Sexuel* (1904). It is a fascinating account of sexual physiology, techniques and customs through the whole range of insect and animal creation. Gourmont's findings were that there are no rules in nature, and that an appeal to nature for support of a theory or code will never succeed. There is, for instance, no such thing as a male role or a female role in life. The notions of aggressive male and passive female are merely faulty conclusions derived from limited study.

> One has noticed in certain species the female more beautiful, stronger, more active, more intelligent; and one has noticed the opposite. One has seen the male larger, or smaller; one has seen and will see him parasite, or provider, permanent master of the couple or the group, fugitive lover, a slave sacrificed by the female after the completion of her pleasure. All attitudes, and the same ones, are attributed by nature to either of the sexes; there is not, apart from the specific functions, a male or a female role.

Similarly one can scarcely speak of the natural or the unnatural in any fruitful sense. There is no conceivable type of
sexual behaviour that is not found in nature. 'One becomes
more discreet when one contemplates the prodigious picture
of the erotic habits of the animal world, and even entirely in-
competent to decide flatly whether a fact is natural or unnatural.' The sexual inventions of humanity are nearly all
anterior or exterior to man. There is not one whose model,
even in perfection, is not exhibited by the animals, even the
most humble of animals. He mentions the spintrian gastero-
pods who copulate in chains, each acting as a male to one
neighbour and a female to another: 'carnal imaginings that
have been the boast of erotic humanity. Facing this light
from animal habits debauchery loses all character and all its
tang, because it loses all immorality. Man, who unites in
himself the aptitudes of all the animals, all their laborious
instincts, all their industries, could not escape the heritage
of their sexual methods; and there is no lewdness which has
not its normal type in nature, somewhere.' The female Alpine
analote, while copulating with one male, will chew another,
probably one with which she has just had intercourse. 'Truly
this cannibal Marguerite de Bourgogne is a fine type of beast,
and gives a fine spectacle, not of immorality, an empty term,
but of the serenity of nature, which permits all things, wills
all things, and for whom there are neither vices nor virtues
but only movements and chemical reactions.'

It will be seen that Gourmont did not even mention the
spiritual aspect of love. Having demolished the morality, it
was self-evident for him that the spirit was an invention,
perhaps of his grandmother. This book was written at a time
when Western Europe was relaxing the moral restrictions
which encumbered sex. The orthodox had a habit of appeal-
ing to 'natural' behaviour when they encountered something
they didn't like. Gourmont was anxious to show that such
people had never examined the terms they used. After Gourmont sex codes had to be defended along different lines, as
human instruments and restraints on nature. For such writers
love acted as a disguise of sex.

Our finikin scruples protest in vain; man and the most disgusting of his parasites are the products of an identical sexual mechanism. The flowers we have strewn upon love may disguise it as one disguises a trap for wild beasts; all our activities manoeuvre along the edge of this precipice and fall over it one after another; the aim of human life is the continuation of human life.

And, let us stress, the only *natural* aim. If there are others, they are self-created. Love is a human invention, some say a Troubadour invention.

Returning to George Moore, we now see the more clearly the action of such brutal reasoning as Gourmont's on the mind of an intelligent man of normal educational background. Moore cannot set aside the delicacies and sophistications of love, so he is compelled to compromise. He will admit that, *au fond*, the animal impulse is the one that sets him in motion, no matter how enjoyable, how enticing, the other things (by-products) are. If you meet a lover from your past, he says, don't talk about literature. Be honest and admit why you talk to her again, and get pleasure from renewing the acquaintance. It is because you went to bed with her. If you hadn't done that, you might not even stop to speak. You should be bold, revert in conversation to the days when you were lovers. Pay no attention to the phrase: 'Is this all you love me for?', or simply answer: Yes. No woman ever asked that question with conviction. Deep down inside her she knows that 'all her earthly existence is comprised in man's love of her, and that if we were to withdraw our love she would become instantly a thing half our size, with sloping shoulders and wide hips and usually short-legged.' As for sexual virtue, it has cruelly enslaved women, turning them into kitchen maids, laundresses, nuns or wives. Moore felt women had a better appreciation of love when they used to form processions and wind through the woods to hang garlands on Pan's enormous member.

Moore was attracted by Shelley early in life but the rough and tumble of existence cured him. It was Gautier's *Mlle de*

Maupin that turned him from spiritual passion; he called physical love a 'great exaltation of the visible above the invisible'. He was able to turn from a world exemplified in lacerated saints and a crucified Redeemer to one where it was possible to raise the flesh to a place as high as any occupied by the soul. They were brave and innocent days, when the flesh was so exalted that at times it seemed to be in danger of etherialising as so much spirit. Moore could not foresee the time when this new love, won through carnal emancipation, would kick back because the frankness was too one-sided, because the lovers were picking and choosing from what nature spread before them. In the words of Helen Gordon in Hemingway's *To Have and Have Not*:

> . . . love is just another dirty lie. Love is ergoapiol pills to make me come around because you were afraid to make me have a baby. Love is quinine and quinine and quinine until I'm deaf with it. Love is that dirty aborting horror that you took me to. Love is my insides all messed up. It's half catheters and half whirling douches. I know about love. Love always hangs up behind the bathroom door. It smells like lysol. To hell with love.

That is sick love. It's not what people are looking for though it may be what they get. The germs may be entirely innocent and entirely praiseworthy. As when Gide and his friend Paul begin to discuss sex, for instance (*If It Die . . .*, by André Gide). They were both virgins and they were determined that pleasure should be dissociated from love. Paul was a Catholic and had been brought up among artists, students and morals, yet remained a virgin until he was twenty-three. How was it possible, people exclaim, but such cases are much more frequent than one supposes, says Gide; no one boasts of it. Many things can stop a young man on the verge: timidity, shame, distaste, pride, ill-judged sentimentality or nervous fright caused by an unfortunate experience. Eventually they shared a young Arab girl in Biskra. When Gide told his friendly uncle Albert, whom he had imagined broad-minded about this arrangement, Albert was shocked.

Albert *was* broad-minded, but only in the orthodox sense. He recognised a young man's need of a woman, but that they should share! This must be wrong—besides, normal male jealousy would not really allow it. (Uncle Albert had not heard of Beaumont and Fletcher.) Yet the two young men concerned felt their friendship strengthened by this new bond. They were not even jealous of the strangers to whom Meriem occasionally sold her favours. In fact, they looked upon the carnal act with cynicism, and allowed no sentiment to dilute it. The trouble with Uncle Albert was not so much that he was an old-fashioned moralist as a romantic of the generation brought up on Musset. There were rules which must be followed and one was this: sensual enjoyment must be regarded as a recompense of love, simple pleasure was contemptible. Here we see the conflict between two opposed points of view: sex as pleasure, the aim of the pagan and the neo-pagan, and sex as a spiritual experience, the (grudging) aim of the Christian.

Lust

I am not concerned here with lust in action but with the frank acceptance of lust, almost as a way of life. I have chosen as the initial exemplar a curious modern novel which seems to owe its existence to the premiss that sexual frenzy is the admitted basis of life. Even when every obstacle is put in the way, tumescence will occur and eventually give way to detumescence.

Nightwood, by Djuna Barnes, was received very favourably by the more advanced critics when it first appeared in 1936. According to T. S. Eliot, who wrote the Preface, its appeal was primarily to readers of poetry. It is written in a quasi-Joycean style, with a series of dream-states with abrupt, sometimes puzzling, transitions. Its subjects are impotence and decadence, social and sexual, the failure to possess in the way that love hopes and claims to possess, the agony of longing. The leading female characters are Lesbians, the garrulous Irish-American doctor is an impotent homosexual. One might

consider this an unpromising contender for a novel that celebrates the ubiquity of lust, yet it is through the negations that
the lust is seen to be dominant. A sexual haze hangs over the
book and it contains frequent references to unusual sexual
practices or aberrations. The doctor tells of a nigger who
worked in a circus and wore nothing except a loin-cloth, 'all
abulge as if with a deep sea catch', who was tattooed from
head to foot. He couldn't do a thing although it was said
that 'at a stretch it spelled Desdemona'. A Count is followed
by a girl in a riding habit and we are told that he suspected
'he had come upon his last erection'. Madamoiselle Basquette
was a girl without legs, 'built like a medieval abuse'. The
doctor knows that life is at the mercy of love, despite his
own unanswered calls. He tells how on one occasion he went
into a church and prayed for Tiny O'Toole, who was lying
in a swoon. 'It is I, my Lord, who knows there's beauty in
any permanent mistakes like me.' The doctor knows, what is
so often forgotten, that lust does not guarantee performance.
'If one gave birth to a heart on a plate, it would say "Love"
and twitch like the lopped leg of a frog.' The woman knows
more about love than the man, and hence Lesbian love is a
finer thing than heterosexual love. It is in sleep that love
makes itself known for then the controlling mind is put
aside. 'When she sleeps is she not moving her leg aside
for an unknown garrison? . . . sailing to some port with a
ship full of sailors and medical men?' Our heads no sooner
touch the pillow than we lose our continence and take a
host of merrymakers. In the last resort man only knows life
through sex; all other knowledge is irrelevant. 'It's a grue-
some thing that man learns only by what he has between the
one leg and the other! Oh, that short dangle! We corrupt
mortality by its industry.'

  D. H. Lawrence's strictures on 'sex in the head' are well
known to our generation, and deserve every sympathy. Sex
can be talked out of court, especially when the talk is concerned with the creativeness of sex. Yet there is a danger in
making this distinction. If the sexual impulse is as powerful
and as creative as is claimed, then it must pervade the mind

as surely as it fires the loins. Lawrence was so intent on
emancipating the sexual impulse that he paid unnatural
attention to and placed undue weight on a part of man that
has really been abstracted from the whole by psychologists
for convenience of discussion and study. This is not what
Lawrence meant to do. Impotence can arise from a prohibition originating in the mind. I can best illustrate this from
the work of a pornographer who would certainly not claim
to be a philosopher but who can claim to be sane because
of his perpetual gaiety and optimism. This is Akbar de
Piombo, about whom I shall have much to say later on. There
is a passage in *The Double-Bellied Companion* where Pike
meets his old friend Czerni at the Grand Orgy for which the
degenerate, exiled aristocracies of half a dozen European
countries have been waiting. The house is falling to pieces
and Czerni can no longer get a hard-on. It is the end of an
era. Pike reminds Czerni, almost reproachfully, of their old
friend Sacha. He never gave a fuck whether the house was
crumbling or not, nor did he ever fail to get a hard-on.
'Fucking is in the mind,' he said, 'do you remember?' Pike
pointed to his head. 'You get a hard-on up here before you
get it down there.' I understand that the causes of impotence
are still unknown but some psychologists believe it is largely
caused by the belief that it will come. You lose your virility
in the mind before you lose it lower down.

This brings up that old teaser, what stimulates? I have
discussed this at some length in chapter 3, but Piombo has
some pertinent words on the subject, which he puts into the
mouth of a Yankee pimp who calls at the *schloss* by accident
and chats affably with Wilma, the Baroness's daughter. She
asks him about his trade. He says plump girls are the most
popular except among whippers, who like 'em skinny. But:

> Never know in advance what makes a hard-on. Little
> things, like garter-belts, fancy clocks, frilly pants, Chanel,
> snaps, French brassieres, fat fannies, big tits, big mouths,
> big eyes, belly-buttons, hairy crotches, smelly armpits,
> protruding assholes, long nipples, hairy nipples; and

some fall for tiny tits, thin backs, small rumps, short legs, fat thighs and no hair.

Lust snaps it all up. Moralists, serious gentlemen, prudes and professional Jeremiahs mutter 'obsession' when they come across such sociology, and imagine that their amateur judgments should be sufficient to certify. The term is idiotic to the biologist. The merest fragment of the matter of life is 'obsessed' with nothing else. In every living cell the chromosomes strive (unless compelled to some other substituted function) after one thing: reproduction. Gourmont gave dozens of examples. Civilised society assumes that man has changed nature—not man's nature, but nature itself.

Long before these arguments became so refined and sophisticated the Wife of Bath had spoken her piece, in opposition to fourteenth century attempts to disguise the obvious about sex. This is how it runs in Coghill's modern translation:

> Tell me to what conclusions or in aid
> Of what were generative organs made?
> And for what profit were those creatures wrought?
> You take my word they were not made for naught.
> Gloze as you will and plead the explanation
> That they were only made for the purgation
> Of urine, little things of no avail
> Except to know a female from a male,
> And nothing else. Did somebody say no?
> Experience knows well it isn't so.
> The learned may rebuke me or be loth
> To think it so, but they were made for both,
> That is to say both use and pleasure in
> Engendering, except in case of sin.
> Why else the proverb written down and set
> In books: 'A man must yield his wife her debt'?
> What means of paying her can he invent
> Unless he use his silly instrument:
> It follows they were fashioned at creation
> Both to purge urine and for propagation.

The good Wife mentioned pleasure but kept on the right side of authority by making the exception 'in case of sin'. By the time of Crébillon and Gourmont, Moore and Harris, the sin was beginning to evaporate. In *Les Liaisons Dangereuses*, by Choderlos de Laclos, 1782, the sinner has become the man of principle. The Marquise de Merteuil writes to the Vicomte de Valmont who is, in her opinion, wasting his time and capacities in the pursuit of a virtuous married woman. He seems to have renounced the bold plans that served him so well in the past; in her view, it is a loss of principle. 'Don't you remember that love, like medicine, *is only the art of encouraging nature?'*

Lust is encountered in every type of relationship, and even in the respectability of marriage it can be sought out and denounced. Marriage is a channel for lust—one feels at times that its opponents must secretly revile God for linking it with procreation. There is an amusing letter from the painter, B. R. Haydon, to Miss Mitford, who had a Malthusian horror of population increase. When Haydon confessed his wife had produced another child she replied with indignation at his irresponsibility. There is a sly leer in his reply:

> You say you cannot account for the weakness of people having more children than they can maintain. Stay, my dear lady, till you marry someone you passionately love, and then you will easily understand the secret.[2] (6 December 1825)

And Baudelaire was equally down-to-earth in his *Journaux Intimes*:

> Une fois, il fut demandé, devant moi, en quoi consistait le plus grand plaisir de l'amour. Quelqu'un répondit naturellement: à recevoir, et un autre: à se donner.— Celui-ci dit: plaisir d'orgueil;—et celui-là, volupté d'humilité. Tous ses orduriers parlaient comme l'*Imitation de Jésus-Christ*.—Enfin, il se trouva un impudent utopiste qui affirma que le plus grand plaisir de l'amour etait de former des citoyens pour la patrie.

This kind of reply infuriates the Miss Mitfords, perhaps because they have never known *le plus grand plaisir*. There is no doubt, however, that marriage itself is based on lust. It can and frequently does keep the lust within bounds but there are many failures. The institution of marriage has to be bolstered by various appeals to religious sentiment and morality; it is called a sacrament, the downfall of society is threatened if it is disregarded. The fury of lust can at times be equalled by the fury of the lust-haters, a sizeable section of a modern community. According to Kinsey, 28% of older unmarried females had never experienced orgasm in their lives. Many of these were sexually unresponsive, and were limited in their understanding of sexual response and orgasm. To them the intimacies of naked men and women were alien and hateful. They disapproved of the sexual activities of females with high rates of outlet (pardon the Kinseyan jargon), and were particularly incapable of understanding male rates of response. One woman indignantly wrote, after publication of the male volume, that the study was a waste of effort for it merely confirmed her previous opinion 'that the male population is a herd of prancing, leering goats'. Such agonised cries are sometimes heard from within the sacred walls of marriage itself. Dr Sophie Lazarsfeld, the Adlerian psychologist, quotes a woman who, after being disappointed in love, married another man. She told him of her past and all went well for a while. Then he told her he must have a virgin—the knowledge that he had not been 'first' became increasingly difficult to bear. He began to reproach her and made her thoroughly miserable until she even considered finding a girl for him. When she suggested he should see a doctor he reacted angrily. 'Had we not settled this matter before?' she asked. 'Despite all my love for him I am beginning to be repelled, to sense the animal in him. Is every man like this? Are they all animals? Is there no soul? Is *that* the principal thing? But he will not hear of divorce. . . .' (*Woman's Experience of the Male*.)[3] Aldous Huxley reminds us in one of his essays that man is an animal that is aspiring to the state of the angels. Much of the misery of men and women

derives from a forgetting of this truth, by acting on the
assumption that man is still completely animal or has already
become an angel.

I will end this section with some references from a modern
poet, practically unknown in this country, who exemplifies
the modern man's acceptance of his animal nature. Irving
Layton started life as a Roumanian Jew and is now a
Canadian. His *A Red Carpet for the Sun* is forceful and impatient of silly social pretences, but he himself suffers from
a plain-man complex which causes him to ridicule poets like
Keats who write of nightingales and who live in an 'unreal
domain'. (He never explains this unreality.) His hatred of
himself (nothing perverted here—how can anyone except a
pervert be pleased with himself all the time?) finds expression
in an obsessive attitude towards the power women wield over
men. He sees them as trying to castrate the male, aided by a
technological civilisation that renders the male's creative role
superfluous. (Again, this weighty statement is never explained,
and it is hard to see how it can be more than figurative and
what reality the figure stands for.) In his introduction he
says: 'We're being feminised and proletarianised at one and
the same time. This is the inglorious age of the mass-woman.'
In a poem he calls women widows because they kill their
men. 'Step back, sucking spiders.' Layton appears to foist
his personal psychosis on to all men. Feeling emasculated
himself he charges the whole sex with impotence, actual or
potential. His condition is best stated in 'A Roman Jew to
Ovid' where he adds yet one more refinement to the comprehensive annals of erotic literature: the costive lover—

> *The very joy of my flooding front*
> *Is to my backside reproach and taunt . . .*

Layton has no illusions about friendship as a check on lust.
Lust is absolutely supreme. This is how he puts it in a poem
entitled 'Obit'.

The hour when I lose life
My friend made ill by grief
At once takes to his bed
With my poor darling Kit;
Laments in her white arms
My cold expired limbs,
And since her naked flesh
Such perfect marble is
Erects betwixt her and him
A towering headstone.

Alas, his mind is grief-crazed
(Interment all its image)
And into her roomy crypt
His rude memorial
With no delay he slips
While kissing rings its knell.
More! Writes on her mound of tit
A friend's flowing tribute
Spurred on by her frequent sighs
And praise of his fine merit:
Till he too all distracted
Groans and with a shudder dies!

Layton is saying more here than that no loyalty is strong enough to withstand lust. He is neither angry nor sad. He sees hope for the human race. Its enemies may yet be frustrated in their plan of reducing us to automata.[4]

Lust does not wither with the flesh, although it is supposed to according to the code of the moralists, who always rejoice when a man grows old on the grounds that he will cease to be a nuisance. Propaganda and training can influence the body so strongly that lust frequently does die when a man gets old (to be accurate, it is smothered) but remember —lust starts in the mind. Cherish it in the mind and it will never desert you—it may even accompany you to the courts when you are so old and disgusting no one will look at you and you are tempted to waylay little girls with Rolos. Layton

writes sadly and bitterly of what the girls do to him ('To the
Girls of my Graduating Class'). He is a college lecturer and is
agonised by the seductive charms of his students, as teachers
all over the world are. Their features demand praise, they
suffer from 'sweet rage in the blood' and 'delicate trouble in
the veins'. And they're in a hurry. No one has to tell them
that Time Marches On.

> Golda, Fruma, Dinnie, Elinor,
> My saintly wantons, passionate nuns;
>   O light-footed daughters, your unopened
> Brittle beauty troubles an aging man
>   Who hobbles after you a little way
>   Fierce and ridiculous.

Who shall we choose for a goddess? Who else but Marilyn
Monroe, in whose shapely bum there was more wisdom than
in the whole of chivalry. She knew forms unknown by Plato
and music of the stars denied to Pythagoras. Thus, in praise
of Marilyn Monroe, 'Earth Goddess':

> I adore you, Marilyn,
> You teach sex is no sin
> Nor that anguishing fire
> To which the saints aspire . . .[5]

The sex-deniers, those lost in politics or misled by the intellect,
the smelly puritans, the sulky christians, 'all those who hate
man's natural estate', they all trail filth.

> O cinema goddess
> More lovely than Venus,
> More explosive than
> Deirdre or Helen;
> O beauteous wench, embrace
> Me in an hour of grace,
> Bounce me like the ocean
> On each surprising limb;

Then let your kisses fall
Like summer rain on all;
Teach us the happiness,
The carnal blessedness,
The warmth, love, sanity
Of your redeeming energy:
Blest of women, earth goddess,
Teach us to delight and praise.

There must be no half-measures about lust. It should make itself quite clear from the beginning: what it wants, what it intends to do, how it intends to do it. The graces belong to gallantry, which I will discuss in a later section. The Countess Fulvia told Stendhal that anything seeking to give pleasure must have a boxer's first virtue—a strong impact. 'Might we not say, as life itself only consists in sensations, that the universal desire of all living creatures is to learn that they are alive by receiving the strongest possible sensations? . . . It is love that gives the strongest possible sensations.' Stendhal's philosophical reply was, 'Do you want the thousandth proof that we are not made by a benevolent Being? It is that *pleasure* does not make half as much impression on our nature as *pain* does—.' (No. 121 of Miscellaneous Fragments, titled Metaphysical Musings, dated 1816.) How very near Stendhal came here to one of Sade's most fundamental conclusions. Lust is the enemy of romance. It is expressed by men of extreme directness, those whose manners have not been refined by society and those who, though refined, have reacted from the dishonesties that inevitably follow on sophistication. In Vivian Connell's novel, *The Chinese Room*, there is an interesting contrast between Nicholas Bude, who has climbed into the middle class, and his father Jock, who had begun life as a labourer and become a gold-miner, making his fortune and buying a bank for his son. Jock's views of sex are earthy and uninhibited, quite unlike those of Nicholas. 'Love is war and bloody murder,' he says, 'and a long sleep afterwards.' And later: 'A man who isn't fit to go into a boat isn't fit to go into bed.' By this he means a man who isn't an athlete; the Countess Fulvia would have said a boxer.

Husband and Lover

Venus finds Adonis dead, gored by the bull, and laments over him.

> *Since thou art dead, lo! here I prophesy,*
> *Sorrow on love hereafter shall attend:*
> *It shall be waited on with jealousy,*
> *Find sweet beginning, but unsavoury end;*
>   *Ne'er settled equally, but high or low;*
>   *That all love's pleasures shall not match his woe.*
>
> *It shall be fickle, false and full of fraud,*
> *Bud and be blasted in a breathing-while;*
> *The bottom poison, and the top o'erstraw'd*
> *With sweets that shall the truest sight beguile:*
>   *The strongest body shall it make most weak,*
>   *Strike the wise dumb and teach the fool to speak.*
>   Shakespeare, 'Venus and Adonis'.

The bitterness of love lies in its cruelty blossoming out of joy. Lovers are appalled by each other. The goddess suddenly becomes a devil incarnate; the devil knifes with a smile and fond words. Marriage based on love will be destroyed. There will be lovers without marriage but marriage actually calls lovers into existence. There is no humiliation that a lover will not deal out to a rejected or discarded partner, no matter how intense and adoring the dialogue had been a little earlier. Alphonse Daudet writes of Jean, who thought Fanny cruel because she mocked one of her old lovers: 'He did not yet know that a woman who loves has no sensibility but for her own love, all feeling of charity, kindness, pity, devotion, absorbed to the benefit of one being, the one only.'[6]

The first writer to face up to the husband-wife-lover complex as an inevitable institution of modern society was Balzac.

His two works on married life accepted the necessity of the
lover and tried to establish rules of conduct for him. These
books are naturally genteel. The bed is almost entirely
avoided. First the husband's, then the wife's point of view
is presented, up to the taking of lovers as the only way to
keep the marriage going. (At about the same time other
writers were defending prostitutions as a protection of wives
and daughters.) The handling of the lover is dealt with at
some length, arising out of a woman's fears about her husband's prolonged absences. Sex is only approached
circuitously, sometimes through double entendre (Zola does
the same) and on one occasion by baby-talk. This is when
the husband rises early and goes out stealthily. When his
wife sees him she says he is a 'naughty ickle boy'. When he
asks why, she replies, 'Because you didn't let your Liline ride
her gee-gee.' One husband gives his views on marriage to
another. 'My dear chap,' he says, 'you are still under the
delusion that marriage is based on passion. I grant you that
women, at a pinch, can fall in love with one man only. But
we men are different! Bless me, society can't control the
natural instinct. Really, it is best, in the case of married
couples, for each to allow the other complete liberty, provided
that both parties keep up appearances. . . .' This view gains
support from a wife who says the only happy families are
quadrilateral. Despite some failures, interchangeable couples
are the answer.

Choosing a lover (or a mistress) should be done as carefully as choosing a husband (or wife). This school of thought
was not libertine and did not advance promiscuity as a way
out of the dilemma. Lust was recognised but it was thought
it could be controlled with the exercise of a little common
sense and tolerance. Sir Owen Asher, who hoped to elope
with Evelyn in George Moore's *Evelyn Innes*, was as moral a
man as you could wish to meet.

> One of his moralities was that a man who did not love
> his mistress was a beast, and that a man who loved a
> woman who wasn't, was a fool. Another was that although

every man of the world knew a liaison would not last for
ever, he should not begin one unless it seemed as if it
were going to. In other words, you should not be able
to see the end before you began.

So long as marriage is the licit-relationship and the liaison
is illicit, feelings about each will remain sharply differenti-
ated. This is probably just as well. There would be little point
in having two equal and simultaneous relationships. One
must ask the Muslims about that but all kinds of difficulties
are likely to arise. In a Muslim marriage, if one wife is preferred, there is no cushion for the other's feelings; she is
obviously considered inferior in an equal combat. In the
husband-lover and wife-mistress comparison, however, the
injured husband or wife can always console himself with the
thought that the scales are weighted against him. Montaigne
says: 'Wedlock hath for his share honour, justice, profit and
constancy—a plain but more general delight. Love hath it
more ticklish, more lively and more sharp—a pleasure
inflamed by difficulty' (Florio's translation).[7]
    It is because love hath it more ticklish that it makes such
an excellent subject for literature. It is a commonplace to
state that novels about marriage are usually deadly dull, because marriage itself is deadly dull. If a marriage appears to
be a continuing excitement you can be certain that the excitement comes from activities that are not a necessary part of
marriage: the other subjects of fiction. Moore writes of a
woman who tells her story and comes to the familiar climax:
'We resisted till flesh and blood could resist it no longer'.
This is the moment the reader longs for and it is not to be
found in any book on marriage, unless it is a marriage that
is breaking up. All love-stories are alike in one thing, says
Moore—they all contain what the reviewers call sordid
details. (They don't trouble to do this any longer, but Moore's
Memoirs of My Dead Life appeared in 1906.) Wasn't it a
good thing that Tristan took advantage of King Mark's
absence on a hunting expedition—not that he took very much
advantage. 'If Wagner had not loved Madame Wesendonck,

and if Madame Wesendonck had not been unfaithful to her
husband we should not have had *Tristan*.' Who would destroy
the score of Tristan for the sake of Monsieur Wesendonck's
honour? Thank God Paris ran off with Helen. The more
Moore develops this idea, the more enthusiastic he becomes.
'Children are born of the marriage, stories of the adulterous
bed, and the world needs both—stories as well as children.'

The medieval Troubadours devised a Code of Love for
the guidance of courtiers and their ladies. It was fitting that
Balzac should attempt the same in the nineteenth century
for husbands and wives. The following axioms are to be
found in his Matrimonial Catechism:

> A man cannot marry before he has studied anatomy and
> has dissected at least one woman.
> The fate of the house hangs on the first night.
> In love, leaving the soul out of consideration, woman is
> a lyre which only yields up its secrets to the man who
> can play upon it skilfully.
> The husband's interest, quite as much as his honour,
> prescribes that he shall never allow himself a pleasure
> for which he has not had the wit to awake a longing
> in his wife.
> The genius of the husband lies in deftly handling the
> various shades of pleasure, in developing them, and
> endowing them with a new style, an original expression.
> Power does not lie in striking hard or often, but in
> striking true.
> Pleasures go from distich to quatrain, from quatrain to
> sonnet, from sonnet to ballad, from ballad to ode, from
> ode to cantata, from cantata to dithyramb. The hus-
> band who begins with a dithyramb is a fool.
> Every night should have its own menu.
> Never begin marriage by rape.

And as marriage requires the lover, Balzac also supplied a
complementary code for him. It makes no claim to originality
but edits proverbial wisdom.

In a lover the most vulgar desire has the appearance of a genuine passion.

A lover has all the qualities and all the faults that are lacking in a husband.

Woman's little affectations invariably impose on a lover, and a lover goes into ecstasies over things at which a husband merely shrugs his shoulders.

A lover panders to a woman's slightest whim, and as a man is never vile in the arms of his mistress, he will adopt methods of pleasing her such as would disgust a husband.

A woman and her lover exchange feelings; the lover returns her feelings with interest, and she is rich in what she has given, rich in what she has received. Husbands spend all the feelings they have and in the end become bankrupts.

A lover says to his mistress, You must forsake the welfare of your children and the happiness of your husband, who is an excellent fellow, because I admire your leg. I will punish you for a sigh more severely than your husband would punish you for adultery. As a reward for sacrifice, I will bring you as much pain as pleasure.

Faithless Women

The News of the World for 1 January 1865 reported the following case. A man was accused at Constantine, in Algeria, of having murdered his two wives. His name was Ali ben Tabar, and his consorts were Fatma ben el Ady Belkassen and Conika ben Lakden ben Kipuf. As they were both remarkably beautiful Tabar had paid large sums for them. One night he awoke in his tent and was surprised to find that neither of his wives was sleeping at his side. On investigation, he heard voices under a clump of trees a short distance away. As he approached the clouds moved away and the moonlight revealed two men, who took to their heels. Tabar did not trouble to pursue them—he had a more urgent task to perform. As he reached the trees two women flashed past him and ran towards his tent: Belkassan and Kipuf. In the tent he ordered them to fall upon their knees. Their prayers and supplications received one answer only from Tabar: 'Their names!' They refused to betray their lovers, whereupon Tabar took a stick and beat them both to death. By this time two other women, both relatives of Tabar, had arrived and witnessed the scene but made no attempt to restrain him. Next morning Tabar went to the officer in charge of the Arab bureau and said, 'I have killed my two wives! I have avenged my outraged honour!' The father of one of the women alleged that Tabar had killed them for idleness, thus hoping to remove the stain of dishonour and to recover damages. Tabar replied: 'I purchased these two women for 600 douros, and by killing them I have lost that amount. If I had considered my money before my honour I should have let them live.' The judge urged that the penal law should be carried out but the council acquitted Tabar.

It is a tenet of Arab belief that a woman cannot be trusted. He also believes that any man will attempt to seduce a woman if he is alone with her. On the face of it, this means there is no difference between the sexes in this respect. The Arab believes, however, that a woman *should* be virtuous. No one can expect a man to be. The point tends to be academic, for it merely states that a woman ought to be chaste but isn't. There is a very strong body of opinion in the West which shares this attitude, although officially (that is, in literary tradition) the virtuous woman exists. The majority view, however, is that just as every man has his price so every woman can be seduced if you are persistent enough. The general tenor of ordinary male conversation, of folk story and of the great bulk of fiction that doesn't emanate from the prevailing moral Establishment of the day, supports this view. It is not always stated directly and bluntly—apart from social and legal prohibitions against the unadorned statement of what most people say and think (consider the attitude, until recently, towards sex words), a great part of the pleasure to be obtained from sex whether in action or in thought, is derived from the overcoming of difficulties. But throughout

literature, once it was emancipated from the priests, there is
a tone that suggests that woman is man's greatest pleasure,
that he is her greatest pleasure, that come what may they
will get together and if they don't, they ought to. (That *ought*
is purely psychological.) Think of Chanticleer saying to
Pertelote:

> For it's as certain as the Creed, I know,
> Mulier est hominis confusio
> A Latin tag, dear Madam, meaning this:
> 'Woman is man's delight and all his bliss'
>   'The Nun's Priest's Tale'.

as nice a contrasting of public and private as you could wish
for. Think of Rosalind scornfully rebuking Phebe for her
haughty rejection of Silvius, urging her to get down on her
knees and thank heaven for his love:

> For I must tell you, friendly in your ear,
> Sell when you can: you are not for all markets:
> Cry the man mercy; love him; take his offer. . . .
>   As You Like It.

What does Balzac write in the Prologue to the second Volume
of his *Contes Drolatiques*?

> Think of woman; woman will heal thy wound, stop the
> waste-hole in thy bag of tricks. Woman is they wealth;
> have but one woman, dress, undress and fondle that
> woman, make use of that woman—woman is everything
> —woman has an inkstand of her own; dip thy pen in
> that bottomless inkpot. Woman lives love; make love to
> her with the pen only, tickle her fantasies, and sketch
> merrily for her a thousand pictures of love in a thousand
> pretty ways.

And from our own century, from Mailer's *The Naked and the
Dead*. While being carried back to the shore after being

wounded, Wilson rambles. There was a woman he could go
back to whenever he wanted, he had told her he was a
'collidge gradjit', and she had believed him. 'Goddam
women'll believe any damn thing ifen you just keep layin'
'em regular.'

These are all common-man pronouncements. The great
majority of the Western world accepts them, although it has
been reluctant to say so publicly until modern times. It means
that, in their hearts, few men trust any women. They know
they are largely to blame for this because, given satisfactory
circumstances, they will do everything in their power to break
a woman's resistance. Shakespeare as usual gives us a brilliant
picture of a man tortured by his own deviousness. In *The
Merry Wives of Windsor* Ford is suspicious of his wife. The
basic situation is that he has every right to be, for they belong
to a society that urges infidelity and jokes about other people's.
But Ford cannot approach the matter directly. He has to pretend to be a Mr Brook and asks Falstaff to seduce Mrs Ford
so that he, Mr Brook, may later take over. Such crookedness
deserves what it gets, which is a few more twists. Falstaff tells
Ford that he has already dated Mrs Ford, who is in fact playing
a trick on the old rascal. As soon as Falstaff has gone Ford
begins to rant as if he has been cheated out of his heritage.
He sees his bed abused, his coffers ransacked and he will go
by a new name—not a respectable one such as Mammon or
Lucifer but Cuckold and Wittol.

> I will rather trust a Fleming with my butter, Parson
> Hugh the Welshman with my cheese, an Irishman with
> my aquavitae bottle, or a thief to walk my ambling geld-
> ing, than my wife with herself: then she plots, then she
> ruminates, then she devises; and what they think in their
> hearts they may effect, they will break their hearts but
> they will effect. God be praised for my jealousy!

God be praised! Yet he turns on his jealousy like a sheep on
a spit and despises his friend Page who is not jealous! The
sexual rage is never shriller than when aggravated by marriage
vows.

Men assume that any woman can be bought, and can always produce evidence. As an illustration, take the career of Lord Jermyn, one of the leading lights at Charles II's court in 1662. According to *The Memoirs of the Count de Grammont*, written by Anthony Hamilton (1713), Jermyn was able to do practically as he pleased because of his uncle's great wealth. The other courtiers could not vie with him in equipage and magnificence. Jermyn was brave and a gentleman, but he had done nothing of note and his rank was not particularly high. As for his figure, it was undistinguished. He was short, with a large head and small legs. Although he was not bad-looking he was rather affected. He had little wit—what he had he had picked up from others. Yet his success in love was astonishing. First the Princess Royal and then Miss Hyde—his reputation was established even before he set foot in England. 'Prepossession in the minds of women is sufficient to find access to their hearts,' says Hamilton. Even when the ladies discovered Jermyn's insignificance they could not break their prejudice in his favour. The Countess of Castlemaine was no fool and saw through him pretty quickly, yet she clung close to Jermyn until the King himself became her lover. The weakness of all this, of course, is that it is written by a man who may well have been a rival of Jermyn, or have been prejudiced against him by his friends. Jermyn may have been as undistinguished as Hamilton claimed, but no man knows what women look for and find.

The scorn of women finally becomes poisonous, as in this poem, 'A Consolatory Epistle to a Friend on his Disappointment in Marriage', taken from the Miscellaney Poems appended to *Miscellaneous Works of Rochester and Roscommon*, 1707.

> At length, when Riches multiply'd on Earth,
> Which gave to all Love Chests their Impious Birth,
> They ceas'd to offer them at Beauty's Shrine,
> And chang'd the Goddess for the Golden Mine.
> Nothing so ugly or deform'd was found,

When the prevailing Mettal did abound,
But they before the monstrous Image fell,
And worshipp'd Furies, for the Power of Hell.
They taught the fairest Sex to love its Charms,
To yield their Beauties up to loathsome Arms,
And equal Passion, and just Worth disdain,
And for a Miser, fly the loveliest Swain.
  Nature debauch'd, Vice then began to Reign,
And most turn'd Prostitutes for Lust or Gain.
That Innocence, that humbles moving Grace,
That mind that still adorns the Fairest Face,
These Virtues all vile Passions have o'ercome,
And foulest Blemishes fill up their Room.

We will never know the truth about Jermyn. I have noticed that my wife rarely finds merit in the women I admire; it is too much to expect one so favoured as Jermyn to have pleased his own sex. But note the consequence. Envy of one's own sex will later become rage against the other (for its folly, or its acquisitiveness) and the end is misanthropy.

The Uses of Gallantry

'In France what passes for love is merely love talk mingled with ambition and the vanities of gallantry.' Thus St-Evremond, in the late eighteenth century, and later confirmed by Stendhal. The French love myth has so often overwhelmed foreigners that they have not noticed the falsity that many Frenchmen have deplored. In France far more emphasis has been placed on technique, courting technique as well as sexual, than in other parts of Europe. It is an extension of the belief referred to in the previous section, that any woman can be had. The rules of gallantry supply the method, particularly the verbal expression of flattery. The result has been that with many men the conquest has brought more pleasure than the possession; in fact, possession sometimes leads to revulsion.

Like most things, gallantry has its place when controlled

and kept in its proper perspective, that is, as an adjunct.
Most of the modern authors of marriage manuals and How
To Enjoy Sex stress the value of skilled love-play before and
after intercourse. (The gallant only troubles about after when
he wishes to continue the affair. He is not an altruist.) But
the reasons for such behaviour are widely different. The
gallant indulges in love-play to make his mistress (one might
be justified in calling her a victim) more pliable; the good
husband does not 'seek to secure his own gratification in the
quickest possible time and without regard to his wife's feelings' (Dr Eustace Chesser, *How To Make a Success of Your
Marriage*). The great heroes and guiding-stars among gallants
were, of course, Don Juan and Casanova. They gained their
reputations by their success. But Casanova should not be
dismissed along with the beaus and bucks and dandies who
believed they were imitating him. He was a warm-hearted
man with a great store of sentiment.

As I am largely concerned with English eroticists, I will
illustrate gallantry from the most thorough-going English
exponent, who was in fact the Irishman George Moore. He
was not one of the heartless type, who flourished in the
eighteenth century, but they are not well represented in
English literature. Moore wanted to use every trick in the
book and yet to retain the affection of the ladies he loved
and seduced. The following illustrations and quotations come
from his *Memoirs of My Dead Life*.

This book is strewn with pieces of practical wisdom and
axioms of love. 'To argue about details with a woman, to
get angry, is a thing that no one versed in the arts of love
does, not after twenty-five.' Very revealing, for details are
meat and drink to the gallant—but he keeps them to himself.
He tells us how he lies awake at night, wondering what
bloomers he may have made—it's not so very different from
the kind of mental torture one goes through after an inter-
view or a brush with a rival. 'Good heavens! how stupid it
was of me not to have used a certain argument. It might have
been well to have spoken more tenderly, displaying a more
Christian spirit, omitting all that talk about nymphs, dryads,

fauns and satyrs.' He says you can win a woman sometimes so
long as you pretend you are doing something else. Stress the
beauty of her breast and she will be unconscious of the sin
as you slip inside. Keep in harmony with nature. Whether
your hand will be allowed to stay on the knee will depend not
so much on her morality as on the moment you have chosen.
Of course, the gallant these days is as dead as the fauns and
satyrs he used to discourse on. There is not much point in
trying to harmonise with nature with a model who has never
seen a tree, except on television. This is a dead, but historic
art.

Moore was particularly attracted by the recapture of an
old love, who had succumbed to a husband or a quarrel
or even the waning of interest. To win her back was the
greatest triumph of all, to hear her say, 'Well, you've got me
again and after all these years!' Once he was particularly
excited because a previous mistress had married, and an
assault on her new-found chastity was indicated. Did virgin
husbands exist outside the pages of French novels? ' "No
doubt", I said, "they do, but so much good fortune can
hardly be my lot".' A large part of Moore's erotic pleasure
came from nostalgia; wallowing in his conquests, dreaming
of them again and again. 'Spring love is but tremor, laughter
and a little ecstasy; an autumn love is enriched with memories;
and its fear of the lean winter coming exalts it.' To be taken
literally and metaphorically.

More typical of the traditional gallant is Moore's concern
with personal appearance, both his and the lady's. A man
must never show impatience with the time a woman takes
over her toilet. It is neither hypocritical nor stupid, he says,
'for it is only with scent and silk and artifices that we raise
love from an instinct to a passion.' Undressing can become an
art with a woman, from the moment she sits in her evening
dress, playing with her bracelets, until the moment she gives
that final little kick to her discarded panties. In fact, Moore
at times becomes a fetichist over underwear; it can make her
'a woman that one would still take a pleasure in making love
to.' The man must also consider his apparel, especially that

to be worn during the battle. (Moore refers to the bed as a battlefield.) Women are unfortunate in having to take men as they are, by which he means few resemble Greek gods. In northern lands there are (I should now say were) men who made matters worse by wearing flannel nightshirts. Pyjamas had not been invented when Moore was a young man, but they are undoubtedly the great redemption. In fact, it had become possible for a man garbed by Hope Brothers, Regent Street, to enter a lady's bedroom without loss of dignity. He relates an amusing story of the time when, in a French provincial town, he discovered that his valet had forgotten to pack his pyjamas. Doris was let into the secret and together they had to find an answer to the appalling question: 'How am I to go into your room tonight, dear?' They agreed that Schopenhauer must be right, that the sum of their pains exceeded the sum of their pleasures. Together they went from shop to shop, scandalising matrons by their requests for the unmentionables, pyjamas. As though Orelay would even allow them to cross the town boundary! They compromised on a silk nightshirt with pink stripes, priced at ten francs; not a mortal sin, like pyjamas, but venial yet meriting a long term in purgatory. And finally, Moore asks the extraordinary question: Should lovers sleep together? Here again we have proof that it was the conquest that counted, not the sentiment. Lovers, in mind as well as body, cannot bear to sleep apart. Moore claimed that he had never slept with anyone in his life, but he was told by someone who should know that not to have waked up in the morning with one's beloved, to have seen the sunlight pouring through the window and to have heard the birds in the vine, was to be ignorant of the rapture and enchantment of lovers' intimacy. What the answer is today I don't know. One risks finding the beloved wearing gloves and a chinstrap.

So much for the sentimental gallant. The hard-boiled, cold-blooded type can be studied to best advantage in a book such as *Les Liaisons Dangereuses*, which we will come to later. A good modern example is Stanley Kaufman's *The Philanderer*. We find Russell Conrad in bed with his girl,

Suzy, just after intercourse. He is still interested, therefore he kisses her on the corner of the mouth (a little trick they shared), 'to show that although he had had all her intimacy, utter and unreserved, he still felt cordial affection for her, tender respect. It never failed.' No matter how often a woman gives herself to a man, he thought, she is always relieved to find he still likes her afterwards. Her hand is on his cheek as he muses. Suddenly, 'My goodness, he reminded himself, her hand is on my cheek. All this time. I forgot to give her a reaction.' He gave a reaction in such a way that he appeared to be exuding gratitude and beatitude without actually looking at her. 'It disposed of her. Considerately but completely. Now she wouldn't disturb the serenity she herself had bestowed on him. Gave him a chance to think.' A little later the affair comes to an end. Now he can afford to express his true feelings. He tells her that he talked her into the affair in the first place. The sex was good enough to make her forget, but not for long. 'I ought to have beat it long ago. Instead of having to sit here and take you seriously, you dumb twerp. With a face out of a medieval tapestry, still a twerp.' Then he feels he's gone a bit too far. After all, she's not a bad kid. Everything seemed to be closing in on them, he told her. All the scheming and conspiring they had to do to meet, and no future in it either. 'Sure it's awful. I understand all that, I think you know I really understand it. But honey, I—'. A little pause here, professor. 'I think you'll admit too, I never said it would be anything else. I can't claim much in all this, but at least I've always been honest with you.'

The gallantry has evaporated. It's used for winning. What remains depends entirely on the character of the man, whether he be as hard as nails like the Vicomte de Valmont, soft-centred like George Moore, or just a goodtime guy, like Russell Conrad.

Pagans

Just a few general remarks. The pagan attitude to sex has never died. In the nineteenth century there was a literary

pagan revival, with which Swinburne is mainly associated in
English. The same thing happened in France, especially in
the work of Théphile Gautier, greatly admired by Swinburne.
D'Albert, in *Mademoiselle de Maupin*, favoured the herm-
aphrodite type as exemplified by Greek statuary. Maupin
herself declared that the ideal has the body and soul of a
woman, the mind and power of a man. D'Albert says:

> I consider woman, after the manner of the ancients, as a
> beautiful slave designed for our pleasure. Christianity
> has not rehabilitated her in my eyes. To me she is still
> something dissimilar and inferior that we worship and
> play with, a toy that is more intelligent than if it were
> of ivory or gold, and which gets up of itself if we let it
> fall. I have been told, in consequence of this, that I think
> badly of women; I consider, on the contrary, that it is
> thinking very well of them.

What, then, is the difference between lust and the pagan
attitude? The pagans were affected by aesthetic considerations, and in turn came to think of love as an art: the art
of the senses. There is a considerable value difference between
the pagan (and the neo-pagan) and the libertine, who figures
so prominently in genuine erotic literature and pornography.
The libertine's feelings are divorced from any sensations of
love. Physical sensation alone counts. All his actions are full-
blooded and violent. On the few occasions when he acts
gently—as, for instance, strokings around the erogenous zones
—it is only to arouse the passions more successfully for
violent action later on. The interesting thing to notice at
this stage is that he believes himself to be a pagan and makes
frequent appeals to classical authors.

The question arises, to what extent is it possible to distinguish between sexual pleasure and other pleasures? Why
should pleasure connected with the reproductive functions
be different in kind from that connected with the excretory
functions? According to Sade, of course, they are not. Nor
are they to a large number of people whose pleasurable

stimulation requires the use of both. Many readers of Sade must feel that he fails utterly to distinguish between sexual pleasure and other forms of pleasure. This is deliberate on his part. His work tends to be a gradual movement away from what is obviously sexual to what appears to be absolutely non-sexual, yet it is difficult to say exactly where the border has been crossed. Although we consider ourselves frank these days we still do not speak frankly about the excretory functions. Perhaps this will be the next hurdle to be leapt. They are regarded as distasteful and dirty. But there is the complication that one excretory function at least is inextricably connected with a sexual organ. If we are honest most of us would admit that among the most pleasurable sensations known to us are the excretory ones, depending to a great extent on need. The vulgar tongue is, as usual, less reticent: 'a good shit' is usually recorded with enjoyment. The sexual pleasure also depends to some extent on need.

Perhaps much of the animus against the homosexual act derives from the physiological associations. The pagans appear to have been less inhibited in this respect than we are. They saw the beauty of the boy; we imagine the shit. Sade (who carried pagan tastes to their logical conclusion) was ruthless enough not to discriminate at all. In fact, his libertines prefer the back passage, but solely because the pleasure is greater, owing to its contraction. (Later he developed a prejudice against females and their specifically sexual organs that was no longer logical.) He was also guided by his perverse pleasure in doing what was forbidden, for part of his philosophy lay in the close connection between sexuality and crime. Roland (in *Justine*) says the pleasure of seducing one's mother or sister is increased by the criminal flavouring. May not crime, one asks, when dissociated from sexual pleasure, be a joy in itself?

> Thus, let me imagine, the abduction of a girl on one's own account will give a very lively pleasure, but abduction in the interests of someone else will give all that pleasure with which the enjoyment of this girl is im-

proved by rape; the theft of a watch, the rape of a purse,
will also give the same pleasure, and if I have accustomed
my senses to being moved by the rape of some girl *qua*
rape, that same pleasure, that same delight will be found
again in the seizing of the watch or of the purse.

The argument is that the libertine, who begins his career
because he is seeking the keenest pleasure, eventually departs,
or partially departs, from sex as his capacity for pleasure becomes refined and also as boredom sets in. Eventually his
pleasure is obtained from actions that are not ostensibly
sexual at all, though he and we have come to associate them.
Some of Roland's pleasures were virtually intellectual, for
his only experience of his 'subject' was visual and his flesh
gained no stimulation.

   This may seem a rather lengthy digression, but the attitudes
associated with Sade are in fact the pagan ones taken to their
logical conclusion. A very important point is at issue here.
The pagan and the neo-pagan keep their minds concentrated
completely on one object: pleasure. The introduction of
spiritual issues by later generations represents a withdrawal
from the object. The romantics claimed that this was done
partially (motives were complicated) in pursuit of a higher
and nobler pleasure. The neo-pagan complained that the
new attitude was impure and muddled. It is a simplification,
of course, to use such terms as 'new' and 'introduction' for
the idea of love. It had always existed but it had been rejected
by those who set the tone of the classical cultures. Love they
regarded as a disease; in social terms, it was a new kind of
slavery. By far the best modern re-creation of the classical
attitude to Eros is to be found in Pierre Louÿs's *Aphrodite*
(1896) and this is how Demetrios refuses the love of Chrysis:

   Slavery! This is the true name of love. You women all
   have but one dream, a single idea in your brain: to use
   your weakness so as to break a man's strength, to make
   your futility rule over his intelligence. What you desire, as
   soon as your breasts start growing, is not to love or be

loved but to tie a man to your ankles, to humble him, to
make him bow his head so you can put your sandal on it.
Then you are able, each according to his ambition, to
snatch his sword from him or his chisel or compass, break
everything you don't understand, emasculate what
frightens you, lead Hercules by the nostrils and make
him spin wool.

But when you haven't succeeded in bending his head
or his will, you adore the fists that beat you, the knee
that thrusts you to the ground, the very mouth that
insults you. The man who has refused to kiss your bare
feet, when he rapes you fulfils your desires. The one who
did not weep when you left his house can drag you back
by the hair. And your love will be reborn in your tears.
For only one thing consoles you for not imposing slavery,
oh loving women! That is to submit to it!

The coming of Passion and Romance and their subsequent
victory entailed the acceptance of the attitude outlined here
by Demetrios. It was one of the major movements in
European development.

The modern approach may be a loftier one, but it is less
straightforward and subject to its own particular abuse. Just
as the pagan abuse is physical, so the romantic abuse is psychological. He who loves sacrifices himself, runs the argument.
The pleasure is his reward (i.e., not the sole aim). Love is a
martyrdom, an absolute sacrifice of the individual for the
species. Pleasure is only the means which the species makes
use of to attain its purpose, a veil to throw over the eyes
of the individual to bring him to the sacrificial altar. The
species forces the individual person by the illusion of pleasure
to an action that will ensure posterity. 'The physical lure of
sex,' says Hugues le Roux, 'is a snare in which the individual
is caught and plays the role of a marionette for the production
of more and possibly better marionettes.' This is the romantic
abuse: hypocrisy. It is tangled with the guilt which will not
allow people to regard sex as a thing good in itself, as worth
the experience for the pleasure derived from it. There is

always the urge to pretend that it is really distasteful, unpleasant and unattractive, and that people only engage in it out of a sense of duty. The human mind is so pliable it is not difficult for pretence to seem reality. One notes too that the pagan and romantic evaluations of love are really identical. The difference lies between rejection and acceptance. Without attempting a judgment at this point, one can safely say that the terminology is faulty. The 'self' is not sacrificed, but is temporarily obliterated. Obliteration involves a complete loss of responsibility and anxiety. It is nirvana. Sacrifice is pain, or hell.

Passion and Romance

'To judge by literature, adultery would seem to be one of the most remarkable of occupations in both Europe and America. Few are the novels that fail to allude to it. . . .' (Denis de Rougemont, *Passion and Society*). Marriage has become a duty and a convenience. Novels and plays depend upon the 'breakdown of marriage'. As we have seen, this is a situation which George Moore regarded as a positive good.

The story of Tristan and Iseult, which Moore used as an illustration, is in fact the type story of this situation; it has become a myth. It is a tale of passion and of the obstacles that the lovers constantly put in its way when there are no natural obstacles. The courtly love of the Troubadours praised a love outside marriage that was never consummated. The demon of courtly love has descended to our own time and has infected the modern novel (says Rougemont). We insist on suffering. But the suffering has been displaced because we also insist on physical consummation.

'Tristan and Iseult do not love one another. They say they don't, and everything goes to prove it. *What they love is love and being in love.*' Therefore whatever opposes love must consolidate and strengthen it. Menander had said that love was a sickness (he echoed his society in this) whenever it went beyond sensual pleasure, which was alone natural. Plutarch called love a 'frenzy'. The romantics glorified passion, which means and is suffering.

The purpose of the Passion Myth was to confine a lawless force in a ritual framework. Passion enslaves: death is the only escape—and Tristan dies. 'The cultivation of passionate love began in Europe as a reaction to Christianity (and in particular to its doctrine of marriage) by people whose spirit, whether naturally or by inheritance, was still pagan.' The Tristan myth and the Troubadours reflect the spirit of the Cathars and the Manichaean heresy. In a period of no more than twenty years there emerged a new vision of woman, as an ideal set above man, and a complex and refined poetry quite alien to antiquity and the Carolingian renaissance. The condemnation of the flesh, now viewed as typically Christian, was in fact Manichaean and heretical.

It is the modern fashion to regard Tristan's passion as sensual. The two lovers never wish for consummation. The passion which modern novels and films have popularised is a flowing back into our lives of a spiritual heresy. Rougemont seems to play down the fact that in most modern novels the passion is sensual and successful, and to emphasise the suffering of the typical romantic. In fact, what he says is truer of the nineteenth century novel than of the contemporary. A relation is assumed between passion and mysticism, for their metaphors are akin. What is not clear is whether passion is a form of mysticism or mysticism a form of passion, although the latter is normally assumed. The modern mind wishes to explain the higher by the lower. Science speaks of mysticism as a sublimation of instinct: it would be truer to regard the 'instinct' in question as the result of the profanation of an early form of mysticism. La Rochefoucauld said that few people would fall in love if they had never heard of it. The physical aspect is natural: the spiritual aspect is learnt.

Romantic love is summed up by Petrarch. Laura is his 'beloved enemy'. (Compare Moore's description of the bed as a battlefield.) Woman, whether present or absent, is the occasion for a torment the lover cherishes above all else:

> *I know to follow while I flee my fire:*
> *I freeze when present; absent, my desire*
> *Is hot.*
>
>> (*Trionfo d'amore*, trs. Anna Hume. Compare
>> St John of the Cross's 'O sweet cautery!')

French authors like to oppose 'gauloiserie' (the ribald and salacious attitude to love) to the conventions of courtly love. But one is as artificial as the other. *Les Cents Nouvelles* and the *fabliaux* equally attempt to substitute a dream (unending lust, an absence of complication) for reality. There is still an appeal to an ideal, though this time it is unchastity. The underlying connection between the two modes is perfectly illustrated in a thirteenth century satire called *L'Evangile des Femmes*—a sequence of quatrains, the first three lines of each extolling woman in the courtly manner and the last being brutally disparaging.

Passion demands an obstacle: between joy and the external cause there must be an obstruction, whether it is society, sin, virtue, the body or the separate self. It is this that causes the ardour of passion. The wish for complete union is indissolubly linked with a wish for the death that brings release. 'It is because passion cannot exist without pain that passion makes our ruin seem desirable to us.' The Portuguese nun Mariana Alcaforado thanked the man who had seduced her from the bottom of her heart. He had brought her despair and she despised the peace she had previously lived in. And Julie de Lespinasse wrote: 'I love you as one ought to love: with despair.' Don Juan, with his personal tally of 2,065 conquests, is an instance of 'perverse sensuality'. He inspires love but can never love in return. Sade is the antithesis of romanticism. He regarded evil as the only element in nature. 'Yes, I hold nature in abhorrence; and this is because I am only too well aware that I detest it. Apprised of its horrible secrets, I have taken a kind of pleasure in copying its dark wickedness' (*La Nouvelle Justine*). He desired to obtain release from the tyranny of sex through excesses of debauchery. The alternatives are to be cruel to ourselves or to others. The romantic

chooses the self, Sade others. The romantic (Petrarch)
punishes himself in order to preserve the beloved, whereas
Sade sought to kill the beloved. How perfect that Laura
should have been biologically a Sade!

Rougemont quotes Stendhal: 'There are very few moral
afflictions in life that are not rendered precious by the
emotion which they excite.' The point is, we like pain and
tend to be bored by happiness,[8] a fact which Sade was quick
to seize on and balloon out of all recognition. Neither a
Hindu nor a Chinese nor a classical Greek would understand
this strange taste in us. The myth has been established but
it has also been profaned and today every messy little
Metalious wants her meed of torture. But the myth, even in
its degeneration, still requires the happy ending and nowhere
has this been more apparent than in the American film of
the nineteen-twenties. There was a fusion of two contradictory wishes—the romantic one that nothing shall be settled
and the bourgeois one that everything shall be settled.

> There can be no love story unless love meets with opposi-
> tion. There is accordingly an abundance of obstructions
> to the fulfilment of love, and it does not matter how far-
> fetched they are,[9] because the wish for romanticism
> renders the spectator impervious to the straining of his
> credibility. For an hour or two, accordingly, the story
> can rebound, and we be full of heartfelt suspense, which
> is what we want. But the obstruction of love must ultim-
> ately mean death and a renunciation of terrestrial goods.
> This we no longer want once we have grown aware of
> what it is. A plot-maker has therefore to devise the
> suppression of any obstacle at some point earlier than
> death, and the result is the ending which novels and
> films commonly have.

In these terms love comes to resemble war. The eighteenth
century was the great period of amorous planning, when a
woman was regarded in the same light as an enemy strong-
hold that had to be taken by cunning or assault. There is no
better study of this attitude than that given by the Goncourt

Brothers in their *Women in the Eighteenth Century.* 'Neglect nothing' was the motto of one of the amorists they quote.

Probably the greatest poet of passionate love in European literature was Racine. For him love was a passion, that is, something suffered by mankind, a thing imposed upon mankind from outside—and ultimately, therefore, an ill. But no writer has systematised this view of love so carefully as Stendhal. The key to Stendhal is contained in an unobtrusive footnote: 'Beauty is *only* a promise of happiness. Happiness for a Greek was different to the happiness of a Frenchman in 1822.' He believed that one could only love beauty, hence the promise created beauty. A more disturbing view of love, and one more consonant with romantic sensibility, could hardly be imagined. We must also bear in mind that there were variations in romantic procedure, depending on the temperature of the lover: gallant romantic love, Stendhal's 'vanity love', tender romantic love, sentimental love. They are all branches of the one tree.

The first edition of *Love* contained a snook-cocking preface, designed to annoy and put off practical men who have no leisure for love: bankers, state counsellors and cotton manufacturers. Stendhal says the book is simply and solely 'an exact, scientific description of a kind of folly which is very rare in France.' The reasons for this rarity are that in France love is always afraid of derision, and is stifled by the national passion, vanity. He quotes Beaumarchais: 'Nature says to woman, be pretty if you can, virtuous if you can, but esteem you must have', and comments: 'In France, if there is no esteem, there is no consideration, and so no love.' According to Stendhal there are four types of love: passionate love, elegant love (the Paris of 1760, Crébillon and Chamfort), physical love (at sixteen you fall in love with a pretty peasant girl in the woods), and vanity love (especially in France). All of these can be tainted by the romantic attitude but only the first is romantic *sui generis*. Rougemont says that Stendhal was tormented by the need of passion. This alone mattered and he accounted for it by his famous theory of 'crystallisation'—the endowing of a woman with virtues she does not possess. We need to love and only beauty can be loved. Ortega y Gasset pointed out that this theory was based on error, but theoretical debate is not my business.

Stendhal quotes an imaginary young lady who falls victim to love's 'lightning stroke'. She is overwhelmed by a young captain she danced with for ten minutes at a ball. As soon as he went she complained of boredom. 'At last I was able to leave,' she wrote to a friend. 'And no sooner was the key turned twice in my door than I wanted to counter my passion. I thought that I could succeed. But ah! dear friend, what a price I paid that evening and on the days that followed, for the pleasure of thinking that I could remain on the side of virtue!' Eventually she committed suicide—and for whom? A young captain who danced well, was gay, lived with prostitutes, had no nobility and even less money.

He cites the passion of the Provençal knight who would spend three years in exile in the Holy Land at the merest hint of his lady. Today men desert their mistresses with equal readiness. 'No self-respecting woman in Paris takes a lover,' he says. Prudence tells the modern woman not to plunge into passionate love. Another voice of prudence tells them to seek revenge in physical love. In Miscellaneous Fragment no. 35 he explains why passion was not found in the ancient world: 'Sappho saw in love only frenzied delight for the senses, or physical pleasure sublimated by crystallisation. Anacreon sought in it a diversion for the senses and the mind. There was too little security in ancient times to give leisure for passionate love.' In no. 106 he writes: 'In a highly civilised society passionate love is as natural is physical love among savages.' He quotes La Rochefoucauld approvingly: 'The pleasure of love consists in loving and the passion a man feels makes him happier than the passion he inspires.' His theory of crystallisation was expressed in these words: 'Passionate love irradiates all nature for a lover in its sublimer aspects, like something fresh and new only invented yesterday.' He believed that Werther got more pleasure from his love than Don Juan.

Although Rougemont attributes the revolution in love to

the Troubadours and goes even further back for its myth, it was in the nineteenth century, after Werther and Chateaubriand, Shelley and Byron, that romantic sensibility became socially dominant. Stendhal gave it the final push. His *Love* was really a complaint that vanity and gallantry had outlived their usefulness, that a civilised society ought to be romantic. But the romantic victory took a long time to establish itself. Shakespeare knew it and wrote of it, but leaves little doubt that he was sceptical of it. In the midst of that triumphantly romantic situation, the love of Romeo and Juliet, we hear the warning voice of Friar Laurence. Romeo awaits Juliet in the friar's cell. He is beside himself with joy. Nothing will ever destroy their love, once it has vanquished the (necessary) obstacles. The Friar is dubious:

> *These violent delights have violent ends*
> *And in their triumph die, like fire and powder,*
> *Which as they kiss consume: the sweetest honey*
> *Is loathesome in his own deliciousness*
> *And in the taste confounds the appetite:*
> *Therefore love moderately; long love doth so;*
> *Too swift arrives as tardy as too slow.*

And in *As You Like It* Rosalind, disguised as Ganymede, but playing the part of Rosalind to her lover, Orlando, rebukes him for saying he will die if he cannot have her.

No, faith, die by attorney. The poor world is almost six thousand years old, and in all this time there was not any man died in his own person, videlicet, in a love-cause. Troilus had his brains dashed out with a Grecian club; yet he did what he could to die before, and he is one of the patterns of love. Leander, he would have lived many a fair year, though Hero had turned nun, if it had not been for a hot midsummer night; for, good youth, he went but forth to wash him in the Hellespont and being taken with the cramp was drowned: and the foolish chroniclers of that age found it was 'Hero of

Sestos'. But these are all lies: men have died from time
to time and worms have eaten them, but not for love.[10]

The playing down of love is a strong element in this play—
another example is when Phebe protests at Silvius's statement that her eyes wound him. She sees no evidence of a
wound. This attitude is never stated openly in the *Decameron*
although it may be deduced from some of the more blatant
stories. But the opposite attitude, of disappointed lovers dying
of frustration, is expressed.

Our own century has seen yet another approach to love,
which I will illustrate in a later section, but refer to briefly
here because it is a product of the romantic episode. When
the mind sickens of romantic posturing and its far-fetched,
unrealistic claims, it turns to cynicism. This is to be distinguished from the older pagan attitude, because it disclaims
pleasure yet acts from a traditional compulsion (a situation
where, perhaps, we may be justified in speaking roundly of
nature over-ruling the individual). The anti-love writer of
our age has been Aldous Huxley, particularly in his early
work. In his poems he came very near to ridiculing love. Two
examples will suffice, both from *Leda*, 1920. First of all,
'Sympathy'.

> *The irony of being two . . . !*
> *Grey eyes, wide open suddenly,*
> *Regard me and enquire; I see a face*
> *Grave and unquiet in tenderness.*
> *Heart-rending question of women—never answered:*
> *'Tell me, tell me, what are you thinking of?'*
> *Oh, the pain and foolishness of love!*
> *What can I do but make my old grimace,*
> *Ending it with a kiss, as I always do?*

(Professor) Russell Conrad would have had a more satisfactory
answer on the tip of his tongue. Romanticism prefers words
to kisses, and sham romanticism takes advantage of this when
necessary. Finally, Huxley's 'Male and Female Created He
Them'.

Diaphenia, drunk with sleep,
Drunk with pleasure, drunk with fatigue,
Feels her Corydon's fingers creep—
Ring-finger, middle-finger, index, thumb—
Strummingly over the smooth sleek drum
Of her thorax.
                    Meanwhile Handel's Gigue
Turns in Corydon's absent mind
To Yakka-Hoola.
                    She can find
No difference in the thrilling touch
Of one who, now, in everything
Is God-like. 'Was there ever such
Passion as ours?'
                    His pianoing
Gives place to simple arithmetic's
Simplest constatations: six
Letters in Gneiss and three in Gnu:
Luncheon today cost three and two;
In a year—he couldn't calculate
Three-sixty-five times thirty-eight,
Figuring with printless fingers on
Her living parchment.
                    'Corydon!
I faint, faint, faint at your dear touch.
Say, is it possible . . . to love too much?'

Prudes

We must get back to the prudes for they are an important
part of the eros-complex. In fact, there are times when Eros
is so busily engaged he does not see the danger creeping up
from behind.

'A woman should expire with shame at the mere thought
of being a woman.' Thus spake Clement of Alexandria. And
let that suffice for what might easily be an anthology of filth
directed against sexual activity and women in particular by
early Christian spokesmen. Let us note in passing that the

spokesmen were always men and that they found fault in the
other sex. An interesting parallel is to be seen in the fact that
pornography is nearly always written by men. The denuncia-
tions of the early Christian fathers were the pornography of
the day. As I said earlier, this type of statement has a stimu-
latory effect on some.

This view of sex being evil (as I believe), it could easily
be turned to the account of evil. Witness Iago's skilful use of
Christian doctrine to justify his own baseness. It could not
be better put than by Huxley in his poem, 'The Moor' (*The
Cicadas*, 1931):

> *Honest Iago's Christian work is over;*
> *Short, short the parleying at the Golden Gate.*
> *'For I am one who made the Night ashamed*
> *Of his own essence, that his dark was dark;*
> *One who with good St Jerome's filthy tongue*
> *Tainted desire and taught the Moor to scorn*
> *His love's pale body, and because she had*
> *Lain gladly in his arms, to call her whore*
> *And strangle her for whoredom.' So he spoke,*
> *And with majestic motion heaven's high door*
> *Rolled musically apart its burnished vans*
> *To grant him entrance.*

The hatred of sex produces filth, in whatever name it is
pronounced. It may speak in the name of theology but it
remains pathology. There is really little distinction to be
made between the outbursts of the Christian Fathers and
later onslaughts by writers such as Aleister Crowley. They
equally loathe women, sex and ultimately life itself. (The
main difference is that the Fathers were more honest because
they admitted their hatred of life on earth.) Take a poem
like 'The God and the Girl', from Crowley's *The Winged
Beetle*, and ask yourself whether Clement would have shrunk
from the sentiment expressed. A young god tries to turn
womanhood into pure gold, but for all his efforts it remains
gilded dung:

> *The younger God essayed*
> *The scheme—and a nice mess of it he made!*
>
> *So that—or trousers, petticoats or tights*
> *Hides what makes honest men turn sodomites.*
>
> *Hence our joints ache, and life is out of joint—*
> *All ways we turn we stumble over coynte,*
>
> *Slip in the slime, and sicken at the stench*
> *Of English widow, wanton, wife and wench.*

When we read the last couplet the centuries slip away: this is the early Church itself, speaking to us through a diabolist. And to see what such a mind is capable of, read Crowley's parody, 'All the World's a Brothel', bearing in mind that basically this is the work not of a libertine but of a prude. Hence the disgust.

> *All the world's a brothel;*
> *And all the men and women whores and buggers.*
> *They have their exits and their entrances,*
> *And one man in his time lets many farts,*
> *His arsehole being an octave. First the Infant*
> *Violently rogered by an aged duke:*
> *And then the frigging schoolboy, with his scrotum*
> *And shining gland, his spend mere slime of snail*
> *Unwilling from his tool. And then the lover,*
> *Fucking like furnace, wth a woeful ballad*
> *Made to his mistress's bottom. Then a soldier,*
> *Full of stiff spunk, and bollocked like the bull,*
> *Jealous of sapphists, sudden and quick to come,*
> *Seeking the bubble gonorrhea*
> *Even in the bitch's mouth. And then the justice*
> *In fair round belly soaked with mercury*
> *With stand severe, and fuck of formal type,*
> *Full of wise tricks and modern aids to love;*
> *And so he lets his fart. The sixth age shifts*

Into the lean and slippered pantaloon
With drooping·penis, balls withdrawn in belly,
His youthful whore well fucked, a world too wide
For his shrunk prick: and his big manly piss,
Turning again toward childish treble, pipes
And whistles in his sound. Last scene of all
That ends this strange eventful history
Is second impotence and mere castration:
Sans prick, sans balls, sans stand, sans everything.

The net effect of the Christian barrage was to teach women (and many men) that sex was only for procreation. Zenobia, Queen of Palmyra, married Prince Odenathus, but refused any sexual activity except that specifically designed to get a child.

> *She would aver*
> *It was no more than lechery and shame*
> *To woman for a man to play with her.*
>   G. CHAUCER, 'The Monk's Tale'.

Who was to blame if the miserable prince started making suggestions to the palace chambermaid or hied himself to the local house of tolerance? Wise old Montaigne spoke out on the subject:

> Who has rendered the act of generation, an act so natural, so necessary, and so just, a thing not to be spoken of without blushing and to be excluded from all serious and regular discourse? We boldly pronounce 'kill', 'rob', 'betray', but the other we dare only to mutter between the teeth.

I shall have occasion to return to this blot on our society, with especial reference to a remarkable study by Legman.

We cannot expect Sade to have any respect for Zenobia's point of view, but his logic is always refreshing. Coeur-de-fer asks Justine to be his mistress. Being Justine, she refuses indignantly. Says Iron Heart:

> Is it not a ridiculous extravagance to assign, as you do, such a great value to the most futile of all things? How can a girl be so dull-witted as to believe that virtue may depend upon the somewhat greater or lesser diameter of one of her physical parts? What difference does it make to God or man whether this part be intact or tampered with? I will go further: it being the intention of Nature that each individual fulfil on this earth all the purposes for which he has been formed, and women existing for naught but to procure men their enjoyment, it is visibly to outrage her thus to resist the intention she has in your regard.

What Nature says to men and women (and this is not the only consideration in a society as artificial as ours) is extremely difficult to discover. From birth, for generation after generation, century upon century, men and women have been trained to adopt a certain attitude towards their bodies. The teaching has come from the Christian Church and few have escaped it or successfully rebelled against it. Many a man and woman who have not been able to accept the intellectual foundations of the Christian argument, have yet been unable to resist its influence when faced with a decision. A classic literary example is that of Evelyn Innes in Moore's novel of that name. She is in love with Owen and wishes to elope with him. Her whole being tells her to. She knows that such an act would involve considerable sacrifices, for him as well as for her. They would have to give up their old friends, pursuits and habits of life. But a voice said: It is not right. Owen had argued with her, had persuaded her that it was indeed right to live together in love, but she could not face it. When Owen asked her why she could give no other reason than that it was forbidden by the Church.

The same reservations are to be found in many serious books on sex which claim to be outspoken yet which are at times downright mealy-mouthed. *Love Without Fear*, a Plain

Guide to Sex Technique for Every Married Adult, by Dr
Eustace Chesser, is not mealy-mouthed but neither does it
call a spade a spade, as it claims. This has been one of the
most successful marriage manuals, having been first published
in 1941 and having its twenty-sixth reprint in 1962. The book
is frank and even got into some trouble with would-be censors,
but Dr Chesser gives the impression of still being rather
scared of the priests.[11] He is needlessly careful in his attitude
to religious susceptibility. After giving his opinion and advice
on sex behaviour, he adds, 'For those who are Roman
Catholics only the permitted methods of contraceptive
technique should be practised.' This is not for him to say.
He is not an RC priest. He should abide by what he thinks
is right, irrespective of other teaching.

Christian objections, plus the necessary obstacles demanded
by the romantic attitude, practically suffocated literature in
the early nineteenth century. Things were never so bad in
France, and in England we owe a great debt to the liberalising
influence of writers such as Flaubert and Zola (even Balzac
—Dickens once deplored the fact, in a letter, that he had not
the liberty of expression enjoyed by Balzac). By 1817 things
had reached such a deplorable state that the following extract
from Scott's Rob Roy could be accepted by the reading public
as natural, healthy and admirable behaviour. When he has
to leave Diana Vernon, Francis Osbaldistone becomes
emotional, seizes her hand and kisses it:

> 'This is folly!' she exclaimed—'This is madness!' and
> she struggled to withdraw her hand from my grasp, but
> not so stubbornly as actually to succeed, until I had held
> it for nearly a minute. 'Hear me, sir!' she said, 'and
> curb this unmanly burst of passion. . . .'

Note carefully: Diana did not want to release her hand but
knew she ought; and it was considered unmanly, in this
perverted society, for a man to show interest in a woman.

From a literary point of view the most Christian society
in Europe today is Soviet Russia. There the distrust of free

sexual activity is as strong as it was among Christians in their heyday. The reason is the same, though the object is different. Communism does not favour erotic themes or treatment because of their emphasis on the individual. They take from God and they take from the State, who are here seen to be leagued together. During the early days after the Revolution there was a cult of sexual freedom, permitted because the emphasis was on revolt and not on discipline. It did not last long. Sexual relations in fiction tended to be mere adjuncts to social and political themes. Even when authors approached the intimacies of love they always drew back at the last moment. For instance, in V. Ashayev's *Far From Moscow*, a big success of the post-war period, Tanya and Mikhail are in love and walk for hours through the Moscow streets. Finally they go to the house of Tanya's parents, who are out of town. They are both very excited, but Tanya suddenly gets nettle rash and Mikhail has to rub her legs with alcohol. This only increases their excitement, naturally, and Mikhail kisses her fondly. Tanya says, 'We are alone in the house. My parents are in the *dacha*. I do not want to do this to them. I am afraid for our love.' Mikhail lays her on the bed like a small child and spends the rest of the night in an imaginary conversation with her father. The romantic obstacles haunt this scientific-Marxist environment like restless Grand Dukes.

Daniel Granin's *Those Who Seek* describes the affair of Andrei Lobanov, an engineer, with Rita, a married woman. Granin's treatment was considered daring. 'Rita moved towards him, but he drew away, demanding an answer. He felt the pain he caused her by this rebuff . . . 'I need you, I need you always, but I can't go on like this. This room . . . your friend . . . Can't you yourself see how sordid it all is?' Rita lay back on the bed and placed her hands behind her head. Her small breasts were clearly outlined under the blouse. Again she sighed wistfully. 'How ungrateful of you. Come to me. Come, dear . . . What are you afraid of in me? . . . He tried not to look at her unbuttoned blouse, at her long, finely-shaped legs . . .' In the end Andrei finds the inner strength

to finish his 'sordid' affair, and is later rewarded for his
virtue. Note how a relationship that could be as beautiful
as anything we are allowed is called 'sordid'. Walter Z.
Laqueur, in 'The Thaw and After' (*Encounter*, October 1955)
wrote that people outside the totalitarian régimes easily forget
that love and sex are discouraged because they impede the
atomisation of society. They are enemies of the régime. When
attention is paid to love and sex, individual's become important. There is emphasis on the inner life. Since this article
was written there has been a slight shift away from the old
rigidity, but the artistic situation in Russia is much too
mobile to know what direction it is likely to take.

Jazz

'Where've you been?' asked Lee. 'You look as if you've
just got out of bed.'
    'I have. I just got out of the bed of some Frenchman.'
    'Take it easy, Zelda. Scotty's been dead for years.'
    'Zop, zop.'

From a play panned by K. Tynan? No, *The Dud Avocada*,
by E. Dundy.
Getting in and out of bed in that casual way is our own
contribution. I think Lenin referred to it as 'the glass of
water' attitude. You feel thirsty, so you have a drink. You feel
a sexual urge so you go to bed with somebody. To quote
Stradella, you charge your batteries. (If you're a woman; if
you're a man, you run off the surplus.) It's the outlook that
comes when sex loses its fears. It's so easy you feel disappointed
and when it's all over you say: Is that all? It's not really
automatic, it needs co-operation. It's the Jazz Age, half unbuttoned, half trance.
It's a cool attitude to sex but not to be confused with the
tough attitude. The tough attitude has a long history—you
can find it in *Romeo and Juliet*, which is a valuable anthology
of outlooks on sex.[12]

Romeo: Is love a tender thing? it is too rough,
           Too rude, too boisterous, and it pricks like
           thorn.
Mercutio: If love be rough with you, be rough with love;
           Prick love for pricking, and you beat love
           down.

The roughness of love is agreed. Romeo will meet it with
tenderness, Mercutio with blow for blow. But this is not
the casualness of Jazz sex.

Sex always gets rough handling from sophistication. The
sophisticate feels a compulsion to change from whatever is
traditional. From treating sex with awe he swings to an
attitude of over-familiarity. It is the background of a thousand
modern novels, of which Raymond Chandler's are fair repre-
sentatives. In *The Long Goodbye* Terry tells Marlowe that
the first kiss is magic, the second is intimate, the third is
routine. After that you take the girl's clothes off. Marlowe
asks if that is bad. No, says Terry, it's excitement of a high
order, but it's an impure emotion—impure in the aesthetic
sense. 'I'm not sneering at sex. It's necessary and it doesn't
have to be ugly. But it always has to be managed. Making
it glamorous is a billion-dollar industry and it costs every
cent of it.' The only thing that isn't wrong here is that sex
is necessary and this has been known for some time. Sex
doesn't have to be managed. It doesn't have to be made
glamorous. When it's made glamorous the glamour comes
first and then you get fast-set sex, which depends on acces-
sories, is boring and falls short of intimacy to such an extent
that eventually the very idea of intimacy is lost sight of.

We're sick of sex! is a familiar cry these days. Naturally.
No one feels terribly excited by a glass of water. To read how
exciting sex is and then to try it under jazz terms is a let-
down, because the environment of the read-about sex was
quite different. In *Lady Chatterley's Lover* Connie goes home
and does something very similar to what Lieutenant Henry
does in *A Farewell to Arms*, which appeared at about the
same time. Henry decided he was through with all the glory

words. Connie finds nothing but disillusion in the big, comfortable words: home, love, joy, happiness, mother, father,
husband.

> As for sex, the last of the great words, it was just a
> cocktail term for an excitement that bucked you up for
> a while, then left you more raggy than ever. Frayed!
> It was as if the very material you were made of was
> cheap stuff, and was fraying out to nothing.

A few more examples from the writing of the past thirty
years.

Mark Benney: Wide People. The petty crooks Benney
mingled with (described in a book that I hope will not be
forgotten, *Low Company*) were never in love or married to
each other. They were 'having it' with each other. 'This "it"
made the sexual union seem as stark, functional and imper-
manent as modern architecture. Love was reduced to the
category of things, a commodity bought and sold like any
other.'

Angus Wilson: Matter-of-Fact. Wilson is the chronicler of the
emancipated Bright Young Things, now getting on in years.
Here is a scrap of dialogue from a story, 'Life and Letters'
(*Partisan Review*, October 1949). ' "Oh what fun!' she cried.
"Now you can tell me all about those house-parties and the
dreadful things that people confess to. I've always wanted to
hear about that. I remember when the Dean of St Mary's
shared once. He got up in public and said that he'd slept with
his niece. It wasn't true, of course, because I know for a fact
that he's impotent. But still, it was rather sweet of him, because she's a terribly plain girl and it gave her a sexual cachet
that brought her successes." ' The approach is not so different
from that of the wide people, except that it is enlivened by
wit and gaiety.

Norman Mailer: American Problems. The Americans manage

to turn everything into a problem. In Mailer's *The Naked and the Dead* Lieutenant Robert Hearn, an intellectual, expresses this particular dilemma. Sex can be good, can be wonderful, but never for long. Poor old Hearn can't forget every time he starts an affair that it's going to end. Some of the women are beastly to him. They get angry because it's all so much a matter of course. 'Nothing ever hits you', one says. One cannot help noticing that such people are trapped by their own devices; in the beginning they thought casual sex was a step forward. When Hearn goes home and meets his old friends, even he is surprised.

> An odd setup. They are nearly all married with one or two children and governesses and the children are sometimes seen at bedtime. There is a migratory party almost every night from house to house along Lake Shore Drive and the wives and husbands are always mixed, always drunk. It is all done in a random, rather irritable kind of lust, and the petting is more frequent than the cuckolding.

Stanley Kaufmann: Sex Education. A Jazz society brings its kids up in the jazz way. At school our old friend Russell Conrad got friendly with a tough gang. Once he met them in the evening. They go to a cellar where a girl of eleven pulls of her bloomers and parades in front of the boys with her skirts up. Jake, the leader, pulled her behind a low partition. The gang climbed on boxes to watch over the top. Russell could see Jake's fat white buttocks 'and he saw Helen's calm, sullen eyes looking up at him.' He wasn't quite sure what was happening, but he got a thrill from it, beat the partition and yelled 'Hot dog!' He knew that it had to be kept secret from his parents. When he got to high school the boys talked of their conquests like notches in their belts. The well-built track-team man said, 'I look at it like I'm a salesman and every girl's a prospect. If I get to first base with ten per cent, I'm doing OK, my average is OK.' These boys grew up hating and despising women. Russell felt it was

typical of American boys. They grew up knowing nothing
about living with women, and taking their social life with
men. They only wanted women when they felt a physical
need. Tolerate them and get rid of them quick. Whiskey neat
and breast-hunting, that was the ticket.

To mistake sex for love is like mistaking the Pope for God,
Paul Potts writes in *Dante Called You Beatrice*, which sounds
pompous out of context but is on the right lines. Some
people have been sickened by the subject. 'Sex as an institution, sex as a general notion, sex as a platitude—all this is
something I find too tedious for words. Let us skip sex.' (V.
Nabokov, *Playboy*, January 1964). It may even be true that
sex—or vital sex, call it love if you can bear it—really does
need obstacles. Freud himself, towards the end of his career,
came to the conclusion that an obstruction is needed to drive
the libido upward. Where there are no natural obstructions,
men have invented them. This is not an argument in favour
of repression, which only twists the libido into unpleasant
channels. The obstruction should be personal, not social. The
partners to intercourse create their own obstacles to quick and
easy satisfaction. Both hold the basic instinct of sex in check
for the purpose of mutual enrichment. This can apply before
intercourse or during intercourse. Those who practise karezza
or Zugassant or coitus reservatus claim delights the Jazz men
never knew.

Chemistry

You can go even further in emptying sex of feeling. You can
regard it as chemical reaction and chew gum while you do
it. It is not easy to distinguish between this and the Jazz
approach; they certainly overlap. Russell Conrad and his
friends in the previous section may have been Chemists rather
than Jazzmen. The Jazzmen still want to do it and get some
kind of kick out of it but they don't want to give the impression that sexual stimulation is any more exciting than any
other stimulation. (It was the mark of the past, of course,
that sexual stimulation was the most extreme man could

experience.) Perhaps the man (or woman) who believes in the chemical theory of sex does it only because life demands a certain amount of chemistry: seed and soil, air and water. Such a lover is Ice-Cold in Eros. There is no better example than Stradella. She didn't pretend to enjoy sex as even the wives along Lake Shore Drive did. Poor Archie loved her in an old-fashioned way, whereas she thought of sex as a method of clearing up pimples and recharging batteries. He asks her how many men she's been to bed with. The subject bores her, she wants to know if she's supposed to keep check. For Archie each time is like a marriage and he never forgets. He asks her if they're just like supplies, like meat, to her.

> That's right, Archie. Studs. Studs, like meat. They're beef steak. All they want is somewhere to put it. You know they say a stiff one knows no conscience. And I like to get my depth charge every two weeks or so at least. Otherwise the battery'd run down.

Archie works out that, if she has had twenty guys a year for the past fifteen years, she's been to bed with three hundred. He's awe-struck. To Stradella it is one of the facts of life, like the number of restaurants you eat in.

I have referred to the neo-Victorian morality of the communist states. Their approach to sex has turned its back on Marxist materialism. One would expect a chemical interpretation to follow naturally but in fact it does not fit in with social requirements. But it is significant that the renegade from the Soviet Union in Koestler's *The Age of Longing*, Nikitin, refuses to believe in love. He believes the relationship to be entirely mechanical and when Hydie protests, he proceeds to persuade her. He pressed his thumb against her nipple. 'Now . . .,' he said. 'It was a grip more than a caress which she knew only too well; he always did precisely this at the precise moment of her physical climax.' Sure enough, Hydie had her orgasm. She felt utterly humiliated.

Discussing sex is rather like walking on quicksands. No sooner have you made a statement than you find yourself compelled to qualify it. Some measure of belief in the chemical and mechanical nature of sex is obviously essential. One is working with a body, which is flesh and blood. Long before Ovid wrote his rules men had realised that certain techniques ensured greater pleasure, that there were better and worse ways of inducing orgasm. The danger of the expert is that everything else will be subject to his expertise, so that a woman may be brought very successfully to climax and will abuse him afterwards. I will have a lot to say about techniques later, but technique alone is a barren affair. It was a mistake the gallants (who had a very healthy respect for technique) never made. It is a modern heresy, arising out of the conceit which the successes of technology have engendered. When Jurgen went to Cocaigne he became the consort of Anaitia, who devoted her time to curious pleasures. The weather remained fair and changeless, with no glaring sunrays anywhere, and with one large star shining alone in the clear daylight. This was Venus Mechanitis. 'In Cocaigne there was no regret and no variability, but only an interminable flow of curious pleasures, illumined by the wandering star of Venus Mechanitis.' It was the world of the sexual technician and it was a bore.

How much technique should a man have? This cannot be answered categorically, but here are two extracts which will help the choice of a satisfactory *via media*. In the first, Lulu is lying frightened in bed, at a hotel she has been taken to by her lover after leaving her husband. She can hear someone moving and she remembers what happened earlier.

I didn't groan. Of course, he finally did bother me with all his feeling around, he knows how; I have a horror of men who know how. I'd rather sleep with a virgin. They take you for an instrument they're proud of knowing how to play. I hate people to bother me, my throat's dry, I'm afraid and I have a bad taste in my mouth and I'm humiliated because they think they dominate me, I'd like to slap Pierre when he puts on his elegant airs and says, 'I've got technique.' My God, to think that's

life, that's why you get dressed and washed and make
yourself pretty and all the books are written about that
and you think about it all the time and finally that's
what it is, you go to a room with somebody who half
smothers you and ends up by wetting your belly.

JEAN-PAUL SARTRE, Intimacy.

But here is what happens when there's no technique. The
anonymous author of A Woman in Berlin meets Ilse, an old
friend and a sophisticated woman of the world. Like all the
other women in Berlin, Ilse has had to submit to the Russians,
and the writer asks her for her opinion of her new cavaliers.

'Miserable,' she said, and pulled a face. 'They're utterly
without imagination. Primitive and crude—one no better
than another, so far as I've been able to gather here
in the house. But maybe you've had better experiences
with your officers.'

'Don't you believe it. Not in that respect.'

'Maybe back in their country,' said Ilse, 'they have the
latest in socialist economic planning, but as far as
eroticism goes they've not advanced since Adam and Eve.
I told my husband this to comfort him.' And she winked
at me. 'Needless to say, with the miserable food we get,
a poor husband isn't up to much. Mine's already getting
complexes about it and thinks that in the long run the
Red Army with its ruthlessness will make a considerable
impression on us women.' We laughed at this idea and
agreed that under normal circumstances not one in a
hundred of our dear enemies would stand the slightest
chance with us. At best we might consider the hundredth
worthy of a preliminary examination.

Depravity?

'Pleasures go from distich to quatrain, from quatrain to
sonnet, from sonnet to ballad, from ballad to ode, from ode
to cantata, from cantata to dithyramb,' wrote Balzac. We must
now briefly consider the cantata-dithyramb range.

There is a strong resistance to any sexual behaviour which lies outside a narrow permitted spectrum. What is permitted varies from age to age and it is usually obscure why one practice is considered more respectable than another. Let us turn to an unofficial arbiter in these matters. Dr Eustace Chesser, in his *Love Without Fear*, attacks the religious view that the sole object of sexual intercourse is procreation but then leaves the issue in considerable doubt. He will not accept substitutes for normal copulation and thus rejects any activity which is indulged for its own sake. 'Many practices can be considered perfectly normal when indulged in as a means to an end—the end being intercourse—but must be regarded as abnormal when indulged in as an end in themselves. In other words the part, as it were, becomes the whole.' (I always think the use of the meaningless 'as it were' signifies intellectual discomfort.) If procreation is no longer the sole object, what is so sacred in the pleasure obtained from coitus as compared with other practices? We eat to stay alive, but many eat for other reasons. Is it ever considered necessary to regulate our manner of eating? Is alcohol banned with meat? Must it only be consumed with one's wife—or brother-in-law, for that matter? In another passage Dr Chesser is more explicit about his fears. 'Frequent repetition of a sexual aberration often results in its gaining a firm grip,' he writes, and then quotes Bloch: 'The normal human being can become *accustomed* to the most diverse sexual aberrations so that these become perversions.' But the argument is weak. As usual, there is no answer to the question: Why single out sex? It is quite clear that we can only live today by perverting the accepted living conventions of every period before our own. Is not pop music a perversion? Was not Beethoven a perversion in his day? What would Hengist and Horsa have thought of Palestrina? Is not need worth consideration? Fashion may create need, but this does not alter the definition of need. Need is a demand for what is necessary.

Psychologists distinguish between inversion and perversion. After ten years of marriage (regular intercourse) the sharp edge of sensation is worn blunt. There are three alternatives:

accept the bluntness and die to sensation; change the method; and change the instrument which is what the moralists do not want us to do. The citizen looks for variety and finds it easily enough. The human body, multiplied by two, presents a splendid array of possibilities. Those who have incorporated sex into religion or their moral outlook (made it the whole of their moral outlook, in many unfortunate cases) feel compelled to confine themselves to the One Hole. Even with this sad limitation, there is enough potential variety to jack up the jaded nerve ends for a lustrum or so. Others, freer, know no bounds. Every male knows a hole is not necessary, even if pressures and priests have caused him to reject such knowledge as heresy. But why can't psychologists accept this theory of boredom? Why must they evolve complex theories absolutely bloated with symbolism? One result is that the study of aberration is a dreadfully dull business, while its literature (in the right hands) can be really joyous.

Now here's a wicked aberration, presented by Stendhal in his nineteenth Miscellaneous Fragment: 'There is exquisite pleasure in clasping to you a woman who has done you great harm, who has long been your cruel enemy and is ready to be so again. Witness the success of French officers in Spain in 1812.' Not an aberration? Ask Colonel Blimp. Ask the patriots who shaved the girls' heads in 1945. Or must an aberration be physical—meaning that spiritual sin can be forgiven but physical, never. (It's alarming how often one is driven to this conclusion in studying the Christian attitude to sex.) The reason why the women of Berlin laughed at their Russian conquerors was not because they were the enemy or communists but because they were such lousy lovers. Suppose the desire of women for the conqueror is to be explained by a masochistic urge to be humiliated. Aren't we getting uncomfortably close to flagellation?

Alphonse Daudet blamed women for the spread of what he called 'depravity'. To him it was a poison which travelled from one person to another, blasting body and soul. Fanny (the Sappho of his *Sappho*) used every device she knew to hold on to Jean. Modesty and coyness were useless. Perhaps they attract a man to begin with but they never keep him. 'Men are all alike, mad after vice and corruption. . . . To stuff them with what they love is still the best way to keep them to yourself.'

As usual, we must turn to the Divine Marquis for the most logical defence of sexual aberration. Here is Clément in *Justine*:

> The man endowed with uncommon tastes is sick; if you prefer, he is like a woman with hysteric dizziness. Has the idea to punish either of them ever occurred to us? let us be equally fair when dealing with the man whose caprices surprise us; perfectly like unto the ill man or the female dizzard, he is, like them, deserving of sympathy and not of blame; that is the moral apology for the persons whom we are discussing; a physical explanation will without doubt be found as easily, and when the study of anatomy reaches perfection they will without any trouble be able to demonstrate the relationship of the human constitution to the taste which it affects. Ah, you pedants, hangmen, turnkeys, lawmakers, you shavepate rabble, what will you do when we have arrived there? what is to become of your laws, your ethics, your religion, your gallows, your Heavens, your Gods, your Hell when it shall be proven that such a flow of liquids, this variety of fibres, that degree of pungency in the blood or in the animal spirits are sufficient to make a man the object of your givings and your takings away?

Finally, I must refer to a shoddy little aberration discovered by Lionel Trilling while lecturing to some graduate students. He was reading Hazlitt's *Liber Amoris* with them and discovered that they had no understanding whatsoever of the author's obsessive attachment to Sarah Walker. 'They could see no reason why a man could not break the chains of a passion so unrewarding, so humiliating.' Neither they nor Trilling called this passion perverted but I am sure that, from the students' standpoint, it deserves the title. The students did not mention morality because it is one of the merits of the younger generation today that they refuse to beg their questions so shamelessly. But I can think of many people who ought to call such an attachment immoral, just as they call an emotionally and physically fulfilled attachment immoral with far less reason.

FOOTNOTES

1. Though it is more likely that the process worked in the reverse direction. See later in this chapter.

2. Erotic literature has little to say about marriage, except to condemn its boredom. I don't intend to treat love and marriage as opposites and irreconcilables. Marriage often results from love, especially among Anglo-saxons. The notion that they are always poles apart is an affectation, whose point is to prove the bohemian emancipation of the person holding it. On the other hand, the kind of suburban propaganda you get in popular songs such as 'love and marriage go together like a horse and carriage' is pathetic twaddle. Love often underlies marriage but I have never known a case where the two co-exist for long. In some cases love is replaced by affection but eros, my theme, can never stand the atmosphere for long. He is a restless fellow.

3. Establish a truth, or a trend, or a disposition, and you can be assured that its opposite will have equal validity. Along with the all-embracing rapaciousness of lust goes the insistence on virginity. Dr Lazarsfeld quotes another woman who had been married for several years yet was still a virgin. Her husband prized spiritual fidelity above his personal pleasure.

4. Friendship is constant in all other things
   Save in the office and affairs of love:
   Therefore all hearts in love use their own tongues;
   Let every eye negotiate for itself,
   And trust no agent. . . .

   W. Shakespeare, Much Ado About Nothing.

5. Layton may have chosen the wrong woman for, reading between the lines, one infers that MM was not really the sexual hedonist her form surely urged her to be. But nothing in life is perfect. She was how a sex goddess should look.

6. Balzac quotes Venice Preserv'd to illustrate how a woman's coldness can make a man ridiculous. Senator Antonio repeats, over and over again at the feet of Aquilina, 'Aquilina, Quilina, Lina, Aqui, Nacki!' with no other reward than a cut from a whip which causes him to cringe and fawn. But Balzac lacks his customary perception here; Aquilina was a courtesan whom Antonio employed for the express purpose of humiliating him.

7. I cannot refrain from quoting this excellent philosopher's view of the nature of love: '. . . when all is done I find that love is nothing else but an insatiate thirst of enjoying a greedily desired subject. Nor Venus other than a tickling delight of emptying one's seminary vessels.' Love, he tells us, is a vain business but it keeps you young.

8. I am aware that 'like' is a weak word here, yet there is no other that accurately describes the sensation: we need pain to the extent of wanting it, we shrink from its actuality yet are fascinated by it. Biologically we like it.

9. Compare those films and novels where one is tempted to cry out, 'Why don't you tell him this?' or 'Why don't you explain that?' So often two or three words of explanation could put everything right. But then the suffering would end.

10. Shakespeare wrote at a time when certain lyrics repeatedly proclaimed love's power to kill, e.g.,

> And I for sorrow dying,
> Dying, dying, dying,
> Since she I love cares nothing for my sighing,

from the Benedictbeuern MS.

11. I am reminded of a talk by an M.O. on joining the Army. 'It's no good talking to you chaps about sexual intercourse because half of you won't know what it means. I'm going to tell you about what you ought to take care of when you have a fuck.' The chaplain was present but in the Army, as the M.O. said, godliness comes next to cleanliness.

12. Cf. the Nurse's cynicism in the same play. Lady Capulet tells Juliet that by having Paris she will not make herself the less. The Nurse puts in, 'No less! nay, bigger; women grow by men.' This is 'glass of water' with a vengeance.

6: *The Female Body*

A woman tells me most female bodies are revolting. Specially
selected bodies have come in for as much literary praise as
landscapes (and have been compared with landscapes by some
authors) but always by men. There has been little change in
what attracts men through the ages. In *The Changing Face of
Beauty*, by Madge Garland, we are told that small waists,
round bosoms, large eyes and curly hair have been permanent
elements of female beauty. Emphasis shifts and details
change: large round breasts, hard firm ones, flat ones and
pointed ones; wasp waists and thick waists; large made-up
eyes, downcast eyes, doe eyes, small and set wide apart; hair
in every conceivable arrangement. Man's interest in the more
intimate parts of a woman's anatomy is not reflected in respectable, family literature. In erotic literature the pudenda
receive their full meed of praise.

The classic of female description, and a model for later
writers, remains the Song of Songs (sometimes referred to as
the Song of Solomon). There is a recent translation from the
original Hebrew by Hugh J. Schonfield, who believes that it
is a straightforward account of sexual desire before and after
marriage. Many attempts have been made in the past to
interpret the book mystically and allegorically. Towards the
end of the nineteenth century, however, the Rev. E. P. Edd-
rupp, Prebendary of Salisbury Cathedral, appeared to grasp
the true nature of the poem for he wrote in a popular com-
mentary on the Old Testament: 'Such a book as the Song
of Solomon may not be fitted for public reading in a mixed
congregation, or even for private reading by the impure in
heart.' The expression 'impure in heart' is puzzling for it is

usually the self-confessed 'pure in heart' who find such writings disgusting. There was considerable controversy among the first century Pharisees on whether the Song should have a place in the Scriptural Canon. It obviously celebrated physical love and made no mention of God. Nevertheless, the view was eventually accepted that it should be interpreted mystically as the love of God for His people Israel. During the Middle Ages the Christians had similar doubts, and there was a school that wished to identify the Shulamite with the Virgin Mary. Others saw in it Solomon's love of Wisdom. Schonfield gives his translation the true Hebrew title of 'Solomon's Incomparable Song'. We do not know who wrote it, although it could not have been King Solomon, to whom it was attributed. Schonfield thinks it was an independent composition (i.e., not an ancient liturgy of a fertility cult), written by a man of taste and education, a man of substance with a country seat. He probably had some knowledge of the Persian court and an appreciation of the Persian way of life, but retained a strong love of his own country. It is probable that the Song was written after the time of Nehemiah but before 350 B.C., perhaps during the reign of Artaxerxes II (404-359), who may have been the King Ahasuerus of the Book of Esther.

People are not so familiar with the magnificent A.V. translation as were their forefathers, but it is still easily available. Here is a brief extract from Schonfield. The bridegroom (or lover) is speaking:

> Your two breasts are as two fawns,
>   Twins of a female gazelle,
> That graze among the anemones.
>
> Until the day sighs to a close
>   And the creeping shadows spread,
> I will hie me to the hill of myrrh,
>   The rounded mount of frankincense.
> You are wholly charming, my own,
>   And there is no blemish in you.
>
>   SCHONFIELD, *A.V.*, *IV*, *5-7*, Canto 6.

THE FEMALE BODY

This rich, highly metaphorical way of writing about the female problem remained the pattern for later writers, but no other race has equalled the Semites in this field. The family resemblance between the Song and my next example is obvious. The following lines are from a *kasidah* which was sung by the onlookers at village weddings in Syria while the bride (called the Queen) danced. Such dances took place in March, the most fruitful month, up till modern times. Each *kasidah* contained *wasfs*, flattering descriptive lines in praise of the bride's beauty. Dr J. G. Wetzstein received a copy of this one in 1860. It had been composed in the early part of the century by the distinguished poet Kasim al Chinn for the marriage of the daughter of the sheikh of Nawa. These lines are from the *wasf*.

> Her neck is like the neck of the roe which drinks out of the fountain of Kanawab.
> Her breasts are like polished marble tablets, as ships bring them to Sida,[1]
> Thereon like apples of the pomegranate two glittering piles of jewels.
> Her arms are drawn swords, peeled cucumbers—oh that I had such!
> And incomparably beautiful her hands in the rose-red of the Hinna-leaf;
> Her smooth, fine fingers are like the writing reed not yet cut;
> The glance of her nails like Dura-seeds which have lain overnight in milk;
> Her body is a mass of cotton-wool which has been shaken into down,
> And her legs marble pillars in the sacred house of the Omayads.

The Arabian Nights are full of extremely fleshy descriptions of female charms, for the Arabs are addicted to rotundities, particularly of the hindquarters. They are also expert at gilding the lily. Here are two brief evocations of the other side, the belly (from the Mathers translation).

From time to time the breeze lifted the filmy chemise to her navel, showing her belly, which was as white as snow, with dimples in delicate places, each large enough to hold an ounce of powdered nutmeg.

'Tale of Kamar al Zaman and Princess Budur', 206th night.

. . . her navel was carved so deep that it would have held an ounce of nutmeg butter.

'Tale of Sympathy the Learned', 270th night.

And here is the uttermost perfection, nature joined by art in the production of incomparable beauty. It is an account of Sweet-Friend's bath. She has been bought for the king and the little slaves know what is expected from them.

After washing her hair and all her limbs, they rubbed and kneaded her, depilated her carefully with paste of caramel, sprinkled her hair with a sweet wash prepared from musk, tinted her finger-nails and her toe-nails with henna, burnt male incense and ambergris at her feet, and rubbed light perfumes into all her skin. Then they threw a large towel, scented with orange flowers and roses, over her body and, wrapping all her hair in a warm cloth, led her to her own apartment, where the wazir's wife waited to wish her the customary wishes of the bath.

'Tale of Sweet-Friend and Ali Nur', 32nd night, trs. MATHERS.

For the Chinese style one naturally goes to *Golden Lotus*, for a description of the lady of that name.

Her hair was black as a raven's plumage; her eyebrows mobile as the kingfisher and as curved as the new moon. Her almond eyes were clear and cool, and her cherry lips most inviting. Her nose was noble and exquisitely modelled, and her dainty cheeks beautifully powdered. Her face had the delicate roundness of a silver bowl. As for her body, it was as light as a flower, and her fingers

as slender as the tender shoots of a young onion. Her
waist was as narrow as the willow and her white belly
yielding and plump. Her feet were small and tapering;
her breasts soft and luscious. One other thing there was,
black-fringed, grasping, dainty and fresh, but the name
of that I may not tell. Words fail to describe the charm
of so beauteous a vision.

The description is not yet complete. We are told of the pins
and combs in her hair, her jade pendants, her gown and her
perfume. Shakespeare is contradicted when we are told that
a glimpse of this vision would cause the souls of men to
flutter away and die. Her feet were graced by tiny shoes. It
should be borne in mind that a handsome Chinese foot was
not more than three inches long.

One can only make very broad comparisons of racial ideals
of beauty, as men of all races love the same things. On the
whole, however, the Arab beauty was more fleshy than the
Chinese. Arab metaphors tended to be taken from fruit, from
whatever was luscious. The Chinese demanded elegance, and
expressed their admiration in linear terms. A Chinese looked
at a willow tree while an Arab sucked a pomegranate. Both
races admired the moon, the Arabs because it looked as
though you might take an enjoyable bite from it, the Chinese
because of its formal perfection. These tastes are probably
reflected by the love-making. Arab lovers (I am told by ladies
who have not exactly enjoyed their favours) lack technique,
like the Russians; I suspect the Chinese practise their
techniques gravely and with a tinge of suspicion.

By contrast, early European approaches to the glorification
of women seem crude, rather unimaginative, and lacking in
the closely observed detail that is the secret of successful
description. In fact, the classical writer was far more likely
to praise his lady in generalised terms than by detailed catalogue. It was believed in Greece that bodily beauty was the
outward manifestation of spiritual beauty, and this idea certainly seemed to inhibit the kind of lingering interest in mere
parts that we find in the East. Of course, there were excep-

tions and over the centuries certain standards of female
beauty came to be accepted. In the sixteenth century Firenzuola actually produced a book on female beauty, in which
he added his own observations, illustrated from the women
and girls he knew in the city of Prato, to the rules of proportion that were already adopted by artists and authors. Once
again the idea that physical beauty mirrored the soul became
dominant. Firenzuola's beauty had abundant hair of a soft
yellow or light brown colour, full dark eyes with dark brows
and lashes, a nose receding gently but firmly towards the
eyes, a mouth small but well-shaped, lips neither thin nor full
and showing in repose not more than six of the upper teeth,
a round chin, well-shaped ears, and a white, round, long
neck. Her limbs were well-proportioned and her hands were
large and white, and her feet were small and as white as
alabaster. Her skin was soft and a clear white, flushed with
pomegranate ruddiness, which would also be seen in the ears,
the tiny red veins in her eyelids, and on her snowy bosom.
There is no lack of detail here, but it is a rather dreary list
which would set no pulse beating. As for the intimate parts,
they had to be imagined.

Luxuriant description was now coming into fashion. An
early example leaves no doubt of its model because it was
actually called 'Song of Solomon'. It is by Bartholomew
Griffin and appeared in a sonnet sequence called *Fidessa* that
appeared in 1596.

> *Fair is my love that feeds among the lilies,*
> * The lilies growing in that pleasant garden*
> *Where Cupid's Mount, that well beloved hill is,*
> * And where that little god, himself is Warden.*
> *See where my Love sits in the beds of spices!*
> * Beset all round with camphor, myrrh and roses.*
> *And interlaced with curious devices*
> * Which her from all the world apart incloses.*
> *There, doth she tune her lute for her delight!*
> * And with sweet music makes the ground to move;*
> *Whilst I, poor I, do sit in heavy plight,*

Wailing alone my unrespected love.
Not daring rush into so rare a place,
That gives to her, and she to it, a grace.

Griffin was only one of many sonneteers who praised his lady
in these terms, but I am trying to distinguish between descriptions which are as neutral in feeling as those of a daffodil or
a skylark and those which appear to be motivated by erotic
feeling. Some of these were so absurd (for this expression of
admiration did not yet come naturally to most European
poets) that writers in both Italy and England resorted to satire.
Richard Linche, whose *Diella* appeared in the same year as
Fidessa, was in revolt against the ridiculous eulogies of
woman's beauty and virtue that were to be found in contemporary sonnets. His work is dedicated to 'the most worthily
honoured and virtuously beautiful lady, the Lady Anne
Glemnham' but it makes no attempt to list her beauties. It is
frank and lustful and praises the lady's physical charms for
their own sake, not for some mystical significance they may
possess. In Italy Tebaldeo had actually travestied physical
beauty in order to make it absurd or obscene.

  Coming to our own day, when it became quite natural to
describe a woman's most intimate charms, without pretend-
ing that they really represented something else, we find George
Moore still reverting to the Song of Songs for his model.
Doris asks if he likes her hat but it is not her hat he is thinking
of. Moreover, he is able to tell her directly what's on his
mind.

> Yes, I like it, but I am thinking of the Doris that lived
> two thousand years ago; she did not wear a hat. It is not
> only the beauty of your face that I desire, but all your
> beauty: the pink breast flowers, the pretty forearms, the
> belly so daintily designed, the round thighs, the well-
> jointed knees, the long calves, the sloping ankles, the
> thin white feet. In those curved hands and thin trans-
> parent fingers with long red nails I see the nymph in
> my imagination, though I may never see her with mortal
> eyes.

It is a frank appraisal, but the language is impoverished. Moore was writing at a time when the female body was not for public view, or description. In France Gautier had more freedom and D'Albert's account of a desirable woman is correspondingly richer.

> As to her figure, she is rather plump than thin. I am something of a Turk in this matter, and I should scarcely like to meet with a corner when I expected a circumference; a woman's skin should be well filled, her flesh compact and firm, like the pulp of a peach that is nearly ripe: and the mistress I shall have is made just so. She is a blonde with dark eyes, white like a blonde, with the colour of a brunette, and a red and sparkling smile. The lower lip rather large, the eyeball swimming in a flood of natural moisture, her breast round, small and firm, her hands long and plump, her walk undulating like a snake standing on its tail, her hips full and yielding, her shoulders broad, the nape of her neck covered with down; a style of beauty at once delicate and compact, graceful and healthy, poetic and real; a subject of Giorgione's wrought by Rubens.

D'Albert shows the European preference for a 'blonde with dark eyes', but despite the peach and the snake this woman cannot compare with the Oriental for seductiveness. There is a tradition in European writing (particularly in verse) of treating a woman's body as a landscape—I will give a few examples in a later section. This device appeared to release the damned up imagery which, on the whole, flowed so easily among the Arabs and Chinese. Just as the Arabs tended to see a desired body as a fruit and the Chinese as a tree, so the Western Europeans turned, characteristically, to landscape, and often landscape on such a scale that it resembled more a map. Here is a recent example of cartography, mingled with more direct praise of Judith Toumignon, the reigning beauty of Clochemerle:

Her breasts were two lovely promontories. Wherever one looked, one discovered soft open spaces, alluring estuaries, pleasant glades, hillocks, mounds, where pilgrims could have lingered in prayer, where they could have quenched their thirst at cooling springs. But without a passport—and such was rarely given—this rich territory was forbidden ground. A glance might skim its surface, might detect some shady spot, might linger on some peak. But none might venture farther, none might touch. So milk-white was her flesh, so silky its texture, that at sight of it the men of Clochemerle grew hoarse of speech and were overcome by feelings of recklessness and desperation.[2]

GABRIEL CHEVALLIER, *Clochemerle*, 1936.

A description attributed to Frank Harris is often amusing because in the middle of his praise he will introduce a criticism of a particular feature, on which he will enlarge and make a general pronouncement. In the course of his *Life and Loves* he was introduced to the daughter of an English officer and Indian mother. She is a *padmini*, or a lotus-girl, i.e., her yoni was like the bud of a lotus-flower and her *kamasalila*, or love-juice, had the perfume of a lily that·was just opening (this was the procuress's description). Now for Harris.

Her hips were smooth and rounded and gave downwards to a pair of soft and shapely thighs on which the hairless mound, naked of hair between their roundnesses, jutted outwards like a soft beak. I must say I found that rather ugly. It is a fallacy to think that a woman's sexual organ is less prominent when it is shaven of its hair. The hair, rising as it does outwards and away from the lower belly, has a tendency to obscure the sharpness of the line of the mound, thus rendering the mount itself less prominent, more subtle in its provocativeness and more modest to a man's lips. Hair is the grass of the human body, the verdure and the beauty of the carnal meadow.

But that was the only imperfection. The breasts were round and rosy like small pomegranates and her belly was really like the heap of brown-flecked wheat on which Solomon must have showered passionate kisses to have written of it in the immortal lines of his *Songs*. The soft indentation of her perfectly formed navel had all my attention. . . .

To sum up: there are, broadly speaking, two ways of describing a woman's physical charms. One, rarely used in Oriental literature and essentially dull, is the straightforward description by shape and measurement. The richer and more stimulating method, of which Solomon's song is still the prime example, is a stream of metaphor. So powerful is the influence of the early model that the pomegranate, rarely seen in Europe, is still invoked to describe the breast by European writers (as Harris above). The different predilections of the different races are seen in their choice of imagery. A new departure may be noticed in the modern West when a woman's faults are also included among her virtues. This is part of the frankness that is deemed an essential part of modern writing. In the past a beautiful woman was usually flawless (always in traditional Oriental literature).

Finally, a magnificent Song of Songs in the modern manner, by E. E. Cummings:

my love
thy hair is one kingdom
the king whereof is darkness
thy forehead is a flight of flowers

thy head is a quick forest
filled with sleeping birds
thy breasts are swarms of white bees
upon the bow of thy body
thy body to me is April
in whose armpits is the approach of spring

thy thighs are white horses yoked to a chariot of kings
they are the striking of a good minstrel
between them is always a pleasant song

my love
thy head is a casket
  of the cool jewel of thy mind
the hair of thy head is one warrior
  innocent of defeat
thy hair upon thy shoulders is an army
  with victory and with trumpets

thy legs are the trees of dreaming
whose fruit is the very eatage of forgetfulness

thy lips are satraps in scarlet
  in whose kiss is the combing of kings
thy wrists
are holy
  which are the keepers of the keys of thy blood
thy feet upon thy ankles are flowers in vases
of silver

in thy beauty is the dilemma of flutes
  thy eyes are the betrayal
of bells comprehended through incense

Vagina

A rather startling heading, perhaps, but there is no doubt
that this portion of the female anatomy is the major interest
in all writing that is genuinely erotic in spirit. With the
vagina goes the Mount of Venus and occasional references
to the clitoris (dealt with separately). These are written of
as the centre of pleasure, though they come in for their full
share of attention in the considerable amount of humorous
and satirical writing about women and sex.

We can start with one of these, after Swinburne. (If not

by A. C. S. himself, but most of his obscene writings were
concerned with flagellation.) A 'Protest by the Medical Profession' complains that although the eminent physicians who
have 'studied the abdomena of various experimental dames'
have given their parts delightful latin names—

> There's the vulva, the vagina and the jolly peroneum,
> There's the hymen which is sometimes found in brides,
> There's the uterus, the clitoris, the ovum and the
>   oviducts,
> The ovaries and lord knows what besides—

and yet, when idle people chatter, they use such a short and
unattractive little word! There is a 'Reply by a Layman in
Defence of his Vocabulary' to the effect that the ordinary
man does not try to cloud the issue with latinity:

> For men have made this useful but inelegant commodity
> The subject of innumerable jibes;
> And whilst the name we call it by is something of an
>   oddity,
> It seems to fit the subject it describes.

Finally, a 'Retort by one of the Experimental Dames' chides
the men for their heated arguments and points out that,
however much scientists and laymen disagree over terminology, in action they're much the same.

> And furthermore, when you describe in phrases so
>   meticulous
> Our relatively simple little vent,
> You take no account of all the names, so rude and so
>   ridiculous,
> Which designate the gadgets of a gent.

She concludes that men are possibly jealous of the ladies'
ability to tuck their privities away so conveniently.

The 'unattractive little word' was, of course, unmention-

able in public literature and polite conversation until quite
recently. Probably the nearest approach to its utterance was
by Malvolio when he read the fake letter from Olivia. 'By
my life, this is my lady's hand: these be her very C's, her U's
'n' her T's; and thus she makes her great P's.' It could not be
much more explicit but there have been critics to argue the
matter.

There is a distinct difference between the Oriental and
Occidental approaches to this gadget. The East has always
treated it as a thing of beauty, whatever else it might be; the
West has seen it first and foremost as the fount of male
pleasure, with a tendency to joke about it. As I have remarked
before, joy and laughter are closely related, and the experience of joy frequently leads to an impulse to joke. This is a
kind of emotional association.

Rufinus of the *Greek Anthology* seemed to stand in awe of
the female pudenda. In two of his epigrams (Book V) he
dreams that he was a latter-day Paris, making a similar judgment. In one the ladies are unnamed. The first was remarkable for her 'bulging pudenda'; the next were spread apart,
like 'a precious snowy rose growing pink, then ruddy, then
redder still'; the third was 'like a quiet sea furrowed by silent
waves, its dainty skin throbbing of its own accord.' In the
other epigram the ladies are named. This time they are
actually arguing about who has the most powerful fanny.
Rhodope's dazzled 'like a rose-garden cut in two by a silver
stream.' Fate has deprived us of a close-up of Melita. Rhodo-
clea's was like glass, 'from the outside it was like some of the
modern sculptures in the temple.'

The Arabs were more delicate, and their imagery is more
exquisite. There is something journalistic about Rufinus
whereas the *Arabian Nights* give the impression of a faithful
report. When Ali Shar put his hand on Zumurrud's thigh,
he felt 'something round and as high as a throne, as fat as a
chicken, warmer than the throat of a pigeon, hotter than a
loving heart; and this round thing was smooth and white,
melting and enormous.' ('Tale of Zumurrud and Ali Shar',
330th night, trs. Mathers.) These stories rarely go beyond the

Mount of Venus in description, though it is frequently passed
in action. When the Khalifah Haroun al Rashid watched
Zubaidah go to the fountain to bathe, he leaned against a
tree, which cracked. In sudden fear she tried to cover herself.
'Now Zubaidah's affair was so remarkable a thing that two
hands could hardly have hidden the half of it; also it was
so sleek and slippery that she could not hold it at all. It
glided between her fingers, and appeared in all its glory to
the delighted Khalifah.' ('Abu Nuwas and Zubaidah's Bath',
379th night, Mathers.) There are two lyrical descriptions in
'The Adventures of Hasan of Basrah', 586th night, Mathers.
In each the spot is called a little rabbit without ears. (Cf
English pussy.) On one occasion Hasan was looking for his
wife and watched a parade of naked beauties:

> O little rabbits, you were fat and plump and round, and
> white and domed and big, and vaulted and high and
> close, and jutting intact, and shut, like thrones, like
> fishes, and heavy, full-lipped and dumb; you were nests,
> you had no ears, and you were warm; you were tented
> and hairless, you were muzzled and deaf; you were little
> and cuddled, you were split and sensitive, you were dry
> and delightful; but you were not to be compared with
> the little rabbit of Splendour' (the missing wife).

The little rabbit is never mentioned by its colloquial
Arabic name through the whole of the Thousand and One
Nights except once in a rhyme, and then indirectly. (Oddly,
the male counterpart, the zabb, is frequently mentioned.
Another sign of delicacy, reflecting that in the Arab world
the female is a china doll, though one that needs watching).
Here is the rhyme.

> *A thing of grace, appealing to the poet,*
> *And four by five, and six by ten will show it.*

Kaf, K, also stands for twenty, and sin, S, stands for sixty.

Together they spell *Kus* (Arabic ignores vowels), a low word for the female organ.

English literature has numerous examples of the metaphorical approach. Here is Herrick, in *Hesperides*, 1648.

> *To Dianeme*
> *Shew my thy feet; shew me thy legs, thy thighes;*
> *Shew me those* Fleshie Principalities;
> *Shew me that Hill (where smiling Love doth sit)*
> *Having a living Fountain under it.*
> *Shew me thy waste; Then let me there withall,*
> *By the* Assention *of thy Lawn, see All.*[3]

But at other times the method is suggestive without being specific. Herrick again.

> *Upon a Crooked Maid*
> *Crooked you are, but that dislikes not me;*
> *So you be straight, where Virgins straight sho'd be.*

A ballad in praise of Nelly, attributed by some to John Gay and by others to Arbuthnot, also proceeds by indirection.

> *For, spite of Lips, and Eyes, and Mien,*
>   *Me, nothing can delight so,*
> *As does that part that lies between*
>   *Her left Toe, and her right Toe.*

One of the few women who rivalled the men at this sort of thing, Aphra Behn, makes a similar approach (though more genteel) in a poem entitled 'An Imperfect Enjoyment', to be found in *Familiar Letters of Love*, 1718. Lysander surprises Chloris in a thicket and 'presses his suit'. He starts with her breast but proceeds until

> *His daring Hand that Altar seiz'd*
> *Where Gods of Love do sacrifice;*

That awful Throne, *that* Paradice,
Where Rage *is tam'd, and* Anger *pleas'd;*
The living Fountains, *from whose* Trills,
The melted Soul *in liquid* Drops *distils.*

Lysander is impotent when it comes to the point. Chloris has
fainted with desire, but not all her charms laid out before
him can restore his virility. Awaking, she seizes his penis by
accident, and flies in shame.

As the century proceeds, writers become more vulgar and
more daring. (It is only fair to assume that readers were
equally vulgar.) The thoroughly licentious *Festival of Love*,
1770, gets near to using the common word itself. First a
description, from 'On Lady T—re—l's Ring', by Mr S——
——, is unmistakably direct.

> *Your husband gave to you a ring,*
> *Set round with jewels rare;*
> *You gave to him a better thing—*
> *A ring set round with hair.*

The E—— of S—— virtually uses the word in a Song, though
he can't quite bring himself to put it on paper. There are
eight stanzas of which this is the last.

> *Your stars and your garters, and ribbands profuse,*
> *And wide coat of arms that a beggar might quarter,*
> *How faint are their splendour, how trifling their use,*
> *Compar'd with the star that shines over the garter!*
> *The star in the front is the emblem of ——*
> *In a lovely field argent, crown'd sable, she glows,*
> *And two rampant —— as supporters we fix:*
> *Here's —— in a bumper wherever she goes!*

In the same volume a young man has to choose between three
beautiful girls. As they all seemed equally attractive he asks
them a question: which mouth is the older, the one in the
face or the one below. The first girl says it must be the upper,

because of its teeth. The second chooses the lower because it
has a beard, and isn't that a sign of age?

> *The youngest sister, smiling, said,*
> *I'm but a young and silly maid;*
> *But yet I think the mouth above*
> *Is elder than the seat of love;*
> *And what I say, I thus evince:*
> *My upper mouth was wean'd long since,*
> *And flesh and fish, and bones can eat,*
> *But mouth below longs for the teat.*
>
> 'Well Judged', by Mr T——l

It appears that there are only three ways of describing the
vagina: the poetic, the vulgar and the humorous. Flat description is useless—it is what makes so many sex manuals so
appalling. The poetic is rare in the European tradition and
when it occurs it reminds one immediately of the Oriental.
Pierre Louÿs, for instance, in *Aphrodite* (a tale set in the
classical world), turns to jewellery, natural beauty and
classical mythology for his metaphors. Chrysis demands three
crimes from Demetrios as the price of her surrender: 'For it
I shall trade you my whole body which is like a mother-of-
pearl shell opening for you, with more kisses in my mouth
than there are pearls in the sea.' Djala, Chrysis's Indian slave,
sings with her mistress a love song enumerating the beautiful
portions of Chrysis's anatomy. They sing alternate verses.
When they come to the lower portions Djala sings: 'Your
navel is a deep well in a desert of pink sand: your belly is
a young kid sleeping on the breast of its mother.' Chrysis
continues: 'My navel is a round pearl on a turned-down
cup; my delta is the clear crescent of Phoebe shining in the
forest.' The slave is now silent, the rest is too sacred to be
left to her. Chrysis continues: 'It is like a purple flower,
scented with honey and perfume. It is a sea-hydra alive and
soft that opens at night. It is the damp grotto, the always
warm shelter, the Refuge where man may repose on his march
towards death.' The prostrate slave murmurs very low, 'It is
frightening. It is the head of Medusa.'

Most writers agree that physical love is a far more significant experience for a woman than for a man. The sexual act is largely outside the body of man but inside the body of woman. The man's essence leaves him at the moment of consummation. Ideally it starts in woman another, mysterious life in which man cannot participate—even in the most beat, jazzy and abandoned intercourse, the very mechanics of a woman's body will involve her emotionally to a greater extent than a man. A man can afford to joke about the sexual act and its appurtenances more freely than a woman. Women can and do joke about sex but they are also reduced at times to another state which a man rarely experiences: one of bitterness and disillusion, the feeling of having been abused (illustrated by some of the women who turned on Lieutenant Hearn's complacency in *The Naked and the Dead*). An occasional literary joke comes from reversing the roles, showing the woman as insatiable and the man exhausted. This is never encountered in libertine literature where exhaustion is unknown. But there is an example in the *Arabian Nights*, where the wife of Goha, the Cairene clown, lies naked in her room and begins to pat her affair affectionately, exclaiming 'Dear treasure, why are there not two or three or four of you, O cause of all my joys?' At that moment Goha entered and heard these words, whereupon he brought out his inheritance and, with tears in his eyes, began to curse it, saying, 'O dog, O pimp, O cause of all my woes, why are there any of you?' ('The Master of Shifts and Laughter', 925th night, Mathers).

The best size is a matter for continual speculation. The degree of pleasure is measured entirely by the size of the parts, particularly in the East. A small vulva and a powerful penis are considered desirable. Egyptian fellahin used to divide women into three groups: in the *Schelenkijeh* the hymen breaks with a long split, and a slight loss of blood at devirgination; in the *Ennabijeh* the hymen is entirely closed but breaks at the slightest poke, like a grape, with slight loss of blood; in the *Kelbijeh* the hymen is thick, fleshy and resistant, and there is considerable loss of blood. A South Slav song describes what happens from the woman's point of view: 'When I was yet a goatsherd my vulva was like the smallest coin. A short time thereafter I was married, they bent me around like a violin bow, drove a thing in me like a crowbar and drew it out like a coulter.' The outsize organ is not appreciated. A Bosnian Pope's wife once accused him of being a sodomite. His excuse was that her vagina was so enormous 'a goose can go in there, two Turkish penes can go in there, and a board of pinewood and a German cat.'

A large one has its extrasexual uses. Cunégonde describes how she and her mother were captured by Moorish pirates. The women were stripped and the pirates poked their fingers 'into a place where we women normally admit nothing but a syringe-tube' (Candide). The Maltese Knights of St John used to examine Turkish captives in the same way.[4] Those men who have been taken as lovers by giantesses must have been faced with a rare problem. There is one in the Arabian Nights. Hasan of Basrah fell among giants and one day the princess undressed him to clean him. She was fascinated to discover that he was equipped as were male giants, and that on being touched the cucumber became a marrow. In the end Hasan behaved with her exactly as a sparrow does with its mate, but we are not given any further details.

Norman Douglas has put into verse the male complaint about the over-large vagina—or, to be exact, he has printed in his book, Some Limericks, one with fairly wide provenance. (Vide 'The Young Curate of Buckingham') In his comment he expresses a good deal of sympathy with the curate, and says that he has been tempted to make the same complaint on several occasions. It must be remembered that the women suffer equally (he quotes a young lady of Twickenham), yet Douglas has little compassion for them.

What is the biggest cunt in literature, outside giantesses? Surely the one to be found in the Nighttown episode of Joyce's Ulysses, when Bella/Bello bares his arm and plunges it elbowdeep in manwoman Bloom's vulva. 'There's a fine depth for you! What, boys? That give you a hardon?' He shoves his arm in a bidder's face. 'Here, wet the deck and wipe it round!'

Sex certainly seems to invite the spirit of hyperbole or what
might be called the surreal instinct, if such exists. This is
quite common in folk sexlore. Lawrence Durrell, in his *Black
Book*, indulges in it.

> Hilda lies open like a trunk in the corner of the room.
> There is room for everything, the gramophone, the
> records, the cottage piano, the microscope, the hair
> restorer, seven sets of clean clothes, manuscripts, a type-
> writer, a dictionary, a pair of jackboots, skates, an ice
> pick, a crash helmet, a sheath knife, a fishing rod, and
> the latest Book Society choice. There is even room for
> a portable God, if you rope it up among the canvases.
> With these labels to assure me of my distinct and unique
> personality, I step down into the red tunnel, to begin
> the journey. For the purposes of simplification, let me
> be known as Jonah. With Hilda as the whale, there are
> implications in the Bible story which have been
> altogether ignored until now. Very well! With that
> knowing look I always imagine the spermatazoa to wear
> on their faces, I slip down toward the womb, carrying
> my belongings with me. It has all been arranged, I am
> going to be walled in. Womb, then, and tomb in one!
> Plush walls, naturally, and a well-furnished house. All
> the genteel possessions of the cultured owl. . . .

Durrell (calling himself Lawrence Lucifer, an idea he picked
up from Middleton) writes of the womb as a prison. The air
is pure and sterile. He is fed through the walls with synthetic
food which passes into him every two hours without his realis-
ing it. He strolls up and down. He has now got beyond
revolution. There was a time when he was tempted to take
the ice axe and smash his way through the walls, but no
longer. There is a similar passage in Miller, with apocalyptic
overtones. It is a typical twentieth century fantasy, which
occasionally appears in a crude form in smutty stories.[5]
Some women have developed their muscles to such an
extent that they can expand and contract their vaginas to

their hearts' desire—or better still, to the desire of their men.
Douglas sings, in his invaluable guide to the Limerick, of a
girl of Detroit who possessed this capacity to a marked degree.
In one of his scholarly comments he remarks that few women
are capable of doing this. It has to be learnt, and a lot depends
on the teacher. Many, chiefly southerners, are unteachable
and others are too lazy. A pretty but phlegmatic English girl
of his acquaintance belonged to the latter class. She was
afraid of losing her lover's affection, but when Douglas
advised her on the best way of retaining it she replied, 'Oh,
but I can't be bothered like that each time.' Later it appeared
that the gentleman in question found someone who could,
and gladly would, be bothered. It is natural, of course, that
a well-used vagina should become slack. Ying Po-chüeh, a
humorous fellow in *Golden Lotus*, tells of a young lady
who found herself in this condition. Somebody told her to
put a piece of alum in, whereupon it would recover its
former tightness. She did this but it tightened her up so much
it hurt. But then, one must be prepared to suffer for love.
The *Kama Sutra* advises a method which, so far as I know,
is not attended by such unpleasant consequences. If you
plaster the vaginal orifice of a she-elephant woman (that's
the kind we're discussing) with the ground fruit of the
kokilaksha plant, the orifice will contract in one night.

Finally, two oddities. Some young women are afraid that
their rabbits will wear away to nothing with over-use. No
need to worry. They are consoled by Sir John Davies in his
eighth *Epigram*.

> *In Katam*
> *Kate being pleas'd, wisht that her pleasure could*
> *Indure as long as a buff jerkin would*
> *Content thee Kate, although thy pleasure wasteth*
> *Thy pleasures place like a buffe jerkin lasteth.*
> *For no buffe jerkin hath bin oftner worne*
> *Nor hat more scrapings, or more dressings borne.*

And at the other extreme, the woman who imagines she has

a penis. She is no heroine of libertine literature but an occasional character out of the casebooks. The Alderians say she suffers from a consciousness of sexual inferiority. She gets sexual stimulation from minor acts of a masculine character, such as sitting on a chair backwards with her legs each side of the back, wearing clothes of a masculine cut, or performing a masculine gesture such as stroking an imaginary moustache. She wishes she had no cunt.

Clitoris

This little organ, though immensely important in the inducing of pleasure, is rarely mentioned in erotic writing. One wouldn't expect it to be, except perhaps in the fantasies of the hyperbolists. But there is one very interesting passage in *Stradella* which is well worth quoting because it happens. Poor Archie is trying to find it and his jaws ache.

> 'Not there . . . up a little . . . that's the spot . . . now easy . . . no, lower. Lower! O! O!' She made some joy sounds, then cursed. 'I don't know what's wrong! You hit the spot every night and morning last week! Now you can't seem to find it at all!'
> 'But maybe it's just not there any more.'
> 'No, it is! It is! You don't know where to try.'
> 'But I am trying. I did try. The spot's moved. Here let me try again. My jowls are throbbing Stell—Stradella. I can't find it. I can't!'
> 'No, it hasn't moved! It hasn't. It's still there! You don't know where to look. Keep trying. Keep looking.'

Yet Archie was right. It does move.

Trust Sade to produce a worldbeater. In *Juliette* there is a lady named Volmar who is fitted with a clitoris three inches long, and, 'destined to insult Nature whichever be the sex she adopts, the whore's got either to play the nymphomaniac or the sodomite: with her, there's no median alternative.'

Breasts

Breasts go in and out of season. At the moment they're in, especially in America. On the whole, opinion is polarised quite positively. Men either find them immensely alluring or repulsive.

Arabs, liking flesh in quantity, naturally tend to admire big breasts, just as they admire big bellies and big buttocks. It is not surprising that the most poetic appraisal of a woman's breasts that I know comes from the *Arabian Nights*. Kamar gazes on his bride and recalls what a poet wrote:

> *Sleeper, oh do not move; your breasts in sleep,*
> *Allah, they dip and fall like waves at sea;*
> *Your breasts are snow, I breathe them like sea foam,*
> *I taste them like white salt. They dip and fall.*
>
> *Sleeper, they dip and fall. The smiling stream*
> *Stifles its laugh, the gold bee on the leaf*
> *Dies of much love and rosy drunkenness,*
> *My eyes burn the red grapes upon your breast.*
>
> *Sleeper, oh let them burn, let my heart's flower,*
> *Fed on the rose and santal of your flesh,*
> *Burst like a poppy in this solitude,*
> *In this cool silence.*

> 'Tale of Kamar al Zaman and Princess Budur',
> 206th night, trs. MATHERS

A typical English appreciation of the breast is to be found in a manuscript poem by Herrick in the Bodleian, called *The Descripcion: of a Woman*. It is very detailed and rich in imagery, sensual but never obscene. The relevant lines are these.

> *Her brest (a place for beawtyes throne most fitt)*
> *Beares up two globes where loue and pleasure sitt*
> *Which headed with twoe rich round rubies showe*
> *Like wanton rose buds growing out of snowe. . . .*

Eighteenth century literature does not enthuse greatly over
breasts, which makes their treatment in one of John Hall
Stevenson's *Crazy Tales* all the more interesting. This is not
poetry but rhyming ribaldry. Stevenson was born in York-
shire in 1718 and died in 1785. He was a friend of Laurence
Sterne and was the model for Eugenius in *Tristram Shandy*.
'Anthony's Tale, or the Boarding House Tale', appears in
the 1894 reprint.

> *Lucy was not like other lasses,*
> *From twelve her breasts swell'd in a trice,*
> *First they were like two cupping-glasses,*
> *Then like two peaches made of ice.*

Her mother worries about the child's maturity.

> *It is a shame, says her Mamma,*
> *To see a child with bib and apron,*
> *At BARE thirteen, an age so RAW,*
> *Grown and furnish'd like a matron.*

> *But if it was a burning shame,*
> *LUCY was not at all to blame,*
> *But they, who in their composition,*
> *Infus'd that warmth, which was the cause*
> *Of such exuberant nutrition,*
> *The work of vegetative laws.*

But the point of the story is that, whatever mother might
feel, a certain Captain of the Guards, who began by courting
the parent, became inflamed by the sight of Lucy's bosom:

> *Contemplating her breasts as round,*
> *And springy as a tennis ball.*

In the following century Madamoiselle de Maupin, posing
as the Chevalier Théodore de Sérannes, muses on the advant-

ages enjoyed by men in love. As Rosette leans back and casts aside her mantle, displaying the upper part of her bosom, Maupin imagined the pleasure of letting her lips wander over the smooth fine skin. Men have nothing as good to offer. Later, when Maupin discloses her true identity and offers herself to D'Albert he is fired by the sight of her bosom, which is no less fine than Rosette's. D'Albert delicately broke the lacing of her dress 'so that the body opened and the two white treasures appeared in all their splendour; upon the bosom which was as sparkling and as clear as silver bloomed the two beautiful roses of paradise. He pressed their vermilion points lightly in his mouth, and thus went over the whole outline.'

After such delicacy it is anti-climax to return to Russian love. The Russians, as might be expected, desire women who are brimming with health and bulging with embonpoint, and for evidence we can go to the anonymous author of *A Woman in Berlin*. The most popular woman in the district was Frau B., the distiller's wife. The janitor's youngest daughter would dash into the flat crying, 'They're after her again.' Frau B. was the fattest woman in the quarter. Among the Russians, we are told, fat equals beauty because it's more female, more distinct from the male body. Our author adds that among primitive people fat women are revered as symbols of abundance and fertility. King Mutesa I of the Baganda used to feed his wives on cream. They became so fat that they could not stand but had to roll round the floor. In Berlin fat women were scarce. Age didn't matter.

Now let's turn to the opposition. There is, unexpectedly, an attack on fat women in the *Arabian Nights*, but it is made by a thin girl in the course of a debate. She addresses a fat friend.

> O mass of grease and flesh, when you walk, you are a duck; when you eat, you are an elephant. You are insatiable in copulation and unreasonable in repose.
>
> What member is long enough to reach the cave hidden so deep between three mountains, your belly and two thighs?

Even if a man wins to it he is immediately bounced
back by your swollen belly.

'Tale of the Six Different Coloured Girls',
337th night, trs. MATHERS

There is no actual mention of the bosom here, but we can
assume it would not win much favour. Nor can we expect
Sade to take much interest in breasts, except as objects of
torture. In *Justine* Roland tells Justine that in 'mammaeist-
ical matters' she is inferior to Suzanne, and impresses his point
by nipping her breasts with his fingers until he punctures
them. A more considered, Chinese view of large breasts is to
be found in *Evelyn Innes*. Owen is a very sophisticated man
who cannot bear the slightest vulgarity—and he viewed a
big bosom with abhorrence. Yet he was in a dilemma, because
Evelyn was an opera singer and he was a dedicated opera-
goer. He often wondered if she was built stoutly enough to
be the great singer he would like her to be, yet if she were
she could not be his mistress. Evelyn was by no means flat-
chested, 'and he remembered certain curves and plenitudes
with satisfaction'. There is elsewhere a hint that Owen
admired buttocks but Moore is one of the least carnal of
writers. All his erotic effects are the result of suggestion.

Summing up, we can't expect breasts to be mentioned by
erotic writers unless they please. The whole basis of erotic
writing is the description of pleasure and by it the giving
of pleasure. Time is not wasted on displeasing effects. If a
libertine dislikes large breasts he ignores them. There is a
type of writer, the fantasist of the Piombo type, who will
devote himself to large breasts because of their very grossness,
but such writers are rare. The realist naturally describes huge
breasts, pore by pore, but that is only because they exist. Here,
for instance, is Zola, writing about the widow Désir who kept
a bar and a dance hall. She was reputedly an ardent lover,
despite her size.

. . . she seemed so vast, with a pair of breasts each one of
which required a man to embrace it. Rumour had it that

nowadays she had to have two of her weekday lovers
each night to cope with the job.

Germinal, trs. L. W. TANCOCK

As we have frequently noticed, literature and popular folklore are like two horses harnessed together. The above passage
recalls a joke current during the late thirties, that a certain
popular film actress, famed for her sex appeal and physical
development, used to take her lovers two abreast when in a
hurry.

Nipples

Red grapes, rubies, rose buds and roses of paradise, vermilion
points—all of these luscious descriptions of the mammary
climax are taken from the short preceding section. Rude men
sometimes refer to themselves as 'tit-men', meaning they love
the softness of the breast and the contrasting hardness of the
roused nipple. Others are indifferent and devote themselves
to other parts. Women also vary. Some can be brought to
orgasm by stroking of the nipples alone; others appear to be
dead to feeling in that region. The glorious variety of sex.

The unrivalled poet of the Nipple is Robert Herrick. One
of his favourite conceits was his description of the female body
in terms of fruits and flowers, especially as regards colour.
To him nipples on the breast were strawberries in cream.
Here are two charming examples taken from his *Hesperides*.

Upon the Nipples of Julia's Breast

Have ye beheld (with much delight)
A red-Rose peeping through a white?
Or else a Cherrie (double grac't)
Within a Lillies Center plac't?
Or ever mark't the pretty beam,
A Strawberry shewes half drown'd in Creame?
Or seen rich Rubies blushing through
A pure smooth Pearle, and Orient too?
So like to this, nay all the rest,
Is each neate Niplet of her breast.

Fresh Cheese and Cream

Wo'd ye have fresh Cheese and Cream?
Julia's Breast can give you them:
And if more; Each Nipple cries,
To your Cream, here's Strawberries.

There is not so much to be said or written about the nipple.
It is there to be enjoyed, to be rolled between thumb and
forefinger, to be caressed by the tip of the tongue, or nipped
by the teeth. They vary considerably in size and astonishingly
in their surrounds. But libertine writers do not spend much
time on this feature; it is, after all, merely a station on the
way to the true cross of all believers. And yet there is a
remarkable discourse on nipples in a book which can certainly not be termed erotic in intent, but I know of nothing
to rival it. The book is *My Happy Days in Hell*, by George
Faludi, and the passage is worth quoting at length. One of
the characters is a *bon vivant* named Lorsy who can talk
endlessly on any subject. He has become friendly in France
with a bawd and matchmaker named Marfa, whom he regarded as much an expert in love as Ovid or Aretino or
Stendhal.

We were talking about the colour of the female nipple.
Dear Marfa told me that she had to ask only middle-aged
men endowed with extraordinary intellectual capacities
what colour of nipple they preferred. With the others
she always knew, from their manners, their character,
their occupation, their appearance; and men were always
flabbergasted when she told them straight away whether
they liked red, pink or brown nipples, small, medium
or large. Here, dear Marfa gave me a few interesting
pointers: according to her, high-class intellectuals and
complex sensualists usually want women with small, pink
nipples; strong male animals prefer brown nipples, while
men who have once been orphan children or are sorrow-
ing widowers, liked to rest in the shadow of large, red

nipples. The real stags—those who don't care what kind of woman they embrace—have, of course, no preferences. Dear Marfa emphasised, however, that the problem of nipples was merely secondary, even the most sensual of men regard the physical-spiritual qualities of a woman as more important than the colour and size of her nipples. Yet the nipple of a woman is like the buffer of a train; when you run after a train it is the buffer you see, and when you recall one or other of your mistresses it is, at least subconsciously, her nipple to which you react.

Dear Marfa found that in the analysis of the highly complex relationship between man and woman the not so very important nipple supplies the only fixed point. Given this fulcrum, to use Archimedes' words, she lifted love out from its orbit and classified men into precise categories according to the nipple they preferred. To be exact—she explained with a very happy smile—all she had to do was to find the coat to go with the button. And this brilliant intellectual feat provided her with the perfect guide in the intricate trade of procuring.

Backside

Big and fleshy for the Arabs, of course—but by no means only for them. The same applies here as I have said already about breasts and nipples. If a writer likes them he writes enthusiastically about them. If he doesn't, he ignores them and turns to more attractive objects. It is, after all, a literature of pleasure.

The Arabs are by far the best in this field of enquiry, and so I confine my illustrations to the *Arabian Nights*. When Land Abdallah visited the underwater king he was asked questions about various parts of his body. He told the king that among human beings nothing is so esteemed in a man as a good weighty zabb and nothing in a woman so much as a jutting backside. "Tale of Land Abdallah and Sea Abdallah', 514th night.) Princess Janharah had an incomparable backside: 'heavy, tender, firm and self-possessed, curved deliciously each way' ('Tale of Pomegranate Flower and Badr Basim', 536th night, trs. Mathers). In 'White Hair' (378th night) we read of a woman whose face is made up youthfully but whose hair is white. She is asked why she does not disguise her hair also, and her reply hints at a possible reason for backside-adulation.

> I used to dye my hair
>   But time undyed it.
>   Now I am sage,
> I show my bottom bare
>   Which does not age.
>   (I used to hide it).[6]

But the two most impressive backsides in the whole of the Thousand and One nights belonged to a couple of slave girls. One was taken to the king. Her beauties were enumerated: 'as for that blessing of Allah, her most desirable bum, it was so vast that the merchant had not been able to find a veil great enough to cover it.' ('Pomegranate Flower and Badr Basim', 526th night, Mathers). And then there is the one who opened the door to Prince Diamond. 'Truthfully, if she had not gone further to meet Diamond it was because the heavy haunches slung to so slight a waist prevented her, and because her backside, dimpled with valleys, was so remarkable a benediction that she could not move easily without it trembling like curdled milk in a Badawi's porringer or quince jelly heaped on a plate perfumed with benzoin.' ('Splendid Tale of Prince Diamond', 911th night, Mathers.)

Legs and Ankles

Legs have usually interested Europeans more than backsides. Backsides are happenings whereas legs are signposts. On the whole, legs are praised during periods when access to more intimate portions is restricted. The modern breast-fetich has replaced the pre-war leg fetich because naked legs are now on show all day long.

That legs can attract the male at a very early stage is made clear by Frank Harris in his *My Life and Adventures*. He used to drop his pencil at school so that he could crawl on the floor and look at the girls' legs. One pair were particularly beautiful, especially as the sunlight shone right on them: 'they filled me with emotion giving me an indescribable pleasure.' At first he thought he liked the thickest legs best, but these were comparatively slender. A few years later one of his sisters, who had just reached puberty, invited him to touch her breasts, but this did not give him the thrill the sight of those legs had given him.

The most interesting accounts of leg-adoration naturally belong to the days when legs were virtually taboo. In *Anne of Geierstein* we find Sir Walter Scott describing a woman whose clothes came down below the middle of the leg 'but suffered the ankle, in all its fine proportions, to be completely visible'. But much more astonishing is this description from an extremely frank erotic work, *The Memoirs of Dolly Morton*.

> Dolly leant back in an easy chair, with her feet, in smart velvet slippers, resting on a stool, and as her skirts were slightly raised, I was able to see her trim ankles cased in pale blue silk stockings.

The narrator is obviously excited by what he sees, and yet he has already fucked her several times.

Anything about a woman can be seductive—a fetich need not even be part of her body. Men do not usually get excited by wrists, yet functionally they resemble ankles. The main difference, of course, is that they are further removed from the object of the pilgrimage. In the 'Tale of Happy-Handsome and Happy-Fair' (*Arabian Nights*) the former actually saw nothing of the latter on their first meeting except 'the joints of her tender wrists'. But it was enough; and 'he loved her hotly, for wrists so beautiful had need belong to an exquisite body'.

Coat and button again. But often we men are deceived,

walking behind a shapely pair of legs or a waggling bottom
or an hour-glass waist or a swanlike neck.

Scent and Taste

The personal perfume of women has frequently been the
object of a man's adulation. It is a recurrent conceit in
Herrick.

On Julia's Breath

Breathe, Julia, breathe, and Ile protest,
* Nay more, Ile deeply sweare,*
That all the spices of the East
* Are circumfused there.*

Upon Julia's Sweat

Wo'd ye oyle of Blossomes get?
Take it from my Julia's sweat:
Oyl of Lillies, and of Spike,
From her moysture take the like:
Let her breath, or let her blow,
All rich spices thence will flow.

Sir Kenelm Digby, looking upon the body of the sleeping
Venetia Stanley, observed how 'out of that darkness did glisten
a few drops of sweat like diamond sparks, and had a more
fragrant odour than the violets or primroses'. It was said of
Sweet Nelly Fowler, a fashionable whore of the 1860's, that
'this beautiful girl had a natural perfume, so delicate, so
universally admitted, that love-sick swains paid large sums
for the privilege of having their handkerchiefs placed under
their Goddess's pillow, and sweet Nelly pervaded—in spirit
if not in flesh—half the clubs and drawing rooms of London'.
Men can be equally admired for the same reason. One of
H. G. Wells's lovers was once asked why she was so fascinated
by him. She was certainly expected to reply on account of
his intelligence or some such quality but instead remarked
that he smelt of 'honey, pure honey'.

It scarcely comes as a surprise to find that Sade also wrote in praise of smell, but in his case it was the viler the better. *120 Days of Sodom* overemphasises coprophagy in the opinion of many critics. On the nineteenth day the diet was changed to produce a superior shit. It was felt that this might have some effect on the breath, but Curval could see nothing in this to disturb them. A mouth without odour gives no pleasure, he said—and so, in the normal Sadian line of reasoning, the more odour the more pleasure. 'However clean may be the mouth, the lover who sucks it assuredly does an unclean thing, and there is no doubt at all in his mind that it is that very uncleanness that pleases him. Give a somewhat greater degree of strength to the impulse and you'll want that mouth to be impure.'

With the breath we must associate the voice. Many men have been seduced by a sexiness in the voice—is it imaginary or is it based on observation? It is usually said to be husky. An obvious association can be noted here, for after intercourse many women's voices drop a tone or two. Men had little doubt about the sexual quality of Evelyn Innes's voice. Apt enough in Wagner, it caused her acute embarrassment when she sang with the nuns while in retreat at the convent. She was surprised to find how expressive the antique chant was when sung by their etiolated, sexless voices. 'She had never known how much of her life of passion and desire had entered into her voice, and she was shocked at its impurity. Her singing sounded like silken raiment among sackcloth, and she lowered her voice, feeling it to be indecorous and out of place. . . .' She was afraid she must have revealed her past life to the nuns and shocked them.

Finally, with smell is associated taste, and the licking of a woman's body and the sucking of certain more succulent portions plays an important part in the lover's routine. Examples are unnecessary, but the unusual and the exotic are always worth recording. Any passionate lover wishes to devour his or her mate, and it is well known that this is taken literally in the insect world. But Giacomo, a red-haired and bearded farmer and cheesemaker in André Pieyre de Mandiar-

gues's *The Girl Beneath the Lion*, made a real dish of it.
When Vanina, a *contessina*, was a child, she would sit on a
ladder in a shed and taste the fresh cheeses. Giacomo used to
plunge his hand into a vat and rub her legs and thighs with
a mixture of cream cheese and whey. Then he took off her
shoes and underclothes and rubbed her whole body up to
her chin under her loose dress. He said this would give her
a smooth skin all over; the *contesse* had always used this recipe
and found it successful. Sometimes he would set the little girl
high up on the ladder and 'he would lick her feet, lick her
thighs, her belly, snorting like a horse, threatening that she
tasted so good he would eat her down to the bones'. Medea
had to do the same to Giacomo, but she used whey. She was
only a bailiff's daughter.

Female Geography

The comparison of the female body with a mysterious land
that lies spread out for the explorer, is a familiar one, particularly during the seventeenth and eighteenth centuries, a
period when literature as a whole was closely concerned with
exploration of one kind and another. One of the best known
is Swift's 'Love's Progress', 1669.

We should love a woman not for her beauty, nor for her
virtue or her soul, but for what she alone possesses. Cupid
dwells underground.

> *Men to such Gods, their sacrificing Coles*
> *Did not in Altars lay, but pits and holes.*
> *Although we see Celestial bodies move*
> *Above the Earth, the earth we Till and love:*
> *So we her ayres contemplate, words and heart,*
> *And virtues; but we love the Centrique part.*

The lover sets sail from the hair, a Forest of ambushes. He
crosses the face and neck and passes between the 'Sestos and
Abydos of her breasts'. Afterwards there

> *Succeeds a boundless sea, but yet thine eye*
> *Some Island moles may scattered there descry;*
> *And Sailing towards her India, in that way*
> *Shall at her fair Atlantick Navell stay;*
> *Though thence the Current be Thy Pilot made,*
> *Yet ere thou be where thou wouldst be embay'd,*
> *Thou shalt upon another Forest set,*
> *Where many Shipwreck, and no further get.*
> *When thou art there, consider what this chace*
> *Mispent by the beginning at the face.*

In other words, it's much better to approach from the foot. Nature has given women two purses. If you want to pay into the lower one, you should take the low road. (Undoubtedly the great popularity of Sir Harry Lauder's song is partly due to its sexual symbolism.)

The following ('A Riddle', by L—— W—— R——), taken from the *Festival of Love*, is cartographical rather than geographical. This appeared almost exactly one century later than Swift's, and typifies the change in imagery that had taken place.

> *In infancy I knew a spot,*
>   *Where flowers ne'er had blown;*
> *Where creeping moss had never got,*
>   *Where seed was never sown:*
> *But when to years maturer grown,*
>   *The spot was deck'd with flowers,*
> *Seed flourish'd whensoever sown,*
>   *And lik'd reviving showers.*

> *Within this little snug retreat,*
>   *A cooling fountain plays;*
> *Here Venus did Narcissus treat,*
>   *And spent their youthful days.*
> *The stream, they nam'd the Milky Way,*
>   *'Cause of its cooling pow'r;*
> *Here Titus sighed to lose a day!*
>   *And I to lose an hour.*

Around this fount a shady grove,
  To lovely Venus dear;
Where all the Loves and Graces rove,
  And wanton all the year.
The only grove where Ida's dove
  Is known to build her nest;
Wherein the little God of love
  Creeps from his mother's breast.

A smoother plain beyond the fount
  Extends thou Tempe sweet,
Whereon appears a little mount,
  Which Cupid makes his seat;
Two snowy mountains rise above,
  Fairest beneath the skies;
Which Venus nam'd the hills of love,
  Because, when prest they rise.

An interesting excursion in this vein is to be found in
Stradella. Here the imagery is agricultural, and rises into a
delirium in the modern manner (see Miller, Durrell, Burroughs).

She folded her arms around me. She lay on her back
and buried my head in her breasts. Tentatively I kissed
her nipples, a weightless fly flitting over her. They
hardened and expanded, a ripe fruit unpeeled in her
bed and laid bare. She plucked me like a dandelion. I
sank my toe in her apple. She spread me over the sides
of the bed, and sat herself down on me, a sea wave,
corking breath. I impaled her with a finger. On her knees
she moaned into the cushions. I held her above me,
speared on my thumb, and spun her. She clutched blindly
at my stem like a lariat and whirled me. Every place that
I touched on her skin broke out like a wound, ripe and
rosy. The tongue in my head, not a word on it, tilled
her furrows and curves. She became a ripe pasture. The
wounds broke out in blossoms. The curves turned to

creeks of sweat. Her whole body ran like ore, a mother
lode of golden bronze tan.

Decoration

> If black, 'tis odds, she's dev'lish proud;
> If short, Zantippe like too loud,
>   If long, she'll lazy be:
> Foolish (the proverb says) if fair;
> If wise and comely, Danger's there,
>   Lest she do Cuckold thee.

'The Wife-Hater', *Pills to Purge Melancholy*

Some of these judgments have remained remarkably constant. The odalisque of the cartoons is always remarkably
long. The dumb blonde is always with us. And yet (so they
say) Gentlemen Prefer Blondes. Ibn Hazm, who wrote *The
Ring of the Dove* in the eleventh century, confessed that he
was mad about blondes. In a chapter entitled 'Of Falling in
Love with a Quality and Thereafter not Approving any Other
Different', he said he knew men who insisted on short necks,
short stature or a wide mouth. But as for himself:

> In my youth I loved a slave-girl who happened to be a
> blonde; from that time I have never admired brunettes,
> not though their dark tresses set off a face as resplendent
> as the sun, or the very image of beauty itself. I find this
> taste to have become a part of my whole make up and
> constitution since those early days; my soul will not
> suffer me to acquire any other, or to love any type but
> that. This very same thing happened to my father also
> (God be pleased with him!) and he remained faithful to
> his first preference until the terms of his earthly life was
> done.

He adds that all the Caliphs of the Bani Marwan (God have
mercy on their souls!), especially the sons of Al Nasir, had
taste. In fact, taste became hereditary for all of them with
the exception of Suleiman al Zafir (God have especial mercy
on him!). He had black ringlets and a black beard.

I have called this section Decoration, and I am thinking
chiefly of the ways in which women beautify themselves. This
is naturally no place in which to go into details. I am trying
to provide the exceptional and the exotic, yet at the same
time to state the norm. The colour of a woman's hair need
not be natural, and in sophisticated societies the colour of
her face rarely is. As for clothes, they belong to Laver. And
so my illustrations will be few and brief. For instance, we
are naturally interested in a whore who refuses to paint. This
was Moll Flanders. Even at the age of forty-two she set herself out to the best advantage 'except painting, for that I
never stooped to, and had pride enough to think I did not
want it'. Some people think that a whore has no right to use
a phrase such as 'would not stoop' but they are wrong. In
her profession Moll behaved as she was convinced nature
intended, but nature naturally had a low opinion of paint.
Yet even Moll succumbed a few years later when trying to
win the favours of an old knight. For the first time she used a
little art: 'I say for the first time, for I had never yielded to
the baseness of paint before, having always had vanity enough
to believe I had no need of it.'
   Here is a really grand painting job, practically Royal
Academy. It comes from *The Barbarians*, by Van Wyck
Mason. The author forsakes Airbase Murders, Legation
Murders and Spy Murders and tries his hand at history. It is
the heyday of Cathage, when the burly Cealwyn, son of Penda
of Mercia but now a slave, is unaccountably selected by the
Suffeta Tiratha (co-ruler of Carthage with her uncle Adherbal)
as a lover. He watches the Roman slave girl, Valeria, paint
her mistress.

> Brushes of camel's hair and swallow's wings deftly painted
> the Suffeta's eyelids with a coating of antimony; her
> cheekbones were touched with crimson rouge, then over-
> toned with a mask of some bronze tint. Tiratha's lips
> were painted with a fresh covering of carmine.
>   The lazily supine woman's shoulders were dusted with
> a powder that sent off a blood-quickening scent. The

matchless breasts were first gently rubbed with perfumed oils, then brightened at their points by the application of a crimson salve. Valeria, the girl slave, next anointed Tiratha's sleek flanks, her hips, her thighs and legs, with glistening oil until the Suffeta gleamed in the uncertain light of the lamps like one of her own leopards and, like the watchful cats, purred her contentment. . . .

The ten finely rounded nails of Tiratha's tiny feet were skilfully made scarlet as Cealwyn watched. Then, as a last ministration, the Roman girl reached for a sandal-wood box filled with gold dust. Using a hare's foot, Valeria brushed the Suffeta's body with light strokes, setting the gleaming particles on the oiled skin in every shadowed hollow. When she was finished, Tiratha lay there, sleek and sparkling, a figure of unreal and extravagant beauty.

Now she has to dress. Her hair is twisted in a heavy coil, nearly a foot high, secured with gold pins and encircled by a rope of matched pearls. She wraps a filmy green chiton round herself, puts on a wide belt set with square-cut agates, soft antelope-hide sandals, heavy silver bracelets in the form of twining serpents, and many rings on her fingers. Finally she fastens the badge of the virgin to her ankles, the fine gold chain. That must have surprised Cealwyn.

Why did Tiratha dress? Perhaps she had an appointment. But clothes (we are told) increase the seductiveness and the mystery. Women never agree among themselves why they wear clothes. Many of them claim it is done to impress other women, but this doesn't agree very well with their tendency, on certain occasions, to wear as few clothes as possible. About the mystery there can be little doubt where children are concerned. Professor Joad told us that as a child he believed women were solid down to their ankles. George Moore said that as a young man he was absorbed in the life of women— 'the mystery of petticoats, so different from the staidness of trousers! the rolls of hair entwined with so much art, and suggesting so much colour and perfume, so different from the bare crop; the unnaturalness of the waist in stays!, etc., etc.'.

In modern times women have been subjected to continual complaints about indecent dress. They show too much bosom or too much leg or too much midriff. It is a good thing to realise that they have not always been the offenders. In 'The Persones Tale' of Chaucer the Sin of Pride expressed itself in luxurious male apparel: 'Upon that other syde, to speken of the horrible disordinat scantnesse of clothing, has been thise cutted sloppes or hainselins, that thurgh hir shortnesse ne covere nat the shameful membres of man, to wikked entente. Allas! somme of hem shewen the boce of hir shap, and the horrible swollen membres, that semeth lyk the maladie of hirnia, in the wrappings of hir hoses; and eek the buttocks of hem faren as it were the hindre part of a she-ape in the fulle of the mone.'[7]

FOOTNOTES

1. Sidon.

2. But apparently didn't die.

3. The Lawn is rarely referred to, but there is one striking example in the American classic, *Memoirs of Dolly Morton*. Miss Dean, a pure Quakeress, is stripped and beaten for helping runaway slaves. Her spot was covered with a 'thick forest of glossy dark brown hair'. The locks were nearly two inches long. One man said, 'By Gosh! I've never seen such a fleece between a woman's legs in my life. Darn me if she wouldn't have to be sheared before man could get into her.'

4. A popular joke goes like this. An old man and his daughter were returning from market, when they were attacked by robbers. After searching the couple, the robbers made off with the horse and cart. The old man began to bewail his luck but the girl produced the bag of gold, representing the day's takings, from her vagina. 'If only your mother had been here,' said the thankless father, 'we would have saved the horse and cart too.'

5. Example: Parsimonious fellow withdraws, leaving his precious french letter behind. Puts in fingers, hand, arm, and eventually climbs in himself. Meets another fellow and asks if he has seen a letter. No, says the other, but have you seen a steam roller?

6. This is true. I have seen a naked woman with the body of a young girl, which I believed her to be, as she covered her face with her hands. When she took them away I found she was sixty.

7. sloppes: loose garments; hainselins: short jackets; boce: protuberance; faren: behave.

7: *Male Virility*

The basic assumption of all pornography and a great deal of erotic writing in general is that the male organ, whatever name we give to it (there are scores in any one language), is the foundation of sexual pleasure. These writings are usually by men, who may be expected to consult their own feelings first; but even when the woman is considered it is also assumed, often quite naïvely that, her pleasure depends entirely upon male equipment and performance. Crudely, the bigger the better.

The eighteenth century, in what it considered polite literature and we still would not, expressed its wonder and admiration at the penis again and again. A favourite convention was a Post Bag anthology. One of these (actually published in 1692) was called *The Post-boy Rob'd of his Mail, or the Pacquet Broke Open*. A group of gentlemen, bored by a wet summer, are provoked into robbing the mail. They read and discuss each letter. The fourth is from a young son of the Muses at the University, with verses, and is addressed to the Ingenious Author of the *Gentlemam's Journal*, to be left for him at the Latin Coffee-House in Ave Mary Lane, London. The verses are sex riddles, suggestive but reserved.

Coll. Magd. Oxon. June, 1962
The RIDDLE
Riddle my Riddle, my ree,
And tell me what my Riddle shall be.
Long, white and slender,
Tickles Maids where they are tender;
Lyes where Hair grows,
And has long slit under the Nose.

Second RIDDLE

Come up, come over, come under,
I'll make thee believe I'll kill thee;
I'll put that that's thine
Into mine,
And make thy Tail waggle behind thee.

I'll inform you what these two Riddles mean; for tho'
they seem a little Roguish, the first is only a *Bodkin*, and
the second the *Milking of a Cow*.

The last item in a ladies' collection, called *The School of
Venus*, 1739, more than seems Roguish. It is. A familiar name
for the male organ at this time was Arbor Vitae, just as the
female organ was sometimes referred to as Frutex Vulvaria.
Both terms are used here. Arbor Vitae, or the Tree of Life,
is a succulent Plant (we are told). It consists of a straight
stem at the top of which is a Pistillum, or Apex, sometimes
Glandiform and resembling a May-Cherry, but at other times
more like the nut of the Avillana or Filbert Tree. Fruit,
two in number, grow near the root, and are contained in one
strong Siliqua, or purse. The whole root of this plant is thick
set with numerous Fibrillae, or Capillary Tendrils.

It is produced in most countries, tho' it thrives more in
some than in others, where it also increases to a larger
Size. The Height here in England rarely passes nine
or eleven Inches, and that chiefly in Kent; whereas in
Ireland it comes to far greater dimensions; is so good,
that many of the Nations intirely subsists upon it and,
when transplanted, have been sometimes known to raise
good Houses with single plants of the sort.

If the Irish soil is the best for it the worst is near Harborough
and the Forest of Sherwood. It is very sensitive in so far as it
rises and extends itself when handled by a lady. But it must
be kept away from a certain poisonous *Vulvaria*, often mis-

taken for the wholesome one. A tall, thriving tree may soon be covered with *fungus Excrescences*. These venomous *Vulvaria* are commonly found in the Gardens about London, such as St James's Park and Vauxhall.

A fairly straightforward description of this tree is to be found in 'The Delights of Venus', which purports to be a translation from Meursius (*The Cabinet of Love*, 1718). Tullia is speaking:

> It is defin'd, a hollow boneless *part*,
> Of better use, and nobler than the heart;
> With mouth, but without eyes; it has a head
> Soft as the lips, and as the cherry red;
> The —— hang dangling in their hairy ——,
> From whence proceed the spring of tickling floods.
> Good —— should be both thick as well as tall,
> Your F—— D—— are a size too small,
> At first they're hardly in our —— contain'd;
> For maidenheads are by much labour gain'd:
> But men, well furnish'd with stout ——, are wont
> To force their passage through a bleeding ——.

The Size of It

Forcing the passage being such an important act, in the view of the average erotic writer, the size of the organ is of prime importance. No true eroteur can abide a small prick, except for humorous purposes. There is fancy within fancy; the inner fancy permits something exiguous and slender. Male reality can become an eroteur's fantasy.

Let us begin with reality, if Van de Velde is to be trusted. He states that the empty vagina, in a state of sexual repose, has an average length of 7½ to 10 cms; 7½ for the length of the front or anterior wall from *introitus* to *portio*, and 10 for the posterior wall up to the *vaginal vault or fornix*. For purposes of insertion or intromission we may reckon the vaginal passage as 10 cms long. But the length of the axis or medial line of the erect penis on the dorsal side is 15 cms. There is

obviously a disparity here but penetration does not take
place up to the root and the vagina is elastic. It may be a
surprise to many to hear that inadequate development in
these regions is rarer among men than among women, for
it is men who tend to worry about inadequacy. Erotic literature may have had some responsibility for these fears. The
two ways in which a man may fall short of what is required
are through defective seminal fluid and smallness of the erect
phallos. Such men are rarely able to satisfy women, partly
because the coitive friction is insufficient and partly because
their coitive urges are slight. It is true that unusually large
male organs are commoner than unusually small ones, but
extreme cases of the kind frequently encountered in literature
are very rare. The state is conspicuously hereditary and runs
in families. It is also racial. The belief that Negroes are better
endowed than Whites is not a myth. There are more 'phallic
giants' among Negroes than among Caucasians. A large penis
must be more agreeable to women but there are exceptions,
particularly at the beginning of sexual relations or where the
vagina is still in an infantile state.

The *Arabian Nights* have their fair share of enormous
zabbs. An amusing poem in 'The Tale of the Yellow Youth',
520th night, trs. Mathers, describes the misgivings of a woman
when faced by something more fearsome than she bargained
for:

> She put down her hands and sighed,
> Clasped the blossom of her middle
> With her fingers and replied:
> 'Fairest teeth need daily scraping
> With an aromatic twig;
> Chastest parts will sigh for raping
> With a something bold and big.
> Mussulmans, has this not wrung you?
> Is there not a zabb among you?'
> Here I felt him crack his joint
> While the vehemence which swelled him
> Lifted up the clothes which held him

To a noticeable point.
So I let him out, but she
Started back in terror:
'I said twig, and here's a tree,
Is there not some error?'

The criterion of male virility is certainly the size of the zabb
but caution is advised in 'The Boy and the Rubber', 504th
night, Mathers, on the grounds that a wise man does not judge
by appearances. The boy went to a hammam where he was
greatly admired by the rubber, except for one unfortunate
circumstance: his prick was minute. 'How can a shepherd
lean on a crook no larger than one joint of his little finger?'
he asks. The boy is ashamed and asks the rubber to bring
a girl so that he can develop the little creature. The rubber
is astonished by his innocence: 'This poor boy thinks that a
zabb is made of soft toffee and can be pulled out immediately
to any length with the fingers. Does he imagine that a cucumber grows in a day or that a banana ripens before it is a
banana!' As the boy has offered money the rubber thinks
he might as well bring along his wife and keep it all in the
family. She is equally abashed; the boy's equipment was
scarcely as big as a nut. But what a surprise they had. The
zabb began to stir and they soon realised that its smallness
was only an appearance, 'since it was of that kind which
retires almost wholly into its father's bosom when at rest. . . .
Suddenly it sprang erect, as great as an ass's or an elephant's,
a powerful sight to see.'

The *Arabian Nights* also possess a variant on the Nordic
tale of the simple woodman and his wife who were granted
three wishes by a fairy. Mathers calls this story 'The Three
Wishes' (502nd night). The wife is to blame in this version,
for whatever Kinsey was to say later in America she herself
wanted something larger than she had in Arabia. 'You know
that the perfection of man and his delight are rooted in his
manhood,' says she. 'No man may be perfect who is chaste
or impotent or a eunuch. It follows that the larger a man's
zabb, the greater his manhood and the further he has gone

upon the road of perfection. Therefore bow humbly before
the face of the Highest and beg for your zabb to grow to
magnificence.' Unfortunately they saw the zabb swell and
multiply until it look like a calabash lying between two
mighty pumpkins. The poor fellow couldn't stand, so great
was the weight. The other two wishes were wasted by asking
for the encumbrance to be removed and then for the original
to be restored.

Nowhere are the cocks so consistently large as in Sade. One
of his most famous heroes was Roland in *Justine*—who was,
incidentally, as hirsute as a bear.

> . . . that part which differentiates men (writes the un-
> fortunate heroine) from our sex was of such a length and
> exorbitant circumference that not only had I never
> clapped eyes upon anything comparable, but was even
> absolutely convinced Nature had never fashioned another
> as prodigious; I could scarcely surround it with both
> hands, and its length matched that of my forearm.

Another man of enormous strength, a friend of Dubois whose
name was never revealed, had an 'amatory goad' roughly a
foot long and above eight inches round. Sade, unlike most
other writers on this subject, is always extremely meticulous
about the circumference as well as the length—yet one more
instance of his rationality, for lateral friction is at least as
important as depth of thrust. 'This incisive, nervous, constantly alerted and oozing instrument, ribboned with great
purple veins that rendered its aspect still more formidable,
was levitated throughout the *séance*, which lasted five or six
hours; never once did it sink or falter.' There are some even
more remarkable engines described and annotated in *The 120
Days of Sodom*. The Duc de Blangis's statistics were identical
with Roland's and in addition, although he was fifty years of
age, he had a virtually constant erection and could eject his
sperm any number of times a day. Later he reserved for himself the initiation of Zephyr, the most delicious of the eight
boys: 'O tender and delicate child,' exclaims the author in

horrid glee, 'what disproportion and what dreadful fate were
for thee in store!' The eight actors in this epic were naturally
extremely well endowed. Hercule was eight and a quarter
inches round, 13 long. This tool was almost always upright
and tests had revealed that it could fill a pint measure to the
brim with only eight discharges. Antinous was 8 x 12, Bum-
Cleaver eight and three-eighths x 8 only—but its head
resembled the heart of an ox and its shaft was so curved it
nearly tore the anus. Skyscraper (with perpetual erection) was
seven and fifteen-sixteenths by 11. The other four were
similar.[1]

Any of these gentlemen could have made an honest living
by exhibiting themselves to select groups. Human beings will
always pay to see freaks and oddities and gigantism in particular wins their esteem. Céline writes of a medical student
in *Journey to the End of the Night* who used to earn a little
easy money in this way. The lucky devil could boast fantastic
muscular development. He used to be summoned to little
parties in the suburbs in the hopes of making them go. The
ladies were particularly interested and used to make a
tremendous fuss over him because they could never believe
that it could be 'as big as that'—not until they saw it, anyway.
Arrested flappers, Céline called them. The police records
referred to him as John Thomas.

It might be expected that the Enemy of man should have
a weapon utterly stupendous, one beyond the capacity of any
woman to receive. It might be expected that it should burn
like a red hot coal and roast its receptacle to a charred mass.
But not so. Perhaps it was the subtlety of his Satanic Majesty
or it may have been a result of the Fall—whatever the reason,
the Devil was not notably a great performer. There is plenty
of evidence for during the Age of Faith he frequently chose a
mortal woman on whom to vent his spleen or his sexual urge.
Not all the witnesses were in agreement but it seems likely
that some were deceived. De Lancre quoted a 17-year-old
witness who said the devil's penis was like a mule (*Tableau
de l'Inconstance des Mauvais Anges et Démons*), but according to Boguet the witches in Franche-Comté had never seen

one longer than a finger and correspondingly thin. De Lancre's dry comment was that perhaps Satan served the witches of Labourd better than those of Franche-Comté. Another of his witnesses gave details of the penis. It was usually sinuous, pointed and snake-like, made sometimes of half-iron and half-flesh, at other times wholly of horn, and commonly forked like a serpent's tongue. He is accustomed to perform coitus and pederasty at once, while sometimes a third prong went into his lover's mouth. The first reference to a devil *cum membro bifurcato* was in 1520.

Similar confessions were obtained from witches in Lorraine and were recorded by Nicholas Remy in his *Demonolatreiae Libri Tres*, 1595. These women complained that intercourse with devils was a very painful affair because they were so large and rigid. Alexia Drigie examined her devil's penis when it was erected, and said it was as long as some kitchen utensils, which she showed to her interrogator but unfortunately not to us. But there was nothing where the testicles and scrotum were supposed to be. In this she was orthodox and perhaps knowledgeable for the devil obtained his semen from men's nocturnal emissions or by squeezing it from corpses. Claudia Fellet said she herself had often experienced something being forced into her, something swollen to such a size that no matter how capacious a vagina a woman might have she would not be able to receive it without extreme pain. Nearly all the Lorraine witches said that they disliked being embraced by demons but it was useless to struggle against them. Note that stupendous male weapons did not bring the undiluted delight to these women that male pornographers usually impute to them. But on the whole the evidence is against outsize demonic pricks. The evidence of Jacquema Paget, a witch of Franche-Comté, quoted by Boguet in his *Discours des Sorciers*, 1602, is fairly representative. When a devil slept with her she often used to take his member in her hand and found it as cold as ice, only a finger in length, and less thick than a man's. Thievenne Paget and Antoine Tornier also asserted that the members of their demon-lovers were the length and thickness of one of their own fingers.[2]

An Arab (or possibly Islamic) demon is called an Ifrit. The only one I have been able to trace in this connection is Kash-kash ibn Fakrash ibn Atrash, of the line of Abu Hanfash, and he had a zabb forty times larger than that of an elephant. It ran between his legs and rose triumphantly behind him. You can find more about him in 'The Tale of Kamar al Zaman and Princess Budur', 182nd night, trs. Mathers.

What Women Want

In erotic writing this tends to be what men say women want. Self-love and self-doubts combine to cause them to insist that fundamentally a woman wants sex and nothing else. Humanity is so constructed that there is much truth in it but women are not so simple as to want nothing else.

Men can naturally find the evidence they want. Stern, in *The Scented Garden*, quotes a Bosnian maiden who is describing the kind of penis she likes: 'Like a worm, neither too long nor too thick, at its end is a wedge which it feels efficiently when it presses into the vagina.' Another maiden (Stern's word), when asked which kind of penis was best, answered: 'Whether a long one has its end stuck up, or a thick one filled out, it matters not as long as it satisfies in abundance.' Such girls are empiricists.

The women, even quite young girls, in the *Arabian Nights* think seriously and speak gravely about the matter. One puts this question to a kadi: 'First I am a bone, then I am a muscle, and finally I am flesh. What am I?' The ignorant old dotard, his mind full of law, cannot answer, proof that he had not read *Alf Layla wa Layla*. A girl of fourteen finally comes up with the answer: 'In respect of vigour and consistency a man's zabb is a bone when he is between the ages of fifteen and thirty-five, a muscle when he is between thirty-five and sixty, and, when he has passed sixty, it is nothing but a useless piece of hanging flesh.' ('The Second Captain's Tale: Al Malik Baibars and his Captains of Police', 940th night, Mathers.) We are told a good way of judging a man's potentiality, that is, if we don't know into what age group

he fits. When Duraid, a mightly but ageing warrior, asked to
marry Tumadir, she called one of her girls and said: 'Go out
now, and watch Duraid. Follow him when he leaves the tents
to satisfy his need; look carefully at the jet, determine its
strength, and bring me news of its track upon the sand. Your
report will tell us whether he be still a man or no.' ('The Poet
Duraid and his Love for Tumadir al Khansah', 974th night,
Mathers.) The girl's report was the single word: Finished.

In a realistic novel women will be found to complain that
the man's weapon is too big. In this respect, and in many
others, *The Golden Lotus* is realistic. When the insatiable
hero, Hsi-mên, who literally fucked himself to death,
attempted to seduce Moonbeam she, like many other women
before and after, was terrified by the size of his prick. 'Honey,'
she said, 'this is the first time we've come together. You ought
to be merciful and only put half of it in. If you shove it all
in you'll finish me off. You did that with your medicine. In
no other way could it be so red, so fiery, so terrible.' Hsi-mên
argues and, as always, gets his own way, but he is too big
to get in. Moonbeam clasped a little pillow and begged the
man to spare her but he just went on shoving the more
fiercely.

The French use a protection against such circumstances
which they call a *bourrelet*. This is rarely encountered in
erotic literature (which, after all, does not like to admit the
need for one) but there is a reference in *Tableaux Vivants*,
translated into English under the same title in 1888. A
woman's vagina has the remarkable property of opening wide
when penetrated but then resisting the later thrusts, as though
the pleasure caused it to swell and placed a *bourrelet* at the
entrance. A footnote describes the *bourrelet* as a small silken
pad, stuffed with cotton and rounded in shape, with a hole
in the middle corresponding in size with the circumference
of the penis for which it is intended. The protection is provided against exceptional length rather than thickness, of
course. The *fouteur* passes his yard through the hole before
penetrating the woman. It is attached to the thighs or the
loins by two ribands which hold it firmly in position.[3] 'Thanks

to this artifice, new pleasures can be enjoyed without fear of wounding the woman, who no longer dreads the approach of the hitherto frightful but henceforth beneficent object,' writes the author of *Le Petit Citateur*, Paphos, 1881. The famous *Gamiani* mentions this gadget when an ass is performing. And the Duc de Roquelaure, who had a member of exceptional size, used to threaten his wife with connection without one when she displeased him.

If a woman complains that the man is too big, the man will naturally complain that she is too small. Such situations are fairly frequent in Sade, where the organs are so often outsize, and in consequence the men are roused to fury. Here is Roland, trying desperately to get up Justine's backside:

> He thrusts, he sweats, 'tis in vain; he prepares the road, 'tis futile; he is too monstrously proportioned, his enterprises are repeatedly frustrated; and then his wrath exceeds all limits; his nails, his hands, his feet fly to revenge him upon the opposition Nature puts up against him; he returns to the assault, the glowing blade slides to the edge of the neighbouring canal and, smiting vigorously, penetrates to the midway mark; I utter a cry; Roland, enraged by his mistake, withdraws petulantly, and this time hammers at the other gate with such force the moistened dart plunges in, rending me.

Nothing infuriates a Sadist more than entering the neighbouring canal.

The size of the man's equipment naturally has some bearing on that old dilemma, what is the best age for a lover? The Arab girl, already quoted, mentioned the Three Ages of the Penis as bone, muscle and flesh. In another tale there is a debate on the question: Which is the better, a youth or a ripe man? One woman asked the other how she could bear the roughness of a man's beard when he kissed her. How is it possible to prevent lips, cheeks and breasts being cut to pieces? The other woman replies that such arguments belong to fools who have neither intelligence nor taste. 'Do you not

know that a tree is only beautiful when it has leaves, and a
cucumber only savoury when it is coarse and pimpled on the
outside? Is there anything more ugly in the world than a
man beardless and bald as an artichoke?' A beard and
moustaches are to a man what long hair is to a woman. This
is a fact so evident that Allah appointed one angel in Heaven
with no other work than to praise the Creator for having
given beards to men and long hair to women. These arguments may be regarded as secondary and, so evanescent is
fashion, they would have little influence today. But now comes
the real advantage of the mature lover:

> Do you think I would ever stretch myself out for love
> below a youth who, hardly mounted, thinks of dismount-
> ing; who, hardly stretched, thinks of relaxing; who,
> hardly knotted, thinks of unknotting; who, hardly
> arrived, thinks of going away; who, hardly stiffened,
> thinks of melting; who, hardly risen, thinks of falling;
> who, hardly laced, thinks of unlacing; who, hardly stuck,
> thinks of unsticking; and who, as soon as he has fired,
> thinks of retiring? Undeceive yourself, poor sister! I will
> never leave a man who enlaces as soon as he sniffs, who
> stays when he is in, who fills himself when he is empty,
> who begins again when he has finished, whose moving is
> an excellence, whose jerking is a gift, who is generous
> when he gives and, when he pushes, pierces!

The Universal Grievance of Womankind, we are led to
believe from an examination of erotic literature and the
popular culture which always echoes it, is of the man who
comes too quick. Norman Douglas illustrates this dilemma
with the following remarkable encounter:

> *There was a young lady of Thun,*
> *Who was blocked by the Man in the Moon.*
> * 'Well, it has been great fun,'*
> *   She remarked when he'd done,*
> *'But I'm sorry you came quite so soon.'*

This gives Douglas the cue for an attack on our educational system. We say our girls should be taught this and that, he says—but what about our boys? An Arab child named Cheira once lamented to him that, much as she liked the European's money, she abhorred his bedside manners: 'they come and go like dogs,' she declared. The copulatory art has to be learnt, like any other business, and no one knows how many marriages founder on a lack of skill. 'Let us hope that some authority like Dr Marie Stopes will expatiate on this great wrong done to her sex, and propose a fitting remedy,' he wisely writes.

It must not be supposed, however, that women are entirely blameless in this respect. Take, for instance, the young man of Natal who had a connection with a Hottentot gal. She complained he was too slow, but the man refused to change his tempo. Douglas confessed he would have liked to shake hands with that young man, who was an example to us all. The words ascribed to the girl are excusable only in the case of a virgin. Here, certainly, we have no virgin, but she unquestionably suffers from invincible ignorance:

> There was a young lady of Kew,
> Who said, as the curate withdrew:
> 'I prefer the dear vicar;
> He's longer and thicker;
> Besides, he comes quicker than you.'

And so we end where we began, with size. Let Douglas have the last word: 'Mere size cannot hope to compete with a rhythmic *ritardando con sentimento*.'

Male Fantasy

Most modern Erotica and all pornography is bragging. 'The standard of potency which a man sets himself is frequently quite impossible,' writes Dr Sofie Lazarsfeld. A man will brag about his own imaginary performances and then persuade himself that the performance of other men in fact equals his own absurd claims. Psychoanalysts are frequently consulted by men who complain of deficient potency, whereas they are found to be quite normal. Women assist men in their delusions. The pathological desire for a virgin, which I shall discuss in a later chapter, leads to disappointment and frustration. In compensation men try to display their energy and ingenuity and the women, knowing how vain men are in this respect, encourage them. This is a sad result of men's conviction that the prolific lover is the most satisfactory lover.

Sade, as usual, rationalises the matter into a glorification of vigour and cruelty. Saint-Florent in *Justine* makes this claim:

> The character of a man's enjoyment is determined by the kind of organs he has received from Nature; a weak individual's and hence every woman's incline in the direction of procuring moral ecstasies which are more keenly felt than any other by these persons whose physical constitution happens to be entirely devoid of energy.

Vigorous beings get enjoyment from powerful shocks imparted to others, and therefore they prefer such stimuli to be disagreeable rather than agreeable—for the other person. The pleasures of the vigorous person are incontestably more lively than those of the meek and mild-tempered. Some men take joy in cruelty just as others delight in benevolence.

Perhaps another reason why men resort so willingly to fantasy lies in their sense of basic inferiority in the aesthetic aspect. Men are agreed that women are physically more beautiful than men. The cause is their unity of line and men's lack of it. In other words, women are more beautiful because of the invisibility of their sexual organs. Even the most magnificent Greek god is blemished, aesthetically, by his sex. When man is ready for love he is ridiculous, and he is normally aware of it. (The feeling is soon dismissed in the crucible of stronger feelings, of course, but it recurs in calmer moments.) Strength is sometimes beauty, or the cause of beauty, but in this case it is more a substitute for beauty. A man brags of the beauty of his woman (again, this is often

as exaggerated as his more personal claims) and the power
of his sexual urge. Remy de Gourmont said the male organ
was made for the race, not the individual. It is the sensitive
point *par excellence*, and the most visible point, particularly
when erect.

This universal male fantasy is the starting point of some
of the most remarkable, the most amusing and also the most
poetic of the literary treatments of sex. Let us end this section
with a beautiful example from the *Hesperides* of Robert
Herrick, entitled 'The Vine'.

> I dream'd this mortal part of mine
> Was metamorphoz'd to a Vine;
> Which crawling one and every way,
> Enthrall'd my dainty Lucia.
> Methought, her long small legs and thighs
> I with my Tendrils did surprize;
> Her Belly, Buttocks and her Waste
> By my soft Nerv'lits were embrac'd:
> About her head I writhing hung,
> And with rich clusters (hid among
> The leaves) her temples I behung:
> So that my Lucia seem'd to me
> Young Bacchus ravisht by his tree.
> My curles about her neck did craule,
> And armes and hands they did enthrall:
> So that she could not freely stir,
> (All parts there made one prisoner.)
> But when I crept with leaves to hide
> Those parts, which maids keep unespy'd,
> Such fleeting pleasures there I took,
> That with the fancie I awook;
> And found (Ah me!) this flesh of mine
> More like a Stock, than like a Vine.

Miscellanea

By far the greater part of male description and fantasy is

concerned with the prick, particularly its size. Inferences from
other parts of the body are sometimes encountered, as when
the Sultan of China looked carefully at the Barber and saw
that he had a large nose (*Arabian Nights*, 34th night). Burton
has an interesting footnote to this in his edition. He says the
Arabs have a saying corresponding to a dictum of what he
calls 'the Salernitan School', which he quotes:

Noscitur a labiis quantum sit virginis antrum:
Noscitur a naso quanta sit hasta, viro

which he translates

A maiden's mouth shows what's the make of her chose;
And man's mentula one knows by the length of his nose

(which is still popular philosophy). Burton adds a line of his
own:

And the eyebrows disclose how the lower wig grows.

These observations, he says, are empirical but, so far as his
experience goes, correct.

Testicles do not get a very wide literary treatment. They
do not contribute to the pleasure and tend to be admired on
the entirely rational grounds that they are a storehouse of
energy. Again according to the *Arabian Nights* they can be
affected by emotional states. When King Samandal was
attacked by his enemies and fearful havoc was wrought ('Tale
of Pomegranate-Flower and Badr Basim', 540th night, trs
Mathers), the king flew into such terrible anger that his
remarkable testicles, which normally hung to his knees, were
retracted to his navel. But then, these testicles were remarkable to begin with and cannot be treated as standards for
comparison.

One of Norman Douglas's limericks is concerned with a
young man who, in effect, had only one testicle. This gives
rise to one of Douglas's more entertaining notes.

> *There was a young man of Devizes,*
> *Whose balls were of different sizes.*
> *One was so small,*
> *It was nothing at all;*
> *The other took numerous prizes.*

Here is the comment:

If one of his testicles was 'nothing at all', then this young prize-winner was monorchous. Such people were credited in antiquity with great sexual vigour, and the three or four of them whom it has been my privilege to know certainly corroborated the old belief. But they are up a tree when their single testicle has to be removed by a surgical operation, whereas most of us have a second one in reserve. Even that is doomed to extraction all too frequently!

The fact is, these objects in their present situation are exposed to so many risks that we may well envy the whales, and in a booklet entitled *Hints for God* I make bold to suggest that, at the next creation of the world, they be located in a position of greater security. If He agrees to my proposal He will earn the gratitude of all save a few little boys whose testicles remain hidden upstairs, and are anyhow too small to be taken seriously.

Whoever wishes to see what this organ can do in the way of size should go to Pernambuco, where it is nothing out of the way to see a man wheeling his testicles in front of him on a barrow. I suspect the disease (elephantiasis) was imported by African negroes.

Seminal smells are frequently referred to in the case of women, rarely in the case of men. Van de Velde, in his usual pawky style, has some interesting information on this point. He says there is a good deal of difference between races. The seminal odour of Orientals is stronger and more acrid than that of Westerners. The semen of healthy West European youths has a fresh and exhilarating smell; in a mature man

it is more penetrating. This seminal odour is very like that
of the flowers of the Spanish chestnut (marrons). At times it
can be extremely pungent and quite disagreeable. Some
women are remarkably sensitive to such odours. 'I know of
one highly talented and delicately sensitive woman,' he writes,
'who abruptly terminated a liaison on finding, at the first
act of sexual intercourse, that the special seminal odour of
the man was intolerably unpleasant to her.'

Finally, a word about a strange male characteristic that I
have only traced among Sadian heroes. One of the monsters
in *Justine* and several in *120 Days of Sodom* ejaculate from a
limp penis. There is nothing in this to attract the erotic
writer, hence its rarity. According to Kinsey it does happen,
but it is scarcely a symbol of that much sought-after virility
mentioned in an earlier section. Kinsey says it is doubtful
if ejaculation can occur ordinarily without a preceding climax.
On the other hand, ejaculation from an erect penis but without a sensation of release is not unknown. It is also said that
ejaculation without erection can be the result of the utilisa-
tion of special techniques in intercourse.

Rich and Poor

Sex, regarded as the best of the games (Alex Comfort), is
valued by philosophical participants because it overrides
class and wealth barriers. The myth of the prince and the
dairy maid has never died and from time to time it gets a
boost from reality. On the surface there is no reason why a
rich man should get more pleasure from the exercise than a
poor man. The rich man can make love in more pleasant
surroundings but the subject is not really amenable to such
rational arguments—in fact, a Hilton suite may even detract
from the central sensation. Healthy young lovers tend to
despise the luxuries of aristocratic lechers and claim that too
much good living will sap a man's virility. This view is
expressed in a modern novel such as Jan Carew's *The Wild
Coast*, where Doorne is contemptuous of his master, Fitz
Bradshaw, who is only forty-eight but has to buy women and

doesn't have enough juice in his back to fill up a mopsy with delight. 'Better to be a beggar with good sap in your limbs than to have money and position and a sugar-stick with no juice in it.'

Money is of course an important ancillary in sex matters. The usual pattern is rich man making rich gifts to beautiful girl—in other words, prostitution. The man who uses his sex to advance himself is a rarer phenomenon but by no means non-existent. One of the most eminent in English history was John Selden, 1584-1654, about whom the diarist Aubrey wrote: 'I remember my Sadler (who wrought many years to that Family) told me that Mr Selden had got more by his Prick than he had done by his practise.' Selden had made head-way through the good offices of the Countess of Kent and a Mrs Williamson, who was one of the Countess's women. But he also reserved some of his energies for 'my Lady's Shee Blackamore', who was perhaps more fun.

Note The idea that class and wealth are levelled by sex has always had its appeal. One of the story-tellers in the *Heptameron*, Parlamente, found its strange that love should torment working people amid their many toils, 'and that so gentle a passion should lodge in hearts so base', but Saffredent quoted Master Jehan de Mehun (better known as Jean de Meun, who continued *The Romance of the Rose*):

> *Those clad in drugget love no less*
> *Than those that wear a silken dress.*

In Apollinaire's *Memoirs of a Young Rakehell* a boy drills a hole in the toilet partition so that he can see the women. Among all the ladies, those of his family and the servants, there was little to choose between them except in size and difference of hair colour. He became convinced of the truth of something said to him by a farm boy who had once fucked a countess: 'The blouse was of finer material, but aside from that just like with any other woman.'

But see chapter 10 for Norman Mailer's views (or his hero's) on the effect on pleasure of sensation resulting from the knowledge that one's partner is desired by the whole world.

FOOTNOTES

1. A worthy rival was Donald, in Burns's *The Merry Muses of Caledonia*:
   The deevil's dizzen Donald drew,
   And Donald gied her a' that.
                              'Put Butter in my Donald's Brose'
2. Useful information on demon lovers can be found in the entry on 'Sexual Relations with Devils' in the *Encyclopaedia of Witchcraft and Demonology*, Robbins.
3. But why should this be necessary when the gadget is already skewered like a piece of *Kebab*?

8: *The Mechanics of Lust*

The popular idea of lust is that it is irresistible, so it may be both interesting and instructive to start with an account of those occasions when it has been resisted. One assumes that when opportunity is present lust is usually the victor, but there are occasions when, for one reason or another, it is beaten off, usually with a great deal of self-admiration on one side or the other. For much of our morality is based on our capacity to not do what we wish to do.

Ancient literature provides many models of lust repelled, but let us first look at a modern one. Lao-Ti works for a shopkeeper and his youthful beauty rouses the passion of his master's wife (*The Rift of the Lute*, by Noel Langley). When her husband is out of the way she coaxes Lao-Ti to sit beside her for tea and is soon talking of love. He confesses he is backward.

> 'It is a passion shared,' said she, 'and you teach it by sharing it,' then slowly she put her hands upon my cheeks and began drawing me close to her until our lips touched, whereupon she kissed me fiercely and rolled upon her side, dragging me with her unexpected strength, so that I lost my balance and kicked the tray of tea bowls over, and all but smothered, while, with her other hand she seized me so roughly by the bamboo-shoot that I thought she meant to uproot me, and tried to escape with a dismal howl.

Lao-Ti, largely through fear and utter ignorance of what the lady is about, turns out to be incorruptible, thus provoking her undying hatred. She murders her husband and success-fully charges Lao-Ti with the crime. This situation was almost

a cliché in the literature of the past—Apuleius made use of
it, for one. Throughout his work Langley demonstrates his
acquaintance with the best erotic models.

The lady suffered from the pangs of lust but we are not
told whether Lao-Ti felt any stirrings, even in his abused
bamboo-shoot. Turning to the *Arabian Nights*, we read of
one Ghanim ibn Ayyub who rescues Kut al-Kulub, but when
he hears that she belongs to the Khalifah he refuses to touch
her, despite all her enticements. Knowing how fiercely Arabs
possess their women, one can hardly blame him. Poor Ghanim
spent a wretched night, trying to explain to the importunate
creature that what belonged to the master could not belong
to the slave. 'Away with this obsolete morality!' she cries,
as ladies in like condition have cried throughout recorded
(and presumably unrecorded) history. 'Let us ensnare the
flying lust tonight!' But Ghanim would not. 'Come, my beloved, all my flesh lies open to you. My desire is crying and
calling towards you. Ghanim of my life, take these blossoming lips, this body ripened by passion!' But Ghanim would
not. 'My skin is moist with my desire, I am naked to your
kisses. My skin breathes like an orchard of jasmine, touch
and smell and be drunken, O my heart!' But Ghanim would
not. ('Tale of Ghanim ibn Ayyub', 40th night, trs. Mathers.)

From one point of view Ghanim is a bigger bore than Angel
Clare in *Tess*. From another, he is obviously a man who
values his bamboo-shoot and has sufficient self-control to
protect it.[1]

The case of Moll Flanders is slightly different. Being
English, even if comparatively early English, she feels constrained to protest her virtue. She knows, however, that her
powers of resistance are limited and as she tells her story we
sense a kind of clinical curiosity about just how long chastity
can maintain itself against nature. Early in her story she tells
how she is thrown upon the bed, and 'then being both well
warmed, he went farther with me than decency permits me
to mention, nor had it been in my power to have denied
him at that moment, had he offered much more than he did.
However, though he took these freedoms with me, it did

not go to that which they call the last favour, which, to do
him justice, he did not attempt; and he made that self-
denial of his a plea for all his freedoms with me upon other
occasions after this.'

We are certainly getting close to surrender, and *Moll
Flanders* does in fact provide us with one of the most realistic,
and at the same time sympathetic, accounts of how it happens.
Her beau was so enamoured of her that he swore he could lie
naked with her and yet sacredly preserve her virtue— and she
told him she believed him. The test came at Gloucester, where
they had to share a room, though sleeping in separate beds.
Mine host made a moralistic speech, saying that it was none
of his business whether they were married or not, but they
could lie as honestly in those two beds as if they were in
different chambers—whereupon he drew a curtain between
them. Now is the time for the lover to prove his boast. Over
he came ('I resisted a little') and they lay together all night
with no more than an embrace between them.[2] 'This was a
surprising thing to me,' remarks Moll, 'and perhaps may be
so to others, who know how the laws of nature work.' And
it was Moll who finally made sure that the laws of nature
should continue to work, 'for I own that I was much wickeder
than he.' They lived together in this way for two years, except
for a few gaps when he went to London; today we should
place him among the perverts, for it appeared he was not
impotent. But:

> It was one night that we were in bed together warm and
> merry, and having drunk, I think, a little more wine that
> night, both of us, than usual, although not in the least
> to disorder either of us, when, after some other follies
> which I cannot name, and being clasped close in his
> arms, I told him (I repeat it with shame and horror of
> soul) that I could find in my heart to discharge him of
> his engagement for one night and no more.
>
> He took me at my word immediately, and after that
> there was no resisting him; neither indeed had I any
> mind to resist him any more, let what would come of it.

Note how, in this male literature, it is the woman who is
the aggressor; when aggression does not pay, she uses cunning.
Male innocence, as well as male chastity, is stressed. The
women are more knowledgeable. Naturally, literature is full
of men who know what they want and are determined to get
it; Lovelace and Tom Jones are stock characters, and whether
we approve or disapprove has nothing to do with their actions,
for they are markedly similar, but with the personality that
accompanies the action. The innocent man victimised by the
determined woman can be paralleled by the innocent girl
victimised by the determined man, but there is a contrast in
manner between the two. The man is usually represented as
a healthy animal following his instincts, while the woman
is frequently portrayed as a creature of cunning. Let us take
a modern example. Otto, a Chinese shopkeeper in a Trinidad
village, decides to take a wife and Berta, a Negress, is brought
for his consideration. He has never had a woman before
(innocence) while she plays canny (cunning). They sleep
separately. One night he looked at her and saw she was
beautiful. Desire stirred in Otto and he could not sleep. He
didn't know what to do, so he shook Berta for a start. Then
the following conversation ensued:

> 'What is it?' the girl asked, rising on her elbow.
> 'You have a nice body,' Otto said, breathing hard and
> wanting to touch it.
> 'Yes,' Berta said.
> 'You ever do anything with anybody?' Otto asked next.
> 'Yes,' Berta said.
> 'I never do anything with any woman,' Otto said,
> reviewing his life and wondering how it was that he had
> missed out on Woman in his experiences.
>
> *Turn Again Tiger*, SAMUEL SELVON

But enough of all this resistance and ignorance of what
makes the world go round. This chapter is primarily about
success, not failure—from the male point of view, the feeling
expressed in another West Indian novel, this time *The Wild
Coast*, by Jan Carew. The sailor returns—one of the basic

situations of life and literature. 'Man, I got so much juice store up in me back, if I don't find a woman quick I will burst,' says Tengar, back from the sea. And, more suavely, but just as intensely, comes this voice from the early seventeenth century: 'the constitution of my body will never hold out till the wedding; I must seek elsewhere.' Thus Prince Pharamond who suggests sleeping with Arethusa, his bride-to-be, because the wedding ceremonies will take so long to complete. But Arethusa indignantly refuses, and in this refusal lies the challenge to lust. (*Philaster,* by Francis Beaumont and John Fletcher: 'better were they named Beau Mount and Lecher,' says Master Dixon in Joyce's *Ulysses.*)

Assault on Innocence

Graham Greene comments somewhere on the agony of child love; it cannot know fulfilment. Many other writers have referred to these same pangs, among them Nabokov in *Lolita.* At the age of nine Humbert Humbert knew and fell hopelessly in love with Annabel. The only privacy they ever had was to be out of earshot but never out of sight on the populous part of the *plage.* There they would sprawl all the morning 'in a petrified paroxysm of desire', taking advantage of every little accident to touch a hand or a knee or to graze lips behind a sand castle. Their healthy young bodies were driven to such a state of exasperation that not even the cool blue water could bring relief.

  'There we were, unable even to mate as slum children would so easily have found an opportunity to do.' It is doubtful, however, to what extent the slum children are satisfied by their mutual caresses. We see them in Zola's *Germinal,* together in holes and corners, trying out the love-making that they saw and heard at home, behind partitions, through cracks in doors. 'They knew everything but could not do much, they were too young; but they spent hours feeling round, playing about, like vicious little puppies. He called it 'playing mothers and fathers'. There was a delicious thrill of instinct, the girl always yielding in the expectation of some wonderful revelation that never came.

The prickings and promptings of sex in childhood were almost universally ignored in literature until modern times. Today childhood reminiscences, whether fictional or autobiographical, are often extremely frank. Let us take an example more or less at random: *Grandad with Snails*, by Michael Baldwin. As an autobiographical sketch it is beautifully sharp and unsentimental. We get the feeling of the boy without adult moralising. There is in fact very little about sex but what there is is as frank as accounts of food or sport in other novels. The boy is evacuated into the country during the war and meets crude, animal-like boys of a kind he has never encountered before. He becomes aware of his genitalia, of their extraordinary, apparently independent behaviour at times, of the inexplicable urges that accompany such exhibitions. He meets Piper, a shaggy lout who loves to uncover himself and make crude sexual remarks in front of females of any age. When he passes girls he undoes a couple of fly-buttons. He likes to take them into a thicket where they can hold his cock for sixpence. When he doesn't feel like this he wears a better pair of trousers. And Piper has his acolytes, all of whom claim that the girls 'like it' and will go readily in the woods for sixpence. But what is it the girls like? And what happens when they hold it? Do they get a shock?

Eventually the boy discovers what to do. Men may legislate against sex but they can't hold it in check or even force it into socially accepted channels. Hector, in Jan Carew's *The Wild Coast*, has wet dreams. He is worried and asks the old woman who looks after him if he ought to see a doctor. She says it's a healthy sign but advises him to see Doorne. And this is what Doorne says:

> When you got too much juice in your back it does have to find a way out and so Nature does make it come out in you sleep. That is the juice that does seed a woman. Couple more years of eating all the rich food you does eat and taking all that exercise and you will have to find a woman.

Hector is still mystified, but Doorne finds it impossible to be more explicit. He hasn't the imagination to realise that a boy may not have the faintest idea what he's talking about. 'You will have to start using the weapon the Good Lord equip you with to use.' And if he doesn't find the woman, the woman will find him. Which she does. It is Elsa, who regarded sleeping with a man as natural as washing your bare feet at the foot of the steps before you enter a house. 'It was his own fault,' she says, 'the boy came into my hut challenging me with his lean brown self. What was I to do but make him dip his wick in the honey so that he could feel what it's like to be a man?' The irony is that Hector did not realise he was challenging her.

Knowing what to do does not always mean you know how to do it. A good example of this is John in J. C. Powys's *The Brazen Head*. John is all desire, all worship, all enthusiasm— and no control. When Peleg asks him what he thinks of girls he says: 'O I adore them! I worship them! I embrace—in my mind, or course, or in my imagination—every single one of them I meet! Off, off, off I slip their pretty clothes! And oh! so quickly I'm hugging them! But that's the worst of it, for it's the whole of the best of it, and the end of it! For I have an ecstasy at once, and all my soul rushes out, and all my seed is gone, in a minute, and I've no strength left to ravish them and take their divine maidenheads!' John is of course very young, and also this is not a realistic novel. He represents the rational intelligence, living in the ideal world rather than the real—rather akin to the confirmed reader of erotica!

Not everyone is taken as simply and satisfyingly as Hector. Some young men feel compelled to answer the call stirring in their loins, and make for the whorehouse. They have heard that these places exist entirely to satisfy these longings, although they are pretty vague about what goes on there. One of the most sympathetic approaches to this aspect of the conflict is to be found in William Saroyan's story, 'Seventeen'. Sam Wolinsky, a young Polak, was suddenly overcome by a feeling of enormous internal strength—which is, incidentally, as good a way as any of expressing the vague power of the feeling. He wanted to hurt and to destroy, and it frightened him.

> He was in love and there was no girl. He was in love with female whiteness, the swelling of female parts, the curve of back, the soft cohesion of limbs uniting in wholeness, hair, smile or strong frown as of passion, female motion, woman, but mostly the idea of woman. He felt no tenderness, and he had no wish to imitate the moving-picture males, touching the females. That was fake. It was fraudulence. They were trying to keep people unaware of the truth, making it a soft event, a thing of no strength. They were trying to hide the animal drive in man, the lust to function violently, but they couldn't fool him.

He knew all about love. It was nonsense. He had read an article about it in *The Haldeman-Julius Monthly*. It was purely physical; all the rest was imaginary, a stupid fake. Strength accumulated in him and had to be released. No mystery there. He felt contempt for the giggling girls and boys in the park. Women weren't like that: he felt they were primarily evil, eternal and ungiggling.

So he went to Chinatown to find a whore. There was nothing vague or indeterminate about that. Here was a man who knew what he wanted. He went into a sleazy hotel, climbed the stairs and rang a bell. A woman of fifty with hair on her upper lip, a white hag with unclean eyes, answered: the thought struck him, this is not evil, this is filth. She said she would bring a girl. Suddenly he saw himself, as from away up in the sky, sitting pathetically in a small room, smoking a cigarette, feeling unclean, as if he had been dirty from his first moment to this present one, yet refusing to get up and go away. He couldn't decide whether he was being strong or weak, whether this was something to laugh or cry about. Just half an hour later he was going down the stairs, remembering all the rotten details, the face, the hands, the way it happened. 'And the ghastly silence as of death, the absence of strength, the impossibility of laughter, the true ugliness of it.'

This was the first experience of one man. Disease and uncleanliness are emphasised, and the brothel is associated with it. But not every writer makes the brothel sound dirty. Brothels vary, as do people and parties, but their effect depends as much on the visitor as on the place itself. To Maupassant and Steinbeck and Henry Miller they can be as comfortable as clubs. For the man who respects women and does not hypocritically regard the passing of money (instead of meals and fur coats) as wickedness, they are as valuable as front parlours and skating rinks. But men who go in despising the women have got a sure way of hating it all. Sam Wolinsky could not possibly have enjoyed his first bash for he had been carefully taught not to.

A sympathetic, attractive girl in a brothel can do more for a young man (providing he is reasonably humble) than a score of respectable aunts and sisters. How many young fellows have fumbled with the situation, holding their genitals in an agony of self-consciousness, wondering how on earth you carry the thing off with at least an air of composure, instead of public awkwardness. (Everyone is looking at you when you are seventeen, and you have spots into the bargain.) Well, the plunge has to be made—only for God's sake let's hope we don't make fools of ourselves. For this situation let us turn to Connolly's *The Rock Pool*. Naylor has decided it must be done. He has one advantage, he is in France, and it is part of the European myth that French girls are all skilled in sex. He is walking with a group of friends, Lola at his side, to Maxim's in Nice. The following conversation takes place.

> 'Lola, comme vous êtes belle ce soir, j'aimerais tellement coucher avec vous.'
> 'Oh, la la!'
> 'Alors ce soir? Vous permettez? Quand on est jeune il faut coucher avec tout le monde, vous savez!'
> 'Ah non, pas tout le monde!'

'Mais je vous aime, vous êtes si jolie, puis-je espérer?'
'Mais qu'est-ce que c'est la vie sans l'espoir, monsieur?'
'Mais cette nuit, vous vous donnerez, s'il vous plait.'
'Alors, c'est entendu.'

What a charming surrender, he felt. He looked at her young
eager painted face and felt a warm affection. 'Vous êtes une
bonne fille, Lola, je te remercie beaucoup.'

Getting into somebody's bed doesn't always provide a solution. It is true, the young usually have some idea of what
has to be done—probably more today than ever before in
our own culture, because it is practically impossible for them
to remain innocent. But the mutual attraction of male and
female may not always suggest the remedy, and we can turn
back to Langley's *The Rift in the Lute* to see Lao-Ti and the
serving maid, Pei, puzzling it out together. They lie down
together innocently after escaping from some drunken
Mongols. Because it is hot they take off their clothes. He
experiences the familiar feelings, his bamboo shoot quivers,
he feels drugged by Pei's perfume, he runs his hand anxiously
along her body until it comes to rest on the threshold of the
Jug of Doubtful Joy. She hastily moves his hand away.
'Brother,' she says reproachfully, 'what did you seek there?'
He replies that he was seeking reassurance that she was a
sister and not another brother. (He had been tricked once
before in this respect.) Pei confesses to be extremely angry
with him, for 'such roughness destroys all trust.' But when
she sees how contrite he is she softens and says he was only
thoughtless . . . but he would not like it if she were to touch
him there . . . like that . . . would he?

'Sister,' said I, in a breathless panic, 'what are you
doing? My head is spinning like a paper kite! Oh mercy,
help me! I believe I am dying!'
'No, no!' cried she softly, leaning over me hurriedly.
'You were never more alive! you quite startled me, so
fast did life spring up! And—shall I tell you the strangest
thing?—all my fear has gone! . . . And . . . oh brother!

What a handsome brother you are!' And she suddenly
flung herself upon me and buried her face against my
neck, twining her arms about me and sobbing softly, and
just as I thought my bamboo shoot would burst, there
was a murderous clatter. . . .'

They are disturbed.

There is a lot of foolish chatter about what stimulates
young men; efforts are made to discover the causes with a
view to banning them. It would be wisest, of course, to ban
young women. For lust is the desire of women (I write from
the male angle, though the women will be given their desserts
shortly), and they are all around us. It is a truth that writers
have always accepted, though at certain times pressures have
been exerted to hide or distort the truth. Today we are
coming into the open again, and with this revived honesty
others may follow. But still Shakespeare puts it at its best,
as when Capulet speaks to Paris, who has asked for Juliet's
hand:

> At my poor house look to behold this night
> Earth-treading stars that make dark heaven light:
> Such comfort as do lusty young men feel
> When well-apparell'd April on the heel
> Of limping winter treads, even such delight
> Among fresh female buds shall you this night
> Inherit at my house; hear all, all see,
> And like her most whose merit most shall be. . . .

It is the word 'inherit' that speaks loudest there.

Irresistible

The message underlying *Romeo and Juliet* is that the healthy
young man is never without desire. Lust dies but is immediately replaced. Not even Romeo was a one-woman man:

> Now old desire doth in his death-bed lie,

> And young affection gapes to be his heir;
> That fair for which love groan'd for and would die,
> With tender Juliet match'd, is now not fair . . .

says Chorus in the Prologue to Act II.

Just over one hundred and fifty years later Robert Herrick notes in his *Hesperides* that there is 'no difference i' th'dark'.

> Night makes no difference 'twixt the Priest and Clark;
> Jone *as my Lady is as good i'th'dark.*

Such statements are profoundly anti-romantic, and are extremely common. They belong to the strain of folk-lore, the world of the medieval *fabliaux* and the smoking room story, which runs parallel to the romantic strain. It owes its strength and persistence to the final irresistibility of lust which, when it realises there is no choice, chooses what is given. Through the length and breadth of the *Heptameron*, to take one example, we see virtuous ladies and hot-blooded young men struggling against their so-called baser natures; whether virtue remains triumphant or takes a fall is one of the major subjects of discussion among the company after each story is told.

Resistance to love came to be regarded as a virtue during the late Middle Ages in Europe, and it was adopted as an essential part of the romantic ethos. The more direct approach of the classical civilisation may be seen in this extract from an early translation of *Daphnis and Chloe* (George Thornley's):

> And I myself, when I was young, was in love with Amaryllis, and forgot to eat my meat, and drink my drink; and for many tedious nights, never could compose to sleep; my panting heart was very sad and anxious, and my body shook with cold: I cryed out oft, as if I had bin thwackt and basted back and sides: and then again, was still and mute, as if I had layen among the dead: I cast myself into the Rivers, as if I had been all

on a fire: I called on Pan, that he would help me, as
having sometimes bin himself catcht with the love of the
peevish Pitys: I praised the Echo, that with kindnesse
it restored, and trebbled to me, the dear name of
Amaryllis: I broke my Pipes, because they could delight,
and lead the sturdy herds which way I would, and could
not draw the froward girle. For there is no med'cine for
Love, neither meat, nor drink, nor any Charm, but only
Kissing and Embracing, and lying naked together.

But it is not only the man who finds himself helpless. In
fact, much erotic literature describes woman as the True
Lodestone, who draws man on, even against his better self.
Women have been given the harder task, both by writers and
priestly legislators, who have assumed that men are less
culpable than women when sexual morality is transgressed:
there is a queer double-world of psychology that argues that
woman is purer, and should therefore be capable of resistance, and is also more lecherous, and is therefore responsible
for male shortcomings. The classic apology for the female
erotic urge may be found in Dryden's *Sigismonda and Guiscarde*, which is based on Boccaccio's story in the *Decameron*
(Fourth Day, First Novel). Sigismonda, the beautiful daughter
of the tyrant, Tancred of Salerno, married but was widowed
while still young. She was young, healthy and amorous, and
'former joys had left a secret sting behind'. She wished to
marry again, but Tancred would not concur. She therefore
chose Tancred's squire, Guiscard, as her lover, although he
was a man of low birth. She married him secretly, a detail
not found in Boccaccio's original, and possibly due to the
growing English desire for sin to be spiced with respectability.
Tancred discovers the lovers, has Guiscard murdered and
sends his heart to Sigismonda in a golden goblet. In despair,
she takes poison, but before she dies she addresses her father:

Thou, Tancred, better shouldst have understood,
That, as thy Father gave thee Flesh and Blood,
So gav'st thou me: Not from the Quarry hew'd,

But of a softer Mould, with Sense endu'd;
Even softer than thy own, of suppler Kind,
More exquisite of Taste, and more than man refin'd.
Nor need'st thou by thy Daughter to be told,
Though now thy spritely Blood with Age be cold,
Thou hast been young; and canst remember still,
That when thou hadst the Pow'r, thou hadst the Will;
And from the past Experience of thy Fires,
Canst tell with what a Tide our strong Desires
Come rushing on in Youth, and what their Rage requires.

And the same argument, put here more bluntly, from the
Arabian Nights. This time from a homosexual, known as
Mahmud Bilateral, reciting a verse to the boy Abu Shamat—
for lust is desire, and is not limited by the object:

Lust is not content with blushes,
  Kisses taken from pure lips,
    Not content with wedded glances:
    Lust must have a thing which dances,
Lust must have a thing which gushes,
  Lust must have a thing which drips.

                              'Tale of Ala al-Din Abu Shamat',
                              260th night, trs. MATHERS

A clergyman, Robert Herrick, has expressed himself both
elegantly and convincingly, in his *Hesperides*, on mankind's
defencelessness against lechery. It is a minor theme in his
work, but a recurrent one. Most of his poems were short and
pithy, and this one (which is complete) is called 'No Lock
against Letcherie':

Barre close as you can, and bolt fast too your doore,
To keep out the Letcher, and keep in the whore:
Yet, quickly you'l see by the turne of a pin,
The Whore to come out, or the Letcher come in.

In more delicate mood he says the same in a poem addressed

'To Virgins'. (It could be claimed that here he is thinking only of the emotion of love, but the imagery is extremely tactile.)

> *Heare ye Virgins, and Ile teach,*
> *What the times of old did preach.*
> Rosamund *was a in a Bower*
> *Kept, as* Danae *in a Tower:*
> *But yet Love (who subtile is)*
> *Crept to that, and came to this.*
> *Be ye lockt up like to these,*
> *Or the rich* Hesperides;
> *Or those Babies in your eyes,*
> *In their Christall Nunneries;*
> *Notwithstanding Love will win,*
> *Or else force a passage in:*
> *And as coy be, as you can,*
> *Gifts will get ye, or the man.*

Like many bachelors, Herrick was full of good advice to wives. He expressed this in 'The Parting Verse, or charge to his supposed Wife when he travelled'—one of his most sustained efforts, reaching 84 lines! He warns his putative wife of the perils that will beset her once he is gone. She will receive gifts and letters and other expressions of the 'itch'. She must know that it will not be Love speaking, but Lust. Yet he feels confident that she will resist all-comers—and one can see the tongue bulging in his cheek as the wife-less Herrick wrote these lines:

> *But yet if boundlesse Lust must skaile*
> *Thy Fortresse, and will needs prevaile;*
> *And wildly force a passage in,*
> *Banish consent, and 'tis no sinne*
> *Of Thine. . . .*

Any wife knows how simple is the passage. The Epigram, 'Upon Scobble', blurts the truth out, with no resort to fancy language:

> *Scobble for Whoredome whips his wife; and cryes,*
> *He'll slit her nose; But blubb'ring, she replyes,*
> *Good sir, make no more cuts i'th'outward skin,*
> *One slit's enough to let Adultry in.*

If the invincible power of sexual temptation is a constant theme with Herrick, it is one of the foundation stones of Balzac's *Droll Stories*. For a brief example of this, let us look at 'The Unwise Chatter of Three Pilgrims'. Three men meet at an inn in Milan, on their way to Rome. Each carried jewelry—a ring, a golden chain and pearls, as religious gifts. Each had sworn a vow to keep away from women, and each told a story illustrating the viciousness of the female gender. The landlady said that vows were useless if men could not resist temptation, and offered to put them to the test. Next morning the maid wore the ring and the landlady had the chain round her neck and the pearls in her ears.

Lust, which is pure physical desire, has always been distinguished from love, and in most cases is represented as being more powerful than love. For instance, lust for the woman who is here will prevail over love for the one who is not. There is also an attraction in the brevity of lust, its combination of extreme sensual pleasure without any demands of personal responsibility. There was once a prince who received as a gift from a fairy the most desirable quality that a man can possess, viz., always to unite with a woman from love and never from lust. For some years he was extremely happy, but one day went to the fairy with a request to be relieved of the gift just for once because he felt a strong desire for a girl he could never love, because she was stupid, lazy and a glutton. The fairy granted the request, though with great misgivings. When she saw the prince on the following day she anxiously enquired what it had been like. He sniggered and said, 'Not bad, not at all bad.' The snigger suggests that the prince was fully aware that he was surrendering to something ignoble in himself and, to make matters worse, not out of ignorance because he, more than anyone, knew the real beauty and satisfaction of love. But there is a side to man which Emilia expresses thus to Desdemona:

> *They are all but stomachs, and we all but food;*
> *They eat us hungerly, and when they are full,*
> *They belch us.*

In many a modern book, such as *The Naked and the Dead*, the untiring persistence of lust is stressed. It is a monster that feeds on itself. Sergeant William Brown recalls nights with his wife, the fretful conversations that take place in the small hours : 'Now go 'way, leave me alone, Willie, I thought we agreed to lay off for a couple of days. . . . You're just an old hound dog, that's all you are. Always wanting to put in something.' Wilson wanting it so much, he seems to be going off his head. 'Listen, men, Ah got an idea. Y'know them Japs've got those rollin' whorehouses they bring right up to the lines. . . . Why don' we jus' sneak over tonight and get in their tail line, and we can knock off a piece of that yellow stuff?' In another novel, *The Circus of Dr Lao*, by Charles G. Finney, the unadulterated lubricity of the contemporary American male is summed up in the figure of a soldier named Larry. Dr Lao changes a wolf into a woman—for his is a fantastic circus, in which the truths of the known world are acted out symbolically. But Larry, instead of being astonished by a miracle, is disgusted because the resultant woman is old and ugly. 'Aw doc!' he says, 'why didn't you tell us she was going to be so goddam old? Jees! That old dame's like somebody's great-grandmother. Hell, I thought we was going to see a chicken. Fer crying out loud, put some clothes on her, quick!' And the doctor replies sternly, 'Sensualist, I might have known your only interest in this would be carnal. You have seen a miracle, by any standard, sacred or profane, but you are disappointed because it gives no fillip to your lubricity.'

It is often assumed, and it is probably true, that lust flourishes in a state of idleness. Give the boys a ball to kick about, and they'll forget the itch in their pants; it will even cease to itch. But once a man finds time hanging on his hands, a neural canalisation seems to take place, and there can be only one result.

> There was a young man of Peru,
> Who was hard up for something to do.
>   So he took out his carrot,
>   And buggered his parrot,
> And sent the results to the Zoo.

'It is always when people are idle or "tired of doing nothing", as they call it, that these things occur,' comments Norman Douglas. This is true, and yet for once I respectfully question the propriety of his judgment. The verb 'do' in English performs many duties; it is possible that the young Peruvian did not lack work of one kind or another, but that he lacked something to bugger—either meaning can be read into the above. Douglas quotes another of the same class:

> There was a young monk of Siberia,
> Who of frigging grew weary and wearier.
>   At last, with a yell,
>   He burst from his cell,
> And buggered the Father Superior.

Douglas writes: 'Half the cases of rape recorded in the newspapers, the epidemics of onanism among schoolboys—to say nothing of a great many murders—would never be heard of, if the perpetrators were not *hard up for something to do*. The larger apes in captivity, notably mandrills, are liable to masturbate themselves into a consumption from sheer boredom, and it is not difficult to guess what would happen in such circumstances, if there were a bird handy.'

I am now encroaching on a subject which I have reserved for later consideration, although as an expression of uncontrollable libidinousness both masturbation and bestialism are supreme. Returning to the more orthodox ways of satisfying lust, it is scarcely necessary to point out that the power of lust increases with the proximity of the object. Lust can be roused by the idea, fed by sight and made ravenous by touch. I will illustrate this by reference to two works that are flavoured with Oriental eroticism. The first is a Western imitation from which I have already quoted, but Noel Langley builds up sexual excitement by the use of verses and songs interspersed through his text in the manner of the *Arabian Nights*. A magistrate and gifted musician, Ming Lin, sings and plays on a one-stringed lute, celebrating the soaring of passion resulting from normal fleshly contact:

> *My first love is but fifteen Springs,*
> *All heaven's in her eyes;*
> *The gift of innocence she brings,*
> *With me alone she lies.*
> *And when upon my kisses she clings*
> *Such rapture does arise*
> *My loins become two beating wings*
> *That clamour at her thighs—*
> *A swan that too intensely sings*
> *A death-song ere it dies.*

> *The Rift in the Lute*

The other source is genuinely Oriental, the famous *Golden Lotus*. Ching-chi fumbles at Golden Lotus's trousers and tells her she must be kind to him. This is playing with fire. Such a connection would be illicit because Ching-chi is a servant. Golden Lotus refuses his advances but makes the fatal error of allowing him to touch her. As she felt his stiff weapon pushed against her single garment her cheeks grew as rosy as peach blossom. As she refused him, she let her hand slip to his weapon—and she was helpless. Ching-chi pulled up her skirt and went in at a single thrust, because the woman had been worked up over a long period and was moist. They stood against a railing and went at it furiously. 'Lie on the ground,' said Ching-chi, 'and I will give you all you want.' Lust was in full command.

Women to Blame

'Every woman is at heart a rake,' wrote Pope, a comforting
philosophy for men. The fact that most writing about the
sexual relationship, until recent times, has been by men has
resulted in an extremely unfair apportionment of blame for
results—for in our morality it is mostly blame. An English
folk song from the Duke of Portland's MSS in Nottingham
University Library, quoted in de Sola Pinto and Rodway's
The Common Muse, sets the tone:

> *You know yt my love is a flame of fire*
> *And Burns when itt Cannott obtane my desire*
> *My Beauty is now in itts Blooming prime*
> *and I cannot nor will nott dellay ye time*
> *I lonng to tastt those tender Joys*
> *Those soft kisses and wanton toys*
> *Thatt every Lasse in her wedding injoys:*
> *Whillst Lads with young Lasses get Lusty boys.*

But superadded to this view of women is the contrasting one
that it is their duty to resist. Man burns, not quite as fiercely
as woman for some reason or other, but he cannot be expected
to resist the fire: woman must and, strangely, can. Medieval
story collections, such as the Queen of Navarre's *Heptameron*,
are an astonishing hotchpotch of these twin notions which
has surely made life hell for many a woman who wanted to
do nothing but please. Listen to poor Juliet, bewildered almost
beyond her limited understanding, telling her Romeo that
she loves him to distraction but not wantonly:

> O gentle Romeo,
> *If thou doest love, pronounce it faithfully:*
> *Or if thou think'st I am too quickly won,*
> *I'll frown and be perverse and say thee nay,*
> *So thou wilt woo; but else, not for the world.*
> *In truth, fair Montague, I am too fond,*
> *And therefore thou may'st think my 'haviour light:*

But trust me, gentleman, I'll prove more true
Than those that have more cunning to be strange.
I should have been more strange, I must confess,
But that thou overheard'st, ere I was ware,
My true love's passion: therefore pardon me,
And not impute this yielding to light love,
Which the dark night hath so discovered.

Not every woman has the courage or the exuberance to admit her love of sexual pleasure and to throw it in the face of the world. The Wife of Bath was certainly one. King Solomon, she said, was fortunate enough to have a thousand wives and one can be sure he 'threw many a merry fit' with each one—and the reason she gives is that 'he was so much alive'. In other words, she equates ardent sexuality with the life force and blesses God that she married five times. 'Welcome the sixth, whenever he appears.' She admits frankly that she cannot remain continent year after year. Let those who can, do. That this was Chaucer's own view we know from the *Lenvoy de Chaucer à Bukton*, where the latter is advised to read the Wife of Bath's prologue: 'bet is to wedde, than brenne in worse wyse.'

That women cannot be trusted is an article of faith among the general run of men, as reflected in literature. It is to be hoped that women will be virtuous and chaste but it is really too much to expect once temptation is placed in their way. This could be illustrated from hundreds of works, but a curious example may be given from the *Festival of Love*, 1770, one of the many collections of rather naughty tales in which that period delighted. A poem called 'Hob in the Well' (which we are told was by Mr H——) tells how Bodkin, a tailor, kept a farm on which Robin, or Hob, was his agent. When Hob came to town he had to sleep three abed, with Bodkin and his wife. Hob had to keep his breeches on. All through the Middle Ages this had been common practice, even among the aristocracy, among whom it was regarded as an honour for the guest. Louis XIII, for instance, shared a bed with the Duke and Duchess of Luynes. It was usual

for the husband to sleep in the middle. This was Bodkin's
mistake—he trusted to Hob's breeches.

> Bodkin's horn soon began to blow,
>   Hob was awake, and she also.
> On certain signals from behind,
>   Hob his mask'd battery disclos'd,
> Summon'd the fort, which was resign'd
>   Upon the terms that he propos'd.

They had a little sleep, then Hob had another go, but this
time too vigorously, for Bodkin was awakened.

> And then put back his hand, and lo!
> He found Hob in the well below.

He warned Hob to get out, on the odd grounds that if Mrs
B woke up she'd be furious and scratch his eyes out. When
Mrs B did in fact wake up she said she'd had a marvellous
dream, just like old times when her husband was young and
virile. There is a *Moral*.

> The sex, said a physician of the college,
>   Like men, are either saints or sinners;
> Like Eve, they long so much for knowledge,
>   They scarce have time to eat their dinners.
> The difference between them and us
>   Is this, the sex, both great and small,
> All look as innocent as puss,
>   The greatest hypocrite of all.
> But men oft glory in their shame,
>   And take our wives for lawful game.
> Put not your trust in leather breeches,
>   Whether your wife's behind you, or before;
> They all can tell, they are such witches
>   Whether you sleep or only feign a snore.
> She knows her time, she gives an intimation
>   To Galligaskins and, if she's inclin'd,

> *He will accept of madam's invitation,*
> *Just as it suits, before you or behind.*

Brantôme, one of the most authoritative writers on the sexual aspect of the society of his time, alleged that the leading role was played by women. It is they who take the initiative, although often very subtly, and no gallant who is worth his salt may decline the challenge. If the woman tires of him or thinks he does not measure up to her standards, she dismisses him. 'There are many ladies,' he writes, 'who make no scruple to show their beauty openly, and to display themselves naked, the more to inflame and intoxicate their lovers, and to draw them ever the more ardently to them.' Corroboration comes unexpectedly from George Moore, writing four centuries later in a time that is commonly believed to have been the most inhibitory, so far as women are concerned, in European history. Views of Victorian social mores and actual, rather than ideal behaviour, are undergoing revision these days. 'The position of a young man in the nineteenth century is the most enviable that has ever fallen to the lot of any human creature,' Moore writes in his *Confessions.* The male was flattered, fêted and adored. He could do no wrong and every house was open to him. The following statement is extremely significant for it hints at the gap between fact and ideal that we are beginning to realise existed. 'To represent in a novel a girl proposing marriage to a man would be deemed unnatural, but nothing is more common; there are few young men who have not received at least a dozen offers, nay, more; it is characteristic, it has become instinctive for girls to choose. . . .'

Actual examples of the woman making the assault are common enough. Gide tells, in *If It Die . . .,* how utterly shocked and bewildered he was when, as a young fellow, he was set upon by a Swiss chambermaid of opulent charms. She used to talk to him a great deal about her fiancé but one day he was imprudent enough to tickle her neck with his quill pen while she hung over him. The effect was like an electric shock. She collapsed into his arms. 'With a great effort I lugged her on to a sofa; then, as she hung on to me, I found myself tumbled unto her bosom between her open legs. . . .' Of course, not every man is as ill prepared as the young Gide, although there is a curious mood of mingled acceptance and disgust that some men assume. It is as though they are themselves torn between the twin attitudes referred to earlier in this section. It is hit off beautifully by Lawrence Durrell in his early erotic novel, *The Black Book*. The hero finds Morgan working on the boilers in the basement of his rooming house. Morgan is obviously very excited.

> 'She come down 'arf an hour ago. 'Ere. By the boiler.' *His face was like a flower.* 'She come to me with nothing under her dress. She said: "Do you want it, *Mister* Morgan?" Gor but it was surprising like. I dint know what to say. Then she lies down here, in front of the bloody fire, as God's truth, sir, in front of the fire 'ere.' He choked on his own spittle and produced a grin. Phenomenon. Then, turning aside, latched the boiler doors fast. In my role of echo I sat and waited. He was angry now, sort of resentful with me for being at all interested. Then he ended with terrific naturalness: 'She was what you might call fruity. Draws it out of you, sir.' Then, as if a little bewildered by such a literary figure, he stared at his feet and blurted out, 'Juicy as fruit, sir, and that's no error.'

The real thing happens but it also happens in the imagination, time and again, so that there are occasions when an ardent young man scarcely knows whether he had a woman or dreamt it. A little known novel, *The Square Within* by Bruce Oliver, presents us with such a case. Arthur Mann is staying at the hotel in Chatterton, a provincial town. He is full of sexual excitability. He romances about the maid who makes his bed and cleans his room. He knows that she is the local coalman's wife and invents meetings, imagines conversations. His lustful imaginings are spiced with humour.

In her primblack drawers, she might well have grappled me in her massive coalheaving arms and bundled me down on the carpet. You'll forgive this intrusion, sir, but my hubby's gone off to a coalman's weekend conference and I usually has it round this time of a Saturday night. Her curved shoulders and pineapple breasts bending over me. Her passive eyes, thirsting. Her plier thighs, round my waist, crushing the breath. What's your answer sir? Madam I have no alternative. Very good sir. Changing back to her maid's humility. I'm grateful sir and you understand my predicament don't you? If my hubby isn't home to pleasure me, come the weekend I'm all of a chatter. And after all these grubby factory hands I likes a bit of college boy occasionally.

This is the majority pattern, then, yet it must not be assumed that the male writer accepts it. He pretends to be shocked—perhaps he has persuaded himself that he really is shocked, that there really should be a double morality for the sexes. In general, the more lustful the society described, the greater the passion with which lust is condemned. The Elizabethan period was by no means the most sexually-orientated in our literature, but no other period gives such an impression of consuming lust, of a lust that is so destructive that it must be contained. No Elizabethan or Jacobean play expresses the sin and its condemnation more forcibly than Ford's 'Tis Pity She's a Whore. Soranzo discovers that his new wife is pregnant by somebody else, and launches into the following magnificent nonsense. (It should be remembered that in those days the word luxury implied lust.)

Come, strumpet, famous whore! were every drop
Of blood that runs in thy adulterous veins
A life, this sword—dost see't?—should in one blow
Confound them all. Harlot, rare, notable harlot,
That with thy brazen face maintain'st thy sin,
Was there no man in Parma to be bawd
To your loose cunning whoredom else but I?

> *Must your hot itch and plurisy of lust,*
> *The heyday of your luxury, be fed*
> *Up to a surfeit, and could none but I*
> *Be picked out to be cloak to your close tricks,*
> *Your belly sports? Now I must be the dad*
> *To all that gallimaufry that is stuffed*
> *In thy corrupted bastard-bearing womb!*

And the itch was never far from the Elizabethan consciousness, as a brief yet pungent exchange from Webster's *The
Duchess of Malfi* illustrates. The Duchess is a widow. Her
brothers, Duke Ferdinand and the Cardinal, urge her not to
remarry. Ferdinand even threatens her with death. Cynically
he tells her that women like that part which, 'like the lamprey,
hath never a bone in't'. The Duchess pretends to be shocked,
whereupon Ferdinand explains that he means the tongue:
'what cannot a neat knave with a smooth tale make a woman
believe?'

   A curious book published in 1660, with the title *The Horn
Exalted, or Room for Cuckolds*, throws the onus of cuckoldry
on the woman. The word can be 'ransackt thus, C for cold,
O for old, K for knave, C for calot, i.e., a lewd woman whereof
we have O or Wo, L for lewd, D for demeanure, so that 'tis
a cold old knave,

> *Cuckold himself weaning,*
> *And eak a calot of lewd demeaning'.*

The whole book is just about as inspired as that. Much nonsense is attributed to classical authors—Plato is said to have
doubted the rationality of women because there is horn in
their natures: 'at least 'twas thought they had a beast within
them, since that part by its brutall intellect or Spirit enormon-
tick will grow raging and angry and querulous, all which is
exprest in that croaking, heaving and setting or moving up
and down, etc., etc.'—altogether an extraordinary rigmarole.
But the main message is clear enough: woman's lust is uncontrollable. Nor can she be satisfied, but cries continually for

more and increased sexual pleasure, so that by the time she is nearing her end nothing will content her. As I have already remarked, the appetite feeds on itself. Shortly after the publication of *The Horn Exalted* Lord Lansdowne expressed the idea in 'Corinna' thus:

> *Thus wisely she makes up for time*
> *Misspent, while youth was in its prime:*
> *So travellers, who waste the day,*
> *Careful and cautious of their way,*
> *Noting at length the setting sun*
> *They mend their pace as night comes on,*
> *Double their speed to reach their inn,*
> *And whip and spur through thick and thin.*

The expression of female desire in literary form is no easy matter. It is not encompassed by a narrative of sexual affairs or a chronicle of promiscuity. Only too often such descriptions leave an impression of cold-blooded mechanism, an activity as passionate as that of Pavlov's dogs responding to the bell. There is a spirit in lust, and it is a spirit that is excellently typified by the classical notion of a ravenous beast on the prowl. Lust exists in and through actions, but it exudes an atmosphere of brooding heat, of suffocating airlessness. And to establish this condition through words is a skilled business which few have managed successfully. Moore nearly did it in *Evelyn Innes* and one feels he would have succeeded totally if he had had sufficient courage to set aside all restraint. It is probable that in modern literature there has been no study of female desire to compare with that portrayed by W. Somerset Maugham in *Catalina*. Dona Beatriz wants Catalina to enter her convent because she has received the grace of the Holy Mother. Catalina wants to marry, but Dona Beatriz tells her that Diego is only a boy like any other, and not to be preferred before God.

'Ah, Madam, you say that because you have never known the pain and bliss of love. I want to feel his arms round me, I want to feel the warmth of his mouth on mine, the caress of his hands on my naked body. I want him to take me as a lover takes the woman he loves. I want his seed to flow into my womb and to create the child within it. I want to suckle his child at my breast.'

She put a hand to each breast and sensuality poured from her in a flame so fierce that the Prioress shrank back. It was like the heat of a furnace and she put up her hands as though to shield herself from it. She looked at the girl's face and shuddered. It was strangely changed, pale, and one might have thought the features were swollen; it was a mask of desire. She was breathless with lust for the male. She was like one possessed. There was something not quite human about her, something even slightly horrible, but so powerful that it was terrifying. It was sex, nothing but sex, violent and irresistible, sex in its awful nakedness.

The Onset

Male prejudice may regard the female as the initiator but it is in her being, not in her action. Lust may transfigure her, as Catalina was transfigured, but transfiguration it remains; and it is the male who is drawn, who is enticed, who is compelled to make the assault. As Laurent, in Zola's *Thérèse Raquin*, saw his mistress many times and then, quite suddenly, saw that she was beautiful. She was the same, yet she was entirely new: 'Tense and swaying, the young woman was beautiful with a strange beauty, a beauty that was all ecstasy. You might have said that her face had suddenly brightened from within, that flames danced out of her body. A warm air hung about her, generated by her burning blood, her tense nerves—a penetrating, pungent atmosphere.' It must, of course, be a partnership, else it is rape. But she is ready: she may find it necessary to set the train going, for he may be slow or cold or stupid, but even when she makes no overt act it is her body, her beauty and its aura that act on him, causing him to respond like a plant to sunlight. 'Let husbands

know,' cries Emilia to Desdemona, 'their wives have sense
like them.' And so it must be, if we are to set aside the idiocies
of sexual propaganda and admit that it is a game that two
can and must play. Only a depraved generation can apportion
blame in these matters. No one blames the cat for catching
the bird. Man may catch woman or woman may catch man—
whatever the pattern, either is behaving as either must. But
there is a tradition, which is that the woman's desirability
must fill the man with such a sense of power that he longs
for the comforts of weakness and loss.

It is best if the woman should be lusty and uninhibited,
aware of her attractions and also aware of her needs. Something as uncomplicated as the Wife of Bath:

> As help me God, I was a lusty one
> And faire, and riche, and yonge, and wel begone:
> And trewely, as min husbondes tolden me,
> I had the best queint that mighte be.
> For certes I am all fulli venerian
> In feling, and my herte alle marcian:
> Venus me yave my lust and licorousnesse,
> And Mars yave me my sturdy hardinesse.
> Myn ascent was Taur, and Mars therinne;
> Allas, alas, that ever love was synne!
> I folwed ay min inclination:
> By vertue of my constellation:
> That made that I coude nat withdraw
> My chambre of Venus from a good felaw.
> Yet have I a marke of Mars upon my face,
> And also in another privee place.
> For God so wisely be my salvation,
> I loved never by no discretion,
> But ever folwed min owne appetite,
> All were he shorte, longe, blake or white;
> I toke no kepe, so that he liked me,
> How poure he was, ne eke of what degree. . . .

An agreeable body and a co-operative attitude are superb
foundations—necessary foundations if the sport is to provide

its most exquisite sensations. For the fullest enjoyment lust must be restrained, refined, transmuted, checked, kept on the leash, mastered; it must be employed as in a game, with a pattern, with elementary rules, check and check mate. The man will be in the position of the lion-tamer, and on his judgment ultimate fulfilment will depend. But when it comes to the arts and the science of the game it is the woman who takes control. She watches the dial, gauges the pressure, handles the stop-cock, manages the stop-go of the sexual economy. She is a carnal Stock Exchange, inviting investment, indulging in a perpetual round of emotional buying and selling. Zainab, daughter of Delilah the Wily, will stand for all, as she proceeds through the markets of Baghdad, a veritable Tart's Progress, 'undulating her hips and moving her eyes beneath their little veil; her path was strewn with destructive glances, with smiles for some, silent promises for others, coquetries and temptations, with eye answers and lashes' questioning, murders with the lids, awakening by bracelets, music of anklets and general fire for all'. (*The Arabian Nights*, 'Tale of the Shifts of Delilah the Wily', trs. Mathers, 453rd night.) Zainab has it all, at least until the fan language was invented in the eighteenth century. And now play begins.

There are kisses, but I have a special chapter for kissing. The man feels and caresses the woman's body. One thing we must admit, irrespective of who shall be regarded as the true initiator and regardless of variant behaviour or changing fashions: it is normally the man who starts the exploration. Literature is full of complaints, for it is the woman's part to protest against what are called liberties. (In other human fields they demand liberties.)

> *Theer on a furm young Jonty Peil*
> *Sat cuddlin Amy Parkin*
> *When up she fleered and cuffed him weel;*
> *Said he, 'Ah's nobbut larkin.'*
> *Said she, 'Thoo felt my knees and wad*
> *Hev doon far mair thoo taistrel';*

runs a stanza from Jonathan Denwood's *Twinter's Wedding*.

Jonty was getting fresh, in the orthodox manner, and Amy moved her pawn in the approved manner. This was fencing, no one could say how the game was going at that stage.

The object is to place the hand on the knee, then to move it up the thigh which is soft and warm, and eventually to reach the Mount of Venus and the vagina itself. Now if a woman wishes to seduce a man, but meets resistance, a common ploy is to accidentally manoeuvre his hand on to her thigh. Once it arrives there, the man will experience such excitement that he will be unlikely to resist longer. A much more direct method, that of seizing the man's penis, is a minority act. J. C. Powys shows us a holy man in the dilemma of the more orthodox situation in his curious novel, *The Brazen Head*. Bonaventura, General of the Franciscan Order, has come to Wessex to discipline the freethinker Roger Bacon. He is preparing to dine at the satanic Lost Towers, the home of Baron Maldung. He noticed that there was a large empty throne near where the Baron was sitting, and that next to this throne sat an enchantress named Lilith, whose entrancing white thighs were exposed in such a way that any man seated on the throne would naturally and inevitably, as he poured out his wine, rest his free hand upon one of those perfect limbs and lightly slide his caressing fingers along its smooth surface. And it was here that Bonaventura was requested to sit. He tied a white napkin over his eyes but it was of no avail. His hand fell upon that soft bare thigh, as it had to, as not only the Evil One but the whole of Nature commanded, 'and a shock of unmitigated lust so overpowered him' as to disrupt all his plans. He either had to consummate his lust or escape. Being a good churchman, if less than a whole man, he chose the latter.

No matter who initiates, the actions are the same and the same end is arrived at. The man may caress the thigh to win the woman, or the man may be urged to caress the thigh so that he may be won.

> *For there are some a money-bag provokes*
> *And some are won by kindness, some by strokes,*

writes Chaucer ('The Miller's Tale', the Coghill version). And
even when the conquest is virtually complete and the thigh
is only an incident on the way, there is still much to be done
in the way of exploration before penetration takes place. In
one of his most famous poems, 'To His Mistris Going to
Bed', Swift lovingly recounts his travels through a friendly
continent:

> Licence my roaving hands, and let them go.
> Before, behind, between, above, below.
> O my America! my new-found-land,
> My kingdome, safeliest when with one man man'd,
> My myne of precious stones, My Emperie,
> How blest am I in thus discovering thee!

No doubt a well-bred lady quivered beneath the Dean's
roaving hands, by that time surely acquiescent. In the vulgar
world of the broadsides it was sometimes necessary to give
the man vocal encouragement, as in this Chorus to 'A Westminster Wedding, or Like unto Like, quoth the Devil to the
Collier', one of the Wood Collection of Broadsides, c. 1600-
1695:

> Tom come tickle me, Tom come tickle me
>   Tom come tickle me once again.

An invitation to feel. Feeling is the penultimate act, the final
rousing to a state of excitement that will overwhelm all resistance—although in the case of the girl who cries Tom, come
tickle me, there must be precious little resistance to overcome. But feeling, like any sexual act, has a dual purpose—
as the man's fingers creep into the moist interior he knows
that something else must soon follow. There is very little
literature of feeling, or frigging. Either it is indelicate, or
the authors have more urgent matters to discuss. But in itself
it is not indelicate, it is one of the preliminaries that a Van
de Velde or a Chesser will permit—and it is time-honoured.
Barton published the following among his Egyptian love

lyrics dating from 2000 to 1100 B.C., in *Archaeology and the Bible*:

> *I am thy darling sister.*
> *I am to thee like a bit of land*
> *With each shrub of grateful fragrance.*
>
> *Lovely is the water-conduit in it,*
> *Which thy hand has dug,*
> *While the north wind cooled us.*

In the Middle East the bride was frequently referred to as sister.

We pause here, on the threshold of the final act, lust about to collect the spoils. The auxiliaries are numerous. There is no point in examining each portion of the body and assigning to each a special function in the work of surrender, to use a term that is in little favour today. Besides, these areas have become monstrously ugly under the title of 'erogenous zones'. Each lover finds his or her speciality. Fanny used to pull Gaussin's head down on her knees and inhale him, breathe in his eyes, his hair, every inch of him, like a bunch of flowers. (*Sappho*, by Alphonse Daudet.) Van de Velde alludes to lovers who taste each other, who find such stimulation in the saliva of the loved one that they cannot progress far without it. And then, to be quite comprehensive, we must include those elderly gentlemen who proposition young maids quite honourably: all they want is warmth. Aubrey wrote of William Harvey, the great physician: 'I remember he kept a pretty young wench to wayte on him, which I guess he made use of for warmeth-sake as King David did. . . .' I only mention this as an example of how two people in search of very different rewards may find themselves in identical positions.

'A Mysterious Attraction'

What is it? Without the mysterious attraction that we call

desire, said D. H. Lawrence, there is only the calculating decision of the mind, sex-in-the-head.

> And this, this desire, is the reality which is inside love. The ego itself plays a false part in it. The individual is like a deep pool, or tarn, in the mountains, fed from beneath by unseen springs, and having no obvious inlet or outlet. The springs which feed the individual at the depths are sources of power, power from the unknown. But it is not until the stream of desire overflows and goes running downhill into the open world, that the individual has his further, secondary existence.
>
> '. . . Love Was Once a Little Boy', *Sex, Literature and Censorship*, ed. H. T. MOORE

The ancients tell us that no one managed to express the intensity of desire more forcefully than Sappho, and some of the fragments of her work that do remain certainly suggest uncontrollable energy. Much depends on the translator, no doubt. Herbert's 1713 translation of 'A Hymn to Venus' transmutes Lawrence's hidden spring into a raging fire.

> *I love, I burn, and only love require;*
> *And nothing less can quench the raging fire.*
> *What youth, what raving lover shall I gain?*
> *Where is the captive that should wear my chain?*

Sappho appears to have been adept at catching the physical signs of desire and pinning them down in her verse. Here is a prose translation by Henry Thornton Wharton, which appeared in his *Sappho* (1885):

> For when I see thee but a little, I have no utterance left, my tongue is broken down, and straightway a subtle fire has run under my skin, with my eyes I have no sight, my ears ring, sweat pours down, and a trembling seizes all my body; I am paler than grass, and seem in my madness little better than one dead.

And here is the same passage put into English verse by John Addington Symonds, two years earlier:

> For should I but see thee a little moment,
>   Straight is my voice hushed;
> Yea, my tongue is broken, and through and through me
> 'Neath the flesh impalpable fire runs tingling;
> Nothing see mine eyes, and a noise of roaring
>   Waves in my ear sounds;
> Sweat runs down in rivers, a tremor seizes
> All my limbs, and paler than grass in autumn,
> Caught by pains of menacing death, I falter,
>   Lost in the love-trance.

It is strange that some of the most sensual descriptions of lust should have come from a woman, for women are not always as whole-hearted in their approach to sex as men. Some men never attempt to restrain their lusts (keeping on the right side of the law, that is) but traditionally women have been expected to show some resistance. It is a common male opinion that no woman can resist for long, providing the pressure is reasonably persistent and/or subtle, and therefore she is usually in a divided mental state. In *Germinal* Etienne sees a girl struggling with a man and resisting with whispered supplications, but cynically he waited for the inevitable end. If the idea came to him that he should go to the girl's defence, he soon banished it; when girls say no it means they wish to be forced, he reflected.

Some authors have shown us women who are in a perennial state of desire, wrapped in it like a cocoon which seems to half remove them from the real life around them. This is a state of erotic dreaming, not forceful and brutal as in Sappho's case (neither the mind nor the body could stand that for long), but overwhelming nonetheless. There is no better example than George Moore's *Evelyn Innes*, whose 'life seemed to run down like the last struggling sand in a glass' when Sir Owen Asher kissed her. Moore himself wrote that this novel was 'one of the most powerful literary aphrodisiacs

ever written . . . though it be little else'. It is hardly that. It
is the story of a woman who has and needs lovers and whose
life is devoted to sexuality. It is decorously written and in the
long run is more evocative of sexual emotion than much of
the more outspoken kind of writing that we call 'erotic'. The
eroticism lies on the book like a heat-haze. But in the end
Evelyn feels the call of religion (it lies in the defeat of sex,
she discovers) and the total effect of the book is a triumph
for the spiritual life.

The rousing of desire can transform a person's whole
temperament, just as the fat, slobby Laurent in *Thérèse
Raquin* was transformed into a person of nervous sensibility
by his mistress's kisses. She implanted a nervous system of
great sensitiveness in his soft, fat body. He lost his calm and
his stolidity and no longer lived in a sleep; for a short time
his nerves and his blood were in equilibrium and he knew
the profoundest pleasures, but then the nerves became pre-
dominant and he was thrown into agonies that racked his
whole system.

Throughout the fundamentally romantic nineteenth century male lust was recognised as the energy that underlay the
whole social structure. Some societies, such as the Victorian
English, tried to ignore the reality. The code of the Parisian
dilettante, on the other hand, insisted on a cynical acceptance
of the fact, but instead of trying to establish a more satisfactory base for operations, deliberately falsified the relationship. It was cynical because it derived not from a desire to
establish the truth but to establish a convention of permitted
male wickedness. Sexually, the period 1830 to 1914 was the
French period. 'A mistress is to me what the *toga virilis* was
to the young Roman' is a statement that an Englishman of
the nineteenth century might have made, but it would have
revealed him as a francophil. It was in fact made by Gautier's
D'Albert, in *Mademoiselle de Maupin*, during his search for
the perfect mistress. Today a new generation, brought up on
D. H. Lawrence's horror of sex-in-the-head, is repelled by
such a pose. For the French attitude to sex, putting aside the
usual claims of logic (in a field where it is notoriously un-

reliable), represented the taming of desire from something
raw and feral to a neat predictable pussycat. Sex became a
game with rules instead of a sport that could not be fitted
into any Olympiad.

Images of Desire

The most didactic piece of work ever written by Shakespeare
was *Venus and Adonis*. Here we see Venus as the destructive
agent of sensual love and Adonis as reason in love. The one
spoils everything it touches, the other makes it beautiful.
Lust must be met by reason in love, truth and beauty, or the
ideas of man will go down before the appetites. When Adonis
is killed, beauty is killed, and the world is left in chaos, for
beauty, the soul of matter, unites all parts of creation.

The images of desire are often pictured as gross monsters
to whom one surrenders in madness bereft of reason. Painters
such as Bosch portray the inward horror of lust. Without the
gift of reason the animal senses are deceived by the meretri-
cious attractions of hideous forces. Until the scales drop from
the eyes the images appear fair; and then, what appeared
fair is seen to be loathesome. Of all our poets none illustrates
better than Spenser how easily man can be deceived. His
fertile imagination was in love with the world of the senses,
its splendour and its beauty, and with the furniture of love.
In later life he turned to religion as a refuge from the fret and
fever of carnal enticements. And so in 1596 this verse was
omitted from the third book of *The Faerie Queene*:

> Lightly he clipt her twixt his armes twaine,
> And straightly did embrace her body bright,
> Her body, late the prison of sad paine,
> Now the sweet lodge of love and deare delight;
> But she faire Lady overcommen quight
> Of huge affection, did in pleasure melt,
> And in sweete ravishment pourd out her sprighte:
> No word they spake, nor earthly thing they felt,
> But like two senceles stocks in long embracement dwelt.

Spenser's main failure comes from his retreat before such forces. Milton claimed that his famous description of the Bower of Bliss displayed the charm of the sensuous in order to emphasise the stern morality that eventually destroyed it. But why? What virtue lies in the destruction of the beautiful? The moralist must convince us that it is done in the interests of a higher and more enduring good. This Spenser certainly fails to do. Like many other writers, he changed and excised his work in later life in the service of a morality that fails to convince.

The images of desire that swarm through the pages of European poetry have usually worn masks. These are to be torn away, so that we may be warned by the evil lurking behind the beauty. At times this becomes a commonplace, so that we are led to look for the inevitable horror, so that we learn always to distrust beauty, so that we glibly pretend that such dubious pronouncements as 'beauty is but skin deep' are true philosophy. We see it in the work of the youthful Aldous Huxley, who was severely agitated by the prickings of sensuality and who was convinced, deep down inside his spirit struggling to free itself, that anything so alluring must be evil. Consider Jove, lying on his bed, tossing with lust for Leda:

> Libido like a nemesis
> Scourged him with itching memories of bliss.
> The satin of imagined skin was sleek
> And supply warm against his lips and cheek,
> And deep within soft hair's dishevelled dusk
> His eyelids fluttered; like a flowery musk
> The scent of a young body seemed to float
> Faintly about him, close and yet remote: . . .

So constant and powerful has this association been that even conscious attempts to exhibit evil usually turn to beauty as the obvious ally. Lust ceases to be a human function, bequeathed by God or Nature according to one's taste in theology, and becomes the Destroyer. In 1911 Ethel Archer brought out a volume of poems entitled *The Whirlpool*. She was one of the group, containing Victor B. Neuburg and George Raffalovich, around Aleister Crowley. By implication many of the poems are Hymns to the Beast. They drip with sensuality, a mingling of occult and erotic rapture. There is nothing overt, certainly nothing indecent, but a tingling of passion, orthodox and sapphic, which is insistently illicit: note the symbolism and the morbid imagery, 'Medusa's dreaded locks', 'poisonous passion of poppies', etc.

> *The heavy perfumed tresses clasp me round,*
> *Like to the tendrils of the early vine.*
> *Thy snaky limbs in sensuous coils are wound,*
> *And like Medusa's dreaded locks they twine*
> *About me—till I nearer thee incline,*
> *Nearer and nearer, and in joy surround.*
>
> 'The Song Virginal': to the Great One of the Night of Time

> *By the rapturous red of the roses, the ruin of rain,*
> *By the poisonous passion of poppies, the perfume of pain,*
> *By the dawn of the faun of desire, by the shudder of sleep,*
> *And the swoon of the moon as she catches the cry of the deep;*
> *I adore thee!*
>
> 'Lines to The Great High Priest of Elemental Passion'

It is not surprising that such images should consciously be used to produce an aura of evil: it is guilt by association.

The Morality of Lust

The Hebrews used to believe that lust was the devil's morality and attributed to him exceptional powers over the genital organs and human concupiscence. There have been occasional

interesting attempts to meet the devil on his own ground and
to destr‿y his allurements by satiety. One of the most
thoroughgoing of these was undertaken by a sect in the
eighteenth century calling itself the Buttlarsche Rotte, formed
under the inspiration of Eve Margaret von Buttlar, a woman
of good family, and her theological mentor, Justus Gottfried
Winter. She was presumably a nymphomaniac who turned
religion to account. As men and women were unable to resist
the lusts of the flesh she proposed to sicken them through
a surfeit. Eve attempted to do this single-handed, calling herself the Lake of Bethesda in which all her disciples were
invited to bathe regularly. Adam was rather more sadistic.
He added mutilation to copulation, his favourite Way to
benediction lying through the application of strong pressure
to his partners' ovaries, rendering them barren. Such tales
are really outside my field of enquiry, being social rather than
literary. Descriptions exist but they have never constituted
more than a very minor section of erotic curiosa.

Nearly all pornography depends ultimately on an accepted
state of lust. Serious writers have to contend with prevailing
conventions, and in some cases this situation provides the
drama essential to majority fiction and drama. Pornography
is concerned entirely with sensual stimulation and usually
rejects all resistance—possibly to its own loss. One of the
few examples in literature of an officially lustful society is
to be found in 'The Tale of Land Abdallah and Sea Abdallah',
in *The Arabian Nights*. Under the sea there are no marriages,
for there are no laws to control desire and inclination.
When a girl pleases a man, he takes her. When she ceases to
please, he leaves her—but usually she goes on to please someone else.

In contemporary society, reflected in a large number of
novels, it is clear that lust has come to be accepted (that is,
not resisted) by a large section of the population on the
grounds that it is natural. Those who have successfully set
aside the restraints of the past, among which they have in
most cases been reared, are probably still few. There is thus
a state of psychomachy existing in the mind of many a

woman who externally behaves with the highest degree of
confidence and moral indifference. (Women have had to fight
for this kind of freedom more vigorously than men.) The
mental agility displayed by the young lady in this limerick
from Count Palmiro Vicarion's *Book of Limericks* is probably
quite common:

> There was a young girl from Sofia
> Who succumbed to her lover's desire.
> She said, 'It's a sin,
> But now that it's in,
> Could you shove it a few inches higher?'

Boswell once suggested an ingenious way of enlisting lust
in the service of virtue. On Saturday 26 March 1763 he was
patrolling the streets in his accustomed manner with his
friend Erskine, when he saw, in a moment of vision, how his
endless sexual desire and his genuine, if weaker, moral desire
might be satisfied at one and the same time. 'If venereal
delight and the power of propagating the species were permitted only to the virtuous, it would make the world very
good,' he said.

> Our pulpits would then resound with noble descriptions
> of conjugal love. Preachers would incite the audience to
> goodness by warmly and lusciously setting before their
> imaginations the transports of amorous joy. This would
> render the pleasures of love more refined and more valu-
> able, when they were participated only by the good.
> Whereas at present it is the common solace of the virtuous
> and the wicked, the man of taste and the man of
> brutality.

What a noble plan, whereby only decent fellows, such as you
and me, should be allowed to have all the best girls. Such
sermons were no doubt preached in the Abbey of Thélème,

and it may still not be too late to draw the Archbishop of
Canterbury's attention to the scheme.

Persistence

There are two classes of persistence in the acts of lust. The
first persistence is that required to persuade the girl at all.
Traditionally she refuses, frequently using the time-honoured
phrase, 'Not the first time.' This may reasonably be regarded
as a promise but the young man may not feel capable of
waiting. Therefore he must use every art to persuade the girl
that there is nothing inherently wicked about the first time.
(It seems likely that, with contemporary standards of licence,
this type of persistence may not now be required to the same
extent.) The second persistence is a different matter altogether.
The young man has intercourse and enjoys it so much decides
he must have it again. But physically he may be in no fit
state. What is he to do? If he just waits supinely, it may take
too long, the girl may have to be in by eleven. There are ways
and means of recovering virility, and the young man resorts
to these in order to double his bliss.

Folk songs and poetry are full of examples of the first
persistence. Very few dairy maids called out to the swains,
Tom come tickle me!—not until they were pregnant, anyway. There was a ritual which had to be followed, and it is
clearly expressed in the following verses from 'The Coy
Shepherdess, or Phillis and Amintas', one of the Roxburghe
Ballads, spanning the sixteenth and eighteenth centuries.
Amintas sees Phillis lying in a wanton posture in a meadow,
and tries to seduce her, but she resists. (The wanton posture
is part of the ritual, and must be regarded as accidental, like
film actress's hair in outdoor epics.)

> Hotly he persued the Game,
> Whilst his heart was on a flame
> She cry'd Pish nay fye for shame
>   in faith you shall not do it
> But the youth her overcame
>   and eagerly fell to it.

> *Thus she strived all in vain*
> *Whilst she felt a pleasing pain,*
> *Yet he by no means would refrain*
>   *but kindly did embrace her,*
> *He kist his love and told her plain*
>   *he never would disgrace her.*

> *In great rage she flung away*
> *Tumbling ore the new-made hay*
> *Whilst he ashamed and breathless lay;*
>   *although he then displeas'd her, –*
> *He rally'd and renewd the fray,*
>   *and manfully appeas'd her.*

Note that this swain needed very little of the second type of persistence, being at the height of his powers.

The more sophisticated poets loved to suggest, with a twinkle in the eye, that it was a matter of routine for them to do it again. To what extent this was merely a cliché it is impossible to say—as I have said before, there is no subject under the sun about which men are more unreliable. The usual convention is that, once the girl has surrendered, she will take the lead in proposing a repeat performance. In fact, she will often be impatient with her lover's inability, although it is not normal for the man to admit any justification for impatience.

> *When with a sigh she accords me the blessing,*
> *And her eyes twinkle 'twixt pleasure and pain,*
> *Ah what a joy 'tis, beyond all expressing,*
> *Ah what a joy to hear 'Shall we again?'*

writes Dryden in *An Evening's Love*. And Sir Charles Sedley, who managed to combine extreme licence in his way of life with great decorum in his writing, falls back on the suggestive power of blanks. Each stanza of 'On the Happy Corydon and Phillis' ends with 'And——', which means: 'And something else, but what I dare not name.' Here is the penultimate stanza:

> *But Phillis did recover*
> *Much sooner than the swain;*
> *She blushing asked her lover,*
> *Shall we not kiss again?*
> *And——*

In this field, so often given over to boasting, there are few
poems so painfully honest as 'The Choise of Valentines',
usually attributed to Nashe, although a friend of mine denies
the possibility. The author goes to a brothel and his mistress
Frances is brought for him. She throws herself on him, kisses
and strokes him—and he comes. This premature ejaculation,
so familiar to young men before they have learnt control (or
perhaps it is not learnt, I suspect they just wait until natural
ardour lessens), is in itself rarely mentioned in literature. But
the author's description of his attempt to rouse himself for
a more successful combat is exceptionally detailed and is
possibly the earliest piece of writing about physical sex in
English that can justly be called realistic.

> *What shall I doe to shewe myself a man?*
>   *It will not be for ought that beawtie can.*
> *I kisse, I clap, I feele, I view at will,*
>   *Yett dead he lies not thinking good or ill.*
> *Unhappie me, quoth shee, and wilt not stand?*
>   *Com, lett me rubb and chafe it with my hand.*
> *Perhaps the sillie worme is labour'd sore,*
>   *And wearied that it can doe no more.*
> *If it be so (as I greate a-dread)*
>   *I wish tenne thousand times, that I were dead.*
> *How ere it is; no meanes shall want in me,*
>   *That maie availe to his recoverie.*
> *Which saide, she tooke and rould it on hir thigh,*
>   *And when she look't on't, she would weepe and sighe,*
> *And dandled it, and dance't it up and doune,*
>   *Not ceasing, till she rais'd it from his swoune.*

Agony

This is blocked or rejected lust. Wilson in *The Naked and the Dead* talks nostalgically of the days when he was a bellboy at a provincial hotel and he used to 'love it up' every afternoon with the singer of a band that had come to town. When it came to women he was a sonofabitch. Lots of women had told him that they had never met a man like him. But what was the use now? 'It jus' plays hell on a man when he ain't got a woman.'

The man may have the woman but she rejects him. This is the case of M. Hennebeau in *Germinal*. Poor Hennebeau was in a much worse position than Wilson, for his wife despised him. Added to physical frustration was the sense of insufficiency, which certainly never troubled Wilson. Hennebeau had a vision, renewed each morning, that during the following night he would possess her as her lovers had possessed her. But it never happened. She was repelled by him and he lived a life of relentless torture. When at last he discovered that she had taken their nephew for a lover he was tempted to make a scene, but what was the use? If it were not the nephew it would be a servant. Anyone but him.

In other words, you could possess the woman but not her appetite. Marriage gave you certain rights, but it was in a commodity that brought no satisfaction unless freely given. This was Othello's complaint:

> *I am abused; and my relief*
> *Must be to loathe her. O curse of marriage,*
> *That we can call these delicate creatures ours,*
> *And not their appetites! I had rather be a toad,*
> *And live upon the vapour of a dungeon,*
> *Than keep a corner in the thing I love*
> *For others' uses.*

Although the image of lust is that of a rough, shaggy beast, it is often diverted from its purpose with surprising ease. The shame of premature ejaculation can be erased by a

successful second attempt, but what of the man whose lust
fades at the critical moment? Naturally, this is not an occasion
favoured by pornographers, nor does it occur very often in
orthodox fiction, though we may expect to encounter it more
often in the franker literary environment of our own time.
It is said that men who are preoccupied with spiritual and
mental problems tend to suffer from sexual incapacity because scientific ideas pass through their minds at the moment
when coition requires complete attention. Apparently lust is
a demanding beast and will brook no dilution of effort. There
was once a mathematician who never succeeded in complet-
ing his embrace because his whole being was so taken up by
problems of geometry and calculus that he would be shunted
from the labour of Venus to the solution of SSSR̈pdpdOdz.
There was also a prestidigitator who was frequently consumed
by sexual longing at the end of his performances in the
theatre. But he was never able to satisfy his desire for just
as he engaged in intercourse a technical trick would come
to his mind and destroy not only his desire but also his ability
to finish what he had started. His case was even worse than
that of the mathematician, for after a while he was so affected
by fear of failure that he was unable to attain his goal at all,
even when no card trick supervened.

It is surprising that lust, which from personal experience
one feels to be all-powerful, and which is represented in this
light in much erotic literature, and which terrifies the law-
givers in many societies, should in fact be so delicate. It is
surprising that lust should be so easily tamed, yet it can be
taught, like a dog, only to operate at certain hours. There
was once a species of French fiction called 'five to seven'. This
was so named from the period in late afternoon when women
found it easiest to meet their lovers. Later, when married and
no doubt respectable, this was still the time when they found
it easiest to please their husbands. It is also surprising that
although lust is like a vast ocean which appears at times to
be about to engulf the human race, there are so many people
who wistfully long for it to come to them and are never
gratified. Lust tends to concentrate on certain chosen targets.

Maupassant writes of two ladies at the Cannes Battle of Flowers in his story 'Rose'. It is nearly perfect. But one thing is lacking. A little love. Marguerite murmurs: 'Without it life is to me unbearable. I must be loved, even if only by a dog. All women are really like that, whatever you say, Simone.' And only a few novels away there is a vibrant young lady who does not know how to manage all the love that is thrown at her. How unfair.

FOOTNOTES

1. Successful female resistance is recorded in the *Heptameron*, but many of the company find it distasteful. By glorying in in their resistance they become 'like inhuman and cruel beasts'. Writing of the same case, Brauvônie says she killed herself, and praises a woman who regained her health by surrendering to her doctor.

2. Modern bundling, in America at least, is on this pattern. 'More special contact may call for more privacy. On occasion, some nudity may be involved, and there are a few records of males who sleep nude with partners with whom they become involved in intensive petting while never having genital intercourse. Sometimes naked genitalia are placed in apposition, again without effecting coitus.' (Kinsey, *Male*).

9: *Kissing*

Probably the most intimate of all personal acts. One is at first tempted to believe that copulation should be so regarded, but copulation is a union of the animal bodies which is hampered by distance. More sheer pleasure is to be gained from copulation but less mental excitement. One is often aware that something is missing—that is when copulation occurs without psychological engagement. A word might be said for fellatio or cunnilingus but they are both partial acts which cannot attain to a true sense of union. But why might they be considered as candidates? Because the mouth is involved. Of all sexual organs, the mouth is the closest to the brain centre, the focus of thought and feeling. This is why I used the word 'distance' in my second sentence. Mouth to mouth brings the lover essentially closer than any other act. The literature of romance is full of such phrases as 'I felt my soul escaping' and 'my senses grew faint', all of which stress the importance of the controlling mind. A kiss is a decision, and has frequently been treated as such by many writers, as I will illustrate. Decisions belong to the upper areas of the body. The reason why it is not regarded as the sum of sexual experience is because it cannot lead to satisfaction. Kissing increases the desire, which is animal. It is intimate but not complete.

The Romans had three words for the kiss: *oscula* (which was applied to the cheek in friendship), *basia* (applied to the mouth in affection), and *suavia* (to the lips in passion). The practice was a comparatively late innovation among the Europeans, and the Celtic languages have no word for it. (The Irish and Welsh *pog* and *poc* were adapted from the Latin *pax.*) The sniff kiss, popular among Orientals, was known in Vedic India about 2000 B.C., and the mouth kiss appears to have been introduced during the Mahabharatic period. From there it spread outwards, but did not become established in Egypt in ancient times. The Chinese used to regard the European kiss as vulgar and suggestive of cannibalism. Africans used to dislike it and Winwood Reade once described the horror expressed by a native girl whom he kissed in the English fashion. But goodness knows what recent Westernisation has done to all this.

Western theorists do not subscribe to the cannibalist origin of the kiss. Remy de Gourmont, in his *The Natural Philosophy of Love* (trs. Ezra Pound), suspected that the practice may have some connection with avian custom. As male birds lack erectile tissue, coition is by simple contact. 'Displeasing as the comparison may be, it is a play analogous to the mouth to mouth kiss or, if one prefer, to the pressure of two sapphists clasped vulva to vulva.' C. M. Beadnell, in an essay entitled 'The Origin of the Kiss', which gave its name to a book of essays, went even further back. Among some of the earliest and simplest of animals, such as the protozoa, he wrote, certain individuals come into contact for a brief while, part company and then go their own way. During such surface apposition—for that is all it has been—a slight exchange of material has taken place, so that after separation each organism contains within itself particles of living matter that have been subjected to the impacts of two different sets of environments. Such dual experience enables the organism to adapt itself better to the varying circumstances of its ever-changing surroundings. It has been enriched by *variation*, one of the cardinal experiences of life. When insects and other small creatures creep into crevices and holes it is not always due to the instinct to hide themselves. Loeb and others have shown that it is in part due to a desire to get as much as possible of the body surface into contact with a solid; given the choice of concealment in a dark but open space, or of contact with two transparent glass plates exposed to a strong light, many of these creatures choose the latter, even though it entails death from isolation. When the *lumbricus foetida* is placed in a glass tank it invariably comes to rest in an angle between the floor and the side, that is, in a situation where the maximum areas of its body surface is in contact with a solid. But if several of these worms are placed in the tank they will lie side by side, the majority thus securing an extra plane of contact. Loeb thinks this habit of crowding together is enhanced by the soothing effect of each other's skin secretions, for if different species are placed together they will not seek contact with each other.

This is not a very convincing argument. Why should the worm prefer a glass wall to the member of a different species? Don't some ladies prefer lap dogs even to members of their own species? Could not this argument 'explain' why one man socks another on the jaw? And why the gap of aeons between the *lumbricus foetida* and the Mahabharas?

Vivamus, mea Lesbia . . .

The most celebrated literary treatment of the kiss is the poem by Catullus beginning with the above words. It is one of the most poignant poems in any language. I intend to reproduce a few renderings in English which will demonstrate, among other things, what translators get up to. First of all, Ben Jonson's version. It should be borne in mind that the habit of kissing in England was noticed and wondered at by foreigners as far back as the sixteenth century. Erasmus wrote to a friend that if he came to England he would be kissed by all the girls all the time. Catullus's poem was a great favourite with the Island Race.

> *Kiss me, sweet: the wary lover*
> *Can your favours keep, and cover,*
> *When the common courtin jay*
> *All your bounties will betray.*
> *Kiss again! no creature comes;*
> *Kiss, and score up wealthy sums*
> *On my lips, thus hardly sundered,*

> *While you breathe. First give a hundred,*
> *Then a thousand, then another*
> *Hundred, then unto the other*
> *Add a thousand, and so more;*
> *Till you equal with the store*
> *All the grass that Romney yields,*
> *Or the sand in Chelsea fields,*
> *Or the drops in silver Thames,*
> *Or the stars that gild his streams*
> *In the silent summer-nights,*
> *When youths ply their stol'n delights;*
> *That the curious may not know*
> *How to tell 'em as they flow,*
> *And the envious when they find*
> *What their number is, be pined.*

This is obviously a very free rendering, even if you have never seen the original. Compare this with Burton's translation, a much more awkward, self-conscious affair. The outstanding feature of this poem is the numbering of the kisses, and in most translations it is the only common factor. That had to be kept; for the rest, each translator creates his own ambience, usually to return to the note of envy in the last lines.

> *Love we (my Lesbia!) and live we our day,*
> *While all stern sayings crabbed sages say,*
> *At one doit's value let us price and prize!*
> *The suns can westward sink again to rise*
> *But we, extinguished once our tiny light,*
> *Perforce shall slumber through one lasting night!*
> *Kiss me a thousand times, then hundred more,*
> *Then thousand others, then a new five-score,*
> *Still other thousand other hundred store.*
> *Last when the sums to many thousands grow,*
> *The tale let's trouble till no more we know,*
> *Nor envious wight despiteful shall misween us*
> *Knowing how many kisses have been kissed between us.*

In Burton's edition of Catullus his poetic renderings were accompanied by prose translations, by Leonard C. Smithers. These are naturally closer to the letter of the original, though the spirit may fall flat. Here is his version of *Vivamus, mea Lesbia*.

> Let us live, my Lesbia, and let us love, and count all the mumblings of sour age at a penny's fee. Suns set can rise again: we when once our brief light has set must sleep through a perpetual night. Give me of kisses a thousand, and then a hundred, then another thousand, then a second hundred, then another thousand without resting, then a hundred. Then, when we have made many thousands, we will confuse the count lest we know the numbering, so that no wretch may be able to envy us through knowledge of our kisses' number.

Technically no objection can be made to the accuracy of this, except in the last two lines—but most translators seem to go astray there. Catullus's *invidere* implies more than 'envy', rather 'to cast an evil eye upon'. It was considered bad luck to count blessings too accurately.

Here is a spirited modern rendering by Jack Lindsay, which appeared in his edition of Catullus Englished:

> *My Lesbia, let us live and strain*
> *our love through all Time's pores, I pray—*
> *till we don't care a tinker's curse*
> *for moral men that slander love.*
> *Suns drop to earth yet lift again—*
> *for us when the quick circle of light*
> *gutters away, the sky above*
> *shuts with a thick unbroken night.*
> *And so, my Lesbia, let's rehearse*
> *our game of kisses while we may . . .*
> *a thousand first, a hundred then;*
> *a second thousand from our store;*
> *a hundred—or a thousand, say;*
> *and then another hundred more.*

> *And while we tot up kisses, let*
> *some endless touch so daze each mind*
> *that what we've counted we forget*
> *and thus may cheat malicious men*
> *who hope, with evil eye, to blight*
> *our kissing, but despairing find*
> *infinity flag far behind.*

This version is one of the few to mention the evil eye. Yet
some years later, in an anthology of Latin erotic writing called
Ribaldry of Rome, Lindsay essayed a new version of this
poem. (This is possibly an indication of the fascination it
exerts over all who know it.) The second version is greatly
compressed, and in my opinion the better for it, but the evil
eye is one of the elements that has been squeezed out.
Incidentally, the original poem contained thirteen lines;
Jonson's version contained twenty-two and Lindsay's first
twenty-one, whereas Burton stuck close to his model with
thirteen. Lindsay's second attempt also contains thirteen
lines. It is in every way the closest of all to Catullus.

> *Quick Lesbia, let us live and love.*
> *At a brass farthing let us reckon*
> *the talk of old, morose-eyed men.*
> *Suns sink, and burn again above.*
> *With us, when the brief light is broken,*
> *there's one long night and sleep that's blind.*
>
> *Give me a thousand kisses then,*
> *a hundred, thousand, hundred more,*
> *and then a thousand from your store,*
> *a hundred, till in kissing-maze*
> *we lose our counting in a daze*
> *and cheat malicious men who find*
> *their wondering envy flag behind.*

Let us conclude with Byron's imitation, inscribed 'To
Ellen'. It cannot be regarded as a translation—the absence

of repetitive numeration is sufficient proof of that. But it introduces the romantic tenor unknown to the Romans, and here signified by 'for ever'. Catullus wrote of an endless night but this was obviously a metaphor. Romantic earnestness insists on the idea being taken seriously. Catullus writes of a night; Byron will only be satisfied with eternity.

> Oh! might I kiss those eyes of fire,
> A million scarce would quench desire;
> Still would I steep my lips in bliss,
> And dwell an age on every kiss;
> Nor then my soul should sated be,
> Still would I kiss and cling to thee:
> Nought should my kiss from thine dissever,
> Still would we kiss, and kiss for ever:
> E'en though the number did exceed
> The yellow harvest's countless seed;
> To part would be a vain endeavour—
> Could I desist?—ah! never—never.

Kinds of Kiss

Rufinus, in the Greek Anthology, shows us that deep kissing was known and appreciated among the Greeks;

> Were it only a butterfly touch
> On the mouth, lightly brushing the lips,
> The kiss of Europa was sweet;
> But she scorns all such marginal sips.
> It's with mouth closely cleaving she draws
> A man's soul from his finger tips.

The translator is Philip M. Pope and in case you think the introduction of finger-tips into the discussion sounds rather odd, please refer to the prose translation below where it becomes clear that this is actually what Rufinus said.[1] Elsewhere in the Anthology the kisses of three ladies are compared by Paulus Silentiarius (in the Cycle of Agathias). We are told that Galatea's kisses are long and strong, Demo's are soft, whereas Doris bites you. Whose is the most exciting? Demo's, says the author, because her mouth is sweet as honey. Incidentally, in the *Arabian Nights* it is stated that a man sucks a woman's upper lip while she sucks his lower.

Deep kissing has remained popular in Europe and particularly in France, hence its alternative name, French kissing. In the Pays de Mont area of the Vendée deep, exploratory tongue-kissing, sometimes lasting for hours, used to be enjoyed by unmarried couples in public. This custom is known as *maraichinage*, after the name of the local people, the *Maraichins*. While there is obviously a wide range between butterfly-stroking (which might be called *effleurage*, which is a technical term used in massage therapy for gentle caressing) and deep kissing, it has never been categorised in our own culture. For this we must turn to the Indians.

The *Kama-Sutra* represents an astonishingly systematic approach to sex, one that has not been surpassed even in our own day, when reduction to system is hopefully regarded as the God that Will not Fail. Vatsyayana observes that the kiss should be given on the forehead, the forelocks, the cheeks, the eyes, the male's chest, the breasts, the lips and the interior of the mouth. Among the people of the Lata country, in Southern Gujerat, there is the custom of kissing the vulva, the armpits and the region above the pubes. The penis, so popular in Europe at certain periods, is omitted.

There are three forms of lip-kiss. These are called Limited, when the girl gently touches her lover's lips but does not attempt to press or suck them; Trembling, when the man takes the lower lip of the woman between his own, and she is uncertain whether to respond or withdraw, thus setting up a trembling sensation; and Exploratory, when the girl covers the eyes of her lover with her hand and shuts her own, then takes the tip of his lower lip between her own lips and caresses the imprisoned lip with a rotatory movement of her tongue. There are also five other kinds of lip-kiss in which the man is generally an active partner. In the Straight kiss he seizes the lower lip of the woman. In the Oblique kiss the face of one of the partners is screwed round a little towards that of the other and the lower lip is held with lips pressed in the form of an O. In the Revolving kiss one kisses the other, while holding the head and chin, and turning them. The Pressed kiss is similar but more robust—there is also a gentler form of this, called Gently Pressed, and a Sucking kiss, known as Drinking the Lip, when pressure is exerted with the tip of the tongue. The fifth variant is called the Super-Pressed, when the lower lip is taken between the thumb and forefinger, and is pressed into the shape of a ball, and is then touched with the tongue, and pressed and sucked by the lips without being bitten.

Vatsyayana suggests love play in the shape of wagers as to who will capture the other's lips first. If the woman loses she pretends to be put out. Then, catching him off his guard, she seizes his lips with her teeth and laughs triumphantly. This heightens sexual passion. If the woman sucks the lower lip of her lover, he may take and suck her upper lip. This is called the Concurrent or Responsive kiss, or the Kiss of the Upper Lips. If one takes both lips of the other and sucks, making a whistling sound, it is called the Cupping kiss. A woman cannot suck a man's upper lip if he has a moustache, because it is repugnant. If lovers brush each other's tongues and palates it is called the Battle of the Tongues.

There are four types of kiss on other parts of the body. These are the Balanced, which is on the pelvis, navel and chest, neither too forcibly nor too lightly; the Forcible, on the breasts, cheek and vulva, requiring a considerable amount of passion; the Worshipful, on the breasts and down to the waist, but always given chastely; and the Mild or Affectionate, which is given on the forehead or the eyes. Kisses may also be named according to circumstances, e.g., the Passion-Arousing, which kindles the female to burning heat, the Starter or Diverting, which is given while preoccupied, to end a quarrel or to stop a man dropping off to sleep, the Signalling, which shows desire when returning home late, the Reflecting, which is blown on to a mirror or water to show intention, and the Transferred, which is given to a child or portrait, hinting at

desire for another. A woman may kiss a man's toes, but the
man must not do anything so abject. If a woman, while massag-
ing a man's body, places her face on his thigh or kisses his
great toe, it is called the Interrogatory or Demonstrative kiss.

Many of these rules are human and amusing, yet the very
idea of classifying anything so intimate as a kiss is repugnant
to traditional European taste. I say traditional, because today
there are signs of an opposite trend, although it would be
truer to call this American. The Indian approach to sex makes
of it a craft, an activity that requires only industry and
patience for the greatest rewards. This is not the European,
essentially romantic idea. This postulates perfection, but perfection is a state that is not to be attained by practice but
by the merciful intercession of the gods. The process is
mysterious, and its glory lies in its mystery. Théophile Gautier
once described the perfect kiss in *Mademoiselle de Maupin*.
It occurred when D'Albert was out riding with Rosette. He
leant over and put his arm round her waist. She laid her head
on his shoulder. It was chaste, delicious and perfect—and
never to be repeated. No amount of rules and instructions
would have brought it back. In fact, they tried frequently,
even going to the extent of returning to the same place in
the same season in the same manner, but fruitlessly. A
romantic kiss is not subject to any kind of diurnal control.

> Nothing in the world could have been more pastoral and
> more simple. Some trees, some clouds, five or six blades
> of wild thyme, a woman, and a ray of the sun falling
> across it all like a golden chevron on a coat of arms.
> I had, further, no sensation of surprise or astonishment!
> I knew where I was very well. I had never come to the
> place before, but I recollected perfectly both the shape
> of the leaves and the position of the clouds; the white
> dove which was crossing the sky was flying away in the
> same direction, etc., etc.

This is sheer platonism. By accident the lovers had, once and
once only (it cannot happen twice) stumbled on the ideal

form of the kiss. To describe it is impossible. One describes
the environment. As Flaubert described Madame Bovary's
amours by a catalogue of the furniture. As one sees one's
own in the dents in the pillow and mattress.

Danger Signals

A kiss is a decision, I wrote earlier in this chapter. It is treated
as such by the libertine and feared as such by the girl who
is still feeling her way.

Those who regard kissing as harmless sport are playing
with fire. It is the first act in a chain which leads to seduction.
Venus knew it well. The speed with which she got to work on
Adonis is alarming. She bore him down and started to cover
him with kisses.

> *And yet not cloy thy lips with loathed satiety,*
> *But rather famish them amid their plenty,*
> *Making them red and pale with fresh variety;*
> *Ten kisses short as one, one long as twenty:*
> *A summer's day will seem an hour but short,*
> *Being wasted in such time-beguiling sport.*
>
> 'Venus and Adonis', SHAKESPEARE

There is not a great deal of literary interest in the kiss,
but there is one outstanding fact. It is practically ignored by
eroteurs and pornographers because it is insufficiently exciting. For public writers it represents permissible sex, and therefore comes in for a good deal of significant, if perfunctory,
treatment. It is that part of sex that need not be concealed by
asterisks, and in some cases it is even used as a metaphor.
(Some French writers, for instance, have used *baiser* as an
equivalent for fuck.) In some cultures kissing is a proprietory
activity; in the wrong place it is a warning of seduction. There
is an example in Plautus's *Asinaria*, or The Ass-Dealer.
Argyrippus needs money to gain Philaenium in marriage. Two
slaves get it for him by a trick. Before handing it over they
insist on being allowed to kiss Philaenium. One says to her
(in the English of E. H. Sugden): 'Transform me to a serpent,

let me have a double tongue', by which he meant, put your tongue between my lips as you kiss me. Diabolus hopes to win her and gets Parasite to draw up a severe marriage contract. It includes:

> If she perchance must cough, she shall not cough
> So as to put her tongue out when she coughs,

which would be regarded as an invitation to kiss. Meanwhile Argyrippus and his father Demaenetus are enjoying the marriage feast with Philaenium. Demaenetus sits next to Philaenium and starts kissing her. Philaenium behaves like a courtesan and appears to enjoy it, much to Argyrippus's discomfiture. Demaenetus's wife, Artemona, witnesses and overhears his behaviour and conversation. When Philaenium asks if her kisses are better than his wife's, he compares the latter to ditch-water. Artemona drives him home in a fury. The Epilogue sums up as follows:

> If the old man did deceive his wife and have a little game,
> That is nothing new or wondrous; other people do the same;
> No one has so strict a conscience or so resolute a breast
> That, if once the chance is given, he won't do just like the rest.

Asinaria is a sexy play but all the implications are made through kissing. We are invited, though not compelled, to understand a more thorough-going degree of sexual activity than the text actually asserts. But if we wish to take the text at its face value, the suggestion is still that kissing is the first act in a chain, and those concerned must be prepared for the consequences. The warning is admirably expressed by Chaucer in 'The Persones Tale'. He discusses the Seven Deadly Sins and says that the devil uses all his fingers to bring people to lechery. I quote from Skeat's version:

The fourthe finger is the kissinge; and trewely he were

a great fool that wolde kisse the mouth of a brenninge
ovene or of a fourneys. And more fooles been they that
kissen in vileinye; for that mouth is the mouth of helle:
and namely, thise olde dotardes holours, yet wol they
kisse, though they may nat do, and smatre hem. Certes,
they been lyk to houndes; for an hound, whan he cometh
by the roser or by other busshes, though he may nat pisse,
yet wole he heve up his leg and make a contenaunce to
pisse.[2]

It is therefore natural that kissing should be part of a
whore's repertoire, though it may only be needed on occasion.
When she stops you in the street and you know exactly what
she wants (and better still, what you want) kissing is neither
expected nor indulged in. But it is quite a different matter
when the whore is engaged in seduction, possibly with a
young man who is not quite sure of himself, and needs a little
persuasion. There is a little known whore's primer in the
English language called *The Whore's Rhetorick*, published in
1683, and purporting to give the accumulated wisdom of
Mother Cresswell, a bawd who is frequently mentioned in
Restoration literature. This is the kind of advice that she
gives to the girls in her charge:

It must be known that this Arrow, the Tongue, shot from
the Bow of the Lips, when kisses are dispensed, does make
a very remarkable impression; and it is worthy observation, with what alacrity the Blood and Spirits correspond
to the raising a lascivious desire, at the gliding of this
Member between the opposite Lips, just so far as to hit
the white, that is, the Lovers Teeth: but it is likewise
true, that some not well informed in this exercise, thrusting their Tongues with impetuosity into the Mouth of
him they kiss, do nauseate rather than please; or using
this appurtenance of a kiss indiscreetly at times, do
render it less pleasing, nay hated sometimes, as not agreeable to the expressions of the sweetest love. . . .
Remember you to frame your Tongue acute, in form

of a Darts head, and so to dispose the motion that the
extremity or tip may only pass to and fro tickling between
the Lips, without forcing too hard on the borders of the
teeth.

Mother Cresswell in fact waxes lyrical on the subject of kissing, claiming that it incites the beloved soul to the table of
Venus as if the tongue spake within. She knew, from years
of experience, that skilled kissing will guarantee results. So
did Lady Booby, in Henry Fielding's *Joseph Andrews*. In her
efforts to seduce chaste Joseph she refers to his reputation
among the parlour maids, and he replies that he has never
gone beyond kissing. 'Kissing!' exclaims the lady, 'do you
call that no crime? Kissing, Joseph, is as a prologue to a play.
Can I believe that a young fellow of your age and complexion
will be content with kissing? No, Joseph, there is no woman
who grants that but will grant more. . . .'

There are so many stages and gradations in the art of
kissing that much may be learnt of a girl's experience of love
as a whole from this one aspect. There is a rather touching
poem by Ovid (but, being by Ovid, the mockery is never far
away) about a girl whom he had lost touch with for a period,
but who, on renewal of contact, showed rather more command
of kissing technique than she had possessed before. What is
the only possible conclusion? Here is Jack Lindsay's translation:

> *The kiss she granted me forgivingly*
> *was a far better kiss than those I'd taught her.*
> *I had the impression she'd learned something new.*
> *Yes, that remarkable kiss was an ominous sign.*
> *I'm worried that she joined her lips to mine,*
> *and mine to hers, with such a loving deftness.*
> *And yet that worry's not the only one.*
> *I don't complain that kisses were exchanged*
> *(although I complain of that as well),*
> *I'm bothered that she couldn't have acquired*
> *such kissing virtuosity without*

a long and close acquaintanceship with someone,
and I have no idea
who was the expert whom she amply rewarded
by kissing back the way he kissed.

There is a long passage in that most torrid of novels, *Evelyn
Innes*, describing the kiss that sealed the union between
Evelyn and her lover. It is the most obviously erotic passage
in the book. She lies in her chair, fascinated as he plays the
love music out of *Tristan* (the novel is terribly Wagnerian)
and speaks of the motif of the love call. She begins to feel
faint; he comes across and kisses her. 'This is very foolish of
me,' she says, and throwing her arm round his neck, kisses
him back. He confesses his love and she asks him when he
first knew it. It was when she returned from Greece, he says,
but in fact it was at the moment when he kissed her, although
he dared not tell her that. She says it is wrong to kiss him,
it will make her miserable, then turns her face to him and
kisses him again. 'She'll be an adorable mistress,' he thought,
'and in four years the greatest singer in England.'

The kiss is clearly an act of enormous potential, a promise,
a danger sign, a decision. That society agrees I can best
express by one amusing, unsensational passage from a newspaper. One passage never proved anything, but there is no
doubt in my mind that the fears that lie behind the legal
action mentioned below are familiar and powerful in a large
sector of our society. Men simply must not be allowed to go
around kissing young girls. The heading for this news item,
taken from *The News of the World* for 11 July 1915, was
'Kissed Breathless':

> Although he said it was only a 'fatherly kiss', Charles
> Franklin, manager of the Southern Optical Company,
> Strand, was sharply fined at Bow Street for assaulting
> Mabel Woodward, 14, a messenger girl. Complainant
> stated that she delivered a parcel to defendant at his
> shop. He took her into a little office in the rear and kissed
> her several times, 'so that she could hardly get her breath'.

When she managed to get away he gave her twopence
and asked her not to tell anyone. She returned to her
firm and told the manager what had occurred. The girl's
mother said she called upon defendant and asked him
what he meant by insulting her daughter. He replied, 'I
only kissed her in a fatherly way. If it is blackmail you
have come for, I know how to deal with you.' He added
that he had kissed other girls, and they had not made
any fuss. Defendant said he gave the girl some coppers
for bringing the parcel, and in thanking him she held
up her mouth to kiss him. He gave her a kiss and she
went away. He thought no more of the matter. The
magistrate said he was satisfied that the girl was kissed
without her consent. In these days, when girls were so
much needed in place of men, it was important that they
should be protected against conduct of this sort, and he
ordered defendant to pay a fine of £3 and 10s costs.

Robert Herrick, the Kissing Poet

I must say that the passage just quoted leaves a nasty taste in
my mouth. There is something disturbing about the high
moral tone adopted by the magistrate and, one suspects, by
the newspaper. One can almost hear the mother asserting that
hers was a good girl, hers was. And what was it all about?
A kiss—and a girl of fourteen. I have no doubt that the girl
was upset, but I am not sure that she would have been upset
if she had not grown up with the belief that kissing is devil's
work.

Poets of the fifteenth and sixteenth century wrote so naturally and consistently of kissing that one is compelled to accept
that in those days it was a custom acknowledged by all and
resented by none. I have already referred to the famous letter
of Erasmus, in which he alludes to the popularity of kissing
in England. Today we shake hands, a horrid carnal act that
might lead the devil knows where. I stated at the beginning
of this section that no act of love can be more intimate than
a kiss, but intimacy is what you make it. I have seen women

whose very glances, whose shrugging of the shoulders and whose perfume have been so provocative that a kiss might have been an anti-climax.

No one deserves the title of Kissing Poet better than Robert Herrick. His *Hesperides*, 1648, vibrates with kisses and kissing. One feels, as when reading certain French authors, that the word 'kiss' is not always to be taken literally. Like so many other poets he produced his version of Catullus' kissing poem, although he made no reference to the Roman. It is addressed 'To Anthea'.

> *Ah my* Anthea! *Must my heart still break?*
> (Love makes me write, what shame forbids to speak.)
> *Give me a kisse, and to that kisse a score;*
> *Then to that twenty, adde an hundred more:*
> *A thousand to that hundred: so kisse on,*
> *To make that thousand up a million.*
> *Treble that million, and when that is done,*
> *Let's kisse afresh, as when we first begun.*
> *But yet, though Love likes well such Scenes as these,*
> *There is an act that will more fully please:*
> *Kissing and glancing, soothing, all make way*
> *But to the acting of this private play:*
> *Name it I would; but being blushing red,*
> *The rest Ile speak, when we meet both in bed.*

From this it is fair to assume that Herrick was more prolific with his kisses than Catullus, and also rather more outspoken. No one can doubt the Roman poet's true meaning. Herrick prefers to be more explicit, which is not really characteristic of him.

The idea of multiple kissing, without the explicit desire, is developed in a poem 'To Dianeme':

> *Give me one kisse,*
>   *And no more;*
> *If so be, this*
>   *Makes you poore;*
> *To enrich you,*

> *Ile restore*
> *For that one, two*
>   *Thousand score.*

Here are other poems on the same theme, all short, for Herrick was a man of fits and starts and little perseverance, one feels.

Kissing and Bussing

Kissing and Bussing differ both in this;
We busse our Wantons, but our Wives we kisse.

A Kisse

What is a Kisse? Why this, as some approve;
The sure sweet-Sement, Glue and Lime of Love.

In the following kissing once again leads to something that 'will more fully please'.

Up Tailes All

> *Begin with a kisse,*
> *Go on too with this:*
> *And thus, thus, thus let us smother*
> *Our lips for a while.*
> *But let's not beguile*
> *Our hope of one for the other.*

> *This play, be assur'd,*
> *Long enough has endur'd,*
> *Since more and more is exacted;*
> *For love he doth call*
> *For his Uptailes all;*
> *And that's the part to be acted.*

Another with the same end in view:

Kisses Loathsome

I abhor the slimie kisse
(Which to me most loathsome is).
Those lips please me which are plac't
Close, but not too strictly lac't:
Yeilding I would have them; yet
Not a wimbling Tongue admit:
What sho'd poking-sticks make there,
When the ruffe is set elsewhere.

Finally, another example of the multiple-kiss conceit, found in a British Museum manuscript.

His Mistris to him at his Farewell

You may vow Ile not forgett
*   To pay the debt,*
Which to thy Memorie stands as due
*   As faith can seale It you*
Take then tribute of my teares
*   So long as I have feares*
*   To prompt mee, I shall euer*
Languish and looke but thy returne see neuer
*   Oh then to lessen my dispaire*
*   Print thy lips Into the ayre*
*   So by this*
Meanes I may kisse thy kisse
*   When as some kinde*
*   winde*
Shall hither waft it and In leiu
My lipps shall send a 1000 back to you.

Now we must go on to 'the part to be acted'.

FOOTNOTES

1. Europa's kiss is sweet though it reach only to the lips, though it but lightly touch the mouth. But she touches not with the edge of the lips; with her mouth cleaving close she drains the soul from the finger-tips.

2. Busshes: some MSS give 'beautees' or 'beauteis'. Holour: lecher, adulterer: Smatre: taste slightly.

Come, pretty one, shall I loue, thee?
Saie, little one, shall I proue thee?
Gentely mouinge, be not crewell!
Wishe louingly, oh my iewel!
Taulke coyely, moue affection!
Toye prettiely, cause erection!
Looke meriely while I woe thee!
Blushe cherefully whilst I doe thee!
Looke prettiely! oh, that's meetest!
Doe feeleingly! oh, that's sweetest!
Fall willingely, and lie flatly!
Keepe close to me, whilst thou ar't at me!
Moue sprightfully, and lie pantinge!
Shewe rightly nothinge be wantinge!
Speake fayntely; fayrely languishe!
Die daintely in sweet angwishe!
Sweare euermore, I shall woe thee!
And euermore, plucke me to thee!

The old ballad tells the whole story. And now we come to consummation, to climax, to orgasm. In terms of feeling it is the cathartic explosion that gives the lover peace. When Hasan Badr al-Din slept in a burial ground he was seen by a charming Jinniyah. She was so delighted with him that she called a Jinni to look, and on being asked what he thought of Hasan he said, 'Allah, Allah! There is not his like any-where! Many a female organ shall, as it were, explode because of him.' Is this perhaps what the popular press mean by the

term 'population explosion'? Sir Thomas Brown admitted, in
his *Pseudodoxia Epidemica*, that 'those learned Arabicks' did
not surprise him when they declared that 'the felicity of their
Paradise should consist in a Jubile of copulation, that is, a
coition of one act prolonged unto fifty years'. So highly do
human beings rank the ultimate sexual pleasure.

The Orgasm

Literary treatment of the orgasm has varied enormously, particularly from one period to another. In the extracts that follow
it will be treated as a matter of ineffable joy and as an affair
of essential violence. It has been treated as a joke and as a
ritual. On the whole, the civilisations of the past found
pleasure in it and the modern world seeks significance in it.
At times it has ceased to be an act and has become a symbol.
At other times it has become an obsession. There is surely
no more important act in life and equally none that has led
to more idiotic pontificating. First of all, let us run through
the various possibilities.

Our own Restoration tended to be so mixed up about sex
that it tried to reduce it to the status of a leisure-time recrea-
tion. Nothing could be more trivial, and ultimately more silly,
than the kind of valuation expressed by the Earl of Dorset
in a poem entitled 'On Dolly Chamberlain, a Seamstress in
the New Exchange':

> Dolly's Beauty and Art
> Have so hemm'd in my Heart,
> That I cannot resist the charm:
> In revenge I will stitch
> Up the hole next her breech
> With a needle as long as my arm.

This is not jollity, but mere vulgarity. I doubt if any other
period in literature has produced anything quite so banal.
Many other literatures have had their periods of lightearted-
ness about sex, without losing all dignity. Lucian, for instance,

author of *Lucius or the Ass*, was the last person in the world
to be solemn or morbid about sex, to invent fantastic theories
(which are surely surrogates for pleasure) or to reduce it to
fodder for a manual of instruction. He was just serious
enough to avoid being silly, which appears to be a difficult
balancing act. Palaestra treats the sexual act as if it were a
wrestling match—and isn't it, if the most is to be got out of
it? 'All right, my boy,' she says to Lucius,' strip and rub
yourself with some of this perfume.' His job is to get his
opponent down and force her legs apart. After a bit of skir-
mishing you pull away, then make a frontal attack with your
teeth, once more into the breach, one big push—but try
not to hurry, wait a bit and then make the final assault. The
special beauty of such matches is, says Lucian, that both sides
invariably win. This is absolutely pagan and, of course, was
never completely wiped out by Christianity. But although joy
remained, jollity became suspect; the doubts of the puritan
have today given way to the absurdities of the theorist—
absurd, because they frequently have no foundation in
observation and are accepted simply because they are
fantastic.

The Wrestlers are Penis and Vagina, and nowhere is their
unending struggle more faithfully recorded than in the
Chinese classic, *The Golden Lotus*. One of the protagonists
is always the tireless Hsi-men, whose champion is one of the
most redoubtable in literature.

> *A warrior of stature not to be despised*
> *At times a hero and at times a coward.*
> *Who, when for battle disinclined,*
> *As though in drink sprawls to the east and west.*
> *But, when for combat he is ready,*
> *Like a mad monk he plunges back and forth*
> *And to the place from which he came returns.*
> *Such is his duty.*
> *His home is in the loins, beneath the navel.*
> *Heaven has given him two sons*
> *To go wherever he goes*

> And, when he meets an enemy worthy of his steel,
> He will attack, and then attack again.

The opposition is varied, but the most stupendous contests
are fought with Golden Lotus. Her part was so exquisite the
whole world desired it.

> Tender and clinging, with lips like lotus petals
> Yielding and gentle, worthy to be loved.
> When it is happy it puts forth its tongue
> And welcomes with a smile.
> When it is weary, it is content
> To stay where Nature put it
> At home in Trouser Village
> Among the scanty herbage.
> But when it meets a handsome gallant
> It strives with him and says no word.

The orgasm is often referred to among writers as a 'little
death', an imagery that needs no explanation. (It is easy to
feel the temptation to expatiate on the death-wish at this
point, but equally necessary to resist it if this work is to
remain sane, that is, an account of what is known.) Axel
Heyst says one never forgets that death, a statement that
requires much qualification. In an Italian film, *Seduced and
Abandoned*, the layabouts of a Sicilian town discuss the
number of times the human male copulates in a lifetime.
One quotes a medical source as saying 30,000 while another
claims that a healthy man copulates daily between the ages
of 18 and 60, but fails to work out the total. (He thought
it was a higher figure. I make it just over 15,000.) It seems
impossible that each of these occasions will be one that will
stay in the memory for the rest of one's life. Indeed, one of
the disquieting things about sex is the way in which an apparently overwhelming experience so quickly slips out of consciousness. But if Heyst means that the act of copulation is
at the time felt to be in a class apart from any other human
experience, he is right.

One can forget many physical experiences, one forgets
the greatest pleasures, the loveliest bodies, the most en-
chanting garments and entourage, but one cannot forget
that feeling of the sinking of the whole world, that feeling of finality when our whole cosmos is blown to pieces,
when one is reduced to some anonymous atoms, when the
great whirlpool of nature and life is taking us to the
bottom of creation. One never forgets that experience
which is a mystic experience and which comes from the
same source of life from which mystics have drunk.

The orgasm is virtually impossible to describe but some
brave attempts have been made. Those in *The Arabian Nights*
are, as might be expected, light-hearted and frequently metaphorical. The contest between Zumurrud and Ali Shar is unusually realistic in its description ('Tale of Zumurrud and Ali
Shar', 330th night, trs. Mathers). Ali Shar leapt on her like
a lion upon a sheep. He remembered the road, and thrust
his shepherd's staff into the food-bag, going straight ahead
without letting the narrowness of the way distract him. When
he got to the end he stood up straight, at once the porter
and the Imam of the gate. This is orthodox Arabian metaphor, but then we come to this:

On her side, Zumurrud did not leave him for an inch;
she lifted with him, knelt with him, rolled and rose with
him, panting and following his every movement. Game
answered game and thrust answered thrust, amid a
hundred charming flirtations of the two bodies. Cry called
forth sigh, sigh called forth cry, until the noise of them
attracted the little eunuchs, who lifted the curtain to
see if the King had not need of their services. Before
their frightened eyes appeared the spectacle of their King
stretched out on his back, intimately covered by the young
man, adopting quick poses, giving snort for snort, thrust
for assault, inlay for scissor work, and for every shiver
a pleasant trembling.

It is necessary to explain at this point that Zumurrud had been
posing as the King.

A combination of metaphor and straight description was
also followed by the Greeks. Dioscorides tells us how he was
'immortalised by a Dorian girl with rosy buttocks' (Greek
Anthology, Bk V). She lay on her little couch with her 'moist
delights spread wide'. Then we have an account of a long
venereal journey, while they jigged up and down, until his
white manhood rushed out and the girl shuddered in orgasm
and her limbs relaxed—entirely satisfactory, one might say.
Another combination type description is to be found in
Nashe's *The Choise of Valentines*, where a genteel traditional
opening is suddenly followed by a poetic spasm which closely
matches the act.

> *Alass, alass, that love should be a sinne,*
> > *Even now my blisse and sorrow doth beginne.*
> *Hould wide thy lap, my lovelie Danae,*
> > *And entretaine the golden shoure so free,*
> *That trilling falles into thy treasurie,*
> > *As Aprill-drops not half so pleasant be,*
> *Nor Nilus overflowe, to Aegipt-plaines,*
> > *As this sweet-streames, that all hir joints imbaynes;*
> *With Oh, and Oh, she itching moves her hipps,*
> > *And to and fro, full lightlie starts and skips.*
> *She jerks her legs, and sprauleth with hir heeles,*
> > *No tongue maie tell the solace that she feeles.*
> *I faint, I yeald; Oh death rock me a-sleepe;*
> > *Sleepe-sleepe desire, entomed in the deepe.*

The Golden Lotus is extremely frank and rarely lubricious
in its treatment of the sexual act, that is to say, there is no
change of tone once the lovers start to copulate as there is
in the work of many self-conscious writers. Critics who object
to the sordidness of much writing about sex ought to welcome
the Chinese book. In it copulation is both natural and noble.
When Hsi-mên makes love to Moonbeam he breathes heavily
and she makes strange little noises, while her hair is spread

out on the pillow like a fan. Then she murmurs, 'My love, do not be so furious'. When they came to orgasm the semen flowed out of him like a river, and a typically Chinese image seals the act: 'the rain ceased and the clouds dispersed.' Hsi-mên suffers from satyriasis, like Maupassant, and therefore sexual descriptions are manifold, but it still remains a realistic work. Having performed with Porphyry, he rushes to the Lady of the Vase and shows her his still enormous penis. She complains that she is not well, that he will wake the baby, but he insists—and he has the power to take whatever he wants. She tells him he must be mad to make love to a woman during her period, it could cause her death and bring him bad luck. He pushes in, rejoicing at the snowy whiteness of her legs, but can only get half way. She is afraid the blood will flow and takes a napkin to stop it. Hsi-mên kept at it for an hour (he doesn't realise that he is killing himself, but he finds it extremely difficult to reach consummation), and finally forced his penis in to its full extent. 'Please go carefully,' she said, 'it hurts me.' Then Hsi-mên took a drink of ice-cold water and his semen rushed out in a stream. His limbs relaxed comfortably and 'he felt as fresh as the spring'.

How different is the Western approach from all this! The erotic act is rarely mentioned, yet alone described, before the enthusiasm of the Elizabethan dramatists began to cast restraint aside. And when there is a reference it is often shamefaced. Even the merrieness of Merrie England (where the adjective has the force of 'amorous' as well as 'jolly') is at times absurdly coy. In fact, coyness rather than stimulation is the effect aimed at. This is seen again and again in English folk song and poetry. I have already quoted the verses on 'Young Coridon and Phillis', attributed to Sir Charles Sedley, which has all the characteristics of folk poetry even if the author is known to us. (This was printed in the collection, Pills to Purge Melancholy, 1719.) Coridon and Phillis sit in a grove, talking of love. It is a tale of seduction, with each stanza culminating with the suggestive 'And something else, but what I dare not name'. I can only give the last stanza here, but it is fully representative.

> *Thus Love his Revels keeping,*
>   *'Till Nature at a stand;*
> *From talk they fell to Sleeping,*
>   *Holding each others Hand;*
> *And something else but what I dare not name.*

Then there is 'The Maid of Tottenham', printed in *Choyce
Drollery: Songs and Sonnets*, ed. J. W. Ebsworth, 1886. The
maid asks a man to tie up her garter, and 'such tying of a
Garter I think was never seen.' In fact, it cost her her maidenhead but this appeared to her to be little loss, insofar as she
had had little benefit from it and had often been troubled by
it while lying on her bed. Again, each stanza has an identical
conclusion, this one being a fine piece of rhodomontade:

> *To fall down together, down*
>   *down, down, derry down,*
>   *down, down, derry dina.*

'Have-at a Venture', from *The Roxburghe Ballads*, 1540-1790,
ends each stanza with a variation of 'he bravely thrust it in',
which speaks for itself. Here boy meets girl and they agree
to 'put it in' without loss of time. There is literary merit in
this song; it has the air of being a celebration of love rather
than a mockery of it.

> *What pleasure is there like to this,*
>   *this Damsel then did cry,*
> *I've heard them talk of lovers bliss,*
>   *O! what a foole was I*
> *So long to live a maid, ere I*
>   *did this same sport begin;*
> *This death I now could freely dye:*
>   *I prithee thrust it in.*

Robert Burns, if *The Merry Muses of Caledonia* may be
attributed to him, brings a welcome forthrightness to the
subject.

> *The sweetest bed that e'er I got,*
> *Was the bellies o' the lasses, O*

he sings in 'Green grow the rashes, O', and

> *The mair ye bang, the mair she squeals,*
> *An' hey for houghmagandie*

where 'houghmagandie' is yet another term to add to our list
of synonyms for fornication. This is boisterous. Rough
humour, without the all too common snigger to be found
in this kind of material, may be illustrated by a song that
begins 'As Oyster Nan Stood by her Tub', which also appeared
in *Pills to Purge Melancholy*. She is visited by a vintner and
they set to work behind the bar, when his services are called
for 'as he was taking pains to please her'.

> *I'm coming, coming, Sir, says he,*
> *My dear, and so am I, says she, Sir.*[1]

And later:

> *She daily ventures at the same,*
> *And shuts and opens like an oyster.*

The Common Muse is not always coy and metaphorical,
and at times forthrightness goes beyond boisterousness and
becomes crudity. Here are two stanzas, not consecutive from
'Black Thing', which is in the Firth Collection of Original
Broadsides, in the Bodleian. A lass tells how Colin wanted
to play with her 'little black thing' and how he started to
fondle it.

> *I dreamt of no hurt but thought him quite blunt,*
> *And gave him the pleasure to play with my c——*
> *Then got up his p—— quite stiff for a fling,*
> *And ran it slap into my little black thing.*

Then I got on the ground and lay on my back
He drew his p—— and b—— my cunt in a crack.
My legs round his body I fired as a spring,
And dragged out the brains with my little black thing.

These manuscripts are amusingly inconsistent with their
asterisks! The last two lines are exceptionally vivid. The
dragging out the brains is an idea that will be encountered
again in a much later production, *Teleny*. And for crudity it
approaches the type of song that was popular in London
in the eighteen-forties, before the clean-up. Moreover, it is
written from the woman's angle. In literature copulation tends
to be a male joy, even a male joke, and in a poem such as the
above the female reaction is notably male. But occasionally
one comes across a song that might have been composed by a
woman (or conversely, by a true poet). One such is 'A Shepherd
Kept Sheep on a Hill so High', which was also in D'Urfey's
Pills to Purge Melancholy. A shepherd accosts a maid, who
refuses, but he forces her down and talks her round. It has
the genuine accent of the ballad that W. H. Auden managed
to catch so successfully two centuries later; it is sensitive and
beautiful and worth lingering on.

Then he took her and laid her upon the Ground, fa, la,
And made her believe that the World went round, fa, la,
Look yonder my Shepherd, look yonder I spy,
There are fine pretty Babies that dance in the Sky, fa, la.

And now they are vanisht, and now they appear, fa, la,
Sure they will tell Stories of what we do here, fa, la, la,
Lie still my dear Chloris, enjoy thy Conceit,
For the Babes are too young and too little to prate,
*   fa, la, la.*

See how the Heavens fly swifter than Day, fa, la, la,
Rise quickly, or they will all run away, fa, la, la,
Rise quickly, my Shepherd, quickly I tell ye,
For the Sun, Moon and Stars are got all in my Belly, fa, la.

Babies in the eyes, the earth moving, planets in the belly—these are all age-old methods of trying to describe the indescribable. One is reminded of Hemingway, poor Hemingway who eventually was compelled to face his own writer's reality, the need to describe love-making. (In the nineteenth century every self-respecting novlist had to describe death; today it is copulation.) How embarrassing that passage in *For Whom the Bell Tolls* sounds today. 'For him it was a dark passage which led to nowhere, then to nowhere, then again to nowhere, once again to nowhere, always and for ever to nowhere, heavy on the elbows in the earth to nowhere, etc., etc.' The defeated realist turns to romanticism. I really don't think one uses one's elbows.

So let us look at the set exercise in a few modern works. In a story called 'The Princess with the Golden Hair' (*Memoirs of Hecate County*) Edmund Wilson describes a fuck that can fairly be called exquisite. Everything about the lady was delicate and aesthetically ideal. The mount was of 'a classical femininity: round and smooth and plump; the fleece, if not quite golden, was blond and curly and soft; and the portals were a deep tender rose, like the petals of some fleshly flower'. Entrance was easy, owing to a 'honeysweet sleek profusion'—how wrong he was to imagine that his caresses had had no effect. It was a most ladylike performance, scarcely felt by him, for there was very little sensation. She herself 'consummated with a self-excited tremor that appeared to me curiously mild for a woman of her positive energy'. And then—'gently enough—I came too'. What a very pleasant change from the Vesuvian orgasms experienced by so many women in contemporary literature.

From quiet, unpretentious observation to the apocalyptic poetry of Lawrence Durrell in *The Black Book*. Lawrence Lucifer takes a girl into the country. They go in a field. We have an unusual situation here for there is snow on the ground. Their copulation sings with nature. 'It is a new nativity when I enter her, the enormous city crouched between her legs'—and the friendly cattle stand around like a Christmas card. When he enters she becomes an image in rubber, her smallest

bone will melt to snow under the friction of his penis. 'When
she comes it is all pearls and icicles emptied from her womb
into the snow.' There is tremendous excitement in this writing, and it does not embarrass like Hemingway's. It may be
the most successful attempt to do what can be done in no
other way. Only poetic luxury can reproduce the fleshly
luxury.

And now let's turn to the big, tough, roaring Twentieth
Century American male, hating all women and himself most
of all. Nelson Algren, *A Walk on the Wild Side*. This is the
regulation shot at the deep, satisfying shag. It's between the
feckless hero, Dove Linkhorn, and the nice storekeeper, Tera-
sina. He starts by hauling her clothes down to the waist. He
studies her breasts one by one (as though she had fifteen),
squeezes them and says they're 'ready for crating'. They get
down to business. Here eyes that had 'darkened with desire
now lighted in electric bliss'. His hide-tight jeans and her
black lace slip lay entangled inextricably (sic) on the floor.

> Right to the precipice's edge he brought her, letting her
> subside only to draw her yet closer to the brink. Prolong-
> ing her pleasure till it verged on pain. Then, needing
> to rid herself of all this, locked him more fiercely in, beat
> at his chest with both her fists, and upon the peak, with
> one flame-like thrust, fell and fell in a weightless delight
> released from all pleasure, all pain.
>
> Down and down in a dream of falling where nothing
> lived but two far-off voices in a Mindanao Deep of peace,
> some bottomless depth of perfect rest. Having a man's
> slow-drawn breath and a woman's grateful sobbing. . . .

Again the descent into a special kind of imagery of falling,
weightlessness, bottomless depth. The modern realist, who
strains every nerve to give us the texture of the life around
him, nevertheless tacitly admits that sex is different. Tacitly,
for it is an article of his faith that there is no quantitative
difference. This may be the reason why so many modern
writers reject sex as pleasure because pleasure is indescrib-

able. Certainly the Father of Realism would have felt more than dubious of his disciples. When Laurent and Thérèse are left together for the first time, no doubt is left in our minds of the animality of their passion. (Presumably animals, whatever their feelings, are never moved to associate with Mindanao Deep or flame-like thrusts.) Laurent bent down and caught the young woman against his chest. Her head fell back as he crushed her lips. 'She struggled for a moment in wild, savage revolt, then suddenly abandoned herself and slipped to the tiled floor. The act was silent and brutal.' (*Thérèse Raquin*, Emile Zola)

The latest move in sex is Hip, of which Norman Mailer is the major spokesman. The greatest thing of all for the hipster is the orgasm. Nothing else matters so long as it's a good one. It is equated with jazz: 'jazz is orgasm, it is the music of orgasm, good orgasm and bad.' No lecher or libertine of the past would have objected to the notion that the orgasm is all-important, but the evaluation has changed. The lecher is an old-fashioned soul who seeks pleasurable sensation and nothing else. The libertine desired conquest and triumph. What does the hipster want? Possibly an extreme. It is difficult to win any extreme of experience without landing in gaol; sex is a way, given a certain amount of common sense—not that that is a quality the hipster cares for. We are entering into a new phase of consciousness, he says, due to our experience of concentration camps, totalitarian terror, mass murder, genocide and the gas chambers. The existentialist, the psychopath, the saint, the bullfighter and the lover are genuine citizens of this new culture, their common denominator being their burning consciousness of the present. Each instant is good or bad. The orgasm is the heightened moment. Incompatibles have mated, 'the inner life and the violent life, the orgy and the dream of love, the desire to murder and the desire to create, a dialectical conception of existence with a lust for power. . . .' The psychopath becomes a model for existence. He 'may indeed be the perverted and dangerous front-runner of a new kind of personality which could become the central expression of human nature before the twentieth

century is over'. The psychopath is not always an extreme
case, and his condition is to be found in a host of admired
people. He is 'better adapted to dominate those mutually
contradictory inhibitions upon violence and love which
civilisation has exacted of us', writes Mailer in 'The White
Negro' (from *Advertisements for Myself*, 1959).

Mailer once wrote a column in *The Village Voice* in which
he gave some hip sexual definitions while playfully interpret-
ing the title, *Waiting for Godot*. After remarking that the
critics had decided it had something to do with God, he
added: 'But Godot also means 'ot Dog, or the dog who is hot,
and it means God-O, God as the female principle, just as
Daddy-O in Hip means the father who has failed, the man
who has become an O, a vagina.' In certain sections of the
community, the traditional, unhipped community, there is a
laconic saying, 'My name's Hunt', which can be interpreted
as follows: 'I may be a fool but not that big. My name's Hunt,
not Cunt.' It sometimes seems to me that Hip is trying to
make conventional, gutter irreverence acceptable.

'The Time of Her Time', an extract from a forthcoming
novel included in Mailer's *Advertisements for Myself*, is about
the orgasm, a Hip preoccupation. It marks a change of
emphasis from the nineteenth century's desire for the virgin
to a new frontier, the first conquest. For the virgin may be
possessed but without orgasm there is no surrender. The
combat described in this piece is marked, as is so much
American literary sex, by resentment flaring at times to hatred,
occasional reluctant tenderness (but always rare) and, fundamentally, an ability to come to terms with one's sexual nature
accompanied by a conviction that the uglier forms of conflict
are essential to such treatment. Hip is not a passing fashion.
It represents something that is real in us, that has been
obscured for many generations, and that may be coming into
the light again because the social environment is favourable.
But, like most new movements, it is awkward and groping.

O'Shaughnessy takes the girl, a Jewess, to his bullfighting
schoolroom three times. The first time was a failure, the
second an utter flop. (The degree of sexual failure is so marked

in modern literature one is tempted to regard it as yet another indication that something new is taking shape.) O.'s honour is at stake, though this is the last term he would use about his determination to be the first to make her come. The battle is described in great detail in all its phases, and with that lack of humour that distinguishes Mailer's frankness from Miller's (who was always happy in his work). You can compare the grimness in this with one of Miller's lyrics:

> And so I took her with a cold calculation, the rhythms of my body corresponding to no more than a metronome in my mind, tonight the driving mechanical beat would come from me, and blind to nerve-raddlings in my body, and blood-pressures in my brain, I worked on her like a riveter, knowing her resistances were made of steel, I threw her a fuck the equivalent of a fifteen-round fight, I wearied her, I brought her back, I drove my fingers into her shoulders and my knees into her hips. I went, and I went, and I went, I bore her high and thumped her hard, I sprinted, I paced, I lay low, eyes all closed, under sexual water, like a submarine listening for the distant sound of her ship's motors, hoping to steal up close and trick her rhythms away.

Inevitably we are back to imagery, not even Hip can manage the job without becoming a riveter or a submarine. But it is the change in the class of imagery that tells us everything. And where will these men seek pleasure? They lost it in poker long ago. Grog is a compulsion. Perhaps they will rediscover the fairy story.

But it wasn't easy. The girl kept coming near but she wouldn't go over. (Algren's hero sought this type of brinkmanship but that is now sentimentality.) She would give a cry of farewell and he would feel the shudders rippling through her, but then she held back. At last the odour began to be sexual, not the smell of sweaty armpits—smells have fetishistic value for Mailer, though he wouldn't like the language of the fetish at all. The momentum mounted higher

and higher but was just about to hang again when he said into
her ear, 'You dirty little Jew'. That did it, proving the
sophisticated Hip notion that social, racial and communal
factors can provide the major sexual inhibitions in a perverse
modern chick. She was now 'loose in the water for the first
time in her life' but he could do nothing, he was nothing
'but a set of aching balls and a congested cock, and I rode
with her wistfully, looking at the contortion of her face and
listening to her sobbing sound of, 'Oh Jesus, I made it, oh
Jesus, I did'''. And was she grateful? Of course not, she hated
him. Which was probably why she, a Jewess, put the onus
of her great pleasure on Jesus.

There could be no greater contrast than that between
the modern hatred of sex, which can only view surrender as
humiliation, and the traditional glorification of sex, based
on the acceptance of surrender as a transcendence of normal
experience. In the past women were transfigured by love, in
the new ethos that is struggling to be born sex tears aside
every mask and reveals the essential mess. The new compre-
hension is frequently allied to violence and crime, as facets
of a whole; the maddened lover of the past would commit
theft, murder and sacrilege to be permitted to love, which
was greater. When Demetrios earned the right, by these
methods, to possess Chrysis, he experienced something more
magnificent than even the most stupendous of natural spect-
acles (*Aphrodite*, by Pierre Louÿs). This was the transfiguration of the loved one, with her head tumbled back, clutching
a corner of the pillow and clinging desperately, as though
suffocating, her eyes like whirlpools, her cheeks aglow, the
swirl of her hair a giddying rhythm. These have been lost and
lost deliberately.

Always at the back of the act is the awareness that love is
ephemeral. It is possible to feel cheated that what seems
divine at the time can pass away like yesterday's breakfast.
Perhaps the hip mood is a determination not to be cheated.
For centuries poets and lovers have accepted *The Compleynt
of Mars*, as Chaucer put it:

> *To what fyn made the god that sit so hye,*
> *Benethen him, love other companye,*
>   *And streyn̄eth folk to love, malgre hir hede?*
> *And then hir joye, for oght I can espye,*
> *Ne lasteth not the twinkeling of an yë.*
>   *And somme han never joye til they be dede.*
>   *What meneth this? what is this mistihede?*
> *Wherto constreyneth he his folk so faste*
> *Thing to desyre, but hit shulde laste?*

And then comes a moment, almost a historical moment, when
a group of people refuse to accept any longer. The idea is
born that perhaps the 'joye' is not worth the effort, that perhaps behind the joye is a meaning that will prepare the way
for the breakthrough that men never cease to seek. That is
where love's *avant garde* stands today.

The Sensation

Omar Haleby played the part of sexual adviser to the Prophet
Mohammed and was a great believer in sexual stimulants.
No stimulant, in his view, was superior to prayer, which he
advocated before coitus along with the shouting of 'Allah'
at the moment of ejaculation.

Treating sex as a rite with religious significance seemed to
be natural to the Arabs, although it was frequently tempered
with more mundane aids to enjoyment. The Khalifah
Muawiyah asked the witty club-foot Abu Bahr ibn Kais what
he did when he wished to lie with his wife. ('The Tale of
King Umar al-Numan', *The Arabian Nights*, trs. Mathers,
62nd night.) Abu Bahr explained that first of all he talked
pleasantly with her, to put her in a good humour, then he
kissed her all over, to excite her, and then he laid her on her
back and charged her. At the critical moment he cried, 'Grant,
O Lord, that this seed be covered with your blessing and
modelled in beauty'. There is no comment necessary, except
to remark that one could hardly imagine Norman Mailer
uttering such a cry. One of his characters in *The Naked and*

the Dead, Wilson, may well have celebrated his pleasure with grunts and animal noises but in reminiscence he became more articulate and poetic. 'Man,' he said, 'it was like dipping it in a barrel of honey.'

Pornography, written almost entirely by men, insists on the pleasure enjoyed by the female and donated by the man. There are times when this kind of writing suggests that sex is a charity. One of the authors of the *Arabian Nights* tells how his hero was half way in when he was stopped by her petulant sighing. Why, he asked. She answered with a laugh, 'Moon of my eyes, I sigh for the other half.' ('Tale of Aziz and Azizah', 123rd night, trs. Mathers.) The men are not necessarily wrong. If we want real authority, we can go to Mary McCarthy, who describes Dottie's first orgasm in *The Group*. First she copulates with Dick, he teases her about having an orgasm the first time, pinches her nipples which stand up. He asks if she would like it again and she pressed her thighs together. She was ashamed of the violent sensation his exploring fingers had aroused. He told her how to handle him, she felt him stiffening, and this gave her a sense of power.

> She struggled against the excitement his tickling thumb was producing in her own external part; but as she felt him watching her, her eyes closed and her thighs spread open. He disengaged her hand and she fell back on the bed, gasping. His thumb continued its play and she let herself yield to what it was doing, her whole attention concentrated on a tense pinpoint of sensation, which suddenly discharged itself in a nervous, fluttering spasm; her body arched and heaved, and then lay still.

She hadn't enjoyed this climax as much as the first one. Some women preferred it, said Dick. It seemed to her almost perverted. The number of descriptions of female orgasm by a woman, even in our vast and recently liberated literature, is few.

The authors of the *Arabian Nights* wrote on the assumption that the female's pleasure was the greater. This was expressed in a peculiar way in the 'Tale of the Sea Rose of the Girl of China', 957th night. King Zain al-Muluk wished to prove to his sons that anything was possible to the Almighty. A king's only child was a girl, but to save him disappointment his wife told him she was a boy and brought her up as a boy. When the time came for her to marry, a Jinni exchanged sex with her on condition that they should reverse the arrangement when the job was done. But when the prince came to return the Jinni's sex he found her pregnant which meant that another exchange was out of the question. The Jinni said, 'One day a fellow Ifrit, the intendant of these regions, passed through the forest and came to see me. He knew by my changed smell that I was carrying a sex hitherto foreign, and fell violently in love with me. When he had excited a like sentiment in my heart, he joined himself to me in the usual manner and broke the precious seal of the packet which I had in care. I felt all that a woman would feel in like circumstances, and determined that a female's pleasure is more durable and more delicate than a male's. . . .' The Kama Sutra also distinguishes between the kinds of pleasure enjoyed by the two sexes. Auddalika claimed that females do not emit like males. This means that whereas the male merely removes his desire, the female feels another kind of pleasure although she cannot describe it. After emission the male is satisfied but the female is not. Another opinion, however, held that the longer a man takes over the act, the more the woman loves him. This would suggest that the female also emits, although the logic is rather obscure.

Nevertheless, that both sexes are capable of satisfaction (the end of desire) is recognised widely. In the poetic language of the sixteenth and seventeenth centuries a lover was said to die when he ejaculated. But they wish to die together, that is, if there is mutual affection. A song in Dryden's Marriage à la Mode (1673) puts the situation accurately:

The youth, tho' in haste
And breathing his last,

In pity died slowly while she died more fast,
Till at length she cried, 'Now my dear, now let us go!
Now die, my Alexis, and I will die too.'

Thus entranced they did lie,
Till Alexis did try
To recover new breath that again he might die:
Then often they died; but the more they did so,
The nymph died more quick and the shepherd more slow.

But what makes an orgasm thoroughly satisfactory as opposed
to merely satisfactory or even unsatisfactory? Pierre Louÿs
attempts an answer in *Aphrodite*. Demetrios loved Chrysis in
a dream and no longer wanted her in reality. The experience,
he feels, will be the same. 'What makes the difference in
mistresses is their individual style of preparing and climaxing
an act which, after all, is as monotonous as it is necessary—
an act which would hardly be worth all the effort we make
to find the perfect mistress, if that were all we had in view.
In this preparation and conclusion you excel among women.
At least I took pleasure in imagining it so. . . .'

So the woman is the effective agent in determining the man's
pleasure, and some of them are so aware of this that they
make it a profession which they take seriously. But we must
never forget the emotional power which may still sweep aside
all other considerations, with the result that either partner
may be reduced to a state of complete will-lessness, where
instincts are in full control. Sex jokes frequently use this basic
truth of sex, but none of them put it more neatly than one
of Aubrey's funny stories, this time about Sir Walter Raleigh,
1552-1618: 'He loved a wench well; and one time getting
up one of the Mayds of Honour up against a tree in a Wood
('twas his first Lady) who seemed at first boarding to be something fearfull of her Honour, and modest, she cryed, sweet
Sir Walter, what doe you me ask? Will you undoe me? Nay,
sweet Sir Walter! Sweet Sir Walter! Sir Walter! At last, as
the danger and pleasure at the same time grew higher, she

cryed in the extasey, Swisser Swatter Swisser Swatter.' (*Brief Lives*, ed. Oliver Lawson Dick.)

Preparation and tempo may be important aspects of technique, but they remain secondary. The initial and fundamental requirement is mutual consideration, which is a part of affection and half way to love. Dr Sofie Lazarsfeld, for the comfort of the poor male, gives away a feminine secret in her *Woman's Experience of the Male*, hoping that her sisters will forgive her, for it is in the interest of both sexes. The allegedly decisive and vital difference between the male and female tempos of sexual excitement need not be taken too seriously, she says, and the consequences need not be tragic. A considerate man who notices that his partner is slow will help her to arrive first by 'substitute acts'. If he performs his role properly she will be pleased to wait for him, and she may even have a second orgasm coinciding with his own. In effect, success is the product of mutual consideration plus technique, or rhythm. 'We are reminded of the popular custom in Thuringia,' writes Dr Sofie.

> There a couple will not marry until the boy and girl have sawn through a log together. If the rhythm of their movements agrees, the marriage takes place, otherwise the association is broken off. Observe the way a man eats or drinks: if he is hasty he will be the same in love. A man who does not throw away his cigarette while making love to a woman will obviously make an inattentive, inconsiderate husband.

This may appear to be a digression from erotic literature but it is essential to keep in close contact with erotic practice and its offspring, the written code. Female frigidity has played an important part in our literature, whether expressed or implied. It is an aspect of sex that cannot be ignored, and even those writers who are personally least inhibited have to come to terms with it. Goldstein, in Mailer's *Naked and the Dead*, has a problem of this kind. He is virile and is afraid Natalie is not getting all she should from it. He stops in the

middle and asks if she's warm. She smiles and tells him not
to worry about it. After a few repetitions he gets angry. In
the end she says she won't be able to tonight, but not to mind
her, just go ahead. This puts him off and he realises that now
he can't do it. She tries to soothe him but he speaks roughly
to her, saying he doesn't want a mother. She cries. 'He realises
after two and a half years of marriage that when she forms
that smile she is close to hysteria and terror and perhaps even
loathing.'

Why is she like it? Who knows? Perhaps it's cultural.
Perhaps she has been brought up to believe that sexual
pleasure is wicked; perhaps this has never been put to her
explicitly but the fag-end of this belief may have been passed
on to her subconsciously. Balzac deals with the situation,
though in reverse, in one of his *Droll Stories* ('The Married
Life of Fair Imperia'). The Lady Imperia married at the age
of forty-five but although she was in perfect health she could
not bear children. A physician from Paris told her that both
she and her husband took too much pleasure in the act to
have a successful pregnancy.

> Hence for some time, good lady, she strove to remain as
> unmoved as a hen under the cockbird, for this doctor
> had pointed out that in the natural state the creatures
> never failed to produce, which was, he said, because
> their females made no use of any artifice, love-play,
> tendernesses or any of the countless ways in which women
> dress the Poissy olives. That, said Imperia, was why they
> were called *brutes*, but she nevertheless took an oath
> never more to play with her beloved coral branch and to
> consign to oblivion all the love delights she had invented.
> Alas, even while she lay stretched out as sober as that
> German woman whose modest bearing resulted in her
> husband mounting her when she was dead, when, poor
> baron, he went to ask the Pope for absolution and the
> Pope issued that famous Encyclical in which he implored
> the ladies of Franconia to move just a little when in the
> act so that there might never be repetition of that sin. . . .

Men have a related but opposite problem. It is their role
very often to restrain themselves, at least for a time. Physio-
logically a man is not equipped to please his woman by
orthodox means after he has had his orgasm. There is therefore
an anti-hero whose duty is prolongation of the act and, with
it, pleasure. Here again we can turn to *The Group* for our
example. Kay's husband Harald was a cool customer. 'Even
in bed he kept his sang-froid; he did the multiplication tables
to postpone ejaculating—an old Arab recipe he had learned
from an Englishman.' Henry Miller has told us how he used
to fill his head with mechanical thoughts in an effort to hold
off. The *Ratirahasyam*, an ancient Indian work, claims that
a man's seed, even though it has moved dangerously close to
the forepart of his penis, will not issue if he thinks of a very
unsteady ape who is moving on the branches of a tree. Irving
Layton, a Jewish Canadian, honours the birth of Christ in
pagan fashion, and in his poem 'Christmas Day' refers to the
problem of the 'considerate man':

> *Holding it in*
>
> *Straining—groaning—sweating—*
> *But holding it in*
>
> *Then the climax*
>
> *As Wilhelm Reich would say:*
> *It was perfect*

The orgasm is an extreme situation and is celebrated in an
extreme manner. Groans, cries, screams—these are all familiar
to the comprehensive reader, but sadly unanalysed in Western
literature. They tend to be ignored or merely mentioned because they exist, an ignorant practice that stems from a narrow
conception of what is realistic in writing. The Indians were
naturally more curious and the *Kama Sutra* lists eight classes
of sound uttered by the woman: hin, thundering, cooing,
weeping, phut, phat, sut and plat. In addition she continually

utters words expressive of prohibition, sufficiency or desire
of liberation, as well as the words 'father' and 'mother'. One
of the few English writers who have considered this aspect of
congress worth attention is, not unnaturally, R. F. Burton,
and the following footnote to his translation of the *Kama
Sutra* has rarity value:

> Men who are well acquainted with the art of love are
> well aware how often one woman differs from another in
> her sighs and sounds during the time of congress. Some
> women like to be talked to in the most loving way, others
> in the most lustful way, others in the most abusive way,
> and so on. Some women enjoy themselves with closed
> eyes in silence, others make a great noise over it, and
> some almost faint away. The great art is to ascertain
> what gives them the greatest pleasure, and what special-
> ities they like best.

An addition to Dr Lazarsfeld's 'secret'. In *Lolita* Humbert
announced that it might interest physiologists to learn that he
had the ability to shed 'torrents of tears throughout the other
tempest'.

Mailer, through one of his characters, suggests that the
sensation is enhanced by what we may term the public quality
of your partner. In *The Deer Park* Sergius, an ex-Air Force
flyer, has an affair with Lulu Meyers, the film star idol of
millions. Every time he makes love to her he is aware that
he is doing what these millions hopelessly long to do. 'To the
pride of having so beautiful a girl was added the bigger pride
of knowing that I took her with the cheers of millions behind
me . . . I knew I was good when I carried a million men on
my shoulder.'

The sensation being so intense, could a woman be fucked
unconsciously? (It is presumably out of the question that a
man could perform unconsciously, though if he were the
passive partner the question could arise.) Suggestions have
been made from time to time that innocent girls have been
'interfered with' in their sleep. The only example I have

come across in literature is to be found in Iharu Saikaku's 'The Almanac Maker's Tale', from *Five Women Who Chose Love*. Osan, the wife, decides to play a trick on the clerk, Moémon, who has arranged, in rather lordly fashion, to sleep with the maid, Rin. The plan is that Osan shall await him in the bed and the maids will stand by with cudgels and staves to assault him. But the plan goes astray and all fall asleep. Moémon arrives, slips in with Osan, and 'in his eagerness for enjoyment, he dispensed with all verbal preliminaries and soon he had acquitted himself to his manly credit'. When Osan awoke later she realised with shame 'that Moémon had taken his pleasure with her while she slept'. Saikaku was famed in Japan for his realism but I can't help feeling that he has slipped up here.

And when it's all over? The storm which turns the world upside down, after which nothing can ever be the same again —let us turn to 'The Chambermaid's Second Song' from Yeats's *Last Poems*, 1936-9:

> *From pleasure of the bed,*
> *Dull as a worm,*
> *His rod and its butting head*
> *Limp as a worm,*
> *His spirit that has fled*
> *Blind as a worm.*

This is from a group of poems based on an incident from the *Historia mei Temporis* of the Abbé Michel de Bourdeille. A lady loves a man and promises to visit him, but in the event her chastity will not allow it. She bids him keep his room in darkness, as she would be ashamed to see herself—and sends her chambermaid. Susan O'Grady and the Colonel's Lady. The sensation is supreme, the giver of little account. To love a film star is to experience the ultimate, but she needn't be a film star—it is sufficient to believe she is one. Demetrios found it sufficient to dream he was with Chrysis. Yeats's poem could be obscene if he were only concerned with description —although it is hard to know how the unadorned truth can ever really be obscene. But it illustrates a conviction that grew upon Yeats as he aged—the primacy of sexual love, of the body, and the dependence of the spirit, however lofty its achievement, upon it.

The Genteel Approach

This is the one we've been accustomed to in all writing about lovers until very recently. (It must be understood, of course, that such statements refer to public writing, not secret pornography.) We can take our first example from Chaucer's *Troilus and Criseyde*, 1379-83. In this story and particularly in Chaucer's treatment of it (for it is partly a translation of and partly an addition to Boccaccio's *Il Filostrato*, which moves much more quickly but hasn't got the same degree of characterisation), most of the erotic excitement lies in the anticipation of Troilus's winning of Criseyde. This point is reached almost exactly half way. Here, in Chaucer's original language, are stanzas 179 and 189 from Book III. About twenty stanzas in all tell the story of the seduction and they rely partly for their effect on allusion and the reader's knowledge of what does happen when a man gets in a girl's bed. But training and knowledge are necessary for understanding. An innocent, or an asexual creature from Arcturus, would have no idea of what was happening.

> Hir armes smale, hir streyghte bak and softe,
> Hir sydes longe, fleshly, smothe and whyte,
> He gan to stroke, and good thrift bad ful ofte
> Hir snowish throte, hir brestes rounde and lyte;
> Thus in this hevene he gan him to delyte,
> And ther-with-al a thousand tyme hir kiste;
> That, what to done, for joye unnethe he wiste.
>
> O blisful night, of hem so longe y-sought,
> How blithe un-to hem bothe two thou were!
> Why ne hadde I swich on with my soule y-bought,
> Ye, or the leeste joye that was there?

> *A-wey, thou foule daunger and thou fere,*
> *And lat hem in this hevene blisse dwelle,*
> *That is so heygh, that al ne can I telle!*

Later Troilus, telling Pandarus about his 'glade night', said, as he was a true knight, 'I hadde it never half so hote'.

The convention of indirect description became so strong and familiar, the reader was rarely left in any doubt. That he occasionally was could be attributed to the author's desire to mystify the reader, although the reader might decide that this was not playing fair. Nor is it fair to be explicit about the whole of existence except one solitary act. In this translation of Ovid's fifteenth *Heroic Epistle* which he entitled 'Sappho to Phaon', Pope left no doubt in the reader's mind:

> *Then with each word, each glance, each motion fired,*
> *You still enjoyed, and yet you still desired,*
> *Till all dissolving in the trance we lay,*
> *And in tumultuous raptures died away.*

Of course, Pope wasn't allowed to go further than this, but now, when writers are allowed and do go further, the results are disappointing. Perhaps the trouble is that only the most fantastically skilled writing could approach the ecstasy of the thing described. Can one expect language that successfully describes a market scene to describe an orgasm with equal success? Hardly. A difficulty is that a sexual orgasm is in the reach of everybody; ecstatic language is not. Straight description reduces the orgasm to something as unanimated as ballroom dancing. Metaphor and abstraction have to be used to induce the correct tone. But once this is acknowledged, another barrier is raised. A certain type of reader, powerful in society, objects to the metaphorical method just because it tends to be successful. It was this that was attacked so fiercely by Buchanan in his *Fleshly School of Poetry*, with particular reference to Rossetti, who was doing what Pope had done in the passage above.

Flaubert never called himself a realist but some of his

admirers did. He introduced a midway method of describing
seduction. Instead of trying to describe the lovers' emotions,
and resorting to metaphor, hyperbole and poeticisms, he
simply described the material environment of love, as though
it received a flavour or impression from the act that was being
performed. Emma Bovary, for instance, met her first love and
second lover, Léon, weekly in a Rouen hotel. They kissed,
talked, gazed into each other's eyes and called each other
tender names. Then we leave them and float round the room.
Again, the experienced man or woman knows what it's all
about.

> The bed was large, of mahogany, in the shape of a boat.
> The curtains were in red levantine, that hung from the
> ceiling and bulged out too much towards the bell-shaped
> bedside; and nothing in the world was so lovely as her
> brown head and white skin standing out against this
> purple colour when, with a movement of shame, she
> crossed her bare arms, hiding her face in her hands.
>
> The warm room, with its discreet carpet, its grey orna-
> ments, and its calm light, seemed made for the intimacies
> of passion. The curtain-rods, ending in arrows, their
> brass pegs, and the great balls of the fire-dogs shone sud-
> denly when the sun came in. On the chimney between the
> candelabra there were two of those pink shells in which
> one hears the murmur of the sea if one holds them to the
> ear.
>
> How they loved that dear room, so full of gaiety, des-
> pite its rather faded splendour! They always found the
> furniture in the same place, and sometimes hairpins, that
> she had forgotten the Thursday before, under the
> pedestal of the clock. They lunched by the fireside on a
> little round table, inlaid with rosewood, etc., etc.

And it is not surprising that the disciple, George Moore,
should have resorted to the same method of recording a
moment and an act, as in his *Memoirs of my Dead Life*, with
an additional comment:

. . . the very wood we burned in the great fireplace, the shape of one log, how it fell into ashes at one end and, leaving a great knotted stump at the other, the moving of the candles into shadowy places so that the light should not fall upon our eyes—all these details are remembered, only the moment of ecstasy is forgotten.

But with George Moore we are not always certain what happened. Evelyn Innes and Ulick Dean leave the theatre together in a carriage, they embrace and kiss as if they would 'annihilate destiny' on each other's lips, knowing only a delirious present, without a future. The question we ask ourselves is, Did they, or did they not? The pellmell school of critics (of whom G. K. Chesterton was one) usually assumed that they did. We do know that this pair of lovers had previously embraced in her dressing room and that later she confessed to a priest that it had been a seduction. We had not known.

With recent literature the act becomes more explicit, although full, one hundred per cent sanction has not yet been granted by either the courts or society. Even J. P. Donleavy, whose *Gingerman* is as daring as any, felt obliged to observe some of the established proprieties. Sebastian is making love to Marion. Her hand is tightening and touching his groin. Then his mind roams to a certain Ginny Cupper who had once taken him in her car to the spread fields of Indiana. As he makes love to Marion his thoughts and feelings are engaged with Ginny. Then he returns to the present. 'I hear the train, Marion's breath in my ear. My stomach's shaking, my last strength. The world's silent. Crops have stopped growing. Now they grow again.' The crops have a metaphorical significance but they also grew in Indiana. A later bout between Sebastian and Christine is described by stream-of-consciousness, rocking from fantasy to reality without warning. You make your own adaptation.

I'm ready and juices in my groin. Dear Chris you're full of soft love spilling on your dark lips. Outside and down that road by St Patrick's Cathedral I hear the Gregorian

chant. It's not far away. She furrowed her tongue and
blew a warm moist air into his ear. . . . Are you cold
Sebastian, I like it slower, we fit so well, keep you from
coming out so much like a disappearing sun, so much my
female pumping body milking gold. . . . O now, tighten
me taste me O good gracious God I love it. Her head
hanging back, words moving her chin in his nook of
shoulder, have you come, I can't care but you're so funny,
could I have a cigarette. Sweat drying on their skins,
and blowing smoke to watch it on the ceiling.

Let us finish this section with a poem, untitled, by E. E.
Cummings which I cannot resist quoting in full. It says everything in the most delicate fashion and emanates a kind of
puckish joy. In the end she says 'Ummmm' which, according
to Aldous Huxley, is all that the most sophisticated criticism
and appreciation ever says, in essence.

> *may i feel said he*
> *(i'll squeal said she*
> *just once said he)*
> *it's fun said she*
>
> *(may i touch said he*
> *how much said she*
> *a lot said he)*
> *why not said she*
>
> *(let's go said he*
> *not too far said she*
> *what's too far said he*
> *where you are said she)*
>
> *may i stay said he*
> *(which way said she*
> *like this said he*
> *if you kiss said she*

may i move said he
is it love said she)
if you're willing said he
(but you're killing said she

but it's life said he
but your wife said she
now said he)
ow said she

(tiptop said he
don't stop said she
oh no said he)
go slow said she

(cccome? said he
ummm said she)
you're divine said he
(you are Mine said she)

Aids to Pleasure

Remy de Gourmont considered the limberness of the human
form well suited to coition but remarked that in all prob-
ability Daphnis was not the only lover to encounter initial
difficulties. He also pointed out that a bull that leaps clumsily
on a lowing cow, bending his useless hocks along her back,
often has to be helped by an indulgent farm hand. The
reproductive organs, in fact, are not always as well adapted
to their purpose as one might expect.

Where they are not, man makes up the deficiency. One of
the most obvious methods is the raising of the female rump.
Some verse in the Percy Folio MS (c. 1620-50), entitled 'Off a
Puritane', tells of a 'puritanical ladd' who met a holy sister
and 'layd his bible under her breeche, & merylye hee kist her'.
After the regulation complaint about such crude behaviour,
the nun says:

my Buttockes thé lye to lowe: I wisht
apocrypha were in itt!

Once the lovers are joined there is a great deal that the woman
can do to enhance the man's pleasure, and presumably her
own. Without resorting to machinery she can use her vaginal
muscles. In Burton's translation of the *Arabian Nights* (387th
night) one woman says to another: 'Verily a woman should
bring her husband, all of which she is mistress, by way of
excitement and rare buckings and wrigglings and motitations.'
In one of his famous notes Burton said that previous translators had ducked this passage, Torrens because he didn't
understand it and Burckhardt because he thought it wasn't
nice. The art of moving in coition, which even the most
modest woman practises to some extent, is taken seriously
throughout the East. 'In China there are professors, mostly
old women, who instruct young girls in this branch of the
gymnastic.'

A modern erotic publication, *Tableaux Vivants*, which was
translated from the French in 1888, calls this activity the
Casse-Noisette. The author becomes lyrical in his description
of how he encountered this rare capacity—rare in the West,
that is.

> I entered, I thrust—Ai'e! Heaven! What pleasure! The
> coynte of this chambermaid was like a rasp! This wait-
> ing-maid had that which Duchesses had not, that which
> I had vainly sought in Marquises—the CASSE-NOIS-.
> ETTE. It tightened on me, it pinched me. And these
> pinches and this vice, acting as a furious suction pump
> on my surprised member, astonished me. I enjoyed, I
> discharged, I sank with all my weight, etc., etc.

Then comes an extended footnote which defines this nut-
cracker and its action, calling it 'a highly prized peculiarity',
the use of the constrictor vagina muscles. 'The *casse-noisette*
can sit astraddle on a man and provoke the venereal orgasm,
not by wriggling and moving, but by tightening and loosening
the male member with the muscles of her privities, milking
it as it were.' This art goes back to highest antiquity, says the
author, and quotes a probably fictitious authority (A.

François) to the effect that the Chinese are shaped in such a fashion that by this method they 'can give enjoyment to the tiniest Chinaman in the Celestial Empire'. Finally, an anonymous courtesan is quoted: 'I possess the art of *casse-noisette*, which would make a lump of granite enjoy.'

If the Indians have gone further than any other race in ordering and regulating sexual practice, the Chinese have no rivals in the use of gadgetry to enhance sexual pleasure. Any reader of *The Golden Lotus* will remember that Hsi-mên kept a set of instruments in a case. His preparations for love are described at length. He drank some spirit and swallowed a pill, then fastened a silver clasp at the base of his penis, with a sulphur ring above it. Then he took a little red powder from a silver box and placed it in what the Chinese call the horse's eye. In a moment it began to act. The penis stood up straight and fearsome, the head swollen and the eye wide open. The veins that crossed it stood out like cord. The glands had a bruised colour, like liver, and the rod was seven inches long and much thicker than usual. (Whether this seven inches is an accurate translation of, first, the Chinese, and second, the translator's Latin, I cannot guarantee —but *The Golden Lotus* is a fairly realistic book and doesn't go in for the kind of exaggeration that erotic writers use so glibly.) Porphyry, the lady for whom these delights had been prepared, now understood why he had been drinking spirits. She laid herself upon the bed with two pillows underneath her. The head was so swollen he could not get it in at first, and then only a little way. When her juices began to flow it became easier. His penis plunged in and gave him an ecstasy that was scarcely bearable, while she cried, 'O darling man, your magnificent prick will be the death of me'. In fact, it was to be the death of Hsi-mên. Not all the women cared for these measures. Tower of Jade told him to take the clasp off, but he ignored her and rammed in with all his strength. 'Soon her venereal juices were flowing out with a noise like a dog gulping down pearl barley.' She begged him not to continue.

Resurrection of the Flesh

Fascination with sex may not be an entirely sensual matter.
There is a symbolism in the recovery and resurrection of the
male organ which will please those of the most philosophical
turn of mind, while those who think in religious terms,
especially the kind of religion which anchors itself in fertility
and the nature cycle, are liable to go some way (occasionally
the whole way) towards identification of the two impulses.

At the crudest level man will think of himself as a Fucking
Machine. There is no aim, no purpose, beyond sensual enjoyment and this will eventually negate itself, for unbridled
pleasure is not given to man. But it requires thought and
mental balance, and in the final resort (but often too late)
experience to realise this. Sergeant Sam Croft in *The Naked
and the Dead* certainly sees no more in life than eternal jig-
jig. (Of course, he sees the Army and its unpleasant duties,
but this is environment, datum, a part of nature.) He reflects
on life back home with his woman, hears her voice: 'Oh,
give it to me, you sonofabitch, give it to me, I'LL KILL YOU
IF YOU STOP.' And the bubble comes out of his head:
'Ah'm jus' an old fuggin machine. (Crack . . . that . . . whip!
Crack . . . that . . . WHIP!)'

It's a dream, not an intelligent, high-class dream, for sure,
but it must be fairly prevalent.

> *There was a young man called McLean*
> *Who invented a fucking machine.*
>   *Concave or convex,*
>   *It would fit either sex,*
> *And was perfectly simple to clean.*

An advance even on Crowley's Automatic Girl. This is an
American limerick and was included by Norman Douglas in
Some Limericks. As with a Burton translation, it is the footnote that counts. Douglas tells us that he circularised 732
persons of the name of McLean asking for details, and received
one reply only. It is the reply that the male always attributes

to the female—that is, when she is possessed by some truth drug.

Williamstown, Mass.
2nd March 1928

Dear Sir,

Your circular of 18th January addressed to my late husband has been opened by myself. I am sorry to have to inform you that he was not the maker of the instrument in question.

Pardon my frankness but, as you seem to be a man of the world, you will perhaps understand that, being now a widow, I am excusably interested in such a machine and would like, just for curiosity's sake, to purchase a specimen, if not too expensive. Should it be of a breakable nature, I might even take two. I will undertake to procure you a good many clients in our county, if the mechanism comes up to expectation.

Will you remember me when you have succeeded in discovering the inventor? Please try not to forget!

Yours gratefully in anticipation,
Eleanor McLean

The young and vigorous lover will curse the dawn, for business calls him from his love. (See Criseyde's lament in Chaucer's *Troilus and Criseyde*, Book III, verses 208-9.) But all men tire in the end and some tire very quickly. After intercourse, says Rufinus, the poet of the *Greek Anthology*, women lose their charm: 'If women had as much charm when all is over as before, men would never tire of intercourse with their wives, but all women are displeasing then' (Book V, No. 77). There are two school of thought here. All are agreed that, for the time being, the man is incapable anyway. Then comes the divide; some follow Rufinus and argue that where the flesh is weak the spirit is unwilling, others claim that the spirit is unquenchable. The true eroteur belongs to the latter school. The former are a bunch of realists, who tend to be driven by their doctrine into a distaste for prolonged pleasure,

even if available. The eighteenth century libertine was a
convinced optimist in this respect—the much heralded
eighteenth century realism about man's physical nature was
often extremely suspect. Here is the last item in *The Cabinet
of Love*, 1718. Actus I, Scena I represents a bed-chamber.
Tarsander reflects on man's gratitude for an erection and his
joy at losing it. Swivanthe replies:

> Do not thy ——, Nature's best gift, despise,
> That girl that made it fall, will make it rise;
> Tho' it awhile the am'rous combat shun
> And seems from mine into thy belly run,
> Yet 'twill return more vig'rous and more fierce
> Than flaming drunkard, when he's dy'd in tierce.
> It but retires, as losing gamsters do,
> Till they have rais'd a stock to play anew.

Women are sometimes unfair, runs the argument. Not subject
to these losses of power, they become impatient when their
lovers appear to be reticent. Surely this betrays an exceptional
ignorance of male physiology, but lust can rarely wait. An
anonymous poem of 1741, aptly called 'The Resurrection',
tells how Chloe, waking in the morning, rebukes her young
husband for being less amorous than he had been the night
before. The poor fellow says he will set to work again as
soon as there is a Resurrection.

> For a Prophet of old (as I'm sure I have read)
> Stretch'd himself o'er a child whom he rais'd from the
>   Dead,
> Now of this I'm resolv'd to make Tryal, d'ye see,
> And, Love, to that End stretch myself over Thee.
> 'Twas done in a Moment, and o'er me she threw
> A Leg of such Shape as Apelles ne'er drew,
> Her Lips to my Lips, and her Breast to my Breast,
> She join'd with a Sweetness which can't be exprest,
> Her arms clasp'd me round—I grew warm in the Strife,
> Till Death gave me up and I kindled to Life;

> But the Nymph found her Pleasure too great to restrain,
> And with Kindness Excessive she kill'd me again,
> So true is that Maxim—I sorrow, I sigh
> To repeat it—'tis this that We Live but to Dye.

The need of resurrection naturally leads to an art of
resurrection, which Hsi-mên of *The Golden Lotus* knew well.
It is universally known that wine is a valuable aid, though
it does not help in the ultimate performance. With Heart's
Delight he drank wine, took some of the aphrodisiac medicine
given him by an Indian monk, and required her to suck
him. On one occasion Golden Lotus upbraids him because
his penis is limp (he has just been with Porphyry). He takes
a pill and asks her to suck him but at first she refuses because he is dirty. Then she wipes it with a handkerchief and
excites him so much with her mouth that he puts a little
red powder on it and plunges in, thrusting some three
hundred times before he comes. Golden Lotus trembles and
says, 'Darling, you should not have put the powder on him.'

Aphrodisiacs are needed by lovers who have over-indulged
and by the ageing whose powers are declining. When does this
happen? Kinsey can always help here (for Americans). He
says there is a decline in the active incidence of orgasm after
forty, a steady decline through the fifties, but no marked
decline until after sixty. In a white, non-prison sample there
was no case of a female experiencing orgasm after seventy-
five, but in the prison, non-white histories there are cases of
females 'responding in their seventies and eighties and, in one
instance, responding to the point of orgasm with frequencies
which averaged between once a month and once a week at the
age of ninety'. But there is no male equivalent.

Ceremonial

Anything that man feels is of especial significance to him
tends to be ritualised and ceremonialised. Sex is no exception.
In the previous section I referred to the symbolic association
of erection, resurrection and the nature cycle. Religion, parti-

cularly Christianity, has tried to separate sex into compart-
ments of man's choosing. This is good sex (children), that is
bad sex (pleasure). Copulation can and should be blessed
if performed for the right purpose. 'The Presbyterian Wedding', from *The Musical Miscellany Being a Collection of
Choice Songs*, 1729, tells how after the wedding the pastor
bade the guests depart, then prayed that the marriage should
be a fruitful one. Giving the bridal pair 'sack posset' he bade
them begin their enterprise.

> *The Bridegroom then drew near his Spouse,*
> *T'apply Prolifick Balm;*
> *And while they strove in mutual Love,*
> *The Parson sung a Psalm.*

The rhythm of copulation has frequently suggested music
and the idea that copulation should be performed to music
is not far behind. It must surely be a perverted mind that
imagines that copulation performed to music is wicked, yet
this is the attitude taken by Emile Laurent and Paul Nagour,
authors of *Magica Sexualis* (trs. Raymond Sabatier, 1934).
According to them, 'perverts' have made use of two works in
particular. One was *Internationale*, 'the Communist (*sic*) rally-
ing song', which provided a fast and spirited beat, while the
other, Handel's *Largo*, was preferred by those who require
something slow and leisurely. Not only this, but erotic verses
have been composed to these melodies, so that couples can
sing during coition, an act which the authors appear to regard
as the depths of infamy. A more serious approach to the
relationship between music and sex is to be found in Moore's
Evelyn Innes, which is to some extent a celebration of music
as a sexual stimulant. This could only be done through its
rhythmic power, because it is non-representational. Here is
Ulick Dean's opinion of *Parsifal*: 'The obtusely religious
could not fail to be moved; the appeal of the chaste kiss,
with little sexual cries all the while in the orchestra, could
not but stir the vulgar heart to infinite delight, and the art
was so dexterously beautiful that the intelligent were

deceived.' Evelyn would have liked to sing an 'Agnes Dei'
but she knew she could not; her voice was too full of sex,
the effect of singing in Wagner and modern operas.

The most famous celebration of the sexual act in Western
literature is to be found in the Song of Songs. A modern
translator, H. J. Schonfield, says that an invitation is given
and accepted to consummate the marriage, and friends and
relations add their blessings. What follows is a ritualised
version of Hsi-mên fitting his clasps, Sergeant Croft cracking
his whip, and Burns heying for houghmagandie. There are
as many modes of sex and thinking about sex as there are (or
have been) cultures.

> She

> *Rise, O north wind! Come, O south!*
>   *Blow softly upon my garden,*
> *To waft its spice on your breezes.*
>   *Let my darling enter his garden*
> *And partake of its luscious fruit.*

> He

> *I am coming into my garden,*
>   *O my sister, my bride.*
> *I am gathering my myrrh;*
>   *I am gathering my spices.*
> *I am licking honey from the comb,*
>   *And quaffing my wine and my milk.*

> Chorus

> *Eat your fill now, you sweethearts.*
>   *Drink and quaff deeply, you lovers.*
>   *Revised Version, IV 16 and V 1, Canto 6,* SCHONFIELD

Even Hsi-mên, despite his unconquerable lechery, observed
a certain amount of ritual. Being Chinese, he could scarcely
avoid it. He employed an old woman named Wang to bring

Golden Lotus to him. According to her, there were ten phases in seduction, and all of them must be properly undertaken if the project is to be successful. We see Hsi-mên and his latest mistress at the tenth and final phase—Wang called them 'points'. It is still necessary to show resistance, on the woman's part, and to overcome it gently, on the man's. They sit together over a meal, and the old procuress leaves them. Hsi-mên takes his coat off, complaining of the heat and asks Golden Lotus to put it on the bed. She smilingly refuses, so he has to lean across and do it himself. While doing this, he brushed a chop-stick off the table with his sleeve. Luckily it came to rest beneath her skirt. He pretended he didn't know where it was but she pushed it with her foot and said with a laugh, 'Isn't this it?' He bent down to pick it up but instead took hold of her embroidered shoe. 'I shall shout if you are so naughty,' cried Golden Lotus. 'Be kind to me, lady,' said Hsi-mên, going down on his knees and stroking her silken garments. She threatened to box his ears but the gallant lover knew the correct response to this: 'Lady,' he said, 'if your blows should cause my death, it would be a happy end.' This was the end of the preliminary. He now picked her up, carried her to Wang's bed, took off his clothes, loosened her girdle and lay down with her. Golden Lotus was enchanted. In her previous experience, with old Chang and Wu Ta, she had never known such a delightful pattern, such an exquisite treatment of the formality which such an important act deserved.

The Festival of Love, usually called Epithalamium, used to be a familiar subject in English poetry. The ones we know from the anthologies are discreet. Others are more frank. The one in the 1770 volume entitled *The Festival of Love* (said to be from Secundus) is a fair example. It is a very long poem and this stanza recurs at frequent intervals:

> *O night of bliss*
> *To equal this*
> *Olympus strives in vain;*
> *O happy pair!*

> *O happy fair!*
> *O happy, happy swain!*

The author can scarcely control his language while describing the climax:

> *They pant, they bleed;*
> *Who shall succeed,*
> *Who best the contest wage;*
> *Now their sole care,*
> *Love's nimble spear,*
> *Provoking mutual rage.*

And so on, for several nervous, jerking stanzas. It is not the god or goddess of war who guides the wondrous spear, it is one more dear (the love goddess) who delights in seeing 'the last great thrust', 'who loves to see coy chastity a bleeding victim lie'. They gasp for breath until a moment's death releases them, and 'love's various tide in streams of pleasure flows'.

This particular poem now takes an unexpected turning. The bride has so enjoyed her raptures that she constantly demands more. The metre lengthens, becomes turgid and slack. Eighteenth century cynicism takes over, and the ecstasy of marriage is replaced by boredom and infidelity.

> *The mossy spot gave exquisite delight,*
> *And, while it warm'd the fancy, pleas'd the sight:*
> *But greater pleasure still remain'd behind,*
> *Which were by Venus' aid for him design'd.*
> *No longer hesitation was his foe;*
> *Nature was strong and told him what to do;*
> *Gently he drew her naked limbs aside—*
> *Where now, alas! Stellina, is your pride?*
> *Your boasted guard is gone, the charm is o'er,*
> *Philander conquers, and shall sue no more.*
> *She felt the tickling rapture at her heart,*
> *And hugg'd the youth, nor wish'd again to part;*

> *Return'd each kiss, and every pleasing move,*
> *Which now he practis'd in the art of love.*

But Stellina begins to grant her favours to any and everyone,
'so cheaply now she holds her C—— ware'.

> *Her rare accomplishments, so highly priz'd,*
> *Are all neglected, or perhaps despis'd;*
> *Lascivious, wanton, in a high degree,*
> *In bagnios and in brothels, who but she?*
> *Her nature, temper and her rural cot,*
> *Her tender parents, all alike forgot. . . .*

The moral is uncertain, except that the author distinguishes
between 'honest love' and 'lustful passions'. The poem could
easily be read as a protest against a too strict unbringing.
There is an Epigram.

> *Did ladies now (as we are told*
> *Our great-grandmother did of old)*
> *Wake to a sense of blasted fame,*
> *The* fig-tree *spoil to hide their* shame,
> *So num'rous are those modern Eves,*
> *A forest scarce could find them leaves.*

The point of this digression is that the ritual of sex can never
be maintained. In later stages it follows its own path.

Unorthodoxy

Van de Velde says that by 'sexual intercourse' he refers
exclusively to normal intercourse between opposite sexes. 'It
is our intention to keep the Hell-gate of the Realm of Sexual
Perversions firmly closed,' he writes rather stridently (*Ideal
Marriage*). 'On the other hand, Ideal Marriage permits normal
physiological activities the fullest scope, in all desirable and
delectable ways; these we shall envisage, without any prudery,
but *with deepest reverence for true chastity.* All that is morbid,
all that is perverse, we banish; for this is Holy Ground.'

Normal; morbid; perverse: difficult words to define. And the introduction of deity immensely weakens the argument for millions of people who have quite definite views on what is holy and what is not. Van de Velde tries to define normal sexual intercourse, and admits it is not easy. His final definition is as follows: 'That intercourse which takes place between two sexually mature individuals of opposite sexes; which excludes cruelty and the use of artificial means for producing voluptuous sensations; which aims directly or indirectly at the consummation of sexual satisfaction and which, having achieved a certain degree of stimulation, concludes with the ejaculation—or emission—of the semen into the vagina, at the nearly simultaneous culmination of sensation—or orgasm —of both partners.'

An immediate objection must be made to the idea of 'nearly simultaneous' culmination. As this is something which cannot always be achieved, with the best will in the world, its acceptance would penalise many innocent people—innocent of seeking pleasures not covered by the above definition, that is.

If one is to persist in the attempt to establish an orthodoxy, it is surely essential to consult nature and what is permitted by nature. That Nature (by this time in our discussion it is recognised as a force, and inevitably assumes the capital N) is determined to achieve orgasm, whatever the circumstances, is clear from the incidence of wet dreams, which probably afflict puritans and comstocks far more often than lechers and libertines. They are not common in literature but Dryden refers to one in the first part of *The Conquest of Granada*, 1672. The poet dreams of his love, who always denies him. Refusing yet again, she fades from the dream.

> *I waked, and straight I knew*
> *I loved so well it made my dream prove true:*
> *Fancy, the kinder mistress of the two,*
> *Fancy had done what Phillis would not do.*
> *Ah, cruel nymph, cease your disdain,*
> *While I can dream you scorn in vain:*
> *Asleep or waking you must ease my pain.*

What satisfies the definition? Dance hall orgasms? Anna, the heroine of Edmund Wilson's 'The Princess with the Golden Hair' (*Memoirs of Hecate County*), worked in a dance hall. Low-grade halls of that type were known as 'rub houses'. Most of the clients, known as 'greaseballs', came to get an orgasm by pressing against their partners. One of the girls came into the ladies' room with it all over her dress. 'They're pigs!' said Anna. This won't pass: only one partner is satisfied. It is also possible that in such cases the wearing of clothes should be regarded as an artificial means of stimulation. Should all intercourse be in the nude? Are pyjamas perverse?

Kinsey reports some very unusual means of achieving orgasm. Some females in his records had been brought to orgasm by having their eyebrows stroked, or by having the hairs on some other part of their bodies gently blown upon, or by having pressure applied on the teeth alone. There may be simultaneous orgasm—we don't know what the man is doing apart from blowing or stroking—and there may even be emission into the vagina.

What about biting?

> Suddenly he pressed his face into her breasts. She fastened her teeth in his neck and kept them there until he had seized her and taken her into the bedroom. Then during the fierce inarticulate conflict of their passion she would grip his shoulder with her teeth and never let go until the end. (*The Chinese Room*, by Vivian Connell)

Van de Velde admits love bites—but when is a love-bite not a love-bite? When it draws blood? ('Their passion was a fierce and exhaustinng struggle and her teeth had drawn blood from his shoulder,' *ibid*).

Toe- and foot-work are enjoyed immensely by some lovers. Prince Mony, in Apollinaire's *The Debauched Hospodar*, meets an actress on a train and sits opposite her in the dining car. She recites Baudelaire's *Invitation au Voyage* to him, and then he felt her small feet moving up his legs until they

reached his prick which was hanging sadly outside his fly.
(He was always prepared.) Taking the sad little object between
them, they moved in a curious little see-saw motion. This
seems a fairly obvious method of titillation, and in fact the
human body is so constructed that a stranger from another
planet might well come to the conclusion that mutual toe-
work would be the 'normal' and 'natural' method of stimulation. Sally and Jane Lambert, in Angela Pearson's *The Whipping Club*, illustrate the posture most effectively. They lie on
a divan with their heads at opposite ends. Each had her big
toe thrust inside the vulva of the other and their bodies
agitated vigorously against the toes. This is the only method
of intercourse which will allow a man to enjoy sexual satisfaction and drink whisky, smoke a cigar and read a book at the
same time. Of course, this would not appeal to Van de Velde.
The methods quoted above break several of his requirements.
In the Apollinaire there can be no mutual satisfaction. As for
the Pearson, the sexual balance is wrong and the girls are
actually being flagellated while they prod each other.

Between the breasts? Certainly not. But many enjoy it,
including the hero of Apollinaire's *Memoirs of a Young Rakehell*. The boy locks himself in a room with Helen, a kitchen
maid. He has a huge erection and she plays with it but tells
him she has her period. He pushed her onto a chair and put
his prick between her breasts. 'A most practical method: it
disappeared among the fleshy folds of her delectable hillocks.
But it would have been better with a bit of lubrication. I told
her so. She spat on my prick and squeezed it tightly between
her boobies. On top the glans peeked out, and at the bottom
my balls were hanging down.' The trouble with definitions of
orthodoxy is that we are seldom told what basis the criteria
are raised on. Why should this method, for instance, open 'the
Hell-gate of the Realm of Sexual Perversion'?

There are a host of 'perversions' and 'aberrations'. Let us
take one to serve as a representative. The man who requires
an auxiliary activity, or a substitute activity, if he is to have
his orgasm. Van de Velde would deny him any sexual enjoyment whatsoever, which seems unnecessarily cruel. Why

should cruelty only be permitted in sexual matters? Isn't it equally reprehensible there? In Nelson Algren's *A Walk on the Wild Side* there is a Black Mammy Freak. He can only get his thrill while being beaten on the backside by a woman. This is because he was often beaten in this way, by a black mammy, when he was a child and always had a sexual thrill. When asked in the brothel exactly what he meant, he said, 'Why, what happens when a man is having a girl, *that's* what happened. And I've never been able to make it happen any other way since.' So Mamma, the madame, 'paddled' him—which is what used to happen in the old slave days, according to *Dolly Morton*, though then an actual paddle was used.) I dare say analysis would eventually have freed this man from his neurosis, but how long would it take?

Finally, a curiosity from Burton, to be found in his Terminal Essay to his translation of the *Arabian Nights*.

> The learned casuist Dr Thomas Sanchez the Spaniard had (says Mirabeau in *Kadhésch*) to decide a difficult question concerning the sinfulness of a peculiar erotic perversion. The Jesuits brought home from Manilla a tailed man whose moveable prolongation of the *os coccygis* measured from seven to ten inches: he had placed himself between two women, enjoying one naturally while the other used his tail as a *penis sucedaneus*. The verdict was incomplete sodomy and simple fornication.

A rather surprising verdict. Presumably the man was committing incomplete sodomy, though I feel this is stretching the definition of sodomy unnecessarily. I fail to see how any existing law could apply to a tail used in this manner, but it does appear that the second woman was using a dildo—of which Van de Velde would not approve.

Time and Place

Paris in the Spring, you might say, but Paris as the Lover's

Mecca is a very recent development, and is already old-fashioned. Here is the longer-standing tradition: Rural Bliss.

> *No youth here need Willow wear,*
> *No beauteous maid will her lover destroy:*
> *The gentle little Lass will yield*
> *In the soft Daisy Field, freely our pleasures we here enjoy:*
> *No great Juno we boldly defie,*
> *With you Cloris' cheeks or fair Celia's eye;*
> *We let those things alone, and enjoy our own,*
> *Every Night with our Beauties lie.*
>   'The Happy Husbandman, or Country Innocence',
>   *The Roxburghe Ballads,* c. 1540-1790, B.M.

The town-country polarisation which is basic to our society is evident here. Now and again it rises to the surface with a touch of acerbity, then sinks back again out of sight. The town thinks the country dull and simple, the country thinks the town wicked and stupid. Samuel Butler (1612-80) wrote in his *Notebooks*:

> Those children that are begotten in the day, are commonly born in the day, and those in the Night by night: for Nature for the most part keepe's a Punctuall accompt of time: and that is one reason, why more are born in the Night than by Day, when men are commonly diverted by many other occasions. And in great Cities men are often in Drink before they goe to Bed which Makes the Children they get prove soe foolish. . . .

It is generally believed that there is a maximum of desire in spring, and even the towndwellers feel it. It corresponds to the breeding season of animals and birds and is manifested in human societies by the spring festivals of primitive races with their overwhelmingly sexual features. 'This vernal efflorescence' (Van de Velde) affects male and female alike. In fact, statistics indicate a maximum number of conceptions in May.

With a race so active as the human, little more can be said about the best time and place for sexual intercourse. They do it all the time and wherever they can. In later years habits are established and they follow the lines of least resistance: hence, bed and night. In an earlier chapter I referred to the Lover's Five O'clock of French romance. Such variations will occur all over the world where local conditions are favourable. Take, for instance, the miner. According to Zola (*Germinal*), it happens after the bath. The woman dries the man while he tells her about the day's events. The children are got out of the way, he puts his arms around her, she laughingly pushes him away. But he won't be denied—he has been stimulated by the vigorous towelling she has given him. He pushes her on to the table and 'takes his dessert—free of charge, what's more!'

Of course, mere humans, even Indians, get it over pretty quickly. It took three nights to conceive Hercules. He was the son of Alcmene and Zeus. Zeus lengthened the night he did the job to three times its normal length.

En Masse

Group copulation is also frowned upon, but where does it start? Is it group copulation when two or more couples perform in the same room? If so, it must have been familiar enough in slum areas. Who are guilty, the couples for not performing in private or the local authority for not providing sufficient space?

Sex in company is probably the first stage towards group performance. Once you have had intercourse in the knowledge that your actions have been overheard and perhaps observed, the prohibition on sharing the act with a third or a fourth or a fifth party could not remain so very strong. Something of the atmosphere that must exist in such circumstances is conveyed in William Faulkner's *The Wild Palms*. Wilbourne and Charlotte share a room with the Bruckners at a minehead, where Wilbourne is the company doctor. It is fearfully cold. Although they place their mattresses in opposite corners they are still too close for Wilbourne and Charlotte to talk to each other comfortably. The Bruckners had no such inhibitions. There was a minimum of preliminary talking and whispering, the blanket-muffled motion led into the woman's moans without a break. Then it got so cold that they moved the mattresses together for warmth and slept as a unit, the two women in the middle. 'And still sometimes before the light was scarcely out (or perhaps they would be wakened by it) there would come the ruthless impact with no word spoken, as if they had been drawn violently and savagely to one another out of pure slumber like steel and magnet. . . .'

Mass copulation has always had its devotees, sometimes for the most admirable of reasons. Those people who have seen a specially intimate link between sex and religion have been drawn to it by the logic of their beliefs. The Bogomils and Fraticelli used to practise sexual promiscuity for the glory of God, the Creator. Among the Fraticelli, the women used to come to meetings in great numbers and the officiating priest, after performing due ceremonies, called for the lights to be extinguished and requested the Holy Ghost to give a sign for the mixing of the sexes. It is said that the children born of these unions were thrown from hand to hand in a circle of the initiates until they perished. The man in whose hands a child died was acclaimed High Priest. One of these children was burned by the priests, its ashes mixed with wine in a goblet and used for the initiation of novices. 'The mixing of the flesh' was also encountered in Russia, among the adherents of a Moslem sect, and another community of this type once flourished near Berlin. The notorious Rasputin belonged to a similar group. Even the restrained English have thrown up their champion of religious promiscuity in the person of Henry James Prince, who founded a Sect of Love (Agapemone) in Bridgewater, Somerset. He was believed to be a saint who was completely inured to the temptations of the flesh. He announced that he would take a virgin and make her a woman 'by the strength of God'—not in shame and secrecy but in public. He did not state who was to be chosen but all his virgin followers were to hold themselves in readiness. To the accompaniment of sacred songs he seduced Miss Patterson.

Religious sanction is by no means necessary for this kind of activity but it is worth bearing in mind that something that most people probably regard with horror has been held acceptable by various groups of people for the best of reasons. Literature is full of references to and descriptions of group sex. In this section a few examples will suffice. There is not a great deal of it in the Chinese classic, *Golden Lotus*, but it probably takes place when Golden Lotus arranged for Chingchi to visit her and they play Turtle Chess with Plum Blossom. In the Chinese code of love a turtle is a lover and sometimes a penis, and it appears likely that Turtle Chess is a threesome.

But it is the full-blooded pornographers who have always rejoiced in descriptions of mass copulation, writers who tend to be bored by simple, everyday coupling. Akbar del Piombo, who is a kind of Olympia Press Yeoman of the Guard, gives an amusing account of one such encounter in *Who Pushed Paula?* It is relatively restrained, a mere two into one. Mrs Smills, the butler's wife, goes down on her knees to suck off Henry and the Baron gets up behind. The shock of his attack knocked them headlong and in the confusion Henry managed to transfer his prick to her cunt. 'She succumbed like jelly and the three of us lay sprawled on the floor, fucking for good. Each time I went in deep I felt, on the other side of the vaginal wall, the head of the Baron's cock. The good woman got her justice double-barrelled and, coming all together, harmony reigned once more in the household.' Mrs Smills had been angry because the Baron had been buggering her husband, who had lost interest in her.

One woman can accommodate several men and Sade was naturally quick to exploit the possibilities. On one occasion, for instance, Justine was the target for four. While the Superior was busy with her rear section, Antonin 'made an offering to the contrary God'. But there was still a place for Jerôme in her mouth while Clément fitted himself between her hands. There were also auxiliaries, the priestesses, who stood around and offered stimulation to those who needed it—but the whole weight bore on Justine and she was a second time 'infamously defiled by the proofs of those blackguards' disgusting luxury'.

It is not so easy for a man to accommodate a plurality of women, though the anonymous author of *Three Mistresses* describes its own favourite threesome, i.e. one man, two girls. It was also apparently a favourite with the girls. One of them lay on her back and another over her, resting on her hands and knees. The latter put her cunt to the mouth of the girl below and presented her buttocks to the man. The lower girl then guided his prick into the cunt, watching its entrance and tickling his balls as they dangled above her nose. While he fucked the lower girl sucked, and he also played with her bottom 'till we all fainted in an agony of spending, which was renewed by changing places'.

Here is how, according to Sade, six women may minister to one man. The man was the monk Antonin who began by seizing Justine's haunches and pulling her down on him. A fifteen-year-old girl, resting on Justine's flanks, offers him her vulva from which he pumps the precious natural juice which has only recently begun to flow. One of the older women bends to the monk's loins and animates his desires with her tongue while, 'to inflame himself yet further, the debauchee excites a woman with either hand; there is not one of his senses which is not tickled, not one which does not concur in the perfection of his delirium; he attains it, but my unwavering horror for all these infamies inhibits me from sharing it. . . . He arrives there alone; his jets, his cries, everything announces it and, despite myself, I am flooded with the proofs of a fire I am but one of six to light.'

Justine and Sade say six but I have only been able to count five.

Dangers

Some are obvious, such as venereal disease. Some are unexpected and even laughable.

There was a young man of Kildare,
Who was having a girl in a chair.
  At the sixty-third stroke
  The furniture broke,
And his rifle went off in the air.

It was presumably one of those cheap Vienna chairs,' comments Norman Douglas, 'which are exported in great quantities to Kildare and other Irish towns, and which should never be used for such purposes. But the young man was also to blame for being so long about the business. Sixty-three strokes! Even London chairs, excellent as they are, will feel that strain. People with such deliberate methods should stick to the floor, where a rug, or preferably the fur of some animal, will be found a welcome adjunct.' But what would Douglas have thought of Hsi-mên and his three hundred?

Breaking furniture is a marginal danger. Possibly the most threatening, after disease, results from discrepancy in size, what might be called the Arbuckle Complex. The anonymous author of *Teleny* mentions a Viscount who had such a huge phallus that even the whores were frightened by it. Roman ladies, who are said to be dissatisfied with the inferior size of the male penis and have been heard to demand something of ass-like proportions, would have accepted it. But there was a rumour that some foreign woman had been so ripped by it that the partition between the front and the back entrance had been torn and the poor wretch had died in consequence. Perhaps something of the same kind happened to a lady mentioned in Count Palmiro Vicarion's Book of Limericks.

There was a young lady named Hilda
Who went for a walk with a builder,
  He knew that he could,
  And he should and he would—
And he did—and he goddam near killed her!

Fortunately, this kind of accident is rare for females are much tougher than they sometimes look.

If we extend the dangers of sex to include domestic trouble, ranging from constant nagging to *crime passionel*, we will never finish. Sexual jealousy can be frightening in its consequences, and suspicion is often worse than discovery. I have referred in an earlier chapter to the importance of the diaphragm in the bathroom cabinet, how its absence at a crucial moment can spark off a war. We live in an awkward transition period. The diaphragm will soon be a thing of the past, and not so long ago its existence was not even dreamed of. In those days the woman would study her partner with anguish in an attempt to divine whether he had been faithless or not. There is an example of this in Louÿs's *Aphrodite*. Demetrios, the sculptor, is the lover of Queen Berenice but he is losing interest in her, partly because he is becoming infatuated with the courtesan, Chrysis. Berenice is suspicious and behaves like any suburban housewife. 'Were you at the Temple?' she snaps. 'You were not in the Gardens with those foreign women? No, I see by your eyes that you have not been making love.' Demetrios breathes again. At least this is not such a brutal method of making sure as the one employed by an aristocratic lady in a nineteenth century *Pearl* story.

The fact of sex is so extraordinary that one can suffer not only for participating in it but even for possessing it. Think of the poor eunuch, although except for a few areas in the Arabian peninsula he is now a thing of the past. The *Arabian Nights* is naturally full of them, often men who had had their yards cut off while still lads and sent to a harem or sold as castrati. Burton naturally has much to tell us about the custom in one of his footnotes. The most prized was the Sandali who had had both his penis and testes removed. Apparently there are various way of making a castrato; it can be done by removing the penis or by bruising the testes or cutting them off altogether. But in all cases the animal passion remains for (according to Burton, and this is what D. H. Lawrence objected to) the *fons veneris* in men is in the brain. (With animals it is not.) The story of Abelard is given as evidence. Juvenal derided the idea of married eunuchs yet most of them had wives with whom they practised the arts of love that Van de Velde proscribed: masturbation, tribadism, irrumation, *tête-bêche, feuille-de-rose*, etc., until orgasm was achieved. Burton claims that a eunuch's wife gave him this information, and added that the couple were greatly to be pitied. At the critical moment she used to give her husband a pillow to bite for otherwise he would have torn her to shreds.

The more one reads the Arabs, the more one realises that sexual intercourse is so fraught with danger, rather like housekeeping, that it is hardly worth while trying to avoid it. In one of Burton's Supplemental Nights we are given a father's advice on copulation ('The History of El Haggaz bin Yusuf and the Young Sayyid').

> Also have no connection with woman in the Hammam for its consequence is the palsy: nor do thou lie with her when thou art full or when thou art empty or when thou art drunken with wine or when thou art in wrath nor when lying on thy side, for that it occasioneth swelling of the testicle-veins; or when thou are under a fruit-bearing tree. And avoid carnal knowledge of the old woman for that she taketh from thee and giveth not to thee.

Burton has a solemn comment to make here when he defines an old woman as one who has ceased to have her monthly period. Orientals are convinced, he says, that no good will ever come of lying with an old woman and he was inclined to agree when he considered the 'old-young faces of men who had married their grandmothers' for money or folly. It was believed that an old woman took everything and gave nothing.

The old Arab believed that love-making on the side was a damaging process. It used to be believed by some English country people that love-making standing up also had definite consequences, though whether they were to be welcomed or abhorred depended entirely on what the lovers desired. In 1563 Henry Moneley took John Cotgreve to the Bishop's Court at Chester, charging him with being the father of a child delivered by his sister Margaret. He wanted to know what Cotgreve intended to do about the child's upkeep. Cotgreve said the child was none of his but Moneley replied that it had been conceived 'behind the Milne dore'. John Cotgreve did not deny the act but added, 'Cockes woundes, can a man get a child standinge? for I never had any thinge to do with her but standinge.'

The Future of Pornography

A rise in the pulse rate is an obvious and recognised result of erotic stimulation, a point that did not occur to Queen Berenice when grilling her errant lover. This is something we only get in medical literature—but the popular sales of medical literature are steadily increasing.[2]

The pulse rate can be easily obtained with automatic recording devices. The few records that are available show that a pulse that normally runs at something between 70 and

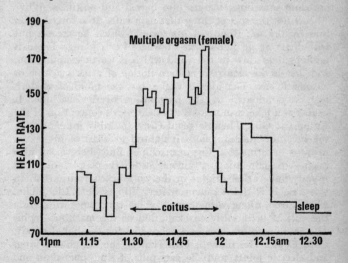

8o per minute may be raised to as much as 150 or more when
there is erotic arousal, and particularly if the reaction proceeds to the point of orgasm. This may approach the pulse
rate of an athlete during his maximum effort, or that of a
man involved in heavy labour. Heart rates can also be
measured—Kinsey reproduced graphs from Boas and Gold-
schmidt, showing the erotic responses before, during and after
coitus between a man and his wife. Here is the rough graphic
record of such an encounter, in which the wife had four
orgasms. (Ecstasy omitted.)

This is a personal document and might be included, in some
form or other, in the individual's dossier of a future police
state.

Wry jokes sometimes have a way of coming true. It is not
a profitable matter to discuss possible future attitudes to sex
but it is sometimes worth while commenting on trends. The
literature of the past does not show any of the boredom with
sex that is apparent in much contemporary literature. This
boredom sometimes merges into hatred and nastiness. Why?
This is not the sort of thing that man wills. It is forced upon
him by the net trends of his society, which he creates but
with little or no knowledge of where he is going. There is
perhaps one straw in the wind which is worth examination,
and that is the recurrent modern notion of a sex machine or
automatic sex. The idea is vague, but the mind of modern
man is dominated by the possibilities of the machine. It
begins as a joke, a sour joke, as in Crowley's conception of the
Automatic Girl. Then Sergeant Croft (possibly influenced by
the inventor Maclean) finds it natural to boast of his sexual
prowess in terms of a 'fuggin machine'. But wherever an idea
begins to gain support among ordinary people, one can
usually find earlier origins in the work of a serious artist. In
this case it is the decadent writer, Villiers de L'Isle Adam,
who moved, along with several of his contemporaries, from
the cult of artificiality to exaltation of the machine. In his
Eve Future Edison creates a robot girl for the bored dandy,
Lord Ewald. Her name is Miss Hadaly, she has golden lungs
and electric joints, and she eats pills of zinc, potassium and

lead. Of her sex life we are told nothing, but there is not much to be left to the imagination in that sphere.

FOOTNOTES

1. Which reminds one not only of Prince Hal's joke with the drawer in *Henry IV* but also of the Plumber of Leigh.

2. At the moment of writing, *Human Sexual Behaviour*, by Dr William H. Masters and Mrs Virginia E. Johnson, seems to be taking up where Kinsey left off.

11: *How Many Times*

Man appears to be proud of his sexual prowess. In no other department of sexual activity is there so much boasting as in the number of occasions he can have an orgasm during a continuous period. Bringing the woman to orgasm is also a matter for boasting, and boasting of a particularly uncontrolled nature, since no man can ever be sure how often a woman reaches a crisis unless she tells him. I have therefore confined this chapter to an account of male boasting about male orgasm, a matter in which there is little truth but where objective reporting is possible.

A nice girl thinks it shouldn't be done too often. Perhaps surfeit is bad for the health, certainly there seems to be a moral prohibition on excessive exercise—known as 'overdoing it'. (It is true, nature itself revolts for the parts get sore and the penis may peel.) This is what might happen when a courtier meets a country girl, according to 'A Pleasant New Court Song' in *The Roxburghe Ballads*:

> Then did I help to plucke
>   of every flower that grew;
> No herbe nor flower I mist,
>   but only Time and Rue.
> Both she and I tooke paines
>   to gather flowers store,
> Untill this maiden said,
>   Kinde sir, Ile have no more.

> *Yet still my loving heart*
> *   did proffer more to pull;*
> *No sir, quoth she, Ile part,*
> *   because mine apron's full.*
> *So, sir, Ile take my leave,*
> *   till next we meet againe:*
> *Rewards me with a kisse,*
> *   and thanks me for my paine.*

Now in this case the maiden wished to stop because she
felt she had had enough. But on other occasions the woman
may wish to husband the man's resources—a good example
of this was Theodelinde, the wife of Agilulf, king of the
Lombards, as reported in the *Decameron*. She was visited by
a groom, who lay with her—as it was dark she believed him
to be the king. Then Agilulf himself came to her and she
expressed surprise at this second visit and begged him to take
care of his health. On the whole, one gets the impression
that Boccaccio's characters are not much concerned with their
health, at least in this respect. Also Agilulf must have been
a man of exceptionally low virility, particularly within the
terms of literary eroticism. Let us turn to Kinsey to establish
some kind of worldly standard. One piece of information in
his Male report aroused tremendous interest among readers
and reviewers: this was the claim of a scholarly and skilled
lawyer that he had averaged over thirty sexual encounters
per week for thirty years. The implication, which brought
joy to many academic hearts, was that a high rate of sexual
frequency was not a sign of animalism. But Kinsey pointed
out that our marriage customs show little consideration for
the possibility that partners may be far apart in their sexual
inclinations, backgrounds and capacities. He claimed that just
as there was an immense difference in rates of sexual performance and of sexual capacity (a difference of several thousand
times between the highest and the lowest), so we might expect
an enormous difference in the degree of interest in and
response to sexual matters.

So let us start cataloguing the possibilities as revealed by

literature, starting at the bottom. It is rather surprising that
when the hero and heroine of Beardsley's *Under the Hill*,
Venus and Tannhauser, met, their performance was anything
but impressive. In fact, at only their third meeting they failed
to raise love and had to be helped. Beardsley was sardonically
aware that it was the custom of romancers to depict heroes
who could give proof of their valliance (his word) to the lady
at least twenty times a night. But this was the kind of crudity
that had no interest whatsoever for Beardsley. He admitted
that Tannhauser had no such 'Gargantuan felicity' and in
fact was rather relieved when, an hour later, Mrs Marsuple
and Doricourt and some others burst drunkenly into the room
and claimed Venus for themselves. It was the quality of love,
not its volume, that interested the *art nouveau*.

What exactly are we to understand by 'Gargantuan
felicity'? Well, Gargantua being a giant of tremendous
appetites, we may guess. But in fact Rabelais discusses the
matter of frequency in a talk between Panurge and
Pantagruel. With a friend, they throw dice to decide whether
Panurge should take a wife. The three dice show a total of
sixteen. This, says Panurge, in true masculine style, means
he will fuck his wife sixteen times on the first night. Pantagruel has a different version. The first bout will be a flop,
and this would be love fifteen (as in tennis). Then the bridegroom would make amends, bringing the number to sixteen.
This sets Panurge off on a fine piece of rhetoric:

> Is it so that you understand the matter? and must my
> words be thus interpreted? Nay, believe me, never yet was
> any solecism committed by that valiant champion, who
> often hath for me in Bellydale stood sentry at the hypo-
> gastrian cranny. Did you ever hitherto find me in the
> confraternity of the faulty? Never, I trow; never, nor
> ever shall, for ever and a day. I do the feat like a goodly
> friar, or father confessor, without default: and therein
> am I willing to be judged by the players.

As for the friars and father confessors, they had such doughty
reputations, I am devoting a whole chapter to them later on.

How many times *ought* a young couple to do it? Ignorance
and lack of experience can put lovers into a devilish difficult
situation. Above all, they must feel they are normal or even
super-normal. There was the Roman lady who was disappointed with her husband because he was not equipped like
a donkey, the only male creature whose sex she had seen.
Balzac writes about a pathetic couple who wedded in all
innocence, the young Moncontour and a girl of the Amboise
family. Neither knew the first thing about sex and so they
did nothing on their first night except pray for guidance,
which was not forthcoming. Nevertheless, next morning the
young bride professed herself very pleased with her husband.
When a lascivious neighbour asked 'how many loaves her
husband put in the oven,' she overdid it and said twenty-four.
('The Danger of Being Too Much of an Innocent', *Droll
Stories*).

The favoured guide and mentor of the French peasantry
used to be Dr Venette, author of *Le Tableau de la Vie
Conjugale*, which was first published in 1696 but continued
to be read for generations, well into the nineteenth century.
He did not think it advisable to make love more than five
times in one period, though he knew that some claimed to
do it ten or twelve times in a night. He also thought that it
was best not to start before four or five hours had elapsed
after a big meal, advice that has rarely been followed by the
libertines. If we accept five, not as a regular diet but as a
maximum figure, let us see it in action—or at least, in literature. Boswell gives us an example in his *London Journal*.
This encounter occurred on Wednesday 12 January 1763 with
Louisa, on whom he had already done some preparatory
work. He left the room while the maid undressed her.

> I came softly into the room, and in a sweet delirium
> slipped into bed and was immediately clasped in her
> snowy arms and pressed to her milk-white bosom. Good
> heavens, what a loose did we give to amorous dalliance!
> The friendly curtain of darkness concealed our blushes.
> In a moment I felt myself animated with the strongest

powers of love, and, from my dearest creature's kindness,
had a most luscious feast. Proud of my godlike vigour, I
soon resumed the noble game. I was in full glow of health.
Sobriety had preserved me from effeminacy and weakness, and my bounding blood beat quick and high alarms.
A more voluptuous night I never enjoyed. Five times
was I fairly lost in supreme rapture. Louisa was madly
fond of me; she declared I was a prodigy, and asked me
if this was not too extraordinary for human nature. I
said twice as much might be, but this was not, although
in my own mind I was somewhat proud of my performance. She said it was what there was no just reason to be
proud of. But I told her I could not help it. She said
it was what we had in common with the beasts. I said
no. For we had it highly improved by the pleasures of
sentiment. I asked her what she thought enough. She
gently chid me for asking such questions, but said two
times.

I sense something of the hypocrite in Louisa. Of course, Boswell was a doughty performer and in his journals was probably
truthful. On another occasion he made love to Thérésa Le
Vasseur, Rousseau's mistress, thirteen times on the trip from
Paris to Dover. This was a matter of days but then opportunity was fairly limited. And while we are still in the realms
of fact I may as well quote the modest rhyme which Gumbril
Junior once addressed to the highly-sexed Myra Viveash:

> Puisque nous sommes là, je dois
> Vous avertir, sans trop de honte,
> Que je n'égale pas le Comte
> Casanovesque de Sixfois.

Now we may start the romance, and we can begin by asking
how the exaggerations begin to grow and how they come to
be accepted. Humanity loves wonders and has an unassuage-
able interest in freaks. A lady once told me that Mellors and
Lady Chatterley performed seven times in one evening. I had

remembered the passion but not the endurance, so read the book again carefully, but found no record of this feat. Is this how folklore begins? Perhaps men and women like to believe that others have performed these feats in the hope that they themselves will be fortunate enough to follow in the path of others. Not that I disbelieve the possibility of seven. I am sure it is well within the powers of many sexual champions, past and present. A friend of mine tells me he managed it once. I have never managed more than five, but sexually I am a weakling, although I do not allow the fact to embitter me. So we may proceed to a literary seven which I take from *Teleny*. 'As true votaries of the Grecian god, we poured out seven copious libations to Priapus,' wrote Teleny of himself and his sodomite lover, Des Grieux. The sodomy does not affect the point but when Teleny adds that 'seven is a mystic, cabalistic, propitious number . . .' we are entitled to wonder if love works in this way.

A couple of interesting nines come from classical literature. Catullus seemed to be in no doubt of his powers when he wrote this (trs. Jack Lindsay):

> *Sweet Ipsythilla, see me soon,*
> *O be a dear, you sweet young thing,*
> *ask me to visit you at noon.*
> *If yes it is, don't change once more*
> *and bid some servant bar the door;*
> *and don't rush out to call or shop,*
> *but nicely wait for what I'll bring,*
> *and then—nine hugs without a stop!*
> *So if you're home, at once reply.*
> *I've lunched and sprawling here I lie*
> *with tunic monstrously awry.*

Quite a different story from Ovid, although when he wrote Elegy VII in his Third Book ('The Poet Reproaches Himself for Having Failed in His Duty Towards His Mistress', trs. J. Lewis Day) he was getting old and the ageing process doesn't help love. He shamefully confesses that he has held his girl in his arms but to no purpose. 'In vain her tongue she thrust against my tongue, and slipped her amorous thigh beneath my own; vainly she lavished on me all her sweetest names, called me her conqueror and said the things that women are wont to say in such a pass; it was as though my members had been rubbed with chilling hemlock and knew no more the way to do their duty. . . .' He is growing old, yes, but he should not be too old to prove himself a man. Why, only lately he has done it twice with Chloe, three times with Pitho and another three with Libas—but best of all, nine times with Corinna. And then, even as he is considering his wretched condition, life begins to stir again. 'And look at it now, and high time it is, see how it is coming back to life again; see how it is asking to be up and doing, to get to work once more. Why are you not overcome with shame, thou vilest part of me?'

These two have a modern French counterpart, Prévan, whose curious story is recounted in *Les Liaisons Dangereuses*. He became the simultaneous lover of three friends, none of whom was aware of his relationship with the others. When their other lovers discovered his activities, they each and separately issued challenges, all at the same place and time. 'That evening he accomplished his triple task with complete success; at all events he boasted afterwards that each of his new mistresses had thrice received the pledge and proof of his love. As you imagine, the story at this point lacks authentication,' writes Laclos in the form of a letter from Valmont to Mme de Merteuil. Valmont's comment is interesting. 'All that the impartial historian can do is to point out to the incredulous reader that vanity and an inflamed imagination may work miracles; and that, besides, it looked as though the morning that was to succeed so brilliant a night, would obviate any necessity to provide against the future.'

We reach double figures but my example is pure fantasy. In Sade's *Juliette* there is a Muscovite giant named Minsky who is forty-five years of age and declares that he never goes to bed without first discharging ten times. 'It is a fact that the inordinate amount of human flesh I eat contributes greatly

to the augmentation and thickening of my seminal fluid.'
Now that our records depend less on fact than on boasting
it is natural that the Arabs, the Americans and the French
should lead the field. In this sphere, no one can rival the
Arabs. In 'The Second Madman's Tale', told on the 842nd
Arabian Night, one wretched lover is dismissed by the woman
because he is too feeble to manage a twelfth orgasm, and is
actually sent to prison as a punishment for his weakness. But
he strove manfully:

> Life and love lived love and life together for thirty days
> and nights, my lord. I crushed and filed and stuffed the
> stuffable, the fileable, the crushable, until a giddiness
> came over me and I dared to say: 'I know not why, my
> saint, but I feel I cannot plant the twelfth great lance
> today.' 'But the twelfth is the most necessary,' love
> objected. 'The eleven do not count.' 'Yet it is impossible,
> impossible,' said I. Then she with a laugh: 'You must
> have rest, my poor fellow, you must have rest!' And when
> I heard that word I lay down and fainted clear away.

A modern American manages (or says he has) the dozen in, I
fear, a grinding, humourless fashion, rather like those wretches
who turn the massive wheel in the slave states of science-fiction
films. It is Wilson from *The Naked and the Dead*. He calls
on a woman whose husband is away when his own wife is in
hospital, having a baby. He tells her that a little while ago he
had a whore twelve times in a night and the way he felt now,
with all that honey stored inside him, he was going to beat
that record. 'Better not drink too much, Woodrow, it'll keep
ya down,' says the woman but the dreary fellow replies,
'Nothin' keeps me down, Ah'm a man likes his lovin'.'
Back to another of Sade's heroes, the Duc de Blangis whose
exploits are recorded in *120 Days of Sodom*. In his youth he
had been accustomed to discharge as often as eighteen times
a day without experiencing the slightest fatigue. He could
manage seven or eight orgasms running even in his fiftieth
year. He was also a champion of passive sodomy and had

once wagered he could sustain fifty-five attacks in one day—
'and so he had', commented Sade, who should know. Incidentally, one of the boys who had been taken to the chateau
reached puberty on the twenty-fifth day, for he shot five or
six jets of sweet fuck white as cream a distance of one yard.
After a repetition of this feat, the four libertines each induced
him to shed another load in their mouths, which he did without difficulty, making six altogether—a very promising start.

But the palm for this sort of thing goes to the Arabs. Not
only do they make greater claims but they describe their
feats with greater style and also a sense of humour. (Humour
tends to disappear as sexual athleticism increases.) On the
fifteenth night, in 'The Tale of the Third Kalandar', we are
told of a man surrounded by forty exquisite girls, one of
whom he is invited to choose for the night. As all were so
desirable, he shut his eyes and seized one. So great was her
beauty his eyes were dazzled when he opened them, and he was
compelled to close them again. They went to bed where 'I
charged her forty times and forty times she charged me, calling at each assault: "Yu! My darling! Yu! My soul!" First
she would caress me, then I would bite her, and then she
would pinch me. So the night wore away.' (Trs. Mathers.)

In this field we see male sexual fantasy at its peak. Realistic
literature may restrict itself to five or seven—in fact, I have
no idea what is realistic in this connection. But in sex, as in
war, man has a thirst for heroism and he expresses it in his
writing. There is nothing odd or unhealthy in this. It is a
situation reflected in the folk literature of the common people,
best expressed these days through the funny story (called dirty
or smutty by some, but this is to ignore man's interest in his
own functions as functions and not as hygiene). Here is one
which might be included in a new Thousand and One Nights.
An English sailor got into an argument with a Chinese sailor
in a low dive in Shanghai. Each boasted about how many
times he could do it. Finally they agreed to put the matter to
the test. Each took a girl to bed and kept a record of the
number of occasions complete intercourse took place. The
Englishman performed once, then again and finally, with

difficulty, for he had drunk far too much, a third time. He marked each one on the wall with an upright stroke. Then he fell asleep. In the morning the door of his room opened and the Chinese crawled in. He looked at the Englishman's tally and said, 'One hundred and eleven! Beaten by one, by God!'

12: 'The Lonely Pleasure'

Masturbation can cover various activities. It is, to begin with, the resort of the man who has no woman or the woman who has no man. Such people may indulge in what used to be called 'self-abuse'. But mutual masturbation is possible, either with a member of the same sex or with one of the opposite sex. In the latter case the activity is obviously a sexual variant, not a substitute imposed by circumstances. Usually masturbation is a solitary activity (hence a 'lonely pleasure'). The term is also used to cover forms of sexual stimulation which do not involve penetration or being penetrated. In fact, male use of inorganic orifices can also be included under this head.

The Kinsey Female Report gives vivid account of infantile masturbation by a mother who had observed her three-year-old daughter. The child lay face down on the bed with her knees drawn up and started rhythmic pelvic thrusts. The genitalia were pressed against a doll and periodic adjustments of position were made. The mother reported audible gasps and then final relaxation. Kinsey commented that the child's method anticipated that used by adults. The contact is primarily clitoral, rarely genital.

The implication is that masturbation is a natural process and is to be encountered along with other sexual manifestations in the infantile period. Such experience may well be forgotten later, but with puberty there comes another phase of masturbatory behaviour. Now such activity will be more conscious and may well be mentally associated with the absence of a partner with whom to indulge in sex activity. But the idea of masturbation, either as a relief or simply as a pleasure, can be suggested from written sources. Kinsey said that 75% of males and 43% of females learnt about masturbation from verbal or printed sources. Females got their information from books more often than men: the chief source seemed to be 'moral and sex education literature' and religious lectures designed to discourage masturbation. Other studies mention the same type of source: Hellmann, 16% from literature, Schbankov, 31% from literature and shows. Moraglia cites religious books as an inspiration for masturbation. Wulffen makes the same claim for the Bible and classics. In this connection, it is worth drawing attention to a familiar error about Onan, who gave his name to onanism, used as a synonym for masturbation. The passage in Genesis xxxviii, 8, 9 reads: 'And Judah said unto Onan, Go in unto thy brother's wife, and perform the duty of an husband's brother unto her, and raise up seed to thy brother. And Onan knew that the seed should not be his; and it came to pass, when he went in unto his brother's wife, that he spilled it on the ground, lest he should give seed to his brother.' The brother, Er, had been wicked in the sight of the Lord and had been slain. It was Onan's duty, according to the Law, to provide the widow with offspring. It seems quite clear from the passage that Onan practised *coitus interruptus*.

How frequent is masturbation? In the stricter definition (i.e., deliberate self-stimulation) it probably occurs in the histories of most males. Kinsey's sample gave the figure of 92% who had pursued masturbation to the point of orgasm. Incidence was higher among the better educated. Kinsey expressed misgivings:

> The general opinion that all males masturbate at some time in their lives, and the easy acceptance of this opinion among many clinicians and educators, are not warranted by the actual record. There are some individuals who do not masturbate for the simple reason that they do not have sufficient sex drive to cause them to go out of their way to find any sort of outlet, and who depend on nocturnal emission for most of their orgasms. There are

some boys, particularly at lower social levels, who do not
masturbate because they become involved in heterosexual coitus at such an early age that they have little
need for other sources of outlet. There are some duller
and slower reacting individuals who find it impossible
to effect orgasm in masturbation, and who in consequence
make no attempt to masturbate after their first
experiments.[1]

But Kinsey really was an obstinate soul. Always half worried
about the reception of such a frank study, he was determined
(rather unscientifically one feels, and sometimes in direct
contradiction to his own statistical evidence) to prove that
popular ideas on sex were always wrong. This usually meant
that a freer interpretation should be placed on sexual activity.
In the one activity where it was almost universally accepted
that depravity ruled, i.e., that everyone masturbated, he went
out of his way to claim that everyone does not masturbate.
With every other sexual aberration he proved that far more
people indulged than orthodoxy cared to think.

There are numerous references to masturbation in literature and I intend to quote some of them. What is rather
surprising is that the majority of references in Shakespeare
are concerned with the woman caressing the man. Eric Partridge enumerates nine terms that allude, or may be presumed
to allude, to the practice: *conjure it down, finger, go to bed,
lay it, mar, rubbing, spin off, take down* and *take off*. Not one
of these alludes to a woman's self-pollution (another term!)
and only one (the second) alludes to a man's so caressing a
woman's genitalia that she is likely to experience an orgasm.
All the others refer to a woman's caresses, leading to climax
and 'love's quick pants'.

Western society has held masturbation in some horror,
which is perhaps why it is rarely described even in erotic or,
a better term in this connection, hedonistic literature. For
the act is only erotic at a remove and by association, although
it may be accompanied by sexual fantasies. Of course, the
thoroughgoing pornographer is not put off by moral con-

siderations but then masturbation is hardly likely to occur to him as a subject. After all, anyone can masturbate; people who like to read about sexual combat are often those who are unable, for whatever reason, to indulge in it themselves. There has probably been more misinformation about masturbation than any other form of sex activity. This was at its height during the period 1760-1890 and can probably be traced, according to F. W. Meagher, to the influence of Tissot's *De l'Onanisme* which was published in St. Petersburg in the last quarter of the eighteenth century. Lallemand, Simon and Voltaire, and Leitner even as late as 1844 wrote in a most exaggerated way about the diseases resulting from the habit. Hippocrates, as long ago as 380 B.C., had written in the same vein, but we do not associate the Greeks particularly with this prohibition. It was not until the last quarter of the nineteenth century that the subject began to be studied in a scientific way, and the real facts concerning the habit were carefully studied. It is to men such as Erb, Fürbringer, Jones, Stanley Hall, Freud and Reich that we are indebted for separating facts from fancies.

The twentieth century has naturally reversed the time-worn attitudes of the recent past. Masturbation is tolerated among the young though still frowned upon as an adult habit. And one writer, at least, has managed to turn it into a joke. This is James Joyce, whose character Buck Mulligan in *Ulysses*, says he has conceived a play for mummers, called *Everyman His Own Housewife* or, *A Honeymoon in the Hand* (a national immorality in three orgasms). The author is Ballocky Mulligan. The characters appear to owe a lot to Arthur Sullivan, said to be the author of *The Bugger's Opera*: Toby Tostoff, a ruined Pole; Crab, a bushranger; Medical Dick and Medical Davy, two birds with one stone; Mother Grogan, a watercarrier; Fresh Nelly; and Rosalie, the coalquay whore.

Male

The discovery of masturbation is a disturbing affair. I well remember my own discovery. Perhaps because I had no father to guide me (the 'gutter' should have looked after my education but unaccountably failed to do so, although I went to school with labourers' sons, who at least suffered from no false gentility), I was unprepared. Looking back, innocence, surprise and fear seemed to make up my emotional reaction. At least no one threatened me with blindness.

One of the best descriptions of this discovery is to be found in Apollinaire's *Memoirs of a Young Rakehell*. This is quite a sincere little book and is not sheer pornography like the author's other essay on these themes, *The Debauched Hospodar*. The early chapters deal with the first stirrings of sex. The boy feels inexplicably excited at the sight of his naked sister. He watches the peasant girls and their men sporting in the fields. He used to get erections, which he examined and played with, without understanding.

One day he was sitting in the library, reading a book which described the female genital organs. He got such an erection that he took it out. He tightened his grip, loosened it, stroked it back and forth, and uncovered the tip to examine the glans, deep red in colour and as shiny as lacquer.

> The pleasure I felt was beyond words. I ended up by discovering the rules for the fine art of masturbation, and stroked my dick regularly and rhythmically until finally something about which I had previously been unaware happened.
>
> The feeling was so voluptuous that I was led to stretch my legs out in front of me and push against the legs of the table. My body slipped down and was pressing against the back of the chair. I felt the blood surging into my face. My breathing was becoming difficult. I closed my eyes; my mouth dropped slightly open. . . .

His mind was filled with erotic pictures. He stroked faster and felt an electric shock coursing through his body. Then his penis began to swell 'and from the dark red glans gushed forth a whitish liquid, first with a powerful spurt, then in a series of less potent jets. I had just discharged for the first time.' He soon discovered that masturbation was like drink: the more you indulge, the more you want.

Not only may it become a habit but it may be preferred to any other form of sexual satisfaction. Agathias Scholasticus asks (in the Greek Anthology) by what road should one seek Love. If you seek him in the streets you will repent the courtesan's greed for gold and luxury. If you approach a maiden's bed, it must end in marriage or you will be punished for seduction. Should one be expected to awake reluctant desire to calm a wife, because it is one's duty? Adultery and unnatural intercourse are out of the question. As for widows, if one of them is ill-conditioned, she is anyone's mistress, and knows all the arts of harlotry, while if she is chaste, she is pricked by loveless remorse, hates what she has done, and having a remnant of shame shrinks from the union till she decides to put an end to it. If you associate with your own servant you must make up your mind to change places and become hers, and if with someone else's, the law which prosecutes for outrage on slaves that are not your own will get you. Agathias fled from all these 'and celebrated his nuptials by hand, never lacking a mistress'.

Such a coldblooded attitude to the device is unusual. Agathias manages to justify it even if he could not make it respectable, but the famous jester in the *Arabian Nights*, Goha, was able to extract fun from it as he did from everything else. He lay in the road in the heat of the sun and held his tool naked in his hand. A passer-by remonstrated with him for such a shameful act, but Goha replied merrily, 'I see nothing shameful in a father taking his son out for a little fresh air.' ('The Master of Shifts and Laughter', 925th night.) Another of the very few writers who managed to treat the whole business as a joke was Mark Twain, who was invited as a guest of honour at the Stomach Club in Paris after the publication of *1601*. His speech on this occasion was published under the title of *Some Thoughts on the Science of Onanism* in 1879. It was short and witty, and its aim was not erotic stimulation but amusement. At the time it appeared to be rather more sensational than it does now because

7 SEX IN LITERATURE

masturbation was believed to be highly dangerous. In fact,
Twain contributed to the destruction of this myth.

As for the amount of masturbation in which a man
indulges, the range is probably as great as that in normal
copulation. A rather mild performer, such as Beardsley's
Tannhauser, was compelled to stroke himself a little when
he saw, on a wall of the Palace of Venus, a print showing
'how an old marquis practised his five-finger exercise, while
in front of him his mistress offered her warm fesses to a panting poodle'. At the other extreme we have Rudolph Redpaw
in *Stradella*, a man of tremendous physical vitality. Address-
ing Archie he said, 'Used to masturbate as many as twelve
times a day when I was your age. Never did a man have the
sex drive I've got. It's been my curse and my glory. I can't
escape it. Ruined me everywhere. At the same time it's given
me the only pleasure I've ever gotten.' Talking of the sex
drive, what on earth does an armless man do? Naturally, such
a question does not often arise but, just as naturally, it is
bound to in the world of Samuel Beckett. Penned in his jar,
the unnamable (in the novel of that name) worries about the
possibility of asphyxiation. His face is blue, his tongue pro-
trudes, his penis is tumescent. He rambles on.

> The penis, well now, that's a nice surprise, I'd forgotten
> I had one. What a pity I have no arms, there might still
> be something to be wrung from it. No, 'tis better thus.
> At my age, to start masturbating again, it would be in-
> decent. And fruitless. And yet one can never tell. With
> a yo heave ho, concentrating with all my might on a
> horse's rump, at the moment when the tail rises, I might
> not go altogether empty-handed away. Heaven, I almost
> felt it flutter.

Yet not masturbation but imaginative effort.

Finally, there are forms of masturbation celebrated in
fiction (or noticed in other forms of literature) which might
accommodate the armless man. In his Terminal Essay to the
Arabian Nights Burton writes of various Chinese devices

including the *merkin*, which is a heart-shaped article of thin skin stuffed with cotton and slit with an artificial vagina. There are tapes above and below by which it can be lashed to the back of a chair. There is also a very curious reference in Rabelais when Kissbreech is giving evidence. This is virtually unintelligible, except for odd phrases, among them these: 'For that having a great desire to obey the pleasure of the king, I armed myself from top to toe with belly-furniture, of the soles of good venison pasties, to go see how my grape-gatherers and vintagers had pinked and cut full of small holes their high-coped hats, to lecher it the better, and play at in and in.'

Female

All psychologists know that perversion figures have great fascination for some people: they may have their guilt assuaged, or they may simply get a kick out of the idea of so many people. . . . Dr Sofie Lazarsfeld tells us that the Advisory Bureau (on sexual matters), set up by a Viennese newspaper and directed by her, discovered that large numbers of men and women continued the practice of masturbation long after puberty. Men outnumbered women by three to one but she thinks the female figure should be higher because many women believe that masturbation necessarily means manipulation by hand. This form of masturbation is less common among women than among men, but she believes the total figures are much the same for each sex.

In America, says Kinsey, about 62% of all females masturbate at some time in the course of their lives. (The figure is for his sample, of course.) About 58% masturbate at some time to the point of orgasm. Other researchers have published figures ranging from 49-80% of American women. European figures have varied even more, but this is probably because they have been obtained from more selective samples. Kinsey tells us something of the female technique. She usually moves a finger gently and rhythmically over the sensitive areas, or applies rhythmic or steady pressure with several of her fingers or with her whole hand. Occasionally her heel or some other object is used to press on the sensitive areas. Regular motion is one of the main stimulants. Men, for instance, often experience erections while on horseback, driving in a carriage, or travelling by rail. Van de Velde says he has known ipsatresses[2] who were driven to masturbation by journeys, although they resisted the idea and strongly disapproved of the practice. He regrets that men, even doctors, have very little opportunity to ask women such intimate questions. Van de Velde was writing in 1928. Since then the research institute and the questionnaire between them have allowed women to express themselves on these subjects in sometimes embarrassing detail.

Turning to non-medical or scientific literature, we are given a picture of a female masturbator by the Japanese novelist, Ihara Saikaku. The heroine of his *Life of an Amorous Woman* is always consumed by lust and cannot always satisfy it in the orthodox manner, particularly when living in the house of a warrior, which is bound by the strictest rules. She is, in effect, a nymphomaniac. 'One day, as I was examining a fascinating depiction by Hiskikawa of an erotic scene, I was stirred despite myself to the most intense excitement. I sought then to quench my amorous flames, now with my heel, now with the middle finger of my hand. These were cold and insensible tools indeed for stilling my wanton lust, and soon I was overcome with desire for a more solid form of love.' Ivan Morris, who edited and translated this work, comments that the use of the heel was not as startling as it may seem to Western readers, when one remembers the traditional Japanese sitting posture and the suppleness resulting from it. But as we have seen, Kinsey reports the same device in America.

Let us conclude with three ladies who masturbated from time to time because it gave them pleasure, and perhaps because it was so easy and demanded no involvement of the type described by Agathias. First there is the girl celebrated in the last stanza of 'Green Grow the Rashes' from *The Merry Muses of Caledonia*.

And ken ye Leezie Lundie, O.
 The godly Leezie Lundie, O,
She m——s like reek thro' a' the week,
But finger f——s on Sunday, O.

A young lady known as Angel Baby in Bruce Oliver's *The Square Within*:

Angel Baby's up and she's down and she's down and she's up and through it behind it over and under it where it hurts and it beats and it throbs and its good and its worse and its better my hillocks are bounding white angels are leaping I'm bad and I'm human not human inhuman big human big mother big father big mother big coming o jiminy Jim-Jim.

To quote this out of context suggests obsession, which is unfair for this is one of those rare novels in which sex is given its true proportion without any hedging in describing sensation. It resembles Hemingway's approach to copulation in *For Whom the Bell Tolls*, and may be contrasted with the following from Mary McCarthy's *The Group*, which stays outside the sensation and adopts a rather cynical pose. It is the story of Libby who is immensely proud of her new aristocratic Scandinavian acquisition, Nils, until he tries to rape her on the sofa. He tears her dress and starts pulling at her skirt. She remembers you are supposed to kick men in the testicles when they misbehave but when she tries he laughs and smacks her face. Hs asks if she is a virgin and when she says she is he stops and tells her she's a bore. Libby was sorry to lose him. At least she would have known what it was like when a man did it to you.

Libby had a little secret; she sometimes made love to herself, on the bath mat, after having her tub. She always felt awful afterwards, sort of shaken and depleted and wondering what people would think if they could see

her, especially when she took herself what she called
'Over the Top'.

And she wondered if Nils had thought she was experienced
because he could see what she had been doing in her face, for
they said it gave you circles under the eyes. Another aspect
of the masturbation myth.

Mutual

When men and women do it together it is obviously a sexual
variant and not a substitute. It is probably in many cases a
sophistication, though it may also be found among young
and inexperienced couples who have not yet brought themselves to full sexual intercourse.

The first story in *Tableaux Vivants* opens with a rather
charming account of clitorisation (what the French call *La
Branlade*) which is worth quoting at some length:

> Ladies, I tell you truthfully, clitorisation is a means of
> enjoyment more efficacious than agreeable. I am firmly
> of opinion that it was invented to triumph over the
> resistance of nature. The first person to tickle a clitoris
> was an unfortunate futterer.
>
> There are disinherited creatures to whom heaven has
> refused the gift of pleasure. The warmest kisses, the
> liveliest embraces, cannot give warmth to these living
> limbs of marble; the finger is the last resource; no woman
> can resist a learned forefinger.
>
> But those to whom this operation is necessary enjoy
> in the same manner as they give birth. In their pangs
> the lover's fingers rake into their gulf, seeking the rebel-
> lious clitoris, touching it, pressing it, furiously rubbing
> it. And she: 'You—you are flaying me!'
>
> And she writhes in a nervous paroxysm. The pleasure
> tears her like the lightning rends the cloud; it is no more
> lasting than the lightning.
>
> There are clitorises, on the contrary, which you need

but graze to give them life. Clitorisation is truly a touch-stone; and if the mare quivers under the first touches of the finger which caresses her, use discretion and art. If she has never been touched before—

Ah! it is a delicate operation tickling a virgin.

There, experience is everything. You tickle at a venture. A sigh, a start, ought to warn you that the crisis is near. Sometimes the ingénue shrinks away: 'You go—you go too fast!'

A man of wit, who was also a great libertine, was accustomed to say, 'God has done me the favour to give me slow fingers!'

Lightness alone does not suffice; you must in addition touch exactly. The clitoris flees, you have to seize it. You have probably never clitorised any of your mistresses without her having said to you in the course of the work, 'It isn't there.'

How clumsy men are! Women know much better how to take hold of it. That is what justifies Lesbos.

Still, even when two women render to each other the eminent service of tickling one another the business is not perfect. The most accomplished tribade sometimes touches on one side.

One is best clitorised by oneself only.[3]

There is quite a lot of masturbation, mutual and otherwise, in *Teleny*. The curious word 'brandle' (presumably from the French) is used three times to denote the stroking of the penis. When the activity is mutual it is between men. As an example, a couple on a balcony are looking down on a homosexual party. 'I suppose your cocks were crowing so lustily that the naked fellows below must have been in great danger of receiving a shower of your holy water,' remarks a friend, 'for you must have brandled each other's sprinklers rapturously up there.' This sounds coarse, but when Teleny and his friend are working on each other there is quite a different tone. There are none of the fantastic jets of sperm that disfigure much pornography (except when the exaggeration is intended

for comic purposes) and there is no suggestion of a lonely
vice; it is an intimate and loving relationship.

> There was, for a moment, an intense pain, somewhere
> about the root of the penis—or rather, within the very
> core and centre of the reins, after which the sap of life
> began to move slowly, slowly, from within the seminal
> glands; it mounted up the bulb of the urethra, and up
> the narrow column, somewhat like mercury within the
> tube of a thermometer—or rather, like the scalding and
> scathing lava within the crater of a volcano.
>
> It finally reached the apex; then the slit gaped, the tiny
> lips parted, and the pearly, creamy, viscous fluid oozed
> out—not all at once in a gushing jet, but at intervals, and
> in huge, burning tears.
>
> At every drop that escaped out of the body, a creepy
> almost unbearable feeling started from the tips of the
> fingers, from the ends of the toes, especially from the
> innermost cells of the brain; the marrow in the spine
> and within all the bones seemed to melt; and when the
> different currents—either coursing with the blood or
> running rapidly up the nervous fibres—met within the
> phallus (that small instrument made out of muscle and
> blood-vessels) a tremendous shock took place; a convul-
> sion which annihilated both mind and matter, a quiver-
> ing delight which everyone has felt, to a greater or less
> degree—often a thrill almost too intense to be pleasur-
> able.

Perhaps the reason why this book was once attributed to
Oscar Wilde is that the author was obviously an earnest homosexual whose writing was in some respects a plea for tolerance
—but the earnestness infects the language and the gaiety
which must never be far away in good writing about sex is
not apparent. Most writers who do trouble to introduce
masturbation are not really attracted by it but use it as a
station on the road of sensation. Angela Pearson, for instance,
allows her hero in *The Whipping Post* to undergo a variant

of it. Arthur Simes has a night-out in Hamburg. He is trying to expose the flagellationists of the Whipping Club but is a mass of perversions himself. He is pissed on by a girl (at his request), then whips her viciously. (The code frowns upon a man whipping a woman.) Then he asks for a boy, but this is not pederasty. The boy says he will use soap. Simes lies on a bed with his trousers down. The boy lathers his hand with hot soap and water and massages gently. Simes lies back and gives himself up to the blissful sensation.

We will conclude with two special occasions on which masturbation may be resorted to. First, Henry Miller finds normal intercourse impossible because he has blisters on his cock and fears it may be pox. Mona suffers similarly. Fucking is painful. Miller is not one to give up easily—in fact, he realised the situation gave the opportunity for a new area of exploration. As he lay with her, one arm round her and his fingers up her crotch, she became strangely confidential. 'It was as though the erogenous zone of her mind was being tickled by my fingers. The juice began to spill out . . . "the dirt", as she had once called it.'

That was necessity but invention is never far behind. Self-abuse can become exhibition, and this is one of the indignities Sir Stephen puts upon O in his enslavement of her (*The Story of O*, by Pauline Reage). He orders her to caress herself. She put her fingers between the already parted fleece, 'the already burning morsel of flesh placed above where the fragile lips of her sex joined together.' But she could not do it. She remembered seeing her friend Marion doing it. O had been only fifteen years old. Marion had sat in an armchair in a hotel room, with one leg flung over an arm and her head sagging to the other, caressing herself and moaning in front of O. She had once done it in her office and her boss had come in and caught her. He locked the door and told her to take off her panties and do it again, and he moved the chair over by the window.

The Great Sin

Go Tell it on the Mountain, by James Baldwin, is the story
of fourteen-year-old John in a Negro household in New York.
He is exploited by religion and the 'saints' who uphold it,
including his step-father. We see him pass through an
emotional crisis, sparked by religious pressures and domestic
insecurity working on a sensitive but immature mind. Masturbation is the weak point through which sin pours into
him and holds him to spiritual ransom. 'He had sinned. In
spite of the saints, his mother and his father, the warnings
he had heard from his earliest beginnings, he had sinned with
his hands a sin that was hard to forgive. In the school lava-
tory, alone, thinking of the boys, older, bigger, braver, who
made bets with each other as to whose urine could arch
higher, he had watched in himself a transformation of which
he would never dare to speak.' Yes, he was a sinner, and he
knew it. But a sense of sin is not always enough. One needs
a sign, tangible proof. He had it in masturbation.

For generations now young men have been threatened with
the direst penalties if they give way to this temptation. Today
more tolerance is shown, and a realistic appraisal of possible
damage is made. But in the past the heaviest battalions were
moved up against the practice.

In 1724 there appeared a book entitled *The Crime of Onan*
(together with that of his Brother Er, punished with Sudden
Death) or, the Hainous Vice of Self-Defilement with all its
Dismal Consequences. There were ten chapters. The first
gave the reasons for publishing this treatise. 'As this Branch
of Uncleanness, viz., Sinning with a Person's own Self, is the
most general of any Sin of Impurity whatsoever, by consequence some instructions concerning it are the most of any
wanted in the World, in order to awake the Guilty, and deter
the Innocent and Unwary from falling into it, through In-
advertence or Ignorance.' Chapter 2 dealt with the Heinous-
ness and Abomination of the Sin of Self-Defilement. A learned
divine is quoted: 'That the Crime in itself is Monstrous and
Unnatural: in its Practice Filthy, Base and Odious to

Extremity: its Guilt is crying, and its Consequence ruinous. It destroys conjugal Affection, perverts natural Inclination, tends to extinguish the Hopes of Posterity, brings on a numerous Train of Diseases on the Body in this World and utterly ruins the Soul for all Eternity in the next.' Chapter 3 treats of the Blindness, and some other Circumstances attending the Commission of this Sin. This, of course, means spiritual blindness but a later age did not scruple to interpret it as physical blindness. Further chapters discuss the situation of an Onanian on his deathbed and his condition in the afterlife. 'Imagine that you see in the Center of the Earth a vast Gulph and Lake of Fire and Flames, and those two unhappy Men Er and Onan, together with all others who have impenitently imitated them in the perpetration of this abominable Fact, plunged and roling in it, all covered and transperced with Fire, which they not only suck in with their Breath, but which enters also at their Eyes and Ears, their Mouths and Nostrils casting forth dreadful Flames, their Skin scorched, their Flesh, Blood, Humors and Brains boiling up with the Violence of the Burning, their Bones and Marrow all transparent with Fire, like a Piece of Iron taken red Hot out of a Furnace, and all the Parts of their Bodies glowing with Fire.' The commentators, says the author, agree that Er's sin was the same as Onan's, but that he did it for different reasons: Er wanted to preserve Tamar's beauty, while Onan did not want a child that would technically not be his. (No arguments are given for this assumption about Er.) Chapter 8 tells us of the Usual Misfortune that attends the Sin of Self-Defilement, and how to Remedy it. Persons of either sex (one of the rare suggestions that women are also guilty) are brought insensibly to a gleet, or some such draining weakness. The last two chapters are about the nature of gleets, and the reader is referred to another book for treatment. Commercial acumen seems to have warred successfully at this point with righteous indignation.

In the same year another publication, entitled *Eronania, or the Misusing of the Marriage Bed by Er and Onan,* also appeared. The early part of this tract appears to be a direct

copy of the previous one, which naturally suggests single
authorship. The unsuspected seriousness of the sin is stressed.
Many people have imagined themselves innocent because they
are not guilty of Adultery or Fornication or other crimes of
Impurity, yet for years they have been extravagantly guilty
of Onan's sin. It is often treated as unimportant because it
happens in private, and so they continue. Yet even the most
dissolute are ashamed of it because it is so vile. 'During Youth
there are the most and strongest Cravings of Flesh and Blood
after Lust, from a more plentiful and every Day increasing
Quantity of warm Blood and vigorous animal Spirits in the
Body, which, from that vast Quantity of Saline Particles,
they (but particularly the *Semen*) abound with, irritate, stir
up, and excite a more than ordinary Ferment in all the Juices
and Fluids of the Body. Being thus in a manner boiling,
working and fermenting, are swelled and frothed up, by
which they cause a larger Repletion of the Vessels being more
than usually distended and stretched out by the Repletion
and Redundancy of these Humours, sets Nature a work,
violently to gratify this carnal and sensual Appetite.'
Practisers of the vice are warned that they are not likely to
bear children, and if they do the offspring will be sickly
creatures, characterised by a lean countenance, pale looks,
hollow eyes, feeble hams, legs without calves, limping with
a stick, gouty limbs and pains in the small of the back.
Masturbation also causes profuse nightly seminal effusions,
from the semen being thin and the parts feeble and loose.
It is a hard habit to break. Next follow letters of advice from
two learned divines. One gives the story of a young man who
had fallen into a deplorable condition through frequent self-
pollution. Onan was also criticised for the time he committed
his sin: 'It seems he stayed not till Night for the Time of
Privacy for such a Purpose, else the Bed might have been
named as well as the Ground.' Both Er and Onan 'satisfied
their Sensuality against the Order of Nature'. In this claim
we can see the complete reversal of the Greek attitude, not
so much in the expression as in its conception of Nature. The
Greeks sought the satisfaction of lust and the gratification of

concupiscence (always within acceptable bounds). In the Christian attitude towards Onan and his sin we see the insistence on the production of children as the sole aim of sex. And so the young men are given advice: to stay in bed only while sleeping; to read a good book until sleep comes; to get up on first awakening; to sleep on one side, not on the back, which heats the reins. 'I know it will cost some Violence at first to Nature to be flung so suddenly out of a warm Bed upon a cold floor, but the difficulty will soon vanish, after five or six Times Practice of it.' And no one should take pleasure in night emissions. 'It is never lawful for any Person to give way to any carnal Delight, in any sort whatsoever, but only in lawful Marriage.' And at this point the divine considers womanhood and declares that women are like fruit, because they can be kept in many ways but once they are bruised they cannot be preserved.

These publications appear to have aroused misgivings among some readers for later in the year there appeared *A Supplement to the Onania*, or the Heinous Sin of Self-Pollution. In his Preface the author says his Adversaries profess an aversion to the sin but extenuate the Crime by saying that it is made to appear more heinous than it deserves, or even make out that the act itself is innocent and that only frequent practice is criminal. It is necessary, they say, 'an easement of Nature', and they even claim that total forbearance can damage the health. Some physicians have said that if the semen is detained for long, some noxious particles may work back into the blood. Some say he has brought the practice to the notice of those who would not otherwise have been acquainted with it. Others regard the mention of self-pollution among women as an insult to their sex, as if it is worse than adultery and fornication, which are practised daily. Our author now hits back at his critics with the histories of two young masturbators of his acquaintance. One did it every night. 'As soon as I heard of it, I quickly prognosticated the Wretch's Fate, which came to pass within eighteen Months after, for he died of a deep Consumption, having lived till he became like a Ghost, or living Skeleton.' The other followed the practice 'till his Seed did indeed come away without any Provocation, and little or no Erection, whereby he fell into a Hectick, and was soon cut off.'

FOOTNOTES

1. In the Middle East Egyptians are sometimes referred to in impolite circles by the code number 31 because they are so thick-blooded and slow-moving as to require 31 strokes of the penis to orgasm. This is in particular contradiction to the Sudanese, who have little self-control.

2. Van de Velde gives a footnote: '*Ipsation* is the more modern and accurate term for what was known as *maṣturbation*. Other accurate terms are *autoeroticism* and *self-relief*.' (*Ideal Marriage*.)

3. The quality of this passage will explain why G. Legman, one of the best living erotic bibliographers, has called *Les Tableaux Vivants* 'one of the most charming erotic books in any language'. It was translated into English by the redoubtable Leonard Smithers, one of Burton's collaborators, and an adaptation was published in New York under the title of *The Amusements of a Fortnight*, by 'Pierre Louys'.

13: *Dildo*

Let me repeat: erotic writing and pornography are male literature which likes to regard the female Oestrus as its starting point. Whether it believes this is doubtful, but as a last resort it is convenient to think of female desire as the true lodestone. None were more certain of this than the early Christian Fathers who, could not think of epithets disgusting enough to describe womankind.

The eighteenth century, in its cynicism, joyfully accepted the views of the Christian Fathers, whom it spurned. The eighteenth century was not unduly serious in its outlook on anything, having come round to the view that the world was what it was and nothing much could be done about it. The men were agreed to get as much pleasure as they could out of their women, and emulated the Romans in tearing female reputations to shreds when anything went wrong. Tom Brown, an underestimated poet and commentator, was representative. Here is a passage from his *Satire Against Women*.

> We need not rake the brothel and the stews,
> To see what various scenes of lust they use,
> Then the lewd punks of want may plead excuse.
> But let us to proud palaces repair,
> And out of choice see what is acted there;
> When, unconstrain'd by want of choice they lie
> Wallowing in all the filth of boundless luxury;
> They set no limits to their wild desires,
> But each possesses what she now admires.
> Footman and groom successively they know,
> The sooty negro, and the pulvill'd beau,
> The brawny coachman and the porter too.

A woman would satisfy her desires where she could and how she could. Cynically Brown writes "On a Blind Man in Love":

> *If Argus with an hundred eyes not one*
> *Could guard, hop'st thou to keep thine, who hast none?*

And as for the how, we have seen her resorting to masturbation. If a man may occasionally resort to a merkin, why not woman to a dildo?

Webster suggests the origin of the word in *diddle-o*, with an ultimate origin in Old English *dyderian*, to deceive or cheat. The French call it *godmichet*, which is said to come from *gaude mihi*, give me pleasure. The polite term is *penis succedaneus*. The Romans simply called it a *phallus* or *fascinum*, the Italians a *passatempo* or *diletto* (which is, of course, another possible derivation, and a more likely one, for our dildo). The classic model was constructed of caoutchouc, but sometimes it was made of horn, leather or even velvet. It is mentioned by Petronius Arbiter, in a passage where an old priestess in the course of her mystical practices thrusts one, smeared with a mixture of oil, ground pepper and bruised nettle seeds into the anus of Encolpius. In *L'Escole des Filles* the story is related of a king's daughter who had made for her a bronze statue of a man, painted flesh colour, and furnished with a phallus of a more yielding material. This machine was erect and hollow, it had a red head and a small hole at the end, with two pendants in the shape of testicles, everything in close imitation of nature. When the damsel was inflamed by the presence of this figure, she approached the phallus and thrust it into her vulva, clasping the buttocks of the statue and drawing herself against it. When she was on the point of discharging she touched a certain spring which projected from the buttocks and the statue immediately squirted a warm and thickened liquor, white like pap, into the lady's vulva, thus satisfying her venereal desires.

It may be asked why a French princess should go to all this trouble. It is not likely that she went to the trouble but that her father did. At certain times in history the mystique

of royalty has reached such extremes that few men, if any,
have been considered fit to touch a maiden of the blood, yet
alone have intimate relations with her. The attitude of men
towards the dildo has been ambivalent. True, it can be
regarded as a rival, but again, it may be useful in cooling the
desires of a too amorous spouse. All the points of view are
expressed in an epic poem entitled *Dildoides*, by Samuel
Butler, author of *Hudibras*. (It is to be found in *The Cabinet
of Love*, 1718.) This poem is said to have been occasioned by
the public burning of a hogshead of dildoes in the year 1672,
'pursuant to an Act of Parliament for the prohibiting of
French Goods'. The poem begins:

> Such a sad tale prepare to hear,
> As claims from either sex a tear.
> Twelve dildoes, meant for the support
> Of aged lechers of the court,
> Were lately burnt by impious hand
> Of trading rascals of the land,
> Who envying their curious frame,
> Expos'd their Priaps to the flame.

They were of various materials and different sizes:

> Some were of wax, where ev'ry vein,
> And smallest fibre were made plain.
> Some were for tender virgins fit,
> Some for the large salacious slit
> Of a rank lady, tho' so torn,
> She hardly feels when child is born.

At an assembly, one speaker spoke on behalf of the dildo

> Are you afraid lest merry griggs
> Will wear false—like periwigs;
> And being but to small ones born,
> Will great ones have of wax and horn.

Their value to women was never in doubt:

> *Did not a lady of great honour*
> *Marry a footman waiting on her?*
> *When one of these timely apply'd,*
> *Has eas'd her lust and saved her pride.*
> *Safely her Ladyship might have spent,*
> *While such gallants in pocket went.*

But another speaker swayed the assembly by reminding them
that the dildo was man's rival. If it could replace the foot-
man might it not also replace all other men, including husbands and legitimate lovers?

Ancient and Oriental

Ezekiel warns against the dildo in these words: 'Thou
didst also take thy fair jewels of my gold and my silver, which
I had given thee, and madest for thee images of men, and
didst play the harlot with them. . . .' Far less fuss has been
made about this sin than about Onan's, and there are probably two reasons for this. In the first place, the use of the
dildo is comparatively rare. Secondly, the great crime in the
eyes of the Church lay in the wanton emission of the male
seed. The woman was regarded as a seed-bed and there was
no question of wastage when an orgasm took place.[1]

In India the dildo tended to be used fairly frequently in
the harem, and again the reason is obvious. The women were
rarely able to have their desires fully satisfied and therefore
had recourse to each other. Masturbation was one possibility
but if greater reality were required the dildo was used. They
used to dress the daughters of their nurses, their female
friends or their female attendants in men's clothes, and then
accomplish their object by means of bulbs, roots and fruits
in the shape of the lingam, or they would lie upon the statue
of a male figure with an erect lingam. According to the *Kama
Sutra*, however, the dildo was rarely used independently. The
dildos described above were makeshifts, suggesting that such

activity was frowned upon. The true Indian dildo was a con-
trivance fitted over the erect penis to increase its size. They
were of different types. One was a hollow body, worn like a
bangle, and having a number of small nodules on the outer
surface to increase sensation. Sometimes a couple of bangles
were worn, with three or four ridges in the surface of each,
for the same purpose as already mentioned. When three
bangles were worn, they covered the whole penis and were
known as a bracelet. Sometimes a piece of metal wire was
wrapped round the penis to increase its girth. Another type
was a cylinder which covered the whole penis; it had small
holes at the lower end through which a line could be passed
to tie it to the body to keep it in position. When the other
end was closed it resembled a Western condom. Finally a
tube was made out of the rind of a gourd, a reed or a bamboo
according to the size required. It was well seasoned in medi
cated oil and tied to the waist with thread. A variant on the
wire method was to wrap a string of beads, either fine or
coarse, round the penis. This effectually increased the size of
the penis and also added to the sensation experienced by the
woman, according to the type of surface.

English and Traditional

'The Maid's Complaint for Want of a Dil Doul' appears
in *The Bagford Ballads*, which roughly covers the period
1600-1715, but some of the songs in this collection are undoubtedly older.

> *For I am a Maid and a very good Maid,*
> *and sixteen years of age am I,*
> *And fain would I part with my Maiden-head,*
> *if any good fellow would with me lye:*
> *But none to me yet ever proffered such love*
> *as to lye by my side and give me a shove*
> With his dil doul, dill doul, dill doul,
>   O happy were I, *etc.*

It is quite clear what a *dil doul* is in this context—but why
is it given this name? In no other song that I know of is it
used. The suggestion is that the maiden was at least
acquainted with the dildo and its use, though presumably had
not used one, else her maidenhead would not have remained
unbroken.

The earliest account of a dildo in action in the English
language is to be found in *The Choise of Valentines or the
Merie Ballad of Nash his Dildo*. Nashe lived from 1567-1601
and a detailed account of such length as this of a sexual act,
particularly a deviate act, is very rare indeed. Of course, there
was a great deal of intermittent bawdiness throughout the
writing of the period, but that was a different matter altogether. The *Works* of Thomas Nashe were edited from
original texts by Ronald B. McKerrow in 1905. This poem
is included among his Doubtful Works. The dedication to the
right Honorable the Lord S. ran:

> *Complaints and praises everyone can write,*
>   *And passion-out their pangs in statelie rimes,*
> *But of love's pleasures none did ever write*
>   *That hath succeeded in theis latter times.*

It seems probable that more writing of this type did circulate,
but it was rare enough for Nashe to believe he was doing
something unusual. Some critics suggest that the dildoic
section was an interpolation, even another poem that was
incorporated into the main body. In a brief epilogue the
author apologises for any offence he may have given, and
blames 'Ovid's wanton Muse'. Anyway, here it is (the lady
has had two orgasms, but wants more):

> *Adiew faint-hearted instrument of lust,*
>   *That falselie hast betrayde our equale trust.*
> *Hence-forth no more will I implore thine ayde,*
>   *Or thee, or men of cowardize upbrayde.*
> *My little dilldo shall supplye their kinde:*
>   *A knave, that moves as light as leaves by winde;*

That bendeth not, nor fouldeth anie deale,
But stands as stiff, as he were made of steele,
And playes at peacock twixt my leggs right blythe,
And doeth my ticking swage with manie a sighe;
For, by Saint Runnion he'le refresh me well,
And never make my tender bellie swell.
Poore Priapus, whose triumph now must falle,
Except thou thrust this weakeling to the walle.
Behould how he usurps in bed and bowre,
And undermines thy kingdom everie howre.
How slye he creeps betwixt the barke and tree,
And sucks the sap, whilst sleepe detaineth thee.

He is a youth almost two handfulls highe,
Streight, round and plumbe, yett having but one eye,
Wherein the rhewm so ferventlie doeth raigne,
That Stigian gulph maie scarce his teares containe;
Attired in white velvet or in silk,
And nourisht with whott water or with milk;
Arm'd otherwise in thick congealed glasse,
When he more glib to hell belowe would passe,
Upon a chariot of five wheeles he rydes,
The which an arme strong driver stedfast guides,
And often alters pace, as wayes growe deepe;
(For, who in pathe's unknowen, one gate can keepe?)
Sometimes he smoothlie slideth doune the hill;
Another while the stones his feete doe kill:
In clammie wayes he treadeth by and by,
And plasheth and sprayeth all that be him nye.
So fares this jollie rider in his race,
Plunging, and coursing forward in lyke case,
Bedashed, bespurted, and beplodded foule,
God give thee shame, thou blinde mischapen owle.

By the end of the seventeenth century the little gadget has developed a personality. He is Italian, which is interesting in view of the controversy about the origin of his name (reviewed above). Signior Dildoe was celebrated by John

Wilmot, Earl of Rochester, in a poem of that name (1678).
There are twenty-three quatrains, each ending with the words
'Signior Dildoe', of which the following are specimens:

> *The Pattern of Vertue her Grace of Cl (eve) land,*
> *Has swallow'd more P——s than the Nation has Land;*
> *But by rubbing and scrubbing so wide it does grow.*
> *It is fit for just nothing but Signior Dildoe.*

> *This Signior is sound, safe, ready and dumb,*
> *As ever was Candle, Carrot or your Thumb;*
> *Then away with the nasty Devices and show*
> *How you rate the just Merit of Signior Dildoe.*

And today we complain about character assassination! And
incidentally, this is the second verse I have quoted which
suggests that the dildo was particularly appreciated by ladies
whose parts were on the large side.

Modern and Experimental

Three modern examples, and one experimental.

Jérôme, in Sade's *Justine*, decided to perforate the unfortunate creature with 'one of those articles of furniture usually
found in nunneries', which he drove in deep with repeated
blows and then replaced with his own organ. The following
morning he produced a much bigger machine, hollow and
fitted with a high pressure pump that squirted a powerful
stream of water through an orifice having a circumference
of over three inches. The monk filled it with very hot water
and buried it in the girl's front end, about two-thirds of the
way up. After fifteen minutes of lacerating action (during
which, needless to say, he is excited by a third person), he
pulled the trigger and a column of boiling water gushed into
the depths of her womb.

Henry Miller discovered one of these instruments among
the possessions of Melanie, a cracked old woman who lived
in his household and who may have been Maude's mother

(Maude being one of the characters in *Sexus*, part I of *The Rosy Crucifixion*). It was tucked away in one of the bureau drawers and could only have been used for one purpose—unless Melanie, in her simplicity, had discovered a wholly innocent usage for it. Whenever the dildo is mentioned in literature there is a tendency to bring in the nuns. Sade did in the passage just quoted, and now Miller wonders 'whether Melanie sometimes whiled away a pleasant hour with this object, as did the nuns of old'. But it is not difficult for Miller's imagination to get to work on such promising material. He was able 'to picture her lying on the filthy quilt clad in her torn chemise, poking this thing in and out of her twat in absent-minded glee. I could even picture the dog licking the juice that slowly trickled between her legs. And the parrot squawking insanely, perhaps repeating some idiotic phrase which Melanie had taught it, such as, "Ever so easy, dearie!" or "Get a move on, now, get a move on!"'

Naturally the great contemporary erotic humorist, Akbar del Piombo, could not be expected to miss such an opportunity. His hero in *Who Pushed Paula?* (how pleasant to record that his name was also Henry!) watched two women using a dildo. It was one of the double type, a big leather thing, extending as far into the 'male's' cunt as into the female's. Clarissa lay on her back and Hortense was on top. Henry was in the bathroom closet. For a couple of hours they tried various positions. Finally they did it doggy fashion, Hortense climbing over Clarissa's back, while rivulets of female come sloshed down her thighs. Hortense's discharge dribbled out of the sides of the dildo's base. Henry could resist it no longer. He dashed out of his hiding place and rammed his own 'real nature-spear' right up Hortense's bung. Then he wrapped both his arms round Clarissa below, holding them both fast. Each blow he drove into Hortense threw the fake cock into Clarissa. Henry met no resistance to his own part in the proceedings.

We end with a curiosity, which deserves the apellation 'experimental'. It is obvious that, just as a male penis can be used on a man in buggery, so a man may use a dildo if he can find nothing better. There is evidence that some men may resort to this method in the correspondence of Flaubert and Louise Colet. He sent her a paperweight which he had found among his father's belongings, 'with a hilarious history'. Dr. Flaubert had extracted it with delivery forceps from an old seaman who had come to him in bewildered discomfort, and quite unable to offer any explanation as to how so large an object had got there. Burton tells a similar story of some English middies in India. It seemed to be an occupational risk of seamen.

Variants

The ladies of the harem used fruit and veg. when they felt disposed. The most popular substitute and one that was always ready to hand in pre-electric days was certainly the candle. Suckling's poem is well known, but this work will not be complete without its inclusion:

> *There is a thing which in the light*
> *Is seldom us'd; but in the night*
> *It serves the female maiden crew,*
> *The ladies and the good-wives too:*
> *They use to take it in their hand,*
> *And then it will uprightly stand;*
> *And to a hole they it apply,*
> *Where by its goodwill it would die;*
> *It spends goes out, and still within*
> *It leaves its moisture thick and thin.*

This is execrable verse, and what is more, is not really intended to represent the candle as a dildo. But in fact the meaning exists on three levels instead of the customary two.

Apollinaire writes of candle-dildoes in his *Memoirs of a Young Rakehell*. The young boy hears his aunt confessing. She says she is still a virgin so far as men are concerned but she once learned that the maid, Kate, was using an exhorbitant number of candles, presumably through reading in bed. The family were afraid of fire. One night, seeing a light in

Kate's room, she went in and found the girl sitting on the floor, leaning forward in the direction of the bed. In front of her was a chair with a mirror on it and a candle burning on each side. She was holding something long and white which she was driving back and forth between her thighs. She was sighing and trembling and then cried, 'Oh, oh, oh! It feels so good!' She explained to the aunt that she did it in memory of her lover who had been drafted into the army. The aunt followed suit and repeated the operation frequently.

Henry Miller also has a candle episode in *Sexus*. He is with Ida, the allegedly frigid wife of a friend. But Henry manages to overcome her scruples and then she wants it again and again. One day they are at lunch. He takes her leg and swings it over the arm of the chair and tells her she's a slut because she never wears undies. He pulls her dress up and tells her to play with herself while he finishes his coffee. She tells him he's filthy but does as she's told. He wonders how her husband ever gets his 'wang' in because she says it's terrific. Then he gives her a candle and asks her if she can get it in all the way.

> She spread the other leg over the other arm of the chair and began to work it in. She was looking at herself intently, her legs parted as if on the verge of an orgasm. She began to move back and forth, then rolled her ass around. I pushed her chair back further, got down on my knees and watched.

Restif de la Bretonne, the great shoe and foot fetichist, naturally prefers a shoe. Most of the men in his *Pleasures and Follies* have the same tendency. A woman named Mezières is fucked by a man who is maddened by his daughter's charms, and has them displayed while he sets to. Taking her shoes off and putting them on again was an important part of the ritual, but sometimes Mezières would seize a shoe and, 'raging with lust, she'd push me on to the bed, lick my cunt and into hers thrust the toe of either my slipper or shoe, wielding it like a godemiche.'

Finally, Molly Bloom, dreaming of a banana. In her famous
soliloquy she remembers how she went out with a man at
Gibraltar. He wanted to 'touch hers with his' for a moment
but she wouldn't let him—you never know, you might get
consumption or pregnant, one drop was enough. '. . . that
old servant Ines told me that one drop even if it got into
you at all after I tried with the banana but I was afraid it
might break and get lost up in me somewhere yes because
they once took something down out of a woman that was
up there for years covered with limesalts. . . .'

1. The interpretation of 'images of men' as a dildo in *Ezekiel* may
seem equivocal but was justified by William Greenhill (*An Exposition
Upon the Prophet Ezekiel*, delivered at lectures in London, 1651) in
this way: 'The Jewish estate being here compared unto a woman, a
whorish woman, who loves and affects the presence, beautie and imbrac-
ings of men, with which she might adulterise and idolise, and satiate her
lusts both fleshly and spirituall.' William Newcome, Bishop of Water-
ford, made everything more explicit in his *An Attempt Towards an
Improved Version*, 1788: 'Thou hast also taken thy goodly jewels of
of my gold and of my silver, and hast made thee images of men, and
hast committed fornication with them . . .' In a footnote he expands
the meaning 'thus showing thy flagitious and shameless spirit'.

Bibliography

Bibliography

This is a selection of works referred to and quoted from in the text of this volume only. It does not attempt to be comprehensive, and many other titles will be listed in future volumes which the author hopes will appear. There is no division into fiction or non-fiction, original English or English in translation, or along any other lines of differentiation. Information about some works is deliberately scanty because they have only been referred to in passing. Fuller information will be given when these books are dealt with in more detail. In much publishing of an erotic nature place and date of publication are not given, or false ones are supplied. Bibliography in this field is full time work for an expert, which I do not pretend to be.   J.A.

Algren, Nelson, *A Walk on the Wild Side*, 1957.
Anonymous: *The Crime of Onan* (together with that of his brother Er, punished with Sudden Death), or the Hainous Vice of Self-Defilement, with all its Dismal Consequence. 1724. *Eronania*, or the Misusing of the Marriage Bed by Er and Onan. 1724. *A Supplement to the Onania*, or the Heinous Sin of Self-Pollution. 1724.
Memoirs of Dolly Morton. An American 'classic', no date, no place of publication. Has the ring of truth, in the way *Fanny Hill* has it. Deals with the sufferings of women who helped slaves escape during American Civil War.
My Secret Life, 11 vols., each containing 375 pages, describing practically every known form of sexual perversion or abnormality: 'Only ten copies of this book, which is believed to be autobiographical, are said to have been published, and of these only one copy, and that in a private collection, is known to be still in existence.'

(Rolf S. Reade, *Reg. Lib, Erot.*, q.v.) Sometimes attributed to H. S. Ashbee, but this suggestion must be treated with caution. There was once a strong tendency to saddle Ashbee, Harris and Oscar Wilde with erotic works whose genesis was unknown. A short version of *My Secret Life*, edited by Drs. Phyllis and Eberhard Kronhausen, is published by Charles Skilton.

Teleny, 1893. Ascribed to Oscar Wilde, an example of the tendency mentioned in the previous entry. It is sufficient to read only one page to know that Wilde was not responsible.

Three Mistresses. Apparently an abbreviated version of the better known *Romance of Lust*. No date.

A Woman in Berlin (trs. James Stern), 1955.

Apollinaire, Guillaume, *The Debauched Hospodar* and *Memoirs of a Young Rakehell*, published in one volume by Olympia Press. No date.

The Arabian Nights (English translation of Arabic *Alf Laylah wa Laylah*). Fuller details of the various translations of this well-known work will be given in a later volume. I have drawn largely from what is usually regarded as the best translation, that of Powys Mathers (although he translated from the French instead of direct from the Arabic), and secondarily from the famous Burton edition.

Archer, Ethel, *The Whirlpool*, 1911.

Ashbee, Henry Spencer (pseud. Pisanus Fraxi). His three volumes of bibliography form the basis of any serious study of erotica. In this volume I only call upon the *Index Librorum Prohibitorum*, being Notes Bio-Biblio-Iconographical and Critical on Curious and Uncommon Books, 1877.

Bibliotheca Arcana seu Catalogus Librorum Penetralium is by Speculator Morum, who has been identified by some as Ashbee, but with what authority I am uncertain. (Being brief notices of books that have been secretly printed, prohibited by law, seized, anathematised, burnt or bowdlerised, 1885.)

Aubrey, *Brief Lives*, ed. Oliver Lawson Dick, 1949. Standard ed., 1898.

Baldwin, James, *Go Tell it on the Mountain*, 1954.

Baldwin, Michael, *Grandad with Snails*, 1960.

Balzac, Honoré de, *Contes Drolatiques* (Droll Stories). Three
volumes with ten tales apiece. Vol. 1, 1832. Purports to
be a picture of French life in the sixteenth century, in
the language of the Merry Vicar of Meudon. 'Triumph
of literary archaeology,' says translator of 1874. *Les Cents
Contes Drolatiques*, completed and published in 1837.
Modern English translation by Alec Brown.
   Physiologie du Marriage, 1829. *Petites Misères de la Vie
Conjugale*, 1845. English edition, *Conjugal Life*, 1957, is
a selection from both. *Misères* translated by Geoffrey
Tickell, *Physiologie* anon., whole edited with Introduc-
tion by Derek Stanford.

Barnes, Djuna, *Nightwood*, 1936. Preface by T. S. Eliot.

Bayle, Pierre, *Dictionnaire Historique et Critique*. First English translation by Des Maizeaux in 5 vols., 1710. Another
trans. 1738.

Bayley, John, *The Characters of Love*, 1960.

Beadnell, C. M., *The Origin of the Kiss*, Thinkers Library,
1942. A volume of essays, the first being the title essay.

Beardsley, Aubrey, *Under the Hill*, 1894-6. One of the finest
pieces of erotic writing in English, though not to everyone's taste.

Beaumont, Francis, and Fletcher, John, *Philiaster*, 1610.

Beckett, Samuel, *The Unnamable*, 1958 (written in French
and translated by Beckett himself).

Boswell, James, *London Journal*, 1762-3. Ed. F. A. Pottle,
1950.

Bradley, Edward, *The Five Books of Sex*, n.d., but *c.* 1940.
This is a grandiloquent title but I have only seen the
first volume. The others may not have appeared.

Brinton, Crane, *History of Western Morals*, 1959.

Brown, Tom, *Works*, 1730 (inc. 'A Satire Against Women').

Cabell, James Branch, *Jurgen*, 1919.

The Cabinet of Love, 1718. Contains 'The Delights of Venus',
said to be translated from Meursius, which is doubtful;
'An Interlude'; 'Dildoides', by Samuel Butler.

Carew, Jan., *The Wild Coast*, 1958.

Céline, Louis-Ferdinand, *Journey to the End of the Night*,
1932.

Chaucer, Geoffrey, *The Canterbury Tales*. Coghill's modern rendering is well known. 'The Wife of Bath's Prologue' and 'The Monk's Tale' of particular interest. *Troilus and Criseyde*, 1379-83.

Chesser, Dr. Eustace, *How to Make a Success of Your Marriage*, 1952. Also *Love Without Fear*. A Plain Guide to Sex Technique for every Married Adult. First published, 1941. 26th reprint, 1962.

Chevallier, Gabriel, *Clochmerle*, 1936.

Connell, Vivian, *The Chinese Room*, 1943.

Connolly, Cyril, *The Rock Pool*. Obelisk Press, Paris, 1936; England, 1947.

Crowley, Aleister, *The Winged Beetle*, 1910. Crowley's erotic writings are hard to come by. The Warburg Institute and Ann Arbor, Michigan, have copies of *Bagh, Snowdrops* and *White Stains*.

Daudet, Alphonse, *Sappho*, 1884.

Davies, Sir John, *Epigrammes*, c. 1600.

Defoe, Daniel, *Moll Flanders*, 1722.

Denwood, Jonathan, *Twinter's Wedding*, 1950.

De Sola Pinto and Rodway, *The Common Muse* (containing songs from the Roxburghe and Bagford Ballads, etc.).

Dingwall, E. J., 'Erotic Literature' (art.), Cassell's *Encyclopaedia of Literature*.

Donleavy, J. P., *The Ginger Man*, 1955.

Douglas, Norman, *Some Limericks*, n.d. Privately printed.

Dryden, John, *Marriage à la Mode*, 1673; *The Conquest of Granada*, 1672; *Sigismonda and Guiscarde* (subtitled 'From Boccace'), 1700.

Duncan, Ronald, Introduction to *Selected Lyrics and Satires of John Wilmot, second Earl of Rochester*, 1948.

Durrell, Lawrence, *The Black Book*. Paris, 1937.

Faludi, George, *My Happy Days in Hell*, 1962.

Familiar Letters of Love, 1718. Includes Aphra Behn's 'An Imperfect Enjoyment'.

Faulkner, William, *The Wild Palms*, 1939.

Festival of Love, 1770. A collection of erotic verse.

Fielding, Henry, *Joseph Andrews*, 1742.

Finney, Charles G., *The Circus of Dr. Lao*, 1948.

Flaubert, Gustave, *Madame Bovary*, 1857.

Ford, John, *'Tis Pity She's a Whore*, 1633.
Frobenius, Leo, and Fox, Douglas C., *African Genesis*, 1938.

Gautier, Théophile, *Mademoiselle de Maupin*, 1835.
Gide, André, *If It Die* . . (trs. Bussy, 1920).
Gourmont, Remy de, *Physique de l'Amour: Essai sur l'Instinct Sexuel*, 1904. Eng. trs., *The Natural Philosophy of Love*, 1926. With introduction by Ezra Pound, 1957.
Griffin, Bartholomew, *Fidessa*, 1596.

Hamilton, Anthony, *Memoirs of the Count de Grammont*, 1713.
Harris, Frank, *My Life and Adventures* (written between 1922 and 1926, published in 1947). Also the famous fifth volume of a series known as *My Life and Loves*, attributed to Frank Harris, but actually written by Alexander Trocchi
Hemingway, Ernest, *For Whom the Bell Tolls*, 1941.
Herrick, Robert, *Hesperides*, 1648.
Heyst, Axel, *Words and Darkness*, 1946.
The Horn Exalted, or Room for Cuckolds. Being a Treatise concerning the Reason and Original of the word Cuckold, and why such are said to wear Horns. Very proper for these times, when Men are Butting and Pushing and Goring and Horning one another. Also an Appendix concerning Women and Jealousie. 1660.
Huxley, Aldous, *Leda*, 1920.
Huysmans, J. K., *Là Bas*, 1891.

Ibn Hazm, *The Ring of the Dove*, trs. A. J. Arberry. First pub. 1027.

Joyce, James, *Ulysses*, 1922.

Kama Sutra, numerous translations, the most famous being that of Burton and Arbuthnot. Full details of various trs. in later volume.
Kaufman, Stanley, *The Philanderer*, 1952.
Koestler, Arthur, *The Age of Longing*, 1951.
Kronhausen, Drs. Phyllis and Eberhard, *Pornography and the Law*, 1967.

Laclos, Choderlos de, *Les Liaisons Dangereuses*, 1782. Trs. P. W. K. Stone.

La Fontaine, *Tales and Novels in Verse*, from the French of La Fontaine, by Several Hands. Ed. Samuel Humphreys, 1762.

Langley, Noel, *The Rift in the Lute*, 1952.

Laurent, Emile, and Nagour, Paul, *Magica Sexualis*, trs. Raymond Sabatier, 1934.

Lawrence, D. H., *Pornography and Obscenity* (Criterion Miscellany No. 5, 1929). Inc. in *Sex. Literature and Censorship*, ed. H. T. Moore, 1955.

Layton, Irving, *A Red Carpet for the Sun*, 1959.

Lazarsfeld, Dr. Sofie, *Woman's Experience of the Male.* Experience, with Case Histories, of a Marriage Advice Bureau in Vienna, tinged with a rather unexpected yet pleasing naïvety.

Lewis, C. S., *The Four Loves*, 1960.

Linche, Richard, *Diella*, 1596.

Longus, *Daphnis and Chloe*, trs. George Thornley, 1657.

Loth, David, *The Erotic in Literature.*

Louys, Pierre, *Aphrodite*, 1896.

McCarthy, Mary, *The Group*, 1963.

Mailer, Norman, *The Naked and the Dead*, 1949. *The Deer Park*, 1957. *Advertisements for Myself*, 1958-9, inc. 'The White Negro' and 'The Time of Her Time'.

Malinowski, Bronislaw, *The Sexual Life of Savages in North-Western Melanesia*, 1929. Preface by Havelock Ellis.

Mandiargues, André Pieyre de, *The Girl Beneath the Lion*, 1959.

Mason, Van Wyck, *The Barbarians*, 1956.

Maugham, W. Somerset, *Catalina*, 1948.

Meagher, F. W., *A Study of Masturbation and the Psychosexual Life.*

The Merry Muses of Caledonia, original edition 1800, collection of songs supposedly made by Robert Burns, some traditional, others by himself.

Metalious, Grace, *The Tight White Collar*, 1960.

Miller, Henry, *The Rosy Crucifixion: I Sexus*, 1949.

Moore, George, *Evelyn Innes*, 1898. *Confessions of a Young Man*, 1888. *Memoirs of My Dead Life*, 1906.

Musical Miscellany. Being a Collection of Choice Songs, 1729.

Nabokov, Vladimir, *Lolita*, 1947.

Nashe, Thomas, *Works*, ed. by Ronald B. McKerrow, 1905.
Contains 'The Choise of Valentines or the Merie Ballad
of Nash his Dildo'.

O'Hara, John, *Appointment in Samarra*, 1934.

Oliver, Bruce, *The Square Within*, 1959.

Ovid, *Elegies*, trs. J. Lewis Day, 1925. There are, of course,
many translations of Ovid. Some of these will be listed
in a later volume.

Partridge, Eric, *Shakespeare's Bawdy*, 1947. Revised ed., 1955.

Pearson, Angela, *The Whipping Club* and *The Whipping
Post*. Both Olympia Press publications, the latter with
more story and variety.

Piombo, Akbar del, *Who Pushed Paula?* Also Olympia. The
author is a master of surrealist sex.

Plautus, *Asmaria*, or The Ass-Dealer. Trs. E. H. Sugden.

Pope, Alexander, 'Sappho to Phaon' (trs. of Ovid's Heroic
Epistle XV).

The Post-Boy Rob'd of his Mail, or the Pacquet Broke Open,
consisting of Five Hundred Letters to Persons of several
qualities and conditions, with observations upon each
Letter. Publish'd by a Gentleman concern'd in the
Frolick. 1692. Dedicated to George Porter by C.G.).

Post-Office Intelligence, or Universal Gallantry, being a
Collection of Love Letters (printed by E. Curll, 1736).

Powys, John Cowper, *The Brazen Head*.

Rabelias, François, The Urquhart trs. of the Pantagruel and
Gargantua tales is deservedly the most famous, but there
have been others. Rabelais, who is in any case marginal
to a study of erotic writing, will be listed in more detail
later.

Reade, Rolf S. (Pseud. for Alfred Rose), *Register Librorum
Eroticorum*, privately printed 1936. Preface (signed
T.O.I.) said Rose died before his classification was complete. It is useful in that it gives the B.M. and Private
Case press-marks (the latter are not known by the general
reader). States that at time of writing Belgium had become chief source of erotic publication. Some of his books
were without any suggestion of evil except to 'those who

would find evil in Paradise'. These were published freely
in France but often proscribed in England.

Reage, Pauline. (Believed by some to be J. Paulhan.) *The
Story of O*, 1959.

Robbins, R. H., *Encyclopaedia of Witchcraft and Demonology*, 1959.

Rochester and Roscommon, *Miscellaneous Works of Rochester
and Roscommon*, 1707, with Miscellany Poems appended.

Rosenbaum, Dr. Julius, *Plague of Lust in Antiquity*.

Rougemont, Denis de, *Passion and Society*, 1938. (Eng. trs.
Montgomery Belgion, 1940, revised 1954.)

Saikaku, Iharu, *Five Women Who Chose Love* and *The Life
of an Amorous Woman*, 1686. Regarded by scholars as a
Japanese Defoe. Edited and trs. by Ivan Morris.

Sartre, Jean-Paul, *Intimacy*, 1949. (Short stories).

Selvon, Samuel, *Turn Again Tiger*.

Sherwood, James, *Stradella*, 1962. Olympia Press, now published in England.

Song of Love. Modern trs. by H. J. Schonfield, with com-
mentary.

Stendhal, *Love*, 1822, with new prefaces in 1826, 1834 and
1842. Trs. Brian Rhys.

Stern, Bernard, *The Scented Garden*.

Stevenson, John Hall, *Crazy Tales*. Written in 18th century,
there is an 1894 reprint.

Stiles, Henry Reed, *Bundling: its Origin, Progress and Decline
in America*, 1871.

Straus, Ralph, *The Unspeakable Curll*, 1927.

Tableaux Vivants, anonymous, but actually written by Paul
Perret and published in Paris, 1870. Trs. into English
by Leonard Smithers, 1888. Greatly fancied by con-
noisseurs.

Taylor, Jeremy, *The Rule and Exercises of Holy Living*, 1650.

Twain, Mark, *Some Thoughts on the Science of Onanism*,
1879.

Van de Velde, Th., *Ideal Marriage: its Physiology and Technique*, 1928.

Vicarion, Count Palmiro, *Book of Limericks*, Paris. A Sunday
paper announced that the Count is actually the poet,
Christopher Logue.

Voltaire (François-Marie Arouet), *Candide or Optimism*, 1758.
    There is a modern translation by John Butt.

Webster, John, *The Duchess of Malfi*, 1614.
Wilson, Edmund, *Memoirs of Hecate County*, 1946.

Zola, Emile, *Germinal*, 1885. (A good translation by L. W.
    Tancock.) *Thérèse Raquin*, 1867.